Memorials of a half-century

Bela Hubbard 1814-1896

Nabu Public Domain Reprints:

You are holding a reproduction of an original work published before 1923 that is in the public domain in the United States of America, and possibly other countries. You may freely copy and distribute this work as no entity (individual or corporate) has a copyright on the body of the work. This book may contain prior copyright references, and library stamps (as most of these works were scanned from library copies). These have been scanned and retained as part of the historical artifact.

This book may have occasional imperfections such as missing or blurred pages, poor pictures, errant marks, etc. that were either part of the original artifact, or were introduced by the scanning process. We believe this work is culturally important, and despite the imperfections, have elected to bring it back into print as part of our continuing commitment to the preservation of printed works worldwide. We appreciate your understanding of the imperfections in the preservation process, and hope you enjoy this valuable book.

VIEW ON DETROIT RIVER FROM OLD KNAGGS HOUSE, WIND-MILL POINT, SPRINGWELLS, 1837.

MEMORIALS

OF A

HALF-CENTURY

BY

BELA HUBBARD

"I have been at a great feast, and stolen the scraps."
Love's Labor Lost.—SHAKS.

"... various, that the mind
Of desultory man, studious of change,
And pleased with novelty, might be indulg'd."
The Task.—COWPER

WITH ILLUSTRATIONS

NEW YORK & LONDON
G. P. PUTNAM'S SONS
The Knickerbocker Press
1887

COPYRIGHT BY
G. P. PUTNAM'S SONS
1887

Press of
G. P. Putnam's Sons
New York

"The notes of a single observer, even in a limited district, describing accurately its features, civil, natural and social, are of more interest, and often of more value, than the grander view and broader generalizations of history.

"In a country whose character and circumstances are constantly changing, the little facts and incidents, which are the life of history, soon pass from the minds even of the present generation."—*Anon.*

PREFACE.

THE writer came to Michigan, a youth, in the spring of 1835, and settled in the town of Springwells, two miles from the western limits of Detroit, then a city of less than 5000 inhabitants. On or near the spot of his first abode, upon the banks of our noble river, he has dwelt for half a century, and until the spreading city has absorbed the intervening farms.

Even a few years ago his present residence was so completely in the country, that the familiar rural sights and sounds were but little banished. The influences thus surrounding him are visible in many of the essays which make up this book, and which are in part compiled from his Diary.

Such are the chapters upon the seasons and upon the inhabitants, human and brute, of the neighborhood. Of the other papers, some will be recognized as having been read before the Detroit Scientific Association, and State and County Pioneer societies, and some have already received publication in newspapers and pioneer collections.

In the essays upon climate, the author ventures to believe, will be found something of merit, in the way of original observation and research. The character of our seasons he has endeavored to portray, less by attempt at vivid description, than by the plain statement of facts. Anything really new, on subjects of such universal interest, may prove of more than local value.

The reflection that many of these memorials may possess a value, at least in the eyes of partial friends—alas! how few now—and may serve a purpose in the preservation of facts and phenomena which are fast being lost with the rapidly passing years, has been the inducement to their compilation into a volume.

B. H.

VINEWOOD, *December*, 1886.

L'ENVOI.

Go forth, little book, bark of destiny, freighted with the records and recollections of many desultory hours. Take thy chance upon the stream which sweeps all things along. Pleasing to the writer has been his task, and little will he take account with fate, whether favoring winds waft thee into a friendly port, or the wayward current drift thee aside, to be stranded on the shallows of oblivion.

CONTENTS.

SCENERY AND DESCRIPTION.

	PAGE.
SCENERY OF THE LAKES....	1–18

Charlevoix, Description of Voyage, 2.—The Lake Plateaus, 3.—The two Peninsulas, topography, 5.—Romance of Early Travel, 7.—The Ocean Lake, 9.—The Straits, before and after Colonization, 12.—River Scenery, 15.

LAKE SUPERIOR IN 1840 19–62

The Exploring Party, 21.—The Route—Mackinac, 23.—Straits of Ste. Marie, 24.—At the Sault, 28.—Coasting, 31.—The Grand Sable, 32.—Pictured Rocks, 36.—Azoic and Mineral Region, 49.—Adventure at the Ontonagon, 53.—La Pointe—Père Marquette, 59.

A MICHIGAN GEOLOGICAL EXPEDITION IN 1837............... 63–90

The Party Introduced, 65.—The Wagon Journey, 67.—River Voyaging, 69.—Descending the Shiawassee—Indian Clearings, 70.—A Primeval Forest, 72.—Saginaw, 75.—*Personnel*—Dr. Houghton—Our Fourth Member, 76.—The Tittabawassee—Midland Solitudes, 80.—The Solitude Broken, 83.—Descending the Saginaw, 84.—Coasting the Bay, 85.—Canoe Voyaging on Lake Huron, 87.

HISTORICAL AND ANTIQUARIAN.

A TIME OF UNIVERSAL PROSPERITY, AND WHAT CAME OF IT.... 91–105

A new Eldorado, 93.—Landlooking, 95.—Eligible Sites—Paper Cities, 96.—Flush Times, 97.—Wild-cat Banking, 98.—Hard Times, 100.—Ruins, 101.—Reverses, 103.—Restoration, 105.

	PAGE.
FRENCH HABITANTS OF THE DETROIT	107-154

Part I.—Introductory, 109.—The old Régime, 110.—Colonization, 113.—The Detroit, 115.—Land-titles and Farms, 116.—First Settlers, 117.—Agriculture, 119.—Farm Implements, 121.—Vehicles, 122.—Canadian Ponies, 124.—Orchards, 125.—Pear Trees, 127.

Part II.—French Homesteads, 131.—Windmills, 135.—Costumes, 136.—Society—Amusements, 139.—White-fishing, 142.—Patriotism, 143.—Education, 146.—Language, 149.—Voyageurs, 150.—Boat Songs, 152.

THE NAMING OF LAKE STE. CLAIRE 155-175
Second Centennial Anniversary, 156.—Historical Address, 157.—Le Sieur de la Salle—His earlier Expeditions, 158.—First Knowledge of the Straits—Incidents, 159.—First Sail-vessel on the Lakes, 162.—The "Griffin" arrives at Lake Ste. Claire, 163.—Origin of the name of the Lake, 164.—The Lady Claire, 165.—The Christening—Surroundings, 166.—Fate of the Griffin, 169.—New Schemes of La Salle, 170.—Discovery of Louisiana, 171.—Death and character of La Salle, 173.—Honors to his Memory—A Suggestion, 174.

INDIANS IN MICHIGAN 177-187
Aboriginal population, 179.—Chippewas of Saginaw, 181.—Pottawatomies and Ottawas, 183.—Trading—Fire-water, 184.—Civilized Ottawas, 185.

POLICY OF THE GOVERNMENT TOWARDS THE INDIANS 187-198
Indian Titles—Treaties, 188.—Indian Character, 189.—Demands of Civilization, 190.—Reservations—Agencies, 192.—Errors in Policy, 193.—Indian Capacity for Civilization, 194.—True Policy, 195.—The Consummation, 197.

THE MOUND-BUILDERS IN MICHIGAN 199-261
Part I.—General Character and Distribution of the Works, 201.—Defensive Works, 203.—Circular Works, 205.—Tumuli, 206.—Modes of Burial—Entombing, 208.—Monument Mounds, 210.—Contents of the Mounds, 211.—Pottery, 213.

Part II.—Indian Antiquities at Springwells, 219.—Tumuli at the Sand-hills, 220.—Exploration—Contents, 222.—Intrusive Burials, 224.—Carsten's Mound, 226.—Circular Earthwork,

227.—The Great Mound at River Rouge, 228.—Festival of the Dead, 231.—Cremation, 233.—Modern Occupation, 234.—Exploration of the Mound, 234.—A Vast Necropolis, 237.—Past and Present, 238.

Part III.—Ancient Garden-beds of Michigan, 241.—Earliest Notice, 243.—Classification, 245.—Beds at Three Rivers, 247.—Kalamazoo, 248.—Prairie Ronde, 249.—Gardenesque Plats, 250.—Botanical Gardens, 251.—Association with other Earthworks, 252.—Origin and Age—Conjectures, 253.—Later Investigations, 254.

FAUNA AND FLORA.

FISH AND FISHING 263–277
Pole and Line, 265.—Prosaic Modes, 266.—Seine Fishing, 268.—On the Upper Lakes, 269.—Whitefish—Life History, 272.—Lake and River Trade, 275.—The Fishing Season, 276.

BIRDS OF MY NEIGHBORHOOD 279–320
Part I.—Aquatic Birds, 281.—Gregarious Birds, 285.—Blackbirds, 286.—Wild Turkeys, 288.—Birds of Prey, 289.—Winter Birds—Harbingers of Spring, 290.—Wild Birds Domesticated, 293.—A Good Talker, 294.

Part II.—Our Birds Further Considered, 297.—The Crow, 299.—A Black Parliament, 303.—Crow Character, 305.—The Turkey, as our National Emblem, 306.—A Pigeon Roost, 307.—Our Northern Mocking-birds, 310.—Song-birds—Game Laws, 312.—Birds as Insect Destroyers, 313.—The European Sparrow, 316.—Bird ways, 317.—Bird Gratitude, 319.

FOUR-FOOTED INHABITANTS 321–343
Predatory Animals, 323.—The Wolverine, 325.—Nut Collectors, 327.—Deers, Wild and Tame, 330.—Traits of Domesticated Animals, 333.—Free Commoners,—Veto, 335.—Medoc—Dash—A capacious mouth, 337.—Dog Chat, 338.—Concerning Cats—Nora, 339.—Tom and Jerry,—A Music-lover, 341.

WILD ANIMALS OF MICHIGAN 345–367
Our existing Mammalia, 347.—Plantigrades, 348.—Carnivores,

350.—Rodents, 353.—Ruminants, 356.—Animals Formerly Abounding, 359.—Trapping—The trade in Furs, 360.

THE BEAVER, ... 361–367
Beaver-made Country, 362.—As an Engineer, 365.—His Social Qualities, 366.

TREES,—THEIR RELATIONS TO US, ECONOMIC AND SCIENTIFIC. 369–388
Our Forests a Century ago, 371.—Results of Settlement, 373.—Forest Destruction, 374.—Fencing—Fuel—Clearings—Lumbering—Forest Fires, 375.—Relations to Climate, 377.—Results of Forest Removal, 379.—Old World Experiences, 380.—New World Experiences, 382.—Forest Economy—Home Efforts, 385.—Legislation—Fencing in of Stock, 386.—Planting, 388.

TREES, IN THEIR SOCIAL RELATIONS............................ 389–415
Natural Forms,—Individual Expression, 391.–Whitewood, 393. Maple, 394.—Ash, 395.—Linden, 396.—Sycamore, 397.—Beech, 398.—Birch, 399.—Oak, 400.—Walnut, 401.—Chestnut—Poplar, 403.—Pepperidge—Willows, 404.—Elm, 406.—Evergreens, 408.—Rapid Tree Growth, 409.—Planting Roadways, 410.—Trees as Scavengers, 411.—Hostility to Trees, 412.—Sylvan Spirits,—Classic Fancies, 413.—Trees as Friends, 415.

CLIMATOLOGY.

CLIMATE OF DETROIT AND THE LAKE REGION. PART I....... 417–450
The Controlling Element—Isotherms, 421.—The Lake Region a Plateau, 425.—Temperature as Modified by the Lakes, 426.—Our Seasons—Comparisons, 429.—Prevailing Winds—The Michigan Fruit Region, 430.—Rainfall—Sources, 432.—As Controlled by the Seasons, 435.—Maximum and Minimum Tendencies, 437.—Monthly Precipitation, United States, 438.—Maximum and Minimum Years of Rainfall, 440.—General Survey of our Seasons, 442.—Comparisons—Contrasts, 444.—Weather Predicates, 445.—Natural Classification of our Seasons, 447.—Peculiarities of our Climate—Advantages, 448.

PART II.—ADDITIONAL OBSERVATIONS..................... 452–461
Temperature and Rainfall since 1874, 452.—Mean Temperature

and Rainfall of the Seasons,—1835 to 1886, 454.—Season Fluctuations, Maximum and Minimum Years, 456.—Grouping of Years, 458.—Annual Fluctuations—Reign of Law, 459.

PART III.—PERIODICAL CHANGES IN THE LAKE LEVELS, RAINFALL, TEMPERATURE AND SUN-SPOTS, AND THEIR RELATIONS TO EACH OTHER... 460–482
Lake Fluctuations, 461.—Periodical Variations, 462.—Lake Erie Fluctuations prior to 1838, 464.—High and Low Levels, 465.—Periodicities, 467.—Temperature and Rainfall Curves, 469.—Sun-spot and Lake Curves,—1769-1834, 470.—Curves of Sun-spots, Temperature, Rainfall and Lake, 1834-1886, 473.—Relationships, 476.—Times of Increase and Decrease, 477.—Summary, 478.—A Meteorological Horoscope, 479.

THE WINTER SEASON.. 483–507
Ordinary Features, 485.—Mild and Open Winters, 487.—Classification, 490.—Cold and Snowy Winters, 491.—Storms of Wintry Time, 493.—Phenomenal Cold, 495.—Unclassifiable Winters, 496.—A Violent Reversal, 498.—A Typical Season, 499.—Forest Occupations, 501.—Visit to the Pine Woods, 503.—Winter Enjoyments, 504.

SPRING-TIDE... 509–524
Characteristic Weather, 511.—Floods, 513.—Transitions—Vicissitudes, 515.—Contrasts, 517.—English Springs, 518.—Indications, 519.—A Spring Morning, 520.—Gifts of Spring—Flowers—Tints, 521.—Progress, 524.—A Typical Season, 525.

OUR SUMMERS... 529–551
Realization, 511.—Tropical Characters, 532.—Insect Life, 534.—Voices of the Night, 535.—Moonlight, 536.—Heated Terms, 537.—Summer Storms, 539.—Gales—Extremes—Frosts, 541.—A Typical Season, 543.—Compensations, 545.—Enjoyment of Summer, 546.—Cloud-land, 547.—Sunsets, 548.—Close of Day, 550.

AUTUMN TIME... 553–571
Before the Frosts, 555.—After the Frosts, 556.—Indian Sum-

mer, 558.—Phenomenal Seasons, 561.—Dry Seasons, 562.—Effects of Drought—Fires—Frosts, 563.—A very Dry Year, 565.—Normal Seasons, 567.—A Typical Autumn, 568.

THE RIPENING OF THE YEAR.................................... 573–581
Autumnal Changes, 575.—Progress—Tree Liveries, 576.—Contrasts—Shrub Tints, 579.—Nature as a Color Painter, 580.

ILLUSTRATIONS.

SCENERY AND DESCRIPTION.

	PAGE
View on Detroit River from Old Knaggs House, Wind-mill Point, Springwells (looking up), 1837	Frontispiece.
Old Knaggs House (author's early residence)	17
Sault Ste. Marie, in 1840	29
Grandes Sables, from the Lake	33
Grandes Sables, from above	35
The Pictured Rocks, distant view	37
La Portaille	41
Gothic Rock	43
La Chapelle, from the Lake	45
La Chapelle, from within	47
View from the Cliff Range	51
Falls at mouth of Montreal River	57
Père Marquette, from the Statue, City Hall, Detroit	61

HISTORY AND ANTIQUITIES.

French Voyageur, from oil portrait, Montreal, 1835	108
French Plough of the olden time	120
French Carryall (carriole)	121
French Pony Cart	123
French Pear Trees, Detroit River	130
Old Clergy-House, Sandwich	134
French Summer Costume (man)	136
French Summer Costume (woman)	137
French Winter Costume (man)	138
French Winter Costume (woman)	139
The Griffin,—First Sailing-vessel on the Lakes	163
La Salle, from Statue at City Hall, Detroit	175
Diagram of Ancient Earthworks, Macomb County	202
Pottery from Mounds at Grand Rapids	214

	PAGE.
Pottery from Mounds, Wayne County	218
Diagram of Ancient Earthworks, Springwells	221
The Great Mound at River Rouge	230
Ancient Garden-beds, Grand River Valley	257
Ancient Garden-beds, St. Joseph River Valley	258
Ancient Garden-beds, Western Michigan	259
Ancient Garden-beds, Kalamazoo County	260
Ancient Garden-beds, Prairie Ronde	261
Ancient Garden-beds (wheel-shaped), Kalamazoo	261

FAUNA AND FLORA.

Trees in Winter:—Whitewood	394
A Forest Whitewood	395
Maple	396
Ash	397
Linden	398
Sycamore	399
Beech	400
Birch	401
White Oak	402
Black Walnut	403
Hickory	404
Cotton-wood Poplar	405
Pepperidge	406
Young Pepperidge	407
White (American) Elm	409

CLIMATOLOGY.

Chart of Isothermal lines, showing influence of the Lakes upon Temperature	420
Diagram, showing Monthly Precipitation, United States	439
Diagram, showing Annual Rainfall, Detroit, 1835–1886	451
Diagram, showing Mean Annual and Summer and Winter Temperature and Rainfall, Detroit	457
Diagram (No. 1) showing Curves of the Sun-spots, and Lake Erie Levels, 1769–1834	460
Diagram (No. 2) showing Curves of the Lake Levels, Rainfall, Temperature and Sun-spots, 1834–1886	466
Winter morning in a Michigan lumber camp	502

SCENERY OF THE LAKES.

"Were we always to sail as I did then, with a serene sky in a most charming climate, and on water as clear as that of the purest fountain; were we sure of finding everywhere secure and agreeable places to pass the night in, where we might enjoy the pleasure of hunting at a small expense, breathe at our ease the purest air, and enjoy the prospect of the finest countries in the universe, we might possibly be tempted to travel to the end of our days.

"Each day a new situation, chosen at pleasure; a neat, commodious house, built and furnished with all necessaries, in less than a quarter of an hour, with a pavement of flowers springing up on a carpet of the most beautiful green; on all sides simple and natural beauties, unadulterated and inimitable by any art. If these pleasures suffer a little interruption, whether by hard weather or some unforeseen accident, it is only to render them more sensibly felt at a second enjoyment."—CHARLEVOIX, *Description of a voyage to the Detroit of Lake Erie*, 1721.

SCENERY OF THE LAKES.

FROM the great Appalachian chain—the mountain region that determines the course of the rivers which fall into the Atlantic on the one side and the Mississippi on the other—the traveller, bound westward, passes abruptly into the immense valley of the Mississippi, and northerly into the famous "Basin of the Lakes," as termed by geographers.

But this term is a misnomer, for, like most fresh-water lakes, these bodies of water occupy an elevated plateau; the summit, in fact, of the vast expanse of land which spreads out between the Alleghanies and the Rocky Mountains. No large streams flow into them, and they drain very limited areas. On the contrary, the Ohio, the Wabash, and other large tributaries of the great Mississippi, have their sources within a few miles of the lake borders, yet drain into the Southern Gulf, while the great rivers of British America, commencing near the lakes, have their outlets in the northern seas. The magnificent St. Lawrence alone, finding its supply in these sources, pursues its eastward way to the Atlantic.

Each lake, it is true, has its separate and deep basin, or, more properly, *chasm*. But, unlike lakes set in the gorges of mountain regions, or streams which collect the drainage of large valleys, these basins are always full to the brim, yet never overflow. No sudden rise of the waters ever swells to destructive floods; a difference of a few feet only being the entire change of level which is occasioned by the extremes of the seasons or the most copious rains and thaws.

The great American lakes may well be considered a distinguishing feature of this continent. They occupy nearly one hundred thousand square miles of its surface, and contain more than one half of all the fresh water on the globe.

Lake Erie is shallow, the mean depth probably not much exceeding 100 feet. But the chasms filled by the lakes above are, in places, 900 to 1000 feet deep; so that while their surfaces range from 232 feet above the ocean —the level of Lake Ontario—to 603 feet—the level of Lake Superior—their bottoms are far below the level of the sea.

From the level of the chief of the lakes, each surface below falls by steps; the water either passing over cataracts, or by swift currents through the connecting channels. Lakes Huron and Michigan are on nearly one level, 25 feet below Lake Superior; Erie is 13 feet below the level of Huron, and Ontario, by the grand cataract and rapids of Niagara, is brought to a still lower descent of 333 feet.

With the exception of Lake Superior, the lake borders are marked by no lofty or rugged cliffs. The lower peninsula of Michigan, bordered by three of the great lakes, partakes of the general undulating character of the Mississippi valley; nowhere rising into mountains nor sinking into deep valleys. In the southerly half, swells of land composing its water-shed attain to from 300 to 600 feet above Lake Erie, and occasionally, rounded knobs rise a hundred feet above the surrounding elevations. The northerly half is more elevated, the general water-shed being 700 or 800 feet, and near Otsego Lake rising to 1100 feet above Lake Erie.

From these water-sheds the surface descends by steppes, or inclines, uniformly to the margin of the lakes. A belt of flat, heavily-wooded country, underlaid with clay, borders the eastern side; while Lake Michigan is margined by steep bluffs of sand.

Beyond these border tracts a varied surface is presented of alternating timbered lands and openings, of flat and rolling surfaces, with numerous lakes and marshes. These are the unfailing sources of many deep streams of clear water.

In the southern part of the State a few rolling prairies occur, the largest being 18 miles in length,—the prelude to the more magnificent prairie country of Illinois and the regions beyond.

The rocks of this peninsula belong to the carboniferous and devonian systems, and are all deeply covered with the drift of the glacial epoch. It is a country of mingled gravels, sands and clays, covering the rocks—which seldom outcrop—to a depth often of several hundred feet; and from these the soils are derived.

Little of the peninsula scenery partakes of the grandeur of primitive and broken districts, but it combines the variety—so essential in a landscape—of woodland, glade, and water in a manner which often seems the result of art, but which is not less truly inimitable.

The character of the "openings" is that of a majestic orchard of oaks and hickories, varied by small prairies, grassy lawns, and clear lakes. They resemble those exquisite pictures of park scenery, where the vision roams amid groups of lofty oaks and over open glades gemmed with flowers; while the distant woodland bounds the horizon, and the velvet-skirted lake reflects the light from the open prairie, or is faintly visible from the bosom of the glen.

Such scenes are destitute of the majesty of mountain aspects, but they have that pervading, tranquil beauty which forsakes the lofty hill-side and the hoary cliff. They present Nature in her simple loveliness, without her sterner aspect and masculine attire.

Of the character of our wooded districts I propose to speak elsewhere.

The topographical features of the upper peninsula of Michigan are very different from those of the lower, and correspond to its different geological character. A large part of the country is rough and broken, though it nowhere composes very elevated mountain chains. Rocks of the silurian and paleozoic systems make frequent outcrops, and rise into steep ledges and sharp peaks. In the Huron and Porcupine mountains they attain heights of 1000 to 1300 feet above Lake Superior. These consist of ranges of broken hills and knobs, often mere naked granite rock, bare of timber, while the valleys between are heavily timbered and fertile.

The lake coast presents a succession of bold and rocky cliffs, with leaping streams and dunes of sand, which give many strange and wild features to the scenery of that wonderful region; wonderful no less in these, than in its mineral riches. Some of these features I propose to notice hereafter.

Though the country of the lower lakes lacks so much of the grand and picturesque of mountain scenery, it has never failed to excite the enthusiastic admiration of the traveller.

No doubt much of the interest which was expressed by

the first explorers is of that romantic character which belongs to a region imperfectly known, and which in the relations of these early voyageurs abounded in marvels. By them the lake scenery was beheld under circumstances very different from those which surround the modern tourist.

The remoteness from the ordinary range of travel; the novel mode of conveyance; the intercourse with Nature in her secret haunts; the freedom from the thousand cares of the busy world, which is felt in her untrimmed forests and upon her heaving waters,—these, to the unaccustomed wanderer, are replete with a rapturous delight, and invest these scenes with a charm apart from their intrinsic interest. All this, too, is aided by the strengthened nerve and vigorous health which are engendered by constant exercise and exposure to pure air. No wonder that the early voyageurs in this region were thus inspired, and often dwelt with enthusiasm even on ordinary scenes.

They stepped into the light canoe and were afloat upon a tide, to the sight boundless as the ocean, but fresh, pure and transparent as ether. They made their way under a variety of incidents; with difficulty escaped the rising gale, and at night encamped upon the beach, where the breaking surf lulled them to sleep; or they sought shelter in the tall forest, and listened to the roar of the night wind in the pine tops.

Day after day, month after month, they continued to traverse the shores, without finding the bounds of these vast fresh-water seas. At one time the shores presented only a dark mass of evergreens, where the tangled cedar spread its innumerable boughs, and the fir shot up its straight, sharp cone. At another, the sight pierced through vistas of openings, disclosing beyond inviting prospects. Again, huge walls of rock reared a threatening front, caverns yawned beneath, and lofty hills, rock-ribbed, rose beyond. They picked up on the shores many curious minerals, precious stones, polished by the waves, beautiful agates, and metallic ores, among which were large pieces of native copper. They found that the savages regarded some of these things with reverence, and eager curiosity pictured a world of hidden wonders.

It was my fortune to traverse these great inland seas in almost the precise manner of those first explorers, and to drink at the same sources of inspiration. Even now, when a few days may suffice to convey the traveller from one end to the other, seeing little of that which is most worthy his observation, so little change have time and the advance of a vigorous race wrought in the features of many parts of the coast scenery, that were the modern tourist to visit these in the only mode possible for obtaining a correct conception,—a coasting voyage in a small boat,—he would find little occasion to reverse those early impressions. He would be surrounded by almost the same solitude and wildness.

There is a sublimity about these vast fresh-water seas which is hardly exceeded by the ocean itself. Lake Superior is 400 miles long, and covers an area of 30,000 square miles. Standing on its shore the eye can embrace not a thousandth part of its surface; yet to the view this small part is a boundless horizon, united only to the sky.

The water of this lake and of those immediately below is of amazing purity and transparency. This is attributable to their rocky beds and the nature of the bordering country, from which so little impurity finds its way.

"The water," writes one of the early journalizers, "was as pure and transparent as air, and my canoe seemed as if it hung suspended in that element. It was impossible to look attentively through this limpid medium at the rocks below without finding, before many minutes, your head swim, and your eyes no longer able to behold the dazzling scene."

From the great extent of surface exposed to so many conflicting winds, the waters in these great basins are seldom quiet. This is especially the case with Lake Superior, which may be styled—par excellence—"the ocean lake."

For some time previous to a gale, even when no wind is perceptible, I have seen its surface agitated by tremendous swells, and the waves "heave their sharp, white helmets" on the dark surface. At times, when calm and glassy, a long, dark line may be observed advancing rapidly, and of a sudden the wind begins to freshen, and finally to blow with vehemence. It is the coming on of the tempest. The dark line is the vanguard of an army of waves, which soon swell into enormous billows and hiss with gathered foam. Owing to the suddenness with which these storms arise, the navigation for canoes and boats is rendered peculiarly hazardous.

The effect of the frequent storms and the almost constant agitation of the water is very observable upon the coast. Where this consists of rock, as is the general case, particularly if it be sandstone, an abrading process is going on, which occasions huge, cavernous fissures, extending to a height often of many feet above the water level, rounded columns, supporting battlements of rock, and a thousand fantastic forms.

We regard rock as the basis of what we are accustomed to designate as the "everlasting hills," but the power of the liquid element is so gradually extending its dominion, that these so-called "sure foundations" present but a feeble obstacle to its violence. It is only in the resistance offered by the proverbially "shifting" sands that an enduring barrier is found to the fury of the storms.

Many miles of the southern shore, near the eastern end of the lake, consist of broad sand beaches, and the phenomena of the sea, as I have there witnessed them, are sublime beyond description. Far abroad the white-caps are seen enlivening the dark blue surface; but as the gale sweeps over the broad expanse, and piles the waters up on the opposing shore, the power of the sea, compressed by the shallow space allowed it, raises huge columns of breakers, which tumble impetuously toward the beach. The line of gathering waves is seen far out, increasing into one long, uplifted billow, that passes majestically on, each moment raising higher its threatening crest, until, no longer able to sustain the accumulated weight, its margin bends smoothly forward, as if rushing over a precipice, then comes thundering down in a tremendous sheet of foam and flying spray, tearing up the sands with a roar that seems to shake the coast. Broken in its majestic march, it now spreads into lesser breakers, and sweeps, foaming, high up the beach. Between the successive ridges the liquid element seems to be drawn away, recoiling from the shoaling sands, and adding height and violence to the accumulating mass. The surf from these breakers is thrown to a great distance up the beach, depositing its suspended sand, and then as instantly recedes, to await the next succeeding lash. It is these breaking surges, with their surf and smothering spray, that are so dangerous to stranded vessels, and that often overwhelm boats in their landing which had outlived, until that moment, the whole violence of the storm.

The sublimity of this scene is enhanced by the continued roar that accompanies it. This is not alone the dash of the waters, however loud. Distinct from the rush of waves and howling of the wind is a deep, bass undertone,—the lowest conceivable note in the music of nature,—distinct, incessant, prolonged, filling up every pause in the awful harmony. The first resembles the roar of the wind in the storm-tossed forest; the dread lower tone is like that which is heard at Niagara, and seems to be produced by a similar cause, the concussion of falling waters.

If, as poets tell us, nature is full of melodies, through all her works are hidden cords that vibrate to the music of the spheres,—strange, deep harmonies that haunt the breast of the woodland; the wind's low sigh; the voice which gushes forth "in concord of sweet sounds" from animated nature: if there is music in the rippling wave and the dashing surge, and even the voiceless sands and dropping caves fill the soul with its eloquence, how more sublime a melody in the deep bass of the tempest, and the rush of the thousand battalions of its army of resistless waters!

The natural beauty of "the Detroit," as the "straits of Erie and Huron" were named by the Jesuit missionaries,—the first white men that set foot in this region,—had been recorded with many words of admiration, long before the day of its colonization. No hills bounded the vision. In many places even the shores spread into wide marshes. But all was on a scale of magnificence to which they were unaccustomed. The banks were densely clothed with fresh timber, such as dwarfed all that the Old World afforded. The straits—though its strong current might claim for it the name of river—varied in width from one to five miles, and was adorned with many green islands, of which the largest was twelve miles in length. Beasts and birds of rare and curious aspect were numerous and tame. Fish of novel kinds and unequalled flavor sported in the waters. Fruits of many sorts and in unexampled abundance grew within sight and reach. Everywhere Nature had spread a feast for all her children, such as she grants only to the most fortunate.

After the first white settlements had been established, and before Christian nations had contended here for empire, the country was not greatly changed. A half century of French occupation had not felled the wide-spreading forests, which remained untouched, except upon the immediate border of the stream. But here the colonists had strung together their hamlets, almost in a continuous village, for many miles, with their little fields and picketed gardens, their orchards and windmills. The single street followed all the windings of the shore, avoiding only the marshes, and usurping the well-chosen sites of the Indian villages. From a central position Fort Ponchartrain frowned its rude protection.

The quiet, Arcadian character of the settlements upon the Detroit had been but little affected by political changes and transfers of sovereignty, even so late as when it became the home of the writer, in 1835. Let me describe the river scenery as it then appeared.

Although Detroit had grown from a mere stockade into a modernized and thriving town, and an energetic class of emigrants had begun to penetrate the interior, the rural character of these straits had undergone but little change. The main roads still ran along the banks, lined with the same kind of habitations, in most cases the very same, that were built there more than a century before. Their possessors were still mainly French, though a few farms had changed ownership, and a somewhat larger extent of fields and meadows had infringed upon the ancient forest.

On the British side of the channel, tasteful English cottages, with green verandas, intermingled with the brown domiciles of the French Canadian, and gave additional charm to its rural character.

The view from the water front of my homestead of half a century ago—known as "Windmill Point"—was both beautiful and animating. The noble stream, which has pursued a nearly westerly course from the Lake Ste. Claire, here bends southerly, and is contracted to three-fourths of a mile in width. Owing to the change in the trend of the shore, this point commands a very extended view, of which my frontispiece will give some idea.

Looking eastward is seen forest-crowned Isle au Cochon (since endowed with the more euphonious name of Belle Isle) two miles above the city, and occupying the centre of the stream. The view embraces both channels. On the south side, the main channel carries the vision onward to the horizon of Lake Ste. Claire, and to Peach Island, the once stronghold of Pontiac. Fronting the northerly channel, lower down, are conspicuous the brick walls and glittering spires of the "City of the Straits."

Following along down stream we discover, on the immediate shore, posts and reels, indicating a fishery, whitefish being at that time largely taken in our river.

Turning the eye down the stream, the widening channel, visible for nearly twenty miles, terminates in the passage between Grosse Isle and the main land on the west, the easterly channel and Lake Erie being shut from view by a wooded point on the Canada shore. The stream, broadened to five miles in width, gives to view Fighting Island, the scene of a savage massacre in the old war times, and many small grassy isles, marked by lighthouses and the huts of fishermen.

The view across the water embraces her Majesty's dominion for a continuous coast-line of thirty miles. The spruce town of Windsor is seen opposite its larger American rival, and contrasts strikingly with the gray and sleepy old village of Sandwich, a few miles lower down.

The banks on both sides of this narrowed portion of the strait are bold, and present, in many places, steep cliffs of twenty to thirty feet elevation.

Between these two villages stands the old Huron Church, a monument of the olden times of French supremacy, and a building of considerable size and architectural pretension for those days.* Its decaying walls are propped by poles, and on the open area in front is planted a high wooden cross. It carries the mental view backward to those halcyon days of simplicity and half feudal domination, when the lord of the demesne required a May-pole to be planted annually before his door, when the practical had not banished the poetical; and when religious ceremonies constituted one of the chief pleasures of the people.

Among the farm-houses and cottages which line the banks, those of the times of the French régime still predominate. From embowering orchards, immense pear

---

*In these days of unrespect, this church has been torn down, and has given place to a brick, gothic cathedral, with an episcopal palace, and the college buildings of St. Benedict.

trees rear their heads, like great elms, or stand in groups upon the banks. Several windmills give animation to the picture, as their white arms sway in the breeze, that seldom fails to ripple these waters, like the pinions of some huge birds.

One of those picturesque structures—the only one in sight on the American side—occupies a low, sandy point in our front, and is a conspicuous object in the foreground of my picture. It is built of timber, the lower story being filled in and encased with stone. Though the best of all the structures of its kind upon the river, it lays no claim to having been the manor windmill, to which, in the earlier days, the settler was required to carry his grist.*

The recently created and already immense commerce of the lakes has brought into being many lines of steam and sailing vessels, which ply daily through the Straits.

Sometimes a crowd of the latter meet at the turn of the river, a little below, awaiting a change of wind; and it is a spectacle most beautiful and inspiriting, when all at once, their wings spread to the favoring breeze, they glide past, a magnificent group, on their way to the neighboring port.

Gulls glancing to and fro, with their long emulous wings, give additional life to the scene; while in a higher zone, flocks of wild ducks and geese are winging their way up, their undeviating, swift and steady flight casting contempt upon those duller-winged sailor craft so far beneath.†

---

* These mills have long since been disused, and all have now (1885) disappeared.

† It is one of the singular mutabilities of civilized progress, that the noble class of passenger steamers—equal in all appointments to the finest now on

While the vernal beauty of this region of wide waters and boundless forests is so often dwelt upon, it does not appear that the impression of tameness or defect is produced by the absence of mountain and rock, and the general level which everywhere meets the eye.

There is a grandeur in Alpine scenery which is elevating to the soul, but this also has its own claim to sublimity. All the parts which compose it are congruous. Land and water are in harmony. These lakes, like the ocean, give the impress of boundlessness, and lake, forest, and prairie unite to form

"a fitting floor
For this magnificent temple of the sky."

Nor is variety wanting. The watery surface is never still and tame. Now tossed at the sport of the wind, now sombre beneath the shadows of passing clouds, now brightening in the sun, and now sleeping with an infant's calmness, it has at all times a charm which belongs not to the "dull, tame shore."

There is a human interest, too, in the white sails, far or near, whether scudding before the gale with bellying canvas, and dashing the white foam from the prow, or slow-moving with full-spread wings before the gentler breeze, which always enchains the eye and betokens man's empire over nature.

In the broad features of the land, also, there is an harmonious charm. If there are no hills to lift us to the clouds there are none to limit our horizon; to shut out the sweet sun at its rising and its setting; to obscure any

---

the ocean—which plied between Detroit and Buffalo a half century ago, should have disappeared. The picturesque groups of sailing craft, also, have given place to prosaic lines of hulls under bare poles, towed by tugs.

OLD KNAGGS HOUSE.—EARLY RESIDENCE OF THE AUTHOR.

of the lesser lights of heaven, or the glories of cloud-land and of sunset, or to interrupt the imagination, when her " magical pinions spread wide " over a domain that from its very uniformity seems the more limitless.

<blockquote>
" The great heaven
Seems to stoop down upon the scene in love,—
A nearer vault and of a tenderer blue,
Than that which bends above the eastern hills." *
</blockquote>

---

* " The Prairie."—BRYANT.

LAKE SUPERIOR IN 1840.

"*Father of lakes!*" thy waters bend
  Beyond the eagle's utmost view,
When, throned in heaven, he sees thee send
  Back to the sky its world of blue.

Boundless and deep, the forests weave
  Their twilight shade thy borders o'er,
And threatening cliffs, like giants, heave
  Their rugged forms along thy shore."
SAML. G. GOODRICH.

LAKE SUPERIOR IN 1840.*

AMONG the pleasantest of all my reminiscences of travel is that of the exploration, in connection with the geological survey of Michigan, of the coasts of our upper peninsula, in 1840.

The party for this expedition was composed of the State geologist, Dr. Douglass Houghton; his two assistants, C. C. Douglass and myself; Fredk. Hubbard, in charge of instrumental observations; and, for a part of the way, H. Thielson, a civil engineer, and Charles W. Penny, a young merchant of Detroit, supernumeraries.

We left Detroit in the steamer "Illinois," arriving at Mackinac, May 23. Here two boat crews were made up, consisting of six Canadians. These belonged to that class so famous in the palmy days of the fur trade and the French régime, now extinct, and known to history as "*courcurs de bois.*" They were of mixed blood, in some, the French, in others, the Indian, predominating. Bred to the business, they would row without fatigue from daybreak until dark,—twelve or fourteen hours,— unlade the boats, pitch the tents for the *bourgeois*, pile up the baggage, prepare the evening meal, and then creep under their blankets in the open air and enjoy the sound sleep that labor bestows.

The principal dependence of these voyageurs for food —we had no leisure for hunting and little for fishing—

---
* Read before the Detroit Pioneer Society, Jan., 1874.

was upon a soup of beans, with a most liberal supply of water, into which a piece of pork was dropped. A cake of hard-bread was allowed to each.

The boats for the passage of the Sault were each about twenty feet long by four broad, lightly constructed of pine and cedar, with sharp bows, and were drawn out of the water at night. At the Sault, to which provisions had been forwarded, one of these boats was exchanged for a "Mackinac barge," sufficiently large to carry two months' provisions and all our baggage.

A voyage to and upon our great lake at the time of my story was by no means the easy journey it is now. North of Mackinac, no steamers and no regular line of sail-vessels traversed the waters. The ship-canal around the waters of the Sault had not then been projected. Furs and fish constituted the only commerce, and the latter found too few customers to make the trade profitable. The American Fur Company had its headquarters at Sault Ste. Marie, where was a village of some twenty or thirty houses, mostly of logs, and the United States maintained a garrison. On the opposite shore was a small English settlement, consisting of a few whitewashed cabins and Episcopal and Baptist mission establishments. Here also the Hudson's Bay Company had a post.

At L'Anse had been established for many years a factory of the American Fur Company, the only buildings being a log house, storehouse, and barn, and near by a Baptist mission, consisting of a dozen neat huts of logs and bark. Near the extreme west end of the lake this company had another factory or trading-post, at La Pointe.

These were the only white settlements on the south

shore of this great lake. At two or three points, transient fishing-camps might be met with. Else, all this region was wild and solitary almost as when, a century earlier, it was traversed by the canoe of the Jesuit missionary or echoed to the rude songs of the wild employees of the fur traders. In a large part of the country, on the southern border, within the territory of the United States, the Indian title had not been extinguished. But the settlements of the aboriginal race were rare; probably the whole region did not number 1000 souls.

Apart from the scientific animus of the expedition, our party, in the ardor of youth, could not but look forward to the new and strange scenes which awaited us with somewhat of the enthusiasm that inspired the first explorers of this region of vast forests and inland seas. We were to voyage almost in the same mode as those travellers, to witness scenes as yet little changed, and partaking of the same character of solitude and mystery.

Though I wander from my narrative, I must linger a moment over the impression produced by the romantic island which was our starting-point, Michilimackinac.

Connected with the story of the early wanderings of the French, their perilous missions in the far wilderness, the fur trade, with its fort, its agents, its *coureurs de bois* and numerous employees, its bustle, show, and dissipation, its traffic and its enormous profits, and with the numerous native tribes which here rendezvoused,—no place in the North-west possesses greater historic and traditionary interest. The town retained, as it still does, much of its old-time character. The crescent bay in front was still a lounging-place for the American Ishmaelite, whose huts often covered the beach; and this was the last place on the frontier where the Mackinac barge might be manned and equipped, as a century ago, by a motley crew of half-breed voyageurs.

The natural beauties and wildness of the island, its situation, enthroned at the apex of the peninsula of Michigan and embracing magnificent views of water and island, its lake breezes and pure cold air, and the excellence of its white-fish and trout, have long made it one of the most attractive of watering-places. The proposal to conserve it as a national park is worthy of its character, and it is to be hoped that thus its natural beauties, and what remains of its woods, will be preserved forever to the nation.

On the morning of May 26 we took our departure from Mackinac, with a moderate breeze and a clear sky,—a thing to be noted where fogs are so frequent,—and coasting by St. Martin's Island, entered les Cheneaux.

The river, or more properly Strait of Ste. Marie, is a series of channels, winding amid innumerable islands. Some of these, as St. Joseph and Drummond, cover many square miles, but the greater number are much smaller, and often occupy only a few acres. They line the whole northern coast of Lake Huron, and are occasioned by the junction between the silurian lime rocks and the azoic or primary rocks of Canada.

These islands are but little elevated above the water, and are wooded to the edge with cedar, fir and birch. The evergreen trees are completely shrouded in a tapestry of parasitic moss. This is a true lichen, and is not allied to the great Southern epiphyte which it so strongly resembles. It hangs in long festoons, giving the woods a fantastic and gloomy appearance, but the effect is very beautiful. What are called "les Cheneaux" are passages among islands of this description. They are seldom wide enough to admit any but the smallest craft, and so intricate as to form a perfect labyrinth, where any but the practised mariner might wander long, "in endless mazes lost."

To the north and east of St. Joseph Island the Ste. Marie parts the two systems of rocks, and an instant change takes place in the character of the scenery. Instead of low, timbered shores, the islands rise in abrupt cones, rounded and water-worn, to the height of twenty to one hundred feet, presenting bare knobs of hornblende and quartz. The surfaces are worn smooth, by the action of glaciers, and are frequently covered with a thick carpet of lichens. Among these is, in profusion, the beautiful reindeer moss. A few miles to the right, in Canada, hills of granite rise to a height of 500 to 1000 feet, and form a background to the view.

To the geologist these low hills and rounded knobs have an absorbing interest. Agassiz tells us that America has been falsely denominated the *new* world; that "hers was the first dry land lifted out of the waters; hers the first shore washed by the ocean that enveloped all the earth beside." The antiquary finds in this portion of America a very respectable antiquity. To its known civil history he adds evidence of the existence of a race of men familiar with this region ages before its discovery by the French, who were by no means despicable cultivators of the arts, and he infers a human history—could he but gather the full record—possibly as ancient as the pyramids. But science points to a period infinitely more remote. We had reached and stood upon what was the skeleton of our earth, when but a crust above the seething fires beneath, not only ages before man had a being upon its surface, but probably ages before what we call the "Old World" had been raised by the forces of nature above the universal ocean. Here was antiquity unmeasured by any human standard. Time itself was young then. This backbone of the earliest continent still stretches unbroken, from the Atlantic to the western plains. During the unnumbered years in which the surface of the earth has been changed by successive upheavals and depressions it has stood unmoved.

Around the base of these low granite and metamorphic hills, in the bed of the river, lies a sandstone rock, which we shall find rising into cliffs along the coast of the lake above. It is the lowest of the paleozoic series, the first rock which brings to our eyes evidence of life upon this continent, and, if geologists speak truth, the first which bears witness to the dawn of life upon our earth. Of the earliest forms of organic life two only have with certainty been found in this rock, the *lingula* and the *trilobite*. And these, in the perfection and adaptation of their structure, equal the most perfect beings of their kind which exist at the present day. Thus the first record of the earliest life, upon the most ancient sea beach which the earth affords, is in apparent condemnation of the development hypothesis of Darwin. Are they then evidence of sudden and independent creation, or must we believe that these forms had their origin in some yet more remote and obscure past, and that we behold in these silurian rocks only their perfect development?

Following the northerly channel, the Ste. Marie soon expands into a broad and lovely sheet of water, twelve miles long, called Lake St. George. We have escaped from the labyrinth of rocky isles, the southern shores are again densely wooded, while the azoic rocks are seen on the Canada side, stretching off to the north-west, and terminating in a series of mountainous knobs,—the vertebræ of the world before the Flood. To this lake the Narrows succeed, and here for the first time the Ste. Marie assumes the appearance of a river, being contracted to less than 1000 feet, with a current and occasional rapids.

We passed frequent memorials of the Indian inhabitants. It is not to be wondered at that this region abounds with them, since with an eye to natural beauty this poetical race selects the loveliest spots for the resting-places, both of the living and the dead. The graves were close cabins of logs, thatched with bark, and the places selected are among the most beautiful and elevated sites, as if the souls of the departed braves could hear the echoing paddle and watch the approach of the distant canoe. The burial-place of the chief is designated by a picketed enclosure, and here it is customary for the voyaging Indian to stop, kindle his camp-fire at the head of the grave, and, on departing, to leave within the enclosure a small portion of the provisions he has cooked, for the use of the occupant. A flat cedar stake at the head exhibits in red paint the figure of some bird or brute,—the family totem of the deceased. Often is seen a small cross, erected as an emblem of his faith in Holy Catholic Church, while close by, in strange contrast, is that evidence of his unalterable attachment to the creed of his fathers,—the basket of provisions that is to support his journeying to the land of spirits.

The camping-ground of the voyageur has been that of the Indian from time immemorial. The wigwam poles are recognized from a distance, in some open glade along the shore, left standing after the vagabond inmates have departed. And there is often to be found an old canoe, a camp-kettle, a cradle swinging from the poles, and invariably a litter of picked bones and dirty rags, completely covering the spot, with the burnt brands and ashes of the cabin fire in the midst. Sometimes we meet a rude altar of stones, on which are laid bits of tobacco and other petty offerings to the Manitou. Sometimes the scene is varied by the cabin of a Canadian Frenchman, who, unable to resist the charm of savage life, is bringing up his family of half-breed children in a condition little akin to civilization.

Early on the morning of May 30 we reached the Sault, and proceeded to encamp at the head of the rapids. This required a portage of several rods. The remainder of the day was spent at the village, in witnessing the novel mode of fishing, and other sights pertaining to this remote frontier post.

Preparations for our lake expedition being completed, on the first of June we took our departure from the head of the rapids. Here lay at anchor a beautiful light brig belonging to the American Fur Company, and which bore the name of its founder, John Jacob Astor. Close by its side was a schooner, which had been built by the Ohio Fishing and Mining Company, at Cleveland, and had just made the portage around the rapids. Another vessel was preparing for a similar transportation. With three such crafts floating on its bosom, our great lake seemed to have already lost something of its old-time character, when, a wide waste of waters, it was traversed only by the canoe of the Indian and voyageur. Its importance as a great commercial highway had thus begun

SAULT STE. MARIE, FROM THE CANADA SHORE.

to be foreshadowed, but, in fact, its waters still laved a savage wilderness.*

Some natural phenomena pertaining to a high northern latitude had begun to exhibit what were marvels to our unaccustomed eyes. One of these was the lengthened twilight, the sun continuing to irradiate the horizon with a bright flash, until nearly midnight. In fact, it was quite possible to tell the hour of the night at any time, by the light which indicated the sun's position. The Auroras, too, were surpassingly brilliant; often the electric rays streamed up from every point of the horizon, meeting at the zenith and waving like flame. I note these simple and common phenomena because they were novel to us, and it is only those who travel and encamp in the open air who enjoy to the full such scenes of beauty and wonder.

A summer temperature had now set in, and we witnessed another characteristic of this high latitude,— the sudden advance of the season. During the three days of our stay at this place, vegetation, which a week before had hardly commenced, sprung into active life. Trees then bare were now in full leaf. This phenomenon, though common to our side of the Atlantic, we had nowhere else seen so conspicuously displayed.

Time will not permit a narrative of our journey, a two-months' coasting voyage along the whole southern side of Lake Superior. Nor can I speak, except briefly, of the beauties of the scenery, most of which is now so well

---

* The immense commerce since built up will appear from the statement, that in 1886 the number of vessels which passed through the Ste. Mary's Falls Canal was 6203, carrying 3,701,000 tons and over 50,000 passengers.

known; of Gros Cap and Point Iroquois, those rock-built pillars of Hercules that guard the entrance, and

> "like giants stand,
> To sentinel enchanted land;"

of White-fish Point and its surroundings; of the grand, wild and varied rocky coast; of the many beautiful streams, flashing with cascades, and filled with the speckled trout; or of our scientific researches and observations. I will venture only to relate an occasional incident, and to delineate some features of the coast scenery which seem to me to have been too little noticed or too imperfectly described by others.

Westward from White-fish Point stretch for many miles broad beaches of sand and gravel, backed by hills clothed with Norway-pines, spruce, hemlock, cedar, and birch. These beaches form extensive fishing-grounds, of which parties had already availed themselves. Every one knows the superiority of Lake Superior white-fish, in size and flavor, over those of the lower waters. Yet in relating the following experience I am aware of the risk which I run of being set down as the retailer of a "fish story."

As we were rowing along the beach, some object was descried at a distance, making out of the water. All, at once, gave vigorous chase. On our near approach, the animal, which proved to be an otter, dropped upon the sand a fish which he had just hauled out, and retreated into the lake. This fish, which was scarcely dead, was of a size so extraordinary that it might truly be called—the fish, not the story—a whopper! It measured two and a half feet in length, and one foot five inches in circumference. We had no accurate means of weighing, but its weight was fairly estimated at fifteen pounds! The flesh was delicious in proportion, and made our whole party several capital meals.

These beaches terminate at a deep harbor called the Grand Marais. Hitherto the hills or dunes of sand have been of no great elevation. But now occurs a phenomenon which, though it seems not to have been classed among the wonders of this region, nor described in any books of travel, so far as I am aware, may well be called extraordinary, and worthy a place among the scenic wonders of America. It is a miniature Sahara, several miles in extent, and in many of its peculiar features resembling those lifeless, sandy deserts which are so distinguishing phenomena in some parts of the world. It is known to the French voyageurs as "*Le Grand Sable.*"

Steep cliffs are first observed rising from the water with a very uniform face, of about 200 feet in height, beyond which are visible barren dunes, rising still higher in the distance. On our approach the whole appeared like lofty hills enveloped in fog. This proved to be nothing less than clouds of sand, which the winds were constantly sweeping towards the lake, and which formed a mist so dense as to conceal completely the real character of the coast.

On ascending these steep and wasting cliffs, a scene opens to view which has no parallel except in the great deserts. For an extent of many miles nothing is visible but a waste of sand; not under the form of a monotonous plain, but rising into lofty cones, sweeping in graceful curves, hurled into hollows and spread into long-extended valleys. A few grass roots and small shrubs in some places find a feeble subsistence, and are the only vegetation. But thrusting through the sand are several tops

GRANDES SABLES.

of half-buried pines, barkless, and worn dry and craggy by the drifting soil, while below the surface their bodies appear to be in perfect preservation. To our imagination they seem the time-worn columns of an antique temple, whose main structure has long ago tumbled into dust, or been buried, like the ruins of Egypt, beneath the drift of many centuries.

The surface sand is mostly packed quite hard, and may be trod as a solid floor. This, in many places, is strewed thickly with pebbles; the deep hollows present vast beds of them. Among these are a great variety of precious stones common to the rocks of the country; agates, chalcedony, jasper, quartz of every shade of color and transparency, with hornstone, trap, and other minerals. All are worn smooth, and often beautifully polished by the sharp, drifting sands, and many rich specimens were obtained. We were reminded of the valley of diamonds in the Arabian tales, which it was the fortune of Sinbad to discover, in a scarcely less singular depository.

In the rear of this desert, about two miles from the coast, timber is again met with. Here, just at the edge of the wood, a small and beautiful lake lies embosomed; on the one side, a rich tract of maple forest; on the other, barren and shifting sand. It broke on our view, from amidst the realm of desolation, as did the unexpected fountain to which Saladin led the weary cavalier, Sir Kenneth, over the sandy plains of Palestine, as told in the magic pages of Scott. We named it, not inaptly, I think, "the diamond of the desert." Around this sheet of water we found snow, on the tenth of June, in large quantities, buried beneath a few inches of sand.

From the diamond lake issues a small stream, which, after making its way through the sand, reaches the clay

GRANDES SABLES FROM ABOVE—SAND FLYING.

that constitutes the base of these dunes, and tumbles a perfect cascade into the greater lake. This rivulet separates the dense maple forest which lies on the east from cliffs of driven sand, which rise abruptly to a height that far overlooks the woodland, and are the commencement of the grand and leafless sables.

The view on ascending these is most entrancing. On the one side stretches beneath, and far away, the verdant forest; while, by a transition as sudden as it is opposite in character, on the other side every feature of the landscape seems as if buried beneath hills of snow. The desert surface might be likened to that of an angry ocean, only that the undulations are far more vast, and the wave crests more lofty than the billows of the sea in its wildest commotion. Looking upward from one of these immense basins, where only the sand-wave meets the sky, the beholder is impressed with a sublimity of a novel kind, unmixed with the terror which attends a storm upon the Alps or on the ocean. The scene, wild and unique, may well claim this brief praise, though hitherto unsung, and lacking the charm of historical association, —"the consecration and the poet's dream."

Twelve miles beyond this singular region the beaches terminate, and the sand-rock makes its appearance on the coast, in a range of abrupt cliffs. These are "The Pictured Rocks." They have been often described, but no description that I have seen conveys to my mind a satisfactory impression of their bold, wild, and curious features. In attempting to convey some clear comprehension of them, I can only hope to impart a faithful, though it be a feeble conception of the peculiar features of this marvel of the Northern Lakes.

These cliffs are composed of the same gray-and-red

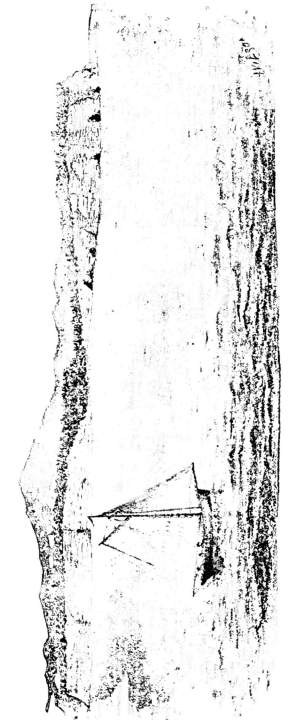

DISTANT VIEW OF THE PICTURED ROCKS.

sand-rock which I have alluded to as the lowest of the paleozoic or silurian rocks. It appears in many places on the coast, and probably forms a large part of the bed of the lake. The cliffs here rise into a mural precipice, springing perpendicularly from the deep waters to the height of from 80 to 250 feet; and for the distance of fifteen miles, except in one or two places, are destitute of a beach upon which even a canoe may be landed. So dangerous is the coast that vessels all give it a wide berth, passing at too great distance for accurate view. A small boat that lingers runs imminent risk, from the liability of this lake to sudden gales, and the traverse is attempted only during a perfect calm. The sand-rock lies in thick strata of varying degrees of hardness, from a coarse crag of the hardest cemented pebbles to a friable rock of aggregated sand. The predominant color is gray, sometimes light, often dark and rusty, and stained by oxides of iron and copper, with which the materials are charged. Bearing in mind these characteristics, the variety of aspects and the strange forms that these cliffs assume will find a ready explanation.

The great diversity of hues that give so beautiful and variegated an appearance to large portions of the surface, and from which the cliffs derive their name, are owing to the metallic oxides which have filtered through the porous stone in watery solutions and left their stains upon the surface. Beautiful as is the effect, it is due to candor to say that to my eyes there appeared but very imperfect representations of those various forms in the vegetable and animal kingdoms which figure in some highly-colored and fanciful descriptions in travellers' tales. Too extravagant an idea could scarcely be conveyed of the exceeding brilliancy of the coloring; but in regard to what artists style the "laying on," the picture presented a much closer resemblance to a house-painter's bucket, upon the outside of which paints of all colors have trickled down in tapering streams. They represent not so much the picture which Nature has painted, as the palette upon which she has cleaned her pencils. Every hue of the rainbow, besides black and white, and in every possible circumstance of shade and alternation, are drawn in long lines, covering thousands of feet of surface.

Near the western extremity of the range, these colors assume a surpassing brilliancy, with a metallic lustre. Streaming over a gracefully curved surface, having an area of several thousand yards, they mimic, on a gigantic scale, the stripes on our national flag, as it waves in the breeze; or, passing down a fractured ledge, are contorted into long zigzag lines.

Upon close examination, these colors are found to proceed from slimy exudations, and to retain their brilliance only while fresh. When the face of the cliff has become dry, they possess a more faint and often mottled appearance. Then may sometimes be found depicted, upon a background of white, yellow or dun, as if rudely dabbed in by the artist, those vague similitudes, in which the imagination may realize verdant landscapes or fierce battle scenes; perhaps, if sufficiently vivid, a full set of Raphael's Cartoons. As a whole, the general effect of the coloring is so striking, that the appellation conferred upon these cliffs is well deserved. Thus strangely drawn, upon as strange a canvas, they add, at least, wonderful beauty and effect to the greater wonders which Nature has here displayed.

But color is far from being the most notable feature of the Pictured Rocks. The disintegrating material of which the rock is composed renders it very susceptible to the effects of the elements. These cliffs present indubitable evidence that the lake once washed them at a height many feet above its present level. And as the strata are of differing degrees of hardness, they have been worn by the waves into a variety of forms. Huge cavernous fissures penetrate the massive wall, often to the distance of several hundred feet, piercing through its great projecting buttresses, and leaving the solid mountain supported by bare pillars. These, in turn, are worn by the eddying waters into cylindrical columns, connected by arches that sometimes spring with great regularity to a vast height.

An immense angular projection of the cliff, known to voyageurs as "La Portaille," exhibits on its three sides arches of this construction, one of which springs to a height of about 150 feet. The openings form passages into a great cavern, or more properly a vestibule, the roof of which is beyond the reach of our longest oars, and which conducts through the entire projecting mass,— a distance of not less than 500 feet. Entering with our boat into this natural rock-built hall, its yawning caverns and overhanging walls strike a sudden awe into the soul. Echo gives back the voice in loud reverberations, and the discharge of a musket produces a roar like a clap of thunder. "Even the slight motion of the waves," writes Governor Cass, "which in the most profound calm agitates these internal seas, swept through the deep caverns with a noise of distant thunder, and died upon the ear, as it rolled forward in the dark recesses inaccessible to human observation ; no sound more melancholy or more awful ever vibrated upon human nerves. Resting in a frail canoe, upon the limpid waters, we seemed

LA PORTAILLE

almost suspended in air, so pellucid is the element upon which we floated. In gazing upon the towering battlements which impended over us, and from which the smallest fragment would have destroyed us, we felt, and felt intensely, our own insignificance. No splendid cathedral, no temple built with human hands, no pomp of worship, could ever impress the spectator with such deep humility, and so strong a conviction of the immense distance between him and the Almighty Architect."* Enthusiastic language! and yet it cannot be deemed exaggerated.

The number and perfection of the wave-created pillars meeting the eye at every turn,—and which seem formed to support the immense weight above,—the various forms of the arches and of the overhanging rock, bear a close resemblance to the orders of human architecture. The rotundity of the columns is, in general, well preserved, and their tops swell into capitals. The supported mass, which is seldom less than 100 feet in thickness, often assumes characteristic forms, corresponding to the mock design. In one instance, for nearly half a mile, it resembles a vast entablature, of which the cornice,—jutting at least 20 feet, with a curve whose grace is not excelled by the best sculpture,—the pictured frieze, the mouldings, metopes, medallions, and other of those forms which pertain to Grecian architecture, are struck out, with a master, but giant hand, in magnificent relief, and with a perfection truly admirable. A portion of the structure had fallen, and lay at the base in heaps of ruins. But even the imperfections appear as if due to the gradual process of decay. It requires little stretch

---

* Discourse before Detroit Historical Society.

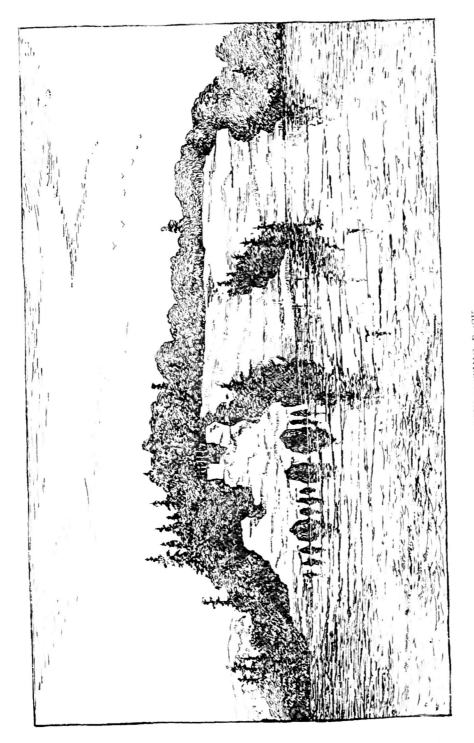
THE GOTHIC ROCK

of the imagination to conceive the whole fabric to be an enormous edifice, the grandest of man's construction, of which the main body has by some convulsion been sunk and engulfed in the waters. We thought of these monuments of ancient art which the volcanic rain of Vesuvius had overwhelmed; but such a temple as this would have enclosed half of Pompeii!

The mind naturally inquires, Are the beautiful forms of ancient architecture the result of long and laborious study, or was some marvel like this exhibited in that distant era, from which cunning sculptors borrowed those designs that immortalize the Parthenon? And if —as the learned have supposed—the marble structures of that age received the addition of a coat of glowing colors,—of which time has left some traces,—we here view the prototype, not only of the graceful forms upon which they labored so successfully, but of the overlay of colorings, in the glory of their original freshness!

These are but single features in the scenic display. The line of cliffs is not uniformly regular, but curves gradually to the south-west, and presents many angles and projecting points. Passing on to harder portions of the rock, the voyageur may encounter at the next angle a vertical and unbroken wall, rearing its solid front from the bed of the lake to the height of from 200 to 300 feet above the surface. The sharpness of the angular projection equals that created by the square and plummet; while the immense thickness of the strata causes the wall to appear as laid in immense blocks, a hundred feet in length. No such blocks were built into their mausolea by the proudest of the Pharaohs.

New changes present themselves as the traveller proceeds. Suddenly he is before the walls of an impregnable

LA CHAPELLE, FROM THE LAKE.

fortress, complete with glacis, bastion, and towers. The western cape of Miner's River exhibits a curious display of this kind. It resembles the dilapidated tower of some time-worn gothic castle. The base rests upon a series of short columns, connected by groined arches, through many of which a boat may pass with ease. There are eight or ten of these pillars; several have large entrances above, and the tower rears its broken battlements to the height of 120 feet.

Among the characteristic features, none is more extraordinary than one to which the French voyageurs have appropriately given the name of "La Chapelle." This rock was originally part of the solid cliff, of which the greater portion has been swept away, causing a valley about half a mile in breadth, through which a considerable stream enters the lake, falling over the rocks in a sheet of foam. Close by, reared upon the rocky platform, about twenty feet above the lake, and conspicuous from its isolation, stands the chapel. It consists of a tabular mass of sandstone, raised upon five columns, whose capitals swell into a uniform arch and support the ceiling or dome of the edifice. Its whole height is 56 feet. The pillars are somewhat irregular in form and position; including their bases, they are about 25 feet in height, and from 4 to 6 feet diameter in the swell. Regular proportions are not altogether preserved, for in most of them the central portion has the smallest diameter, like an hour-glass. Two uphold the front, and from these the arch springs to the height of 30 feet, allowing to the roof a thickness of five or six feet. The span of this arch is 32 feet, as viewed from the water, in which direction the spectator looks completely through the temple into the woodland beyond. The strength

LA CHAPELLE, INSIDE VIEW.

of the roof thus upheld must be considerable, since it is clothed with timber, and from the very centre shoots, spire-like, a lofty pine. The cliff on which the edifice stands forms a proportionate pedestal, ascending from the water in steps, which may be easily mounted.

This solemn natural temple might contain a congregation of several hundred persons. Nor are the usual accommodations for the preacher wanting. A column, the upper half of which has been broken, projects from a recess in the walls, and is worn into a curve behind, like the half of a letter S, creating a stand which would serve the purpose as admirably as it strikingly resembles the old-fashioned pulpit, the base of the column affording convenient steps.

Upon the cliff, just without, a column stands detached, and worn into the form of an urn, no bad representation of the baptismal font.

At what epoch of the world, or for what class of worshippers, this almost perfect temple was created, we might ask in vain of geologist or theologian. Certainly it is well designed to raise in the beholders thoughts of adoration for its all-skilful Architect, while they assign to it a chief place among the wonders of his workmanship.

An urn-shaped mass, similar to the one here observed, of great regularity and beauty of form, and not less than 50 feet in height, may be seen at another point of the coast. Several rills of water leap from the very top of these precipitous cliffs, and add much to the charm of the view. Indeed, taken in connection with the wide-sweeping lake, the distant mountain ranges, and the woodland, crowning the cliff, the scene presented is of the most picturesque and wildest character.

> "Where'er we gaze, around, above, below,
> What rainbow tints, what magic charms are found!
> Rock, river, forest, mountain, all abound,
> And bluest skies that harmonize the whole;
> Beneath, the distant torrent's rushing sound
> Tells where the volumed cataract doth roll,
> Between those hanging rocks, that shock yet please the soul."

Against these huge ramparts in the hour of the storm the billows of this impetuous lake dash with terrific fury, rumbling beneath the open arches, until, from the hollow caverns within, the sounds return like distant echoes, and at times their spray is thrown to the very summits of the cliff. Woe betide the bark that is overtaken by the tempest before these hopeless barriers!

But when the winds are down, lulling the lake to gentlest murmurs, the cautious boatman plies along the lone rampart, and with beating heart ventures to explore its awe-inspiring recesses, those

> "Worn and wild receptacles,
> Worked by the storms, yet work'd as it were planned,
> In hollow halls, with sparry roof and cells."

From this sketch some correct idea may perhaps be gathered of a few of those strange forms which Nature, in her sportive hours, has here carved out of the solid fabric of the globe, as if in mockery of the efforts of man, gigantic monuments of that immeasurable Power who formed the wonders of the universe.

Thirty miles west from the Pictured Rocks, at Chocolate and Carp rivers, we first met, in their approach to the shore, the azoic or primary rocks, which from here onward constitute so interesting and important a feature in the geology of the country. Of their scientific or their economical character it is not my purpose to speak, further than to say that to them belong the iron beds, which are such a mine of wealth to our State. Here, a few years after our visit, sprang into being the busy and thriving city of Marquette. But at the time of which I speak, all was a solitude.

From hence to Keweenaw Bay ranges of granite knobs rise into considerable hills, and around them lie a series of quartzites, slates, and metamorphosed sandstones. The granites are pierced by dykes of trap, which in some cases form straight, narrow, and often lofty walls, in others have overflowed in irregular masses. Here Pluto, not Neptune, has been the controlling spirit, and has left the witness of his rule upon the face of the country. Ascending the knobs of granite and quartz, the change is most striking. To the east the eye embraces a tract lying in immense broad steppes of the sandstone, extending beyond the Pictured Rocks; while to the west are seen only rolling hills and knobs, terminating in the Huron Mountains.

I can add nothing to what is so well known of the mineral riches of this part of the country. But there is in its building-stones a wealth that is hardly yet begun to be realized. No more beautiful and serviceable material than the easily-worked and variously-tinted sandstones is found in the West; and her granites, already broken by natural forces into convenient blocks, and as yet untried, will command a market in the time coming, when the solid and durable shall be regarded as chief requisites to good architecture.

Following our westerly direction to Point Keweenaw, we find the dominion of Pluto established on a most magnificent scale. Not only is his energy displayed in

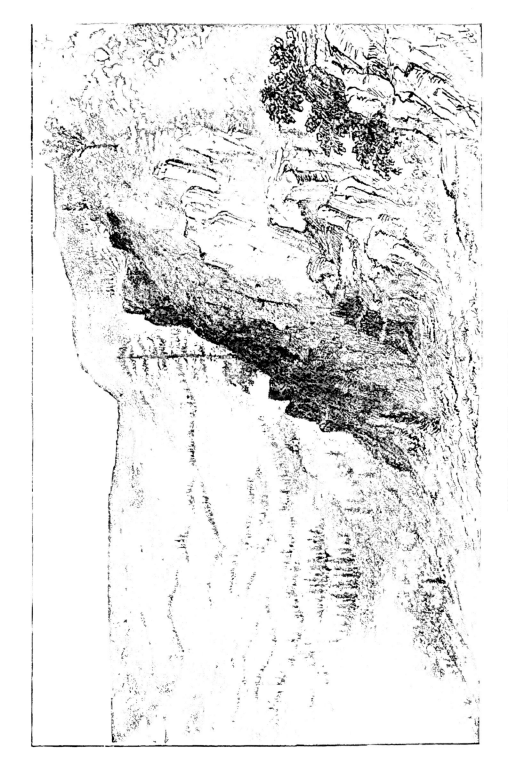

VIEW FROM THE CLIFF RANGES.

the stern and rock-bound coast, but in the lofty ranges of trap, which rise into rugged hills of from 400 to 900 feet above the lake. Within these are secreted, but scarcely concealed, those wonderful veins of native copper, here quarried rather than mined, in masses such as the world has nowhere else produced.

But of all this wealth nothing was then known, except that traces of copper were visible at a few places along the coast, and that a large mass of the native metal lay in the bed of Ontonagon River, long revered by the Indians as a Manitou, and mentioned in the relations of the early French historians.

I will but add, as the result of this season's explorations, that the report of the State geologist, published the ensuing winter, unravelled the whole subject of the mode of occurrence of the copper and its associated minerals, in the most complete and scientific manner. It first made known the immense value which Michigan possessed in its hitherto despised Upper Peninsula; and its immediate effect was to arouse an interest in this then wild and uninhabited Indian territory, which has led to the opening up of its mines, and its present teeming prosperity.

On the third of July we encamped at Copper Harbor, and spent several days in exploration of the surrounding country, and in blasting for ores. Several blasts were got ready for the great national jubilee, which we commemorated in the noisy manner usual with Americans, by a grand discharge from the rocks. We succeeded in producing a tremendous report, and the echo, resounding from the placid water as from a sounding-board, pealed forth in corresponding reverberations for several minutes. Later in the day we retired to our camp and partook of an equally grand dinner. It consisted of pigeons, fried and stewed, corn and bean soup, short-cake and hardtack, pork, and—last but not least—a can of fine oysters, which had been brought along for the occasion. Truly a sumptuous repast for a party of wilderness vagrants, even on a Fourth of July anniversary!

But time warns me to hasten my journey. I will therefore proceed at once to the Ontonagon, where an adventure befel, which it becomes a true knight-errant to relate. It was our purpose to pass up this river to the large mass of copper already alluded to. As we landed at the mouth there were noticed, on the opposite side of the river, several Indian lodges. As soon as we had dined, a few of the occupants crossed over in canoes, shook hands with us, giving the usual greeting of "Bo jou," and received a small gift of tobacco and bread. Accompanying were half a dozen young boys, some of whom had remarkably fine features. We could not but notice, as an unusual circumstance, that several of the men were painted black. One athletic fellow in particular, in this grimy coloring, and naked except the clout, made a very grotesque though savage appearance. The devil himself, however, is said not to be so black as he is painted, and this fellow seemed rather to act the buffoon than the noble warrior.

The party proved to belong to the Buffaloes, whose chief we had met at River Tequamenon, near the eastern end of the lake, and were under the command of the son of that chief. The latter was a resolute-looking fellow, of about 26 or 30 years of age. His face was painted red, and he wore a medal bearing the likeness of John Quincy Adams. We paid little attention to the Indians, although aware that on several occasions exploring parties had been stopped at the mouth of this river and turned back.

We had made but two or three miles progress up the stream when the rapid stroke of paddles was heard, and a canoe, manned with Indians, shot quickly around a bend below and came into sight. The savages were seated, as their custom is, in the bottom of their bark, so that only heads and shoulders were visible. As each applied his whole strength the canoe skimmed over the surface like a young duck, while the dashing of so many paddles caused her to seem propelled by a water-wheel.

Our leader's boat, which was ahead, immediately lay to and raised her American flag. "If they want to fight," said the Doctor, "we'll give them a chance." Our two boats moved into line, and the doctor's assistants armed themselves, one with a revolver, the other with a rusty shot-gun, our entire military resource. The canoe was soon alongside, and the heads and shoulders proved to belong to the bodies of eight stout natives, headed by the young chief. Dr. Houghton held out his hand to be shaken as before. He then asked, through an interpreter, if they recollected the man who had put something into their arms when they were sick, a number of years ago. This something was vaccine for the small-pox, Doctor H. having accompanied the Schoolcraft expedition, in the capacity of physician and botanist. To this the chief, who doubtless well knew, made no reply, but demanded our errand up the river, and said that he and his men had been stationed at the mouth by his father, the head of the tribe, with orders to allow no boat to pass up without that chief's permission. He added further, that we had not paid him, the son, the respect that was his due, by calling at his lodge and leaving a present. Our leader replied that he was sent hither by their great Father, whose instructions he should obey; that he should ascend the river as far as suited him, and that he did not recognize in them any authority to stop him.

Chief. You must wait at the mouth until the Buffalo comes up. Else I and my band shall go with you, and see that you take nothing.

Doctor. I have been here before, and shall go now, as I am ordered by your great Father. I know the country and do not need a guide.

Chief. This country belongs to us.

Doctor. I know that the country is Indian territory, but the treaty of 1826 allows citizens of the United States to visit it. Neither shall I ask consent of the chief to take what I please. But, being acquainted with the Buffalo, I have no objection to showing him what I bring away.

At this stage of the altercation another canoe came in sight, which proved to contain the boys. By this time two of the Indians had made free to step into our small boat, where they seated themselves with great appearance of familiarity. The affair would have had enough of the ludicrous mingled with its serious aspect to warrant us in making light of it, and holding no further parley, but for two considerations, which we could not afford to overlook. Owing to the numerous rapids, the barge, which contained our whole stock, could be got up only ten miles, while we had to proceed to the forks, twenty miles further, in our smaller boat, and thence five miles by foot. And in case of a trial of strength with the Indians, no dependence could be placed upon our hired voyageurs, most of whom were allied to the opposite party, both in blood and training.

Pointing to a bend in the river, our detainers now said, "We are determined that you shall not go beyond that point to-night." This audacious order determined us to at once break off all conference, so asserting our intention to be no longer hindered or delayed, we prepared for immediate departure. After some consultation among themselves, the chief answered, that if we would then and there make them a present of a keg of pork and a barrel of flour we would be allowed to proceed, but should be expected to bestow a further present to the head chief on our return.

To this bold demand, which plainly appeared to be a levy of blackmail, an act of piracy, Dr. Houghton replied that he would give them *as a present* such things as they stood in immediate need of, but nothing more. Nor should he recognize the shadow of a right to demand even that. Accordingly, a bag filled with flour, and some pork and tobacco were offered, and the leader agreed to accept his present in powder, lead, and provisions at La Pointe, whither we were bound.

The parley being at an end, we drew off and pushed up the stream. The hostiles remained awhile in consultation, and then withdrew in the opposite direction. A few miles above we encamped for the night.

It was a necessity, as I have stated, to leave our barge behind with all our stores, while the exploring party were absent for two days and a night. Of course this dilemma was known to the enemy. Holding a council of war the next morning, it was resolved to leave with our goods four of the men, together with the gun. They received most positive orders to fire upon the first Indian who

FALLS AT MOUTH OF MONTREAL RIVER.

touched the baggage, in case any of them should return, as we had reason to expect. And our captain added with solemn emphasis, that if any man failed in fidelity, his own life should pay the forfeit. Having thus played upon their fears, we pursued our laborious journey, reached the Copper Rock at nightfall, and, tired with the day's toils, laid down beneath the cover of the forest and slept soundly.

The next morning we proceeded to the difficult task of detaching portions of the metallic mass, which was successfully accomplished, and we brought away about twenty-five pounds of it. I will here add, that this copper boulder was, a few years afterwards, removed through the agency of Mr. Eldred, of Detroit, and taken to Washington, where it enriches the museum of the Smithsonian Institution. It is now no novelty to see very much larger masses brought down and landed on the dock at our smelting works.

But to conclude the narrative: on reaching camp, on our return, we learned that the chief, with several of his band, had been there, but had touched nothing, and according to his own account, had taken the trail for Lake Flambeau, in order to join a war-party, then organizing, of the Chippewas against the Sioux. Notwithstanding this story we fully expected to meet these fellows again at the mouth, and to whip them there if we could. But when we reached the place all was silent, and the lodges deserted.

I will only add to this long story, that our captain's order was never presented. We learned further, on reaching La Pointe, that the party which waylaid us had known of our journey from the first; that they had "smoked over it," had dogged us the whole way up the lake, subsisting themselves by fishing, and that when we met they were nearly starved.

I will take my hearers but one stage further before closing this excursive ramble.

A few days brought us to the islands called by Carver "The Apostles." On one of the largest of these, Madeline, at La Pointe, is located a general depot of the American Fur Company, for all the western parts of the lake, and the chain of lakes and rivers leading into it. It had become, in consequence, an asylum for all the old traders of that part of the country, and the temporary abode of great numbers of Indians. After pitching our tents on the beach, in front of the fort, amid a crowd of Indians and equally idle half-breeds, we were welcomed by the company's factor, Dr. Borup, Mr. Oakes, the factor from Fond-du-lac, and Mr. Bushnell, the Indian agent, and invited to all the hospitalities of the place.

During our whole voyage from the Sault we had not seen the face of a white man, except at the mission of L'Anse, and a casual fishing party. But here, at the end of our wandering, far from what we had been accustomed to consider the limits of civilization, we were greeted, in the families of these gentlemen, not only by features to which we had been so long strangers, but by all the attendant civilized refinements. The dress and manners of the East, the free converse with friendly voices of our own and the gentler sex, the music of a piano, the sound of the church-going bell and Christian services, seemed to us rather like a return to our homes than the extreme of a two-months' journey in the wilderness.

It may interest my hearers to know in more detail

what composed a post so remote, and which was to me so much a surprise.

La Pointe at that period was one of those peculiar growths known only to an era which has long passed away, or been banished to regions still more remote. What is called the company's "fort" consisted of two large stores painted red, a long storehouse for fish, at the wharf, and a row of neat frame buildings painted white. The latter were occupied by the half dozen families in the company's employ. These dwellings, with the two stores, formed opposite sides of a broad street, in the centre square of which was planted a large flag-pole. Upon this street also clustered sundry smaller and unpainted log tenements of the French and half-breeds. Half a mile from the fort were the Protestant and Catholic missions. The former boasted a good frame mansion of two stories, attached to which was a school, numbering thirty scholars. The Catholic mission had a large number of followers, including the French and Indians. In all, the settlement contained about fifty permanent tenements. Beside these were perhaps an equal number of Indian lodges, irregularly disposed in vacant spaces, and adding to the size and picturesque character of the village. Several hundred Indians usually found constant employ in the fisheries at this place.

This was the oldest, as well as most remote, of the Jesuit missions in the North-west, having been established by Father Allouez, in 1665. It was then a gathering place of many Indian nations, and was hundreds of miles from the nearest French settlement.

It has additional interest from the fact that it witnessed the youthful and zealous labors of Pere Marquette, who came, in 1669, to take the place of Father Allouez, among

PERE MARQUETTE. (FROM THE STATUE AT CITY HALL, DETROIT.)
J. M. DONALDSON, SC.

the Ottawas, Hurons, and other tribes of the neighborhood. It was at La Pointe that Marquette planned that voyage of first discovery, exploration and missionary enterprise down the Mississippi which has rendered his name illustrious.

In the families I have mentioned might be detected an intermixture of Indian blood, which detracts little even from the fairness of the daughters, and the ladies as well as the gentlemen are intelligent and highly educated. Their lives, when not occupied in business, are spent in reading and music; and during the long, cold winter, frequent rides are taken on the ice, upon which they pass from island to island in sledges drawn by dogs.

I could not but picture to my mind, outside of this intelligent circle, the festivities which marked this distant post, at that season, in the more palmy days of the fur trade; when it would be crowded with the hangers-on of such an establishment, returned from their sojourn in the trapping grounds, or their toilsome voyages to and from Montreal and Quebec, bent on lavishing away their season's earnings in days of idleness or debauch, and in "long nights of revelry and ease."

Much of this old-time character still remained. The motley population, the unique village, the fisheries and furs, the Indian dances and pow-wows, the mixture of civilization and barbarism, the isolation, broken only by occasional and irregular arrivals from the world below,— made up a scene for which we were little prepared, which will not be easily forgotten, but of which I can give only this meagre description.

A MICHIGAN GEOLOGICAL EXPEDITION IN 1837.

"Primitive liberty, at last I have found thee! I pass like that bird which flies before me, which pursues its way at random, and is embarrassed only by the choice of shades. While the inhabitants of the rivers accompany my canoe, those of the air sing me their hymns, the beasts of the earth salute me, and the forests bow their tops as I pass.

"Who can describe the feelings that are experienced on entering these forests, coeval with the world, and which alone afford an idea of the creation, such as it issued from the hands of the Almighty."—CHATEAUBRIAND, *Travels in America*, 1791.

A MICHIGAN GEOLOGICAL EXPEDITION IN 1837.*

A RECENT paper read before this society, giving an interesting description of the Saginaw Valley as seen in 1850, suggests some incidents of an expedition into the same valley, in which the writer of this had a share, thirteen years before. At the request of your president, I have undertaken to jot down some of my reminiscences of that journey. These, if they have no other interest, may serve to show the progress of enterprise and settlement in that region, and bring into contrast its feeble beginning and privations of the past, with its present abounding prosperity.

In 1837, the State of Michigan, then in the first year of its young but vigorous existence, organized a State Geological Survey; but the scanty appropriation sufficed only to enable its projector to accomplish, during that year, a limited reconnoissance. This extended, nevertheless, to some degree, into the almost unexplored portion of the lower peninsula.

Salt springs were known to exist, particularly in the vicinity of Grand and Saginaw rivers, and the few facts known of the rocks which constituted most of the coast lines, and made occasional outcrops in the interior, were sufficient to indicate the probability of the existence of coal and gypsum.

---
* Read before the Detroit Pioneer Society Jan., 1872.

It was required, by the act establishing the survey, that an examination and report upon the salt springs should be made at the end of the first season.

It is my intention to relate some of the incidents of a trip—or short campaign, if I may so term it—made in the fall of 1837, for the purpose of making an examination of these springs, and such other geological discoveries as might be made, in the country traversed by those great natural highways, the streams tributary to the Saginaws.

The party consisted of four individuals: Dr. Houghton, the State geologist, and three assistants,—Mr. C. C. Douglass, the writer, and—a dog.

The latter was no inconsequential member of the corps, and had, like the rest, his appointed duties to perform. *Dash* was his name; indicative also of his nature.

This was before the day of railroads, although the young State had already projected its magnificent scheme of internal improvements, and for a considerable part of our contemplated route there were no highways but the streams. Our plan was to reach, by private conveyance, some point on the Shiawassee River, whence we could embark in a canoe and descend to the Saginaw.

Loading into a wagon at Detroit our few traps, which consisted of a tent, provisions, an axe and a gun, in the afternoon of Sept. 13, 1837, we proceeded as far as Royal Oak, where we encamped by the roadside, in the independent mode common to immigrants at that period. To the writer the situation had the charm which youth always finds in novelty.

I will not detain you with incidents, and will only mention the few villages through which we passed.

Prominent among these was Pontiac. The first settler, Mr. Williams, came to this place in 1817 or 1818, with an exploring party, among whom was Governor Cass. This whole region was then supposed to be an interminable morass, and so wild and dangerous was this expedition thought to be, that the party, before setting forth, took leave of their friends with all the solemnity befitting so grave an occasion.

At the time of my visit, Pontiac was a pretty, business-like place. It had been settled 13 years, but had just received incorporation by the legislature. It has always retained its bustling character, while growing rapidly from a thriving hamlet into a beautiful and well built city.

The surrounding country seemed to our eyes far enough removed from the gloomy morass which wild imagination had depicted it, 20 years before. It appeared to me the most beautiful the sun ever shone upon. It was of the character then beginning to be classed as "openings," characterized by a gravelly soil and a sparse growth of oaks and hickories. I speak in the past tense, because, though the rural beauty of the country is still unrivalled, little remains of the original character of the openings. This is a result partly of the process of cultivation, and partly of the thick growth of small timber that has covered all the uncultivated portions since the annual fires have ceased, which kept down the underbrush.

Elevated 400 feet above Detroit River, broken into hills and knobs, which rise frequently 100 feet and more above the surrounding surface, with intervening vales and hollows, forming basins for lakes of the clearest water; in the midst of a park of nature's sole forming, inimitable by the hand of art, this lake region of Michigan deserves its celebrity.

But at the period I allude to, no straight-fenced roads

shut in the highway, and travellers might wind at will through the superb natural park, trampling down only the flowers that in many places created glowing parterres; catching many a bright reflection from the limpid lakes, and sometimes stealing distant sight of a herd of deer, scarcely more wild than the peaceful landscape over which they roamed. Climbing a tree on one of the most elevated knobs, I had a view over probably the whole of Oakland County: seven lakes lay at my feet; on the north and west undulations, like heavy swells of the sea, and on the east a level plain, stretching to the horizon like an ocean's verge.

Byron, in the south-east corner of Shiawassee County, was the termination of our wagon journey. The name had long occupied a prominent place on all the *old* maps of Michigan,—at that time a decade was antiquity,—and held out to the newcomer the promise of a large and thriving village. The reality was disappointing. It possessed—all told—a mill and two houses.

Fentonville, though of more recent origin, had outgrown it, and boasted a tavern, a store, and several frame tenements.

At Byron we exchanged our wagon for a canoe, and commenced a descent of Shiawassee River.

From Byron to Owasso, about twenty miles direct (but many more by the course of the stream), our way lay mostly through land more heavily timbered, but varied with openings and occasional plains. Through this part of the county roads had been opened, and settlements had made rapid progress.

We were now to make our way by the aid of the current, but this meant not all plain-sailing nor luxurious enjoyment. The river was interrupted by numerous rapids, of difficult if not dangerous navigation, and over these shallows we had to drag the canoe. As this necessitated getting into the water, we were provided with water-tight boots, that turned up to the thighs.

At the approach of night a favorable landing was selected, and a new division of labor took place. While one cleared the spot and pitched the tent, another cut wood for the fire, and a third prepared the evening meal. Your humble servant, being installed into the ancient and honorable dignity of cook, had this duty to perform. Any one who has sweetened his food with the sauce of hunger knows how little culinary art is requisite to satisfy famishing guests. Indeed, a piece of fat pork, fried upon a stick over the camp fire, after hours of labor in the wilderness, is a morsel sweeter than any which the pampered epicure knows. To this standard dish our one gun enabled us to add such small game as we chose to take the trouble to obtain.

But my position involved also a duty which might be supposed of less easy accomplishment; viz., the cleaning of the dishes. Fortunately, I was permitted to make free of the assistance of the fourth member of our family. Dash, being properly educated to this service, was not allowed his own dinner until he had thoroughly and impartially scoured our tin plates and sauce-pan; in which duty, I must do him the justice to say, he proved a skilful adept. Indeed, after long experience, I am prepared to recommend a dog's tongue as more effectual than any dish-cloth, with all the aids of hot water and soap. After this process, a simple rinsing in the clear water of the river constituted all the additional operation that the most fastidious could demand.

Several years had passed since the extinguishment of

the Indian title to the lands of the Chippewas, who had claimed this part of the peninsula. But many and extensive reservations lined the Shiawassee and other of the tributaries of the Saginaw, and the natives had as yet felt too little of that fatal spell which falls upon them with the very beginning of the white settlements, to have abandoned much of their old habits.

As we followed down the stream, memorials of the present and recent Indian occupation were frequent. Sometimes we passed huts, constructed of poles, and thatched with bark, but only a few squaws and children were visible. At one place on the bank were ten graves, over which a sort of tomb had been erected, built of logs. Trails were frequent, and on one of these we came upon a tree containing an Indian symbolic epistle. There were figures of men and horses, but we were unable to decipher the meaning. At another place was a cache or pit for hiding provisions.

Many of the Indian clearings stretched for several continuous miles, and many acres bordering the river were covered with the luxuriant maize,—the chief cultivated food of the natives. These plantations receive the name of villages, because they are resorted to by the tribes at the periods of cultivation and harvest. But, in fact, these people had no fixed habitations, but wandered, like the Arabs—their Eastern cousins—from place to place, in patriarchal bands, finding such subsistence as the woods and waters afforded, and pursuing the occupation of trapping and barter with the Indian traders.

At this time, also, they were much scattered by the small-pox, a disease recently introduced by the whites, and which had proved very fatal to the aboriginal inhabitants of this part of Michigan.

Indian trading-houses were a frequent feature, that served to connect the wildness of savage life with the incoming civilization.

Five miles above Shiawassee town was a small Indian village, upon what was known as Knaggs' Reservation, and at a short distance was the house of a trader—Beaubien. Williams, the first settler, came here six years before (1831), and opened a trading-store, as an agent of that extensive enterprise—the American Fur Company. A frame house had since been erected, and a few acres cleared,—the small beginning of one of those invasions of the Saxon upon the Savage which, in an incredibly short period, will leave the latter not even his grave.

Shiawassee town, at this time, contained a dozen log cabins, and as many frames unfinished. One of these was of quite superior construction, and indicative of the era of speculation through which the country had passed. It was three stories in height, and designed for a hotel. The whole village was under mortgage, and was advertised to be sold at public vendue.

Corunna, the county seat, we found to consist of *one* log house, situated upon the bank of the river, and occupied by a Mr. Davis, who, a year before, and soon after the organization of the county, had made an entry here. A steam mill was in process of erection. About twenty acres of land had been cleared and planted; and never did crystal stream lave a more fertile soil.

Three miles below was "located" the village of Owasso, already a thriving settlement, containing a dozen log buildings, one frame one, and a saw-mill.

With the exception of a few scattered settlers upon the plains, south of the line of the present Detroit and Milwaukee Railway, such constituted the entire white population of Shiawassee County.

In the early part of the season, during the progress of the geological survey, beds of bituminous coal had been discovered in the bank of Grand River, in Ingham and Eaton counties, and the rocks met with through the central part of Shiawassee—belonging to the "coal measures"—gave hope of finding an outcrop. Prospecting was accordingly commenced by us at Corunna, but, with the slender means at command, did not prove successful. Yet sufficient was determined, from the character and dip of the rocks, and other indications, to warrant a recommendation to the settlers to continue the investigation. The result was the finding of coal at Corunna, soon after; which, though not of very remunerative thickness, has been used to considerable extent ever since.

I will add, that the year's explorations determined the boundaries of the southerly half of the coal basin of Michigan. Its extent to the north yet remains a problem, to be solved by the hardy pioneers and explorers, who, for a few years past, have been at work so determinedly to bring into the markets of the world that rich and important portion of our State.

A mile below Owasso we passed the last of the white clearings, and made our night's encampment within Big Rock Reservation, twelve miles below that village, and twenty miles from Saginaw.

We had now entered upon the wild and primeval forest, extending in a solitude unbroken by any human sight or sound, except the cabin of the natives and the hut of the Indian trader, to the shores of the upper lakes. For the first time I was startled in my slumbers by the "wolf's long howl," mingled with the hooting of an owl.

Hitherto we had encountered at every few miles the cabin of some adventurous pioneer, for whom the forests had no terrors, but now we were alone with Nature. We could appreciate, in its full extent, the solitude, the boundlessness, the sublimity of this earliest of earth's offspring,—the grand, old, untutored forest.

He who has only traversed woodlands where, at every few miles, he meets a road leading to civilized belongings, knows little of the sense of awe inspired by a forest solitude that has never echoed to the woodman's axe, and where every footstep conducts only into regions more mysterious and unknown.

The woods of this part of Michigan comprised a very mingled growth. Oaks, not gnarled and spreading, as in more open lands, but at once massive and tall, and centuries old; the elm, that most graceful and majestic of trees of any land; the tulip or whitewood, magnificent in size and height above even the Titans of the forest; the broad and green-leaved linden; the clean-bodied beech; the saccharine maples, so superb in their autumnal dresses, —dyed like Joseph's coat of many colors; the giant sycamore, ghost-like, with its white, naked limbs;—these are the common habitants of the forest; with other kinds, each possessing its peculiar grace, and a use and beauty almost unknown in other lands.

We had reached, too, the latitude of the evergreens, which from hence northward, to the farthest limits, become a distinguishing feature of the Michigan forests, imparting to them a more wonderful variety and majesty. Many a towering pine, 150 feet in height, now began to lift its head above its fellow inhabitants, green through youth and age, through verdure and frost. In many places the desert gloom was deepened by the dense and sombre shade of hemlocks, which bent their graceful spray to the earth, and almost shut out the light of day

We took the measure of a white oak that stood at the border of the timbered land and the openings, which I here note as worthy of record. It was thirty-five feet in circumference,—nearly twelve feet diameter. A very respectable tree to be found out of California.

No kind of travel can be imagined more romantically charming than that of floating down the current of one of these large and rapid streams that water this portion of Michigan, piercing the heart of the trackless wilderness. The trees along the banks, instead of forming upright walls, exhibiting the naked trunks of the tall woodland monarchs, throw out thick branches to the sunlight, which bend gracefully to the water, as if to form a screen to the forest depths. Wild fowl are easily approached at almost every bend, affording an ample supply of fresh food without the fatigue of hunting, and at night the camp is made beneath the leafy arches, and lulled by the murmur of the stream or the roar of the wind in the pine tops.

Descending now a wider stream, with a smooth and gentle current, we passed, successively, the mouths of these long feeders to the greater stream,—the Flint, the Cass and the Tittabawassee,—and on the 23d September were opposite Saginaw City.

The last few miles had presented to our view the first irreclaimable marsh we had seen, and here there was plenty of it. The "City" occupied what seemed to be the only considerable elevation for many miles, being about thirty feet above the river.

The paper read to you by Mr. Jennison gave so full

and minute a history of the settlement of the Saginaw Valley that I avoid repetition. I will only refresh your recollection, by stating that the general Government erected a fort here in 1820, and at the same time was established a centre of Indian trade, by the American Fur Company. The country had been visited by General Cass the year previous, and a treaty effected with the native chiefs, by which the lands of the Chippewas were ceded to the United States.

The oldest settlement for farming purposes was made about 1829, and the present site of Saginaw City laid out in 1835. This was just before the height of that mad fever of speculation into which so many plunged wildly, and which built in the wilderness many prospective cities, most of them existing only in the privileged future or on paper plots. Saginaw was one of the few that had good foundation for its celebrity; though as yet there had been little realization of its dreams of future greatness.

My notes record that the city comprised nearly fifty frame houses, four stores—one a handsome dry goods and grocery store, on a large scale—two warehouses, and another in progress, a small church, two steam saw-mills, and, in process of erection, a large edifice, to be called the "Webster House"; this already made a sightly appearance, being 60 by 80 feet. All were of wood. The stockades of the fort still remained; they were some ten feet in height, and surrounded about an acre. I believe that the abandonment of this fortress was occasioned by sickness among the troops, in 1824, three-fourths of the garrison being ill at once of the fevers of the country.

I can add but few to the list of names illustrious in the Saginaw annals, already given you, but I met there, and I well remember, the Littles—Norman and William P.; Hiram Miller and James Fraser, Judge Riggs, Mr. Watson and Mr. Lyon;—men to whose energy and practical wisdom the valley owes so large a share of its prosperity.

It has been stated that the mill known as Emerson's was erected in 1834. I have no recollection of any mill on the east side at the date I record, and the distinguished individual whose name it bears was, at that time, still delighting the happy citizens of Detroit by his *curt* and vehement eloquence. If three mills existed at Saginaw in the fall of 1837, they were certainly the only ones (with one exception) upon that river, as the "City" was the only settlement, if we except a few solitary cabins.

Where now the busy and populous cities of East Saginaw, Bay City, Winona and Portsmouth, numbering their many thousands, stretch almost into a continuous village, for twenty miles below, where the clangor of a hundred mills mingles with the puff of steamers and the scream of the locomotive, and a scene of industry, enterprise and thrift is exhibited which few spots on this earth can rival, was at the period of my visit a solitude, resonant only with the grand, still voices of Nature. Beyond the settlement immediately about the "City," extended the untrimmed forest, as vast and almost as undisturbed as when, to the eyes of De Tocqueville, it was "a real desert."

Having advanced so far with my narrative, I ought, perhaps, in the manner of story-tellers,—though mine is no fiction,—to give a description of the personal appearance of my personages.

Though nearly a generation has passed since the death of Dr. Houghton, no doubt most of those here present well remember the peculiar characteristics of one not easily forgotten;—his diminutive stature—his keen blue eye,—his quick, active motions,—the strong sense and energy of his words, when dealing with matters of science, and his indomitable perseverance in carrying out his designs. They well remember, too, his love of fun, and his hilarious manner of telling a comic story. Of such he had a large fund, and a happy way of using; preserving a grave countenance until he got through, and then joining in the laugh with a peculiar cachination, so contagious as to be alone sufficient to set every one in a roar.

He was no carpet knight of science, and on his geological excursions never flinched from hard work and exposure.

On these occasions he usually wore a suit of gray, the coat having large side-pockets, and hanging loosely upon his small frame. The hands and feet were very small, but the latter were incased in boots that came almost to his thighs. His shocking bad hat was broad-brimmed and slouched, almost concealing his face, and his whole appearance was that of a battered, weather-worn backwoodsman.

I remember meeting him a few years later, when his scientific mind and energetic body had unravelled the mysteries of the mineral region of Lake Superior, and when the new fame of that region had called hosts of scientists to those yet wild shores. He had just landed at Eagle River, fresh from one of his rough expeditions, and was immediately hailed and surrounded by men known over the whole land for their scientific learning, to whose figures and bearing his own presented a striking contrast. Yet these men bowed to his superior knowledge,—sagacity I might term it; and one of them frankly said in my hearing, that the little, rough-looking Doctor carried more true knowledge in his cranium "than all the big heads put together."

I am the more reminded of the personal appearance of our party by an incident which occurred, on occasion of our return to Saginaw from a similar expedition, in the following spring. We happened to be there at the time of the marriage of a sister of Mr. Little, and were among the *distinguished* guests invited to the wedding. Now it chanced that one of the corps—I will not say who—had, with false economy, donned for the expedition a suit of old clothes, which proved to be unequal to the rough usage imposed upon them. When we reached Saginaw he was literally in tatters. A hole garnished each elbow; another became visible when either arm was raised. I have already alluded to the uncouth boots we wore. They were outside the pantaloons, and when not on river service, the wide tops were turned down from the knee. The soles had uncommon width, the rule which regulated surveyors' boots being that these shall project so far beyond the uppers that a mouse might run round on them.

As the other members of the corps were in little better condition,—none of us having a wedding garment,—we would gladly have tendered our regrets, but the persuasive words of our host were not to be withstood.

When I say that we went, I shall only add, that although an apparition so unusual, among a company of well dressed ladies and gentlemen, might well have occasioned remark, the good sense and true politeness of our host and his guests saved us mortification, and left no cause to repent the venture.

As I have undertaken to describe the personnel of our party, I must not omit some further mention of its fourth member. Dash was of spaniel breed, and fond of the water. In the supply of our larder he performed the service of bringing to our boat the wild-fowl that we occasionally shot, and which was abundant in these waters. Nature had furnished him with capacious jaws, which no game could escape, when once within their grip. He had a habit of coming upon game with his mouth wide open.

On one occasion, seeing what he supposed to be a bird floating, he swam towards it, with mouth stretched as usual, and making a grab, his jaws came together with a sudden and loud snap over a piece of foam. Never was dog more puzzled. He looked about with an air of great amazement, and returned, very sheepishly, to be drawn into the boat.

I will relate another anecdote, as showing how he improved in his scientific education. On a future occasion, being sent out for a wounded "diver," and not comprehending the resource of that active and sharp-witted fowl, on the dog's near approach the duck suddenly dived out of sight. Dash was in evident bewilderment, and unable to account for the sudden disappearance. But he was not a dog to be discouraged by so difficult a problem, and after the trick had been several times repeated, a glimmer of the true state of the case entered his canine brain. This accomplished, he was equal to the emergency; for when the diver again went down Dash followed, and both were for some time out of sight. But the dog came up victor, with the bird in his mouth.

As it was in our plan to inspect the salt springs on the Tittabawassee, we had forwarded to Saginaw from

Detroit supplies of biscuit, relying upon the country for our pork. But none was to be had, and we were compelled to resume our journey as destitute of that important item as were the poor inhabitants themselves, who, with a large stock of merchandise, and the great name of *City*, were awaiting the arrival of a schooner to obtain the common necessaries of life. It was to be hoped they were better off for intellectual food, for the place supported a public journal.

Having obtained an order for a more suitable canoe and a guide, we bade temporary adieu to Saginaw (September 25), but were forced by a heavy rain to seek shelter at the house of a Mr. Gardner, a short distance above, where, fortunately, we procured a few pounds of pork. Here, at evening, a few neighbors dropped in, and we consumed the time pleasantly in tales of hunting adventures and fearful Indian murders!

The next day found us at a village of the Chippewas sixteen miles from Saginaw. It consisted of a few lodges, mostly deserted, small-pox having nearly exterminated the band.

At the forks of the Tittabawassee and Pine rivers we found several log cabins, one of which had been occupied as a trading-post. They were inhabited by half-breeds. A Frenchman, with his two Indian wives, occupied the trading-house.

It was still common enough to find, along the shores of the great lakes and rivers, which had been so long the highways of those lawless rangers,—the Coureurs de bois,—during the flourishing period of the fur trade, the cabin of a Canadian, who, with his Indian wife or wives and a troop of half-breed children, had completely adopted the native habits. He lived a half-vagabond life, depending upon fishing and trapping, and sometimes finding employment as a voyageur.

A fair specimen of this class was our guide, Pierre Gruet. Of mixed French and Indian blood, it was hard to tell of which character he most partook. Equally at home in the Canadian cabin and the Indian wigwam, he seemed to be acquainted with every individual of either race that we met, and had a world of talk to unburden himself of whenever we passed a lodge or met a canoe. French joviality was in him united with savage wilfulness. Well enough when confined to his profession of guide and interpreter; as a worker, one American was worth a dozen of him.

Opposite these forks of the river had been " located " the village of Midland;* but it was a village without inhabitants.

Ascending to Salt River, we completed such examination of the springs as the heavy rains of the season permitted. The year following, the State commenced a boring for a salt well near this point, but after a season's labor, with favorable results, the many discouragements attending the work caused its abandonment. Not the least of these was the necessity of sending to Detroit, with long delays and great expense, for everything needed, even for repairs of the augers. It was not until many years afterwards, and when along these vast watercourses populous towns had sprung up, that the conclusions of science were brought to a full practical test, by the establishment of salt wells on the Saginaw; with what success you are all familiar.

I will only say, that in strength and purity the salt of

---

* Now a flourishing city of four thousand inhabitants (1885).

the Saginaw Valley is fully equal to the celebrated article so extensively made in Central New York; that it can be more cheaply manufactured; and, with the increasing facilities for market, is destined to be a very important part of the wealth of Michigan. Already Saginaw furnishes a supply one-half as large as the famous Onondaga.

We had now penetrated into the wilderness, many miles beyond the most remote of the settlements of the Anglo-Saxon. Wild game was very abundant, but we had not the time nor means to pursue it. Besides deer, we had often seen along the shore tracks of the elk, and sometimes of the moose,—an animal almost extinct. Occasionally an otter raised his head above the water, or plunged into it from the bank. We found fresh marks of the labors of the beaver,—that most interesting creature, once existing hereabouts in immense numbers, and now quite hunted to the death. We had shot a snow-owl and driven an eagle from his eyry, and had been regaled with bear's meat, furnished us by the Indians.

How lovely, to our unaccustomed eyes, did nature appear in these solitudes! The first frosts had fallen, and tinged the maples with yellow, orange and crimson; the beech was beginning to assume its russet coat, and the hickories their brilliant yellow, gleaming, in the softened autumn sun, like towers of gold! The river banks, densely wooded, and overrun by the scarlet ivy, were truly magnificent. In strong contrast with these brilliant colors of the autumn was the dark green- almost black, in the shadow of the thick woodland—of the hemlock and fir, amid which shone the white bark of the silver birch, and above all reared the verdant heads of many a lofty pine.

As yet no lumberman's axe had sought to desecrate these glorious shades, nor the speculator to count the dollars that lay hid in the hearts of these mighty pines.

But marvellous changes were in the not distant future.

The traffic in lumber, in the region watered by the Saginaw and its tributaries, which had hardly its beginning a decade after the period I am describing, has in our day reached dimensions of which the wildest brain could not then have dreamed. The main river, for twenty miles from the city of Saginaw to its mouth, is lined with mills. Mainly from this source of wealth numerous cities have sprung into vigorous existence, and five hundred millions of feet of lumber are sent annually, by water and rail, south, east and west, thousands of miles. Michigan pine is in demand, even within the sound of the lumber woods of Maine and Pennsylvania.

I recently visited Midland, not, as before, by the slow progress of a little boat propelled by hands, but in the magnificent cars of the Flint & Pere Marquette Railway, transported by the wings of steam. Where, in 1837, was laid the wilderness city of Midland,—a site without an inhabitant, and approachable only by the river,—now stands the busy, prosperous county seat. A railway connects it with Saginaw, and is rapidly bearing its iron-shod feet far beyond, and joining hands with those vigorous pioneers on our western coasts, that are rapidly pushing on to the Straits of Mackinac. A street of shops, hotels and public buildings, parallel with the river, forms the centre to a town which covers, scatteringly, a mile square, with its churches, mills and comfortable homes.

I passed forty miles further on to the north-west. The scene was a revelation. We are accustomed to regard the railroad as a creation that follows in the wake of man's progress. Here it is the pioneer, the precursor of civilization. It has pierced the heart of the hitherto unbroken wilderness; cutting for itself a narrow path, where, on either side, tall pines and other trees rise into a straight and lofty wall, admitting no prospect, except the narrow line of light that diminishes to a thread in the distance. No time has been allowed for clearings and the ordinary attendants of cultivation. These are all to follow. But saw-mills have sprung up along its magic path, and line the road so thickly that, for nearly the whole distance, I might count an average of two mills to every mile; and all this accomplished within little more than a year.

Having accomplished our river explorations, we prepared for an expedition attended with some danger at that late season, for the month of October had come. This was a coasting voyage, from Saginaw to Port Huron, performed in the canoe which had been procured at the Chippewa Reservation. It was a "dug-out" of wood, thirty feet long, but so narrow, that, seated in the line of the centre, we could use a paddle on either side. In this puny craft we were to undertake, in the middle of autumn, a lake journey of 150 miles.

We descended the Saginaw, which then exhibited few indications of its coming greatness.

East Saginaw had no existence. The village of Carrolton had been plotted, four miles below Saginaw City, and consisted of a two-story log house, used years langsyne as a trading-post.

Portsmouth contained a steam mill, four log cabins and two board shanties, lying just above high-water mark.

Lower Saginaw—now Bay City—occupied somewhat

higher ground, and boasted a pretty frame office used as a chapel, and two or more log huts. It was an infant of one year. In preparation was the frame of a hotel, which, in accordance with the usual custom of the flush times,—already sadly gone,—was large enough to accommodate half the county.

I must here mention a fact which I have never seen alluded to; viz., that we found at several places along the river, and sparingly on the Tittabawassee, *apple trees*. They produced agreeable fruit, and some were apparently of a century's growth. I will not speculate upon their origin; whether the seeds were brought here in the fruit, and accidentally planted, by the voyageurs and coureurs de bois, from the French orchards of Canada, or whether they have a date still more remote. It is curious to notice that some of the earliest travellers allude to orchards, then in profuse bearing, upon islands in the Detroit River. I leave the problem to the antiquary.

Emerging into the bay we encountered, at the Kawkalin River, the last trace of civilized footsteps which we were to see for many days. It was a camp of United States surveyors,—the Rousseaus,—where we were entertained for the night, with all the hospitality which it is common to find among those who dwell beyond the pale of "good society." Unfortunately for our appreciation of these good fellows, it subsequently appeared that the returns of these surveyors were so made-up and false that entire townships had to be re-surveyed by the Government. Corruption in places of public trust is not alone of modern origin.

Memorials of the native inhabitants were still frequent. Upon a swelling knoll overlooking the bay, in the midst of a tract of country from which all the timber had been burned, was a spot which seemed to have been dedicated to the evil Manitou. Here an altar was erected, composed of two large stones, several feet in height, with a flat top and broad base. About were smaller stones, which were covered with propitiatory offerings,—bits of tobacco, pieces of tin, flints, and such articles, of little value to the Indian, as, with religious philosophy, he dedicates to his Manitou. The place had witnessed, doubtless, many an Indian powwow.

In the interest of the scientific object of our tour I will here observe, that near Au Gres River we discovered, beneath the clear waters of the bay, a bed of gypsum. Subsequently, an outcrop of this mineral was found on the neighboring land, and has been long quarried with profit.

Some islands lay several miles from shore, upon our approach to which, immense numbers of gulls, that had here their secure retreat and breeding-places, wheeled about us, uttering loud cries. The young ones were easily caught, and we found a few eggs. Here also sport of an unusual kind awaited us. In the waves that broke among the boulders along the shore, sturgeon were gambolling. So intent were they upon their play, and so ignorant of man's superior cunning, that, springing in among them, after a vigorous tussle we threw one ashore, with no other aid than our hands. It stocked our larder for several days, with its variety of meat,—fish, fowl and— Albany beef.

Of our further voyage, until we rounded Point Aux Barques, I have nothing to note, beyond the usual adventures and delays that attend mariners in so perilous a craft, upon the treacherous waves of Saginaw Bay. The toils of the day were compensated by the sweetest of slumbers, when, having supped on pork and hard bread, wrapped each in his blanket, we fell asleep beneath the soft influence of the Pleiades.

At the point alluded to the coast is iron-bound, affording no harbor, and being thickly wooded with evergreens, its aspect was forbidding and gloomy. Add to this, that the waves are incessantly lashing the rocks, which receive the whole fury of the sea, whether the wind be from the lake on the right or the broad bay on the left. This action of the waters has caused channels to be worn through large masses of the friable sandstone, which, tumbling into the lake, form small islets.

In doubling the cape, the voyageur is struck with the singular appearance of two projecting masses, detached from the main, and covered with timber. They bear close resemblance to the bows of vessels, with the hulls exposed down to the keel. The bowsprit and sides are nearly perfect. They are about 50 feet in the beam, and 16 to 20 in height. Nature seems often to delight in such mimicry of the works of man. The name which was bestowed by the French, at an early day, continues still significant of the mimic resemblance.

Near White Rock, on the Lake Huron coast, 50 miles from its outlet, at the boundary of the then surveyed portion of Sanilac County, we found a settler,--the first we had met since leaving Saginaw River. Mr. Allen had been here three months, and, with five hands, was erecting a saw-mill on a dashing little brook that had nearly swamped us in entering. He had no neighbor, but the mistress of the house informed us they had been all summer in expectation and promise of the settlement at White Rock City of 200 families.

The annals of this place constitute one of the chapters of romance, of which the records of 1835 and 1836 are so replete. Before the rage of real-estate speculation was at its height, and all through that wild fever, we had known of "White Rock City."

Maps, executed in the highest style of the topographic art,—displayed in hotel bar-rooms and other public places, where congregated the thousand seekers after the fortune that courted the happy possessor of valuable lots and water privileges,—had announced its unrivalled situation and advantages. They depicted the magnificent harbor, at the mouth of a large stream, into which steamboats were entering. Saw-mills were converting the forests into houses. Around the Public Square clustered a Court-house, churches, and other public buildings, not omitting the inevitable Bank, and the air of prosperity which pervaded the place was evident at a glance. Auctioneers had sounded its praises, and struck off its lots, at popular prices, to eager buyers. None of the rising cities for which Michigan had become famous had so wide a celebrity, and distributed stock so liberally.

And now we were to see, with our own eyes, this western marvel, or at least its ruins.

A large white boulder in the lake marked the entrance, and gave name to this modern Karnac. We found the entering river. It hardly admitted our log canoe. Harbor there was none. Churches, houses, mills, people, —all were a myth. A thick wilderness covered the whole site. Excepting Mr. Allen, it was 40 miles to the nearest inhabitant. Where the Public Square had been depicted stood several large beech trees. On one of these we carved the names of our party, who were thus registered, for the benefit of future visitors, as the first guests of the "White Rock Hotel."

It may serve more fully to show the adventurous character of our expedition, if I close this narrative by some detail of our last day's experience,—perhaps not a very unusual one in canoe navigation. It may serve, too, to illustrate the risks incurred by our daring chief; sometimes too rashly, and, alas! once too often!

On the night of October 11, we encamped 22 miles from Fort Gratiot, and congratulated ourselves on the near conclusion of our journey. For this there was reason, as our provisions were gone and the weather was stormy. Here a hard wind detained us a day, and the morning succeeding showed the waters risen several feet, and rolling in huge breakers. To proceed by water seemed impossible, but there was no travelled road to Black River, and our provisions were exhausted. For several days we had been on rations, and our poor canine friend, who at the outset could not eat duck meat, was glad to swallow a wing,—feathers and all. A council of war decided to trust once more to the boisterous waves, which our frail craft had hitherto borne us over in safety.

Raising the boat upon rollers, we packed in tent and bags—the latter now heavy with "specimens"—so arranged as to make three partitions, established Dash in his place, while the rest took each his station. Thus appointed, we ran rapidly out into the water, leaped aboard, and pulled from the land. The launch was neatly effected, but danger was ahead. Encountering the breakers we at once shipped a sea, which completely filled the foremost division. This was occupied by the Doctor, who cried, "We are swamped." But a pail stood ready to each hand. The Doctor bailed while the others pulled stoutly on their paddles, and we were soon beyond the breakers. Return was now impossible. The temperature was at freezing, and we received a ducking from many a white-cap that chilled us to the marrow. Our little boat was a morsel for the waves, and when one of those huge swells—the three sisters, as sailors call them—lifted us up, we seemed hurrying inevitably to the shore, and when it receded its crest concealed everything but the sky and the watery horizon. We could not raise sail without danger of running under, and many a wave-crest must be beaten back with our paddles, and our pails were seldom idle.

But "the longest day will have an end," and after five hours endurance, wet, exhausted and hungry, we landed at the light-house. Thence we descended to Black River, two miles below, where the village of Port Huron was in the second year of its infancy. From here a steam-boat conveyed us to Detroit.

Thus ended our adventurous journey, "by flood and fell."

I have only to add, that if my long-drawn gossip has contributed to your entertainment, or given any clearer impression of the Michigan of 34 years ago, it will not have proved altogether idle.

A TIME OF UNIVERSAL PROSPERITY, AND WHAT CAME OF IT.

"Few and evil were the days of this banking, and the history of the system of wild-cat banks would be humiliating, but perhaps profitable, reading now, although the sharpers and rascals of 1876 are undoubtedly more adept in knavery than their ruder predecessors, and would not be proud of such small swindling. The crash came as soon as the general business panic began to spread through the Union; and within five years after the State was formed, the financial ruin of the people was complete."—Chief-Justice CAMPBELL, "Outlines of the Political History of Michigan," 1876.

A TIME OF UNIVERSAL PROSPERITY, AND WHAT CAME OF IT.*

WHILE the errors of the past constitute the wisest lessons of the future, the following episode in Western history may be read with profit. The story is not new, but may derive some additional interest from the individual experience of the writer.

The years 1835, 1836 and 1837 were to Michigan one of those "periods of unexampled prosperity" with which our country has been periodically favored. In its character and results no better example has occurred in our history. This prosperous condition had begun to manifest itself in the extraordinary demand for wild lands, and in the sudden appreciation of the immense advantages possessed by a great number of places in the "West," and particularly in newly opened Michigan, for the building up of large cities. That the Peninsula possessed unequalled "water privileges" could not be doubted by any one who recognized its position on the map of the United States, almost surrounded by the waters of the Great Lakes. Interior lakes, too, were numerous, and large and rapid streams everywhere intersected the land. At least this was the case so far as the country was known, for the Government surveys had extended over not more than one-third of its surface. These surveys had opened to sale, at the low price of one dollar and twenty-five cents

---

* Published in the *Magazine of Western History*, January, 1886.

per acre, a most beautiful and varied country of "oak-openings" and timbered lands, with occasional small rolling prairies, all interspersed with lakes and streams. What a mine of wealth lay in a few thousand, or even a few hundred acres of such lands at the low price of a dollar and a quarter per acre!

From the very beginning of the period we are considering, and even before, a steady stream of immigration had begun to pour into the territory. It consisted mostly of people of means and respectability from the older States, led by the prospect of cheaper lands. Wagons loaded with household goods and surmounted by a live freight of women and children—the men trudging on foot—were constantly entering by the almost only door, Detroit, in great numbers, bound for some paradise in the new Eldorado. A curious spectacle at one time presented itself—literally a *drove* of men—Frenchmen from lower Canada—taken on by an adventurer to be settled upon the River St. Joseph, at the mouth of which, in the olden time, their countrymen had built a "fort" among the savages. Each had his pack, bound up in a blanket, upon his shoulders, and the baggage followed in a wagon; for the United States Government had opened a road in that direction, leading from Detroit to Chicago.

Men who never before saw a wilderness were tempted to set forth, on horseback and on foot, in the spirit which prompted so many gentlemen adventurers, in the early settlement of the New World, to swell the ranks of the colonists—the prospect of speedy and golden fortunes. The numbers that crowded to the search soon converted the ordinary slow process into a race.

Three land-offices had been opened by the Government in Michigan—one at Detroit, one at Monroe, another near the western extremity of the known portion of the territory at Kalamazoo, then called Bronson. The strife and eagerness which prevailed at these offices passed all sober bounds. They were besieged long before the hour arrived for opening; crowds of anxious faces gathered about the doors and blocked up the windows, each eager to make "entry" of some splendid tract of farming land, or better still, some magnificent site for a town, before an equally greedy speculator should discover and pounce upon the treasure.

One of these land-lookers, who had been for days traversing the woods and "taking notes," if he chanced to fall in with some one who was suspected of having seen the coveted tract, secretly hurried off, in the dead of night, determined to steal a march upon the others and secure the prize. Often, after an exhausting ride and a still more tedious waiting for his turn, he obtained his chance at the window, only to learn that a more wary applicant had been beforehand with him. What exultation if he found himself in time! What execration upon his ill fate if too late!

At the hotels were gathered animated crowds, from all quarters of the country, of speculators in lands. Every one who had secured some fortunate entry was busily proclaiming his good luck, and calculating his gains. The less fortunate, and those who were unable to convert themselves into woodsmen, were satisfied to take the accounts of others on trust, and buy at second hand, of course at a very large advance, expecting in their turn to realize a handsome increase.

Beautifully engraved maps of new city plots were executed in all haste, on which the contemplated improvements were laid down. Hotels, warehouses and banks were here erected, like palaces in fairy land; piers projected into the harbors, and steam-boats were seen entering. Wherever a crowd could be collected auctioneers were knocking down lots to eager buyers, and happy was he who secured one with a "fine water privilege," at a price a thousand fold beyond its first cost of a few days before. Nor were these improvements all upon paper. In an incredibly short time small clearings had been effected, a town plat surveyed—often half a hundred miles from the nearest actual settler—and shingle palaces arose in the wilderness, or amid the burned stumps that were left for time to remove. Prominent among these, and often the only buildings erected preliminary to the sale of lots, were a hotel and a bank.

At the admission of Michigan into the Union, in 1836, the territory contained fifteen chartered banks, with a population estimated at nearly one hundred and fifty thousand. These banks were all authorized to issue "currency." Why should these few enjoy a monopoly of so good a thing as money, which benefited all alike, and of which there could not be too much? Consequently one of the first acts of the new State government, March, 1837, was to pass a general banking law. Thus by a bold stroke monopoly was abolished, while bill-holders were made exceptionally secure by a pledge of real estate. Of this everybody held large quantities, and nothing had proved so convertible. Confidence in it was unbounded. Of course every proprietor of a "city" started a bank.

These became so numerous that money was one of the most plentiful of commodities. The new currency was made redeemable in gold and silver, and every bank was required to keep in its vaults thirty per cent. of its circulation in the precious metals. When to these precautions was added the real estate, pledged for the redemption of the bills, and the whole placed under the supervision of commissioners specially appointed, and who were to visit and examine the banks every few months, could reasonable man ask for more ample security?

The banks of Eastern States, also, had a large circulation in the West, and they expanded to the full extent of their powers. The effect of such rapid increase of the circulating medium was to enhance prices of all commodities, and to stimulate speculation. Money became flush in every pocket, and all who had "the fever"—and few had not—were anxious to invest and own one or more of these farms and city lots that were held at such high value, and were making every holder rich. Poor women, who had accumulated a little spare cash, widows and sewing girls, were only too thankful when some kind friend volunteered to put them in the way of realizing some such fortunate investment. The southern counties of Michigan were speedily bought up, and the Government surveys were not rapid enough to satisfy the greed.

Stimulated by the abounding sunshine, the State, too, had entered the arena, in its official capacity, and undertaken a vast system of internal improvements, for which its bonds were outstanding to the amount of five million dollars. But already storm-clouds were gathering, which were soon to darken the whole heavens. As a ship, which for many days has sailed gallantly on its course under favoring winds, with all of its canvas spread, is forced to take in sail when a shift of the wind threatens a gale, so the banks, which had so greatly "expanded" in the breezes of universal prosperity, found it necessary to "contract" at the first suspicion of a change. Suddenly the storm fell. At the first demand to realize for their bills in specie, the banks were compelled to call in their circulation. As the whole amount of specie in the country was far below the amount of paper in circulation, many banks broke under the large demand which fell upon them as soon as the public became suspicious of their ability to pay. All were forced to contract their loans, and money was rapidly being called in, instead of being liberally paid out as before.

Money speedily became "tight." As few banks were able to sustain the pressure, it became necessary, in the view of the public authorities, to exercise the power, where it existed, to suspend specie payments. Accordingly an act was passed to that effect by the State Legislature, which was summoned for that purpose by the governor, June, 1837, only three months after the passage of the general banking law. It was thus hoped to tide over the pressure, which was believed to be but temporary.

Prior to the passage of this act, about twenty banks had registered and gone into operation under the general law. As the act did not repeal this law, many more took advantage of the privilege afforded by it of issuing irredeemable paper; so that before the inevitable end came no less than fifty banks were scattering their worthless notes as far and as widely as means could be found to effect it. But the end was close at hand. Prices fell with as magical a facility as they had risen. The real estate security of the new banks, which was supposed to be so stable, was suddenly found to be the weakest security possible. In the matter of the percentage of specie required to be kept in the vaults, it was found that the grossest frauds had been practised. Kegs filled with nails and broken glass, and having only an upper layer of coin, had been substituted in many instances, and were passed as genuine. In other cases, one institution loaned temporarily to another that was about to receive a visit from the commissioners, and the favor was reciprocated when its turn came. One by one, in rapid succession, the banks toppled to the earth from which, like mushrooms, they had sprung, as it were in a night. They were known universally under the name of "wild-cats." The most worthless were styled "red-dog." The bills fell to a mere nominal value, or greatly depreciated, as it became known that the real estate held would suffice to redeem only a small fraction of the circulation. Much of this was found to be of no value whatever, as it represented merely swindling operations. Many a poor man thus lost all his available means of livelihood.

Many anecdotes were told of these hollow institutions, and many a joke was perpetrated at their expense, which would be laughable enough were there not, in sober sadness, less occasion for mirth than for tears and curses. I vouch for the authenticity of the following:

One of the Michigan banks had gained an unusual share of notoriety, under the name of "The Bank of Sandstone." It was "located" at a place of that name, situated in the central part of the State, where quarries of a fine grit-stone had recently been opened. These constituted the entire commerce of the little burg, and the solid corner-stone of the new institution, whose promises to pay were in wide circulation. An old resident of Michigan held a large quantity of these bills, and learning that the bank was "broke," came to my informant, in great distress, for advice. He was advised to go immediately to Sandstone and demand redemption, as it was understood the bank had some means, and the usual way was "first come, first served." The advice was followed. The man, on his return, called on his adviser, who inquired after his success, and was assured that it was quite complete. "I presented my roll," said he, "and was paid as follows: For every ten-dollar bill, a millstone; for every five-dollar, a grindstone, and for every one-dollar bill a whetstone!"

The year 1838 saw as "hard times" in Michigan as the two previous years had witnessed a seeming prosperity. Men of supposed large wealth, and who owned thousands of acres of wild lands, valued at hundreds of thousands of dollars, were unable to buy provision for their families, and knew not where to look for the supply of their daily wants. Farmers had neglected to cultivate their farms in the struggle to amass land. The new cities, which the magic wand of speculation had created, were left without inhabitants. Trade was paralyzed for want of money, and prices fell below the old standard. To add to the depreciation of real estate, a strong feeling arose among the actual settlers against non-resident proprietors. These were called "speculators," and many contrivances were resorted to to throw on them the burden of taxation. Thus, in opening new roads, the resident was permitted to work out his tax, at an easy rate, by an understanding with the overseers, while the law compelled the non-resident to pay a higher rate in money. Under the name of school-houses, large edifices were built and used for town-meetings and religious worship. The non-resident land-owner was charged with keeping out settlers by raising the price of land, in forgetfulness of the fact that the very tide of speculation had been the means of opening up the country to future settlement. Land which had constituted the sole wealth of thousands became a drug. Large tracts were frequently abandoned to the tax-gatherer for a sum which a few years previous would not have bought a single acre. The banks did not outlive the destruction of the wealth they had fictitiously created. In two years from the act which gave them birth, it is believed, not a "wild-cat" nor "red-dog" of them all was in existence. But they left from one to two millions of dollars of their worthless bills in the hands of creditors. Four or five chartered banks only survived, and they proved fully sufficient for the wants of the population for years to come.

The year following the crash of 1838, the writer had occasion to visit the *ruins* of several of those renowned cities that had flourished so magnificently—on paper. One of these was situated on a small stream which discharged into Lake Michigan. Most of the streams on this side of the Peninsula have lakes near their outlets, originating in the setting back of the water, occasioned by the sand-bars at their mouths. These lakes are often large and deep enough for very fine harbors, but which can be made available only by the construction of piers.

The village of Port Sheldon was "located" at the outlet of one of these streams—the smallest of its kind, and without depth of water sufficient for a harbor. But one road led to it from the nearest and still distant settlement. It was in the midst of a tall forest of pines and other timber, very few of which had been cut away. The clearing disclosed a large frame building, handsomely finished outwardly, but a mere barn within, and by its side a smaller one, decorated with Grecian pillars. These were the hotel and the bank. And they were the only buildings in the place, if we except a few shanties scarcely decent for the abode of the most poverty-stricken. The bank had collapsed; the hotel was without guests; the splendid bubble had burst, and its brilliance vanished suddenly and forever. In 1865 the whole town plat, consisting of two hundred acres of very poor land, was sold for a petty sum. The long abandoned and desolate site, of which its projectors had published with prophetic foresight so many years before—" Nature seems to have done almost everything for this point, and the time is at hand when her eminent advantages will lift her to the first rank among our cities of the lakes "—was now the owlish abode of a solitary Dutchman.

Another of these town sites, which had made a great noise, was situated near the mouth of Maumee Bay of Lake Erie. It was on low, marshy land, which had been regularly laid out in streets and some twenty or more buildings erected. The high water of 1838 had converted into a marsh the whole site. All the buildings were deserted and the city was without an inhabitant. Two of the houses were pointed out—among the handsomest in the place—that had been built by poor milliner girls, who had invested in them all their earnings. They could not be approached, except by boat. This was the Port of Havre, the rival of its namesake, in the dreams of its founders and of their credulous victims, for one short year, before the waters of desolation swept away its glories.

One of the first found and most famous sites was "White-rock City." It was upon the shore of Lake Huron, at the mouth of a pretty rivulet. Maps of this "city" had been scattered far and wide, and lots sold and resold at fabulous prices. These maps represented a large and flourishing town upon a magnificent river. Piers projected into the harbor, which was filled with steam-boats, and it was evident that a thriving commerce had begun. I visited this place, during a coasting voyage, in the fall of 1837. The only approach was by the lake, for it was far removed from any road and forty miles from the nearest inhabitant, except a solitary backwoodsman. A large boulder rock in the lake marked the "harbor." The "river" was insufficient for the entrance of our log canoe. An unbroken and unsurveyed forest covered the whole site. We could not find even a solitary ruin standing alone, like that at Heliopolis, in the Egyptian desert, to mark the place of departed grandeur.

At a few of the really "eligible" sites thriving villages have since sprung up, the Government having aided to build harbors, or natural advantages existing. But most of these town sites still retain their valuable privileges unimproved, and their owners have either abandoned hope, or continue to pay taxes on some undivided one-hundredth part of a fractional "forty," purchased at city prices, that is not even marketable as farming land.

The financial reverses of 1838 were followed by another calamity, which added greatly to the distress of the settled population of the State. The season of 1839 proved very sickly. Among the permanent improvements made during flush times were numerous mills, almost every one of which formed a nucleus for a settlement. No labor or thought had been bestowed upon clearing the stumps and fallen timber from the mill ponds, and this proved a formidable source of malaria.

In the fall of that year I passed through many hamlets, and even considerable villages, where a quarter part of the population were down with fever and ague. I had often to ride miles beyond my intended resting-place, because at the tavern where I applied the family were too ill to wait upon me. At others I was enabled to find supper and a bed for myself, but had to seek accommodation for my horse where I could find it. Having myself had a touch of the ague, I carried a stock of quinine in my saddle-bags. These old-fashioned appurtenances sometimes caused me to be hailed as "doctor." On one of these occasions, finding what was the medicine required, I did not hesitate to allow the mistake to go uncorrected, made the professional visit, administered the pills, but, undoctor-like, departed without my fee.

Reaching Monroe late one evening, I anticipated no difficulty in finding comfortable quarters, for this place was, in name, at least, a city, and second only in importance to Detroit. As I entered the street, I overheard a conversation, in which occurred the not very comforting remark—"Tom, you must make the next coffin; I have worked myself almost to death at it the last week." Even in this old city it was only after much trouble that I succeeded in quartering myself in one place and my beast in another.

Most persons only laughed at those who were so unfortunate as to be seized with "fever and ager," as the popular term was for this diresome disease, as if it were matter of course that every one must have his turn at shaking like a lamb's tail. The rival cities of Monroe and Toledo were constantly bantering each other upon the insalubrity of their neighbor's location. But this year the subject was one almost too serious for joking. Who has not noticed that we are often most inclined to make merry when we have greatest cause for sadness? So jokes carried the day. Saw-mills were spoken of as driven by fever-and-ague power. Villages were told of where the church bells were rung every half hour to mark the time for taking the inevitable quinine. On one occasion, a traveller is said to have entered a village and searched in vain for a tavern. He found the streets deserted and grass-grown. At last he followed the one which showed the most marks of travel, and it led him to—the graveyard.

Since that period a great change has taken place in the salubriousness of the country, and, though intermittent diseases continue to be a prevailing type, it is acknowledged that Michigan has proved to be as healthy a State as any in the Union. As great a change has taken place in the face of the country. The fever of speculation over, resident land-owners applied themselves diligently to the cultivation of the soil. New settlers continued to pour in, though the stream was in part diverted to territory nearer the setting sun, the discovery being made that Michigan was too far east for emigrants bound westward, ho! The mania of speculation which had been considered by the new settlers so serious a drawback, proved a substantial benefit, from the numerous and solid improvements it brought about in a very brief time, that would otherwise have been delayed many years. The hard times continued for almost a decade. It was not until a general bankrupt law had wiped out the load of debt which had overwhelmed a great part of the country, and the sufferers, taught by sad experience, had learned to pursue business in safer channels, that we date the return of substantial as well as universal prosperity.

FRENCH HABITANTS OF THE DETROIT.

"Les Canadiens, c'est-à-dire, les Creoles du Canada, respirent en naissant un air de liberté, qui les rend fort agréables dans le commerce de la vie, et nulle part ailleurs on ne parle plus purement Notre Langue. On ne remarque même ici aucun accent.

"On ne voit point en ce Pays de Personnes riches, et c'est bien dommage, car on y aime à se faire honneur de son bien, and Personne presque ne s'amuse à thésauriser. On fait bon chere, si avec cela on peut avoir de quoi se bien mettre; sinon, on se retranche sur la table, pour être bien vêtu. Aussi faut-il avouer que les ajustements sont bien à nos Créoles. Tout est ici de belle taille, and le plus [beau] sang du Monde dans les deux sexes; l'esprit enjoué, les manieres douces and polies sont communes à tous; et la rusticité, soit dans la langage, soit dans les façons, n'est pas même connuë dans les Campagnes les plus écartées."—CHARLEVOIX, *Histoire de la Nouvelle France*, 1720.

FRENCH HABITANTS OF THE DETROIT.*

PART I.

I HAVE undertaken to occupy your attention with a subject in the details of which general history is very meagre, namely, the character and habits of the first colonists of Michigan.

From time to time many interesting items have been given to the public by noted citizens, including some "to the manor born," but they are mostly of fugitive character, or are buried in the columns of old newspapers.

To these materials, scanty as they are, I am aware that I can add but little that is valuable, out of the stores of my own observation and research. Yet there are fields not wholly gleaned, and if I have discovered any new grains of truth, or can bind the scattered materials into an acceptable sheaf, I may at least be excused from following where others have so worthily led.

Of the present generation how few appreciate the character of the people who laid the foundation of our beautiful city; who for more than half a century constituted the sole population of the Territory of the Lakes; and whose descendants, whelmed in the overflowing tide of Anglo-Saxons, still retain, to a good degree, their old tongue, and somewhat of their ancient customs. But these are undergoing a rapid change. They are destined, at no distant day, to be absorbed into the general

---

* Read before the Detroit Pioneer Society, 1872, and published in the State Pioneer Collections.

element, and the peculiar features which characterized the French of the olden times will soon be utterly obliterated and forgotten.

Without going into historical detail, which would lead into too wide a field, I propose to notice some facts of general application, which will prepare us better to understand the character and customs of those who claim the honors of pioneers in the settlement of Michigan.

The story of the settlement of Canada by the French is full of stirring incident, of marvellous adventure,—of life amid deep forests, and upon the vast rivers and inland oceans of our continent,—almost as wild as that of their savage associates. It has been often told, and nowhere with more fidelity and graphic power than in the captivating pages of Parkman.

English, and sometimes American, historians are not always just toward the race who first peopled the territories of New France. They notice the complete subjection and willing obedience of the French *emigré* to the home government; his recognition of the Indian claims, and ready affiliation and sympathy with the savage tribes; and they compare with these,—unfavorably to the Frenchman,—the energy, enterprise, and individual independence which brought to our Atlantic shores the New England immigrants; which led them to subdue the wilderness, and have impressed their character upon the institutions and fortune of these United States.

The flourishing period of French colonization was that of the long and brilliant reign of Louis XIV. In the home country it was an age of corruption, of despotic arrogance in the high places of the kingdom, and of unreasoning obedience on the part of those below. No successful clashing had occurred between the ruling and the ruled between despotism and liberty—such as conspired to drive the first English emigrants—pilgrims from arbitrary power—to the wild shores of the New England in America. Here, thrown upon their unaided resources, all the energy of which the Anglo-Saxon nature is capable was called forth to enable them to establish a home in the wilderness. They struck at once upon the source of an enduring prosperity, the culture of the soil.

While New France was the cherished care of the Grand Monarque, it did not escape the corruptions of that court and age. The principles which lie at the base of successful colonization were little understood, and ill applied. Glory and gain to France, not the permanence and good of the colony, were the objects sought. The French pioneer came with a purpose, beyond which neither he nor his Government looked. This was not—with some exceptions—to found permanent communities, by the practice of agriculture and the arts, but to establish and extend the gainful traffic in peltries. The first French settlers were communities of fur traders.

To the profitable traffic in furs the religious zeal of the age added another motive, almost equally powerful, the Christianizing of the native population. This was an aim which—with all their religious fervor—did not inspire the emigrants to New England. Equally intolerant with the Catholic *emigrés*, but without their enthusiasm, they gave feeble encouragement to missions among the heathen around them. In the eyes of most, the savages were a race of heretics, to whom was denied alike the consolations of the Christian faith and the benefits of civilization. The spirit of freedom is not always winged with charity.

Strikingly in contrast was the conduct of their neighbors of Canada, in the genius to plan and the courage and endurance to carry out the most toilsome expeditions, for founding missions in the wilderness. Though little remains of the missions established by the Jesuits, their long, unremitting and solitary labors, and severe sufferings and martyrdom, have written their names in glory! History has nothing brighter on her records, than the deeds of these Christian heroes.

> "The order of the Jesuit,
> In rigid compact firmly knit,"

is inseparably interwoven with the fortunes and fate of the French Empire in America. Its character is well described in the following graphic lines, from the poem '*Teuch sa Grondie*,' by our fellow-townsman, the president of this society,—Levi Bishop:

> "A school of strictest self-denial;
> Obedient unto every trial;
> Invincible and calmly bold,
> A social problem to unfold;
> In vigils long; in rigid fast;
> Beneath the scourge in penance cast:
> With constant, never-failing zeal
> That all the woes of man can feel;
> With self-sustaining fervor blest,
> That long devotions well attest;
> With deep enthusiastic glow,
> That blazes on the polar snow;
> With master policy refined,
> To rule the world of human kind;
> In closest league with royal state,
> Wide conquest to accelerate;
> With grasp of universal plan,
> Embracing every race of man:
> Such was the order shrewdly sent,
> To seize the western continent."

With such traits, unhappily, Jesuitism did not confine

itself to the Christianizing of the Indians, but became intimately associated with the political fortunes of the country, for evil as well as good.

In the genius of discovery, in establishing depots for trade and forts for protection, and in opening to the knowledge of civilized man a world vast and unknown, the French, too, were without a rival. The leading spirits in these enterprises would have been men of mark anywhere. With what a handful of men they invaded the savage wilderness! How indomitable their resolution. How judicious their selections of sites for forts and towns. How far-sighted the sagacity with which they secured to France, as they had reason to believe, a mighty Empire in the New World!

The great body of the colonists, it is true, were of the lower orders, uneducated in independence, moral or political. Many came as soldiers, and were induced to remain as settlers. A few were from the gentry; men who claimed an ancestry, and had names of which even yet their descendants are proud. No convicts were sent out, and there were no drones. All were accustomed to seek, and seldom failed to find, a living for themselves.

The colonization of "the Detroit," or Straits of Lakes Erie and Huron, dates from the first year of the 18th century, nearly two centuries after the discoveries of Cartier, on the St. Lawrence, and a century after the founding of Quebec.

The object of Sieur de la Motte Cadillac, in the settlement of Detroit, was not only to establish a military post, which should overawe the natives, check the advance of the English and Dutch, and secure the Indian trade, but to found an agricultural community, and obtain a permanent foothold upon the soil. It was a step further into the wilderness than any colony had yet ventured. It was an intrusion into the stronghold of savage tribes, many of whom were hostile to the French, and in the interest of their enemies. It was within reach of the English settlements, with which an eager contest had commenced for the Indian trade of the lakes, and the vast country to which these opened the gate.

A varied fortune awaited the new colony. From the first there was strong opposition, from political opponents of the measure, and personal enemies of Cadillac, among whom the Jesuits were conspicuous, and those who were interested in the older settlements. Nor was it easy to distinguish between their allies and their foes in the numerous tribes whose villages crowded closely about the fort, and who beset the colony on all sides. No less than four times, the destruction of the fort was the subject of conspiracies and machinations, urged on by rival interests; and for the first half century the security of the peasantry was too precarious to permit extensive or successful agriculture.

Hardly had the settlers begun to feel secure in their possession, when, with the capitulation of Montreal (1760), followed the downfall of the Empire of France in the New World, and the transfer, almost without warning to its inhabitants, of the sovereignty of Canada to its lifelong enemy—the English. The lilies of France were never to float again triumphant upon these waters.

Thirty years later saw the flag of England lowered to the Stars and Stripes of its rebel colonies. In less than two decades more the Cross of St. George resumed its sway over this region, for a brief period, to be again, for the last time, succeeded by the triumphant banner of the new republic.

Few people, and no portion of America, had, in so brief a period, experienced so many and singular reverses. None ever accommodated themselves more gracefully to the mutations of their fate. In their own way they continued to prosper, and had lined the banks of the Detroit with pleasant homesteads.

Little more than the third of a century has passed since the writer's first acquaintance with the region which, not many years before, the author of McFingal had described as,

> "Where Detroit looks out amid the wood,
> Remote, beside the dreary solitude."

Making my abode in the country, at some remove from the City of the Straits,—then boasting its 5000 inhabitants, of many nationalities,—I found myself amid a people mostly French,—the descendants of those who had braved the dangers of the remote wilderness, in following the fortunes of Cadillac.

As yet the inroads of the Anglo-Saxon had but little disturbed the quiet river settlements; but a day of change had arrived, which, in a very short time, was destined to destroy this old-time character. Since that day the Arcadian simplicity and content that had so long continued to prevail, in spite of contending sovereignties, has yielded rapidly to the restless energy of the invading Yankee; as did aforetime, to the conquering Briton, the dream of French Empire in the New World.

While the colonists on the Detroit retained many of the characteristics of their countrymen in the Old World, modifications necessarily took place, in the adaptation to so different an abode. Taking possession of a vast wilderness, families neither gathered into hamlets, as is the custom of the peasantry of France, nor did they seek an independent existence, like the backwoodsmen of New-England stock; but their dwellings—each on its own farm—were in such close proximity as almost to constitute a continuous village for many miles of river shore. Originally motives of protection against the savages, and afterwards those of social intercourse, led to this near neighborhood.

The original titles to these lands were variously derived. Of those below the city, as far as the River Rouge (3 miles), three are from grants of the Marquis du Quesne, Governor-General of Louisiana and Canada—1740; ten from Marquis de la Jousire, vested with like powers—1750. Ten others are from Indian deeds of gift, subsequent to the occupancy by the English—1770 to 1780,—confirmed by the British commandant. Few of the French grants actually received confirmation of the King, although this was required by the *Coutume de Paris*, which was the law of the country. Permits to occupy were sometimes granted by the French commandants. These grants and rights of occupancy were confirmed by the United States Government, early in the present century, through a commission sitting at Detroit; and upon these, patents were issued. The tracts thus confirmed vary in width from two to five arpents, and were about eighty arpents in length.*

I have heard old habitants say they could shout to each other from their door-steps. And this mode of telegraphic message, passing rapidly from house to house, served the purpose of modern methods, in case of apprehended danger, and even for social converse.

---

*The arpent is a measure of length, as well as area. It is a square, the side of which is 192 feet, three inches.

An American backwoodsman thinks settlements crowd too closely upon him—that he has not elbow-room enough—if a neighbor establishes himself within a mile of the spot which he has selected for his hearth-stone. A Frenchman so situated would die of ennui. He must have facilities for regular and frequent intercourse with his neighbors; and, as roads are execrable in a new country, he best accomplishes his object by fixing his habitations upon the streams—highways that nature has created. The canoe is his carry-all, in which he and his family move easily to and from even distant settlements. What glorious opportunities for the gratification of these desires was presented by those grand highways of the New World!

From the water also came a large part of his food; for fishing and trapping were more favorite employments than agriculture. The object of the first settlers being the fur trade and Indian traffic, these lakes and rivers supplied a natural channel through which those operations were conducted.

It was along the chain of the mighty lakes and rivers of our continent that France sought to maintain her foothold in America, by the erection of forts at points widely separated, but selected with wonderful foresight. In the vicinity of, and under the protection of these, were the early settlements made. As this protection became less needed, as the Indian trade declined, or was further removed, the peasant farmers made more distant settlements. They retained, however, the practice of inhabiting only the banks of streams accessible from the great lakes. I know of no original French settlement which is not so situated.

As a hunter the French settler had none of the renown of the American backwoodsman, but to his skill in trapping the great fur companies of Canada owed a large part of the smaller peltries that were so considerable a source of their revenues.

Like the beaver and muskrat, the Canadian not unfrequently lived almost in the water of his favorite streams and marshes, and built his cabin in a spot which could be approached only by canoe. The dwellers in habitations so little superior in architecture and site to the houses which these ingenious little architects contrive for their accommodation in their native marshes, and denoting so little degree of mental advancement, deserved the soubriquet, bestowed upon them by the contemptuous Yankee, of "muskrat Frenchmen."

We have seen that the kind of enterprise which characterized the French *emigré* was very different from that which marked the Anglo-Saxon settler; which has converted the wilderness into fertile fields, and, almost in a single lifetime, constituted this nation one of the formidable powers of the earth.

After more than a century of settlement, the farms along the Straits exhibited only a narrow strip of cultivation. This rarely extended half a mile from the water's edge. From their doors the family had a view of the untrimmed forest, where the deer roamed, and wild beasts prowled frequently to the very barn-yards.

Even this limited extent of field received very imperfect culture. It was almost never manured, and so little was high culture understood or regarded, that instances are well known where farmers, whose manure heaps had accumulated to an inconvenient degree about their barns, adopted the most ready means of relief, by carting the incumbrance on to the ice in winter. The offensive material was thus washed away without further trouble, when the ice broke up in the spring. I have it on undoubted authority, that in some cases even the barns were removed, to avoid the piles that had accumulated!

This limited agricultural improvement did not originate from the extreme subdivision of the land, for each proprietor possessed acres enough; though his farm, in its proportion of length to breadth, bore a resemblance to his pipe-stem.

As this great national interest flourished so little under the kind of encouragement bestowed by the French Government, it may be curious to compare the terms by which grants of land were bestowed by the commandants, with the tenure by which, under the fostering care of the present Government, each householder may secure a homestead. One runs in this wise: 'The grantee was bound to pay a rent of 15 livres a year, in peltries, to the crown forever; to assist in planting a May-pole, on each May-day, before the door of the mansion-house. He was forbidden to buy or sell articles of merchandise, carried to or from Montreal, through servants, clerks, or foreigners; to work at the business of a blacksmith; to sell brandy to the Indians, or to mortgage the land without consent of the Government. The Crown reserved all minerals and timber for military purposes. The grantor reserved the right of hunting rabbits, partridges and pheasants. All the grain raised was to be ground at the manor windmill, where toll was to be given, according to the custom of Paris. On every sale of land a tax was levied, and the Government reserved the right to take precedence of any buyer, at the price offered.' Under so many restrictions we see one reason why agriculture, as an independent pursuit, should not flourish.

Having spoken so disparagingly of French agriculture, it is but just to observe that the Canadians were speedy to adopt the superior implements and modes of cultivation used by the Anglo-Saxon settlers; and the present generation see little difference between the tools and the methods belonging to the one or the other. But half a century ago the old methods were still practised.

The *cart* was the universal vehicle for farm and family use, wagons being unknown. The *plough* was of wood, except the share. Its long beam and handles extended ten or twelve feet, and it had a wooden mould-board. In

OLD FRENCH PLOUGH.

front were two wheels, also of wood, of different sizes: a small one to run on the unploughed side, and a larger one in the furrow. There were neither chains nor whiffletree: oxen were fastened by a pole, which had a hinged attachment to the beam. And very good, though shallow, ploughing was performed by this rude but ingenious implement.

Both oxen and horses were employed in the various operations. The harness was very simple, and constructed of ropes or withes of twisted rawhide. No yoke was used, but a rope of the kind mentioned was passed around the oxens' horns, and they pushed with their heads. It was maintained by those who employed this seemingly singular method, that it was the most natural and effective, and gave greater freedom of action to the cattle. Possibly scientific agriculturists of the present day may get a useful hint from the simple ideas of the olden times.

The *hoe* was a very heavy iron implement, having a long shank. It was the same that was used by the Indians, after the introduction of iron among them. The latter never ploughed, and were ignorant of the method of laying out the field, in parallel rows; hills of corn being planted without regard to regularity, though at tolerably

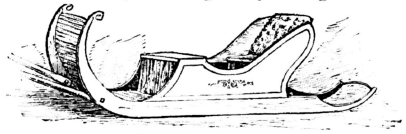

FRENCH CARRY-ALL.

uniform distances; and though the Frenchmen used the plough effectively, their ordinary mode of planting corn was precisely that of the Indians.

The winter *carry-all* was a strong but narrow box, placed upon runners, which spread widely and were iron-shod. Sometimes these were adorned with fancy heads. The thills, which were of hickory or ash, were so fixed as to spring outwardly, and when the horse was harnessed in, the ends were brought together and tied. The strain, consequently, prevented any rubbing against the horse's sides, and allowed a large liberty of action, which was of great service to their keen trotters and pacers. It was constructed for two persons only, although a seat for a third was sometimes placed in front. Horses were sometimes driven *tandem.*

The *traineau* was of rougher construction, made for work, and the runners did not spread.

For summer pleasure-driving a few had the *calèche.* It resembled the modern chaise, and had a movable folding top.

The *cart*, of which I have made mention, is worthy of commemoration. It was the common vehicle for all

FRENCH CALECHE.

classes, and even in the city, long after my arrival here, was almost the only kind of carriage. It was a light two-wheeled vehicle of the ordinary cart construction, and the sides were protected by a low railing. The gentry sometimes had chairs placed within, but commonly all rode after a more primitive style, with a buffalo robe only for seat. In this simple mode ladies were taken to church, to parties and calls, or carted over the mud wherever the roads were in a condition unfit for dainty feet. The stiff clay soil which prevailed along the only road was often almost impassable for pedestrians. There were no pavements, nor even that convenient Western resource—plank walks. Nor was there a stone crossing, nor a public hack in the city, thirty years ago.

Many were the curious scenes, and many the laughable stories

"——legends store
Of strange adventures, happed by—"

mud: the suffocation of dogs; the loss of shoes; the discomfiture of neat gallants, who ventured aid to the weaker sex, in their rash attempts to cross a street. Even those who were so fortunate as to obtain the use of a cart

PONY CART.

did not always escape the danger or the fun; for sometimes the loosely-made lynch-pin gave out, when the living cargo was unceremoniously dumped, of course in the very deepest puddles. But such accidents in those days were a subject of mirth rather than of chagrin. The French cart was an article of real convenience, and well adapted to the wants and tastes of the people and times. It was a legitimate descendant of the cart of Normandy, where, in recent times, I have been interested to see it in common use, of precisely similar construction. Among us its use is now almost confined to Canada. But now and then one may be seen on the American side, on its way to market, with fifty pounds of hay, or a quarter cord of wood, drawn by a shag of a pony, whose back reaches scarcely above the thills, and a little weazen-faced Frenchman mounted on the top.

The stock of the French farmer consisted almost exclusively of horses,—that dwarfed, hardy race, so well known as Canadian ponies. These roamed at large, beyond the enclosures, picking up an independent living by browsing. Even in the winter they seldom received any but a stolen aid from the barns or stacks of their owners. Each pony bore its master's initials, branded upon the shoulder, and was caught and broken to the bit as he happened to be wanted. Whether these horses were obtained originally from the Indians of the plains, or had any relationship with the Mexican mustang, seems not to be determined. They were peculiar to Canada.

To some extent this mode of raising horses has prevailed, even down to present times, in the towns adjacent to Detroit, where the French are still a large element in the population. They receive literally no care whatever, and roam in bands, scouring along the roads with the speed of liberty, and often making night hideous with the uproar. The following lines from a manuscript poem by Hon. James V. Campbell (I hope his Honor will pardon the theft), thus well describes these nightly races through the town :

> " Unchecked, with flying leap and bound,
> The savage courser spurns the ground.
> No venturous horseman leads the ranks,
> No spur has galled their heaving flanks,
> No master's hand has grasped the mane,
> No champing jaw has known the rein ;
> But in a countless host they press,
> Free as the storm, but riderless ;

> Compact as when an army's tramp
> Bears down upon a foeman's camp;
> While the ground trembles, like the shore
> Where foaming lines of breakers roar!"

That the Detroit habitants of an early day were not altogether open to the reproach of being neglectful husbandmen, good evidence has come down to our own times, in the fine orchards of apple, pear, and cherry trees, that gave beauty and value to nearly every farm.

Our view of Canadian agriculture would be incomplete indeed without a particular notice of these old orchards, which are so distinguishing a feature in the river landscape, and in which the Canadians showed such commendable enterprise.

Though many of the farms, so closely crowded along the river banks, had orchards comprising several hundred of these fruit trees, and few were entirely destitute, it is singular that little is known of their history. In answer to inquiries, old people will tell, that their ancestors obtained the trees from Montreal, to which place they were brought, at a still earlier day, from Normandy or Provence; but they have no knowledge when, or from which. The prevailing opinion is, that the seeds were brought from France, and planted as soon as the first permanent settlements were made on the Straits, about a century and a half ago. The present generation remember well the days of their boyhood, passed beneath the shade and in the enjoyment of the fruit of these trees, which, in their recollection, were even then of great size.

Before further considering the mystery of their origin, the character of these orchards claims our attention. When we recognize that from the orchards on this river have originated many noted kinds of apples, still extensively appreciated throughout the Northern States, it will be apparent that they contained no wild or common fruit. From hence were disseminated the famous "Calville"—both red and white; the "Detroit Red"—*Roseau* of the French; the "Pomme de neige," or *Fameuse*—the celebrated "Snow Apple" of America; all fruits that have established a wide reputation. Besides these are several not so well known,—the gray apple, russets, noted for long keeping; pearmains, and others. Almost every orchard had one or more of these noted kinds.

As cider fruit, these apples maintained a reputation long after the influx of settlers from the Eastern States. In this respect they were considered to surpass the apples of New England, and to be second only to the celebrated New Jersey product.

Forty years ago a few cider mills of the French construction were in existence. They were quite unique. The crusher was a large stone or wood cylinder, six to eight feet diameter, and from six to ten inches thickness. It turned on a wooden axis, fashioned to a centre-post, and was carried around by horse-power. It ran in a trough, dug out of a large tree, and put together by sections. The press consisted of a long wooden lever, acting upon a platform, and held down by tackling.

But the crowning glory of the French orchard was the pear tree. Nearly every homestead possessed one, some two or three, few exceeded a half dozen. Such was its wonderful size and productiveness, that one specimen usually amply satisfied the wants of a family.

These pear trees were, and still are, conspicuous objects in the river scenery, and, for size, vigor and productiveness are truly remarkable. A bole six feet in girth, and a height of sixty feet, are only common attainments.

Many show a circumference of trunk of eight to nine feet, and rear their lofty heads seventy, and sometimes eighty feet from the earth! They bear uniform crops, thirty to fifty bushels being often the annual product of a single tree. The fruit is of medium size, ripening about the end of August, and though as a table fruit superseded by many sorts which an improved horticulture has introduced, it still holds a fair rank, and in some respects is not surpassed, if equalled, by any. The flesh is crisp, juicy, sweet and spicy. For stewing and preserving it is quite unrivalled. Individual trees differ a little in their period of ripening, and in size and flavor of fruit, but the variety is well characterized.

It is not a little remarkable that so little should be known of the history of a tree of such extraordinary character. The earliest travellers from whom we have published records, such as Charlevoix, Henry and Carver, make none, or only casual mention, and give no clue to their date and origin. The memory of the oldest inhabitant is only traditional in regard to them. Along the St. Lawrence and about Montreal, whence these trees are, by some, supposed to have been brought to Detroit, no specimens exist, and the orchards are few and inferior. In a hasty journey across Normandy, I saw many fine and large pear trees, but I looked in vain for any of the size or character which might be supposed to have originated the Detroit pear tree.

The prevailing opinion, that the pear and apple trees of the Canadas originated from *seeds* brought from France, is founded on the supposition that nursery trees could not have withstood the long sea voyage of that period. Yet this opinion cannot be accepted without hesitation. It is a law well understood by fruit culturists, that trees raised from the seed of these fruits tend to revert to their original wild state. They are, with rare exceptions, inferior to the cultivated varieties, and besides, are of almost as many different sorts as the seeds which produce them. Neither the pear nor apple trees of the French orchards have the character of seedlings; and the fact that almost every orchard contained several trees of the same, and of well-known kinds, militates against that supposition. On the other hand, it is improbable that they are seedlings raised here and *grafted*. For the art was then little practised in America, and not at all among the Canadians.

The Detroit pear tree is found also on the River Raisin, at Monroe, and, so far as I am informed, exists nowhere else in America. The trees on the latter stream were planted by the early settlers there, many years after the colonization of the Straits. In 1786, Col. Francis Navarre, of Monroe, travelling on horseback from Detroit, carried in his hand six or more trees, which he planted on his farm. They attained large size, and are still bearing immense crops. One of these is said to measure, at two feet from the ground, nine feet two inches circumference, and at four feet, separates into two branches, one of which is seven feet four inches and the other five feet in circumference.

We have ample testimony to the great size of these giant pear trees half a century ago. I am informed by an old resident that in 1812 or 1813 he saw one cut down which was in the way of a battery that was being built just above the city, and which measured nearly two feet diameter of trunk. Such a growth could hardly have been acquired in less than a century.

I know not by what fatality, but our old French pear trees seem destined to have no successors to their fame, as though unwilling to survive the Americanization of the race who nurtured and so long enjoyed their stately munificence. Appreciated by all, no one has thought of continuing the species, or else all attempts have failed. No young trees are to be found in the extensive plantations of the present century, which includes so many vastly inferior. None of the nurseries contain it. It is even yet without a name in the dictionary of American fruit trees. Still, however, the pear trees flourish, in a green old age, while the apple orchards are fast disappearing, partly from natural decay, but more perhaps from neglect; while many are annually swept from existence by the relentless besom of modern *improvement.**

The old pear tree belongs to Detroit and her old habitants, and will perish with them, and with their homesteads, which are so fast disappearing. Another half century will see the last of those magnificent trees,—the pride of the French orchard; the mammoth of fruits,—of which the world does not afford its equal!

Having given this imperfect view of French out-door occupation, their social character claims our attention; but this demands a separate chapter.

---

* Since the above was written many of the pear trees begin to show decay from old age, and are now in dying condition.

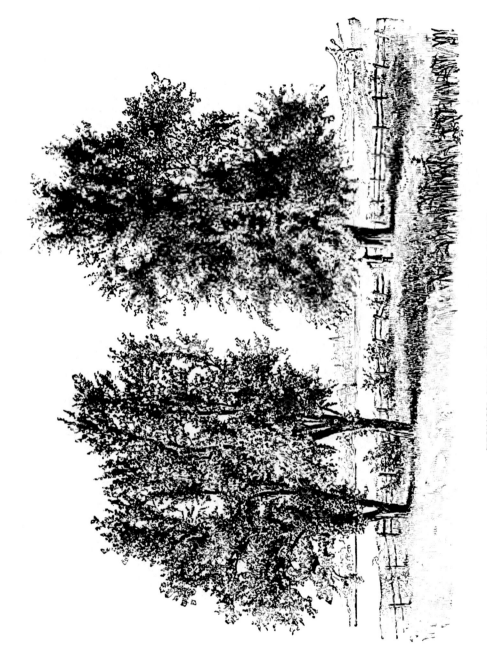

FRENCH PEAR TREES, DETROIT RIVER.

FRENCH HABITANTS OF THE DETROIT.

PART II.

FROM our consideration of the agriculture of the early French settlers on the Detroit, we turn naturally to their homesteads. We form some judgment of a people from the houses they live in.

The better class of dwellings of the French habitants were of quite a substantial character, considered as mere timber structures. They were built of logs, squared and covered with clapboards, and the roofs shingled with cedar. They were of one or two stories, according to the need or ability of the owner, but were never ambitious. Generally they were one *full* story, the upper, or half story, being chiefly within the roof, which was high, and lighted by small dormer windows, projecting on the front and rear sides. The entrance was in the centre, and a hall ran from front to rear. A low and perfectly plain veranda was another usual feature.

One of the oldest and most noted structures of this class was the "Cass house," which had been used by several of the territorial governors of Michigan, and exhibited many marks of the tomahawk and bullet, received during the Indian wars. It stood on the Cass farm, and was built of cedar logs, weather boarded; about fifty feet front and one story in height, with steep roof. A heavy stone chimney rose out of the centre. The position, when I first saw it, was very beautiful. It was upon the immediate bank of the river, here quite abrupt and high, and shadowed with trees. No wharf or building obstructed the view, which commanded many miles of the river channel and shores, and in the rear were smiling gardens, and green slopes, between which flowed the little river "Savoyard," since diverted into a covered sewer. This old mansion is still a comfortable dwelling, or dwellings, on Larned Street. It stands but little removed from its old site, but in front and in rear are stony streets, thickly lined with houses. It is remote from the present border of the river, and its time-honored character is lost in new boards and white paint. Its age is probably not less than 150 years.*

Another old domicile of the times of French régime—the Lafferty house—stood half a mile below, and was torn down in 1861, to give place to structures better suited to the wants of modern times. It was erected in 1747, and was, at the time of its destruction, in excellent preservation; the timbers heavy and solid, and the stone chimney exhibiting the large, open fire-place which marked an age of hospitality and good cheer.

The Knaggs house, another well-known mansion, was for several years my own residence. It consists of two parts: one a low structure of a single story, with an attic, and containing two rooms and a pantry. It is of unknown age, and, like the Cass house, bears marks of Indian outrages. The other portion is of comparatively modern date, and consists of three considerable rooms, separated by a central hall. It has a second half-story, with dormer windows, and also windows in the gables, and is throughout well finished. The front door is um-

---

* It was torn down in 1883, and the site occupied by brick buildings.

braged by a square portico, which had seats, and commanded a delightful look-out upon the river, in its immediate front. Both parts of the mansion are built of squared pine timbers, clapboarded. The newer portion had, when I took possession, a coat of paint, white in front, red in the rear. If there had ever been paint on the older portion it had long disappeared. The panes of glass throughout all the windows were a curiosity, being of a size entirely disused and no longer sold by dealers, —six and a half by seven and a half inches.

I will allude to another, and one of the few French mansions in the city,—the old "Campau house." It is built upon the foundations of the original dwelling burned down by the fire, which consumed the entire city in 1805. Though an interesting relic, and a good specimen of its class, it belongs to the present century. It will give a good idea of the contrast between the old town and the new to state that the avenue of 120 feet wide, upon which this house fronts, corresponds here with the old St. Ann Street, on which it formerly stood, but which (though the largest street of Old Detroit) had a width of only 30 feet.*

Few such memorials of the "good old days" now remain in this vicinity. But on the Canada side of the channel comparatively little change has taken place in the appearance and condition of many old French homesteads. The village of Sandwich wears much of its old-time character, and a dreamy quiet pervades the place, worthy of Sleepy Hollow, and singularly in contrast with the bustling, wide-awake activity which distinguishes most American villages.

---

* This mansion, too, has disappeared, having (1885) given way to the demands of another race and times.

CLERGY HOUSE, SANDWICH.

Most French dwellings had yards, fenced by pickets of red cedar. These were often 10 or 12 feet in height, and were intended and often served as a stockade for protection during the troubles of the war times, as well as against wolves.

Some of these defences were standing along the river, between my house and the town, as late as 1837, and consisted of very closely set, large and mostly round posts, which were generally still sound. They were so deeply sunk that the axe was used rather than the spade, when their removal became expedient. Few if any of these posts can now be seen in this vicinity, but the stumps of many still remain, as landmarks of a past age, below the soil, where the axe has left them.

Another feature of the old settlements has disappeared,—the *windmills*, which once marked every few miles of river shore, and were an animating part of its picturesque scenery.

These institutions of primitive times were in full operation, down to the stirring period of Yankee improvements,—(1836-37). Until then there were no flouring-mills of any other description within many miles; though we have the authority of Judge Campbell for stating, that a watermill was built as early as 1734, on May's Creek, below the city, and one on Mill or Conner's Creek, above, and that as late as 1830 one was standing in ruins upon Bloody Run, where it is crossed by Jefferson Avenue.

The windmills served sufficiently well all the needs of the French era; but with the advent of larger wants, more capable structures were demanded. The neglected windmills fell to decay, and at the present time a few only survive, in ruins.

From these brief notices of the dwellings of the French land-owners it will doubtless, and with truth, be concluded that the occupants lived in reasonable style and comfort; and that the personal appearance of our French progenitors corresponded to the simple and comfortable character of their homesteads.

The gentleman's dress of the olden time, in winter, con-

SUMMER COSTUME.

sisted of colored shirt, with vest, and pantaloons or leggings. A belt or sash held up the trousers, and over all was worn a *capote*, or heavy blanket coat, with a sack or loose cap attached, that was thrown back or over the head, as required. The latter extremity was bound with a colored handkerchief, while the lower were protected by shoe-packs, and sometimes by moccasons.

On dress occasions the sash was richly ornamented with beads, in the Indian fashion, and sometimes was of wampum. It was spread widely over the body, outside the coat, and tied behind, the ends hanging down two feet or more. In warm weather, pantaloons were worn without vest, and were sustained by a belt, generally of

SUMMER COSTUME.

leather. The feet were bare, and hats of straw completed the covering.

The voyageurs, or boatmen, often wore shirts over the trowsers, made of leather, with ruffles in the bosom, of the same material. They had bright-colored cloth caps, which hung over on one side and terminated with a tassel.

The dress of the women consisted of short gowns or *habits*, falling no lower than the knee, and showing the petticoats, which reached to the feet; and they had ample straw hats. For cold weather they had fur hats or bonnets. They received the fashions from Montreal, but the changes were so slight, that probably less varia-

WINTER COSTUME.

tion had occurred in a century than takes place in the costume of our modern belles in a single year. In fact, the costume I have described continued almost unchanged, from the earliest period, down nearly to the time of my own personal observation. The straw hat maintains its repute even yet, as a permanent and wholesome style abroad, its merits having given it a wide adoption; and it would be well if, in other particulars, the convenient fashions of our Canadian dames could be preserved.

The French people continued to preserve, down to a very recent date, a good degree of their ancient character. There was much of the "beau monde" at the rival but neighborly cities of Detroit and Monroe, and a constant

WINTER COSTUME.

intercourse was kept up, until the preponderance of the former city and the overwhelming influx of foreigners.

Amusements were of the social rather than literary kind, and the social virtues never shone more brightly among any people. Nor were these confined to their own kin, but were extended to the newly come, of whatever nationality. The old habitants of the better class still retain a vivid recollection of those happy days, and will tell that no people ever enjoyed life so keenly.

During the winter—which comprised nearly half the year—the settlements on the Detroit and River Raisin were almost shut out from the Eastern world. River craft were all laid up; railroads were not in being; and travel to the nearest Eastern cities was a long and painful journey. I have myself known Detroit to be without a New York mail for more than two weeks at a time, and have found it a week's journey, travelling by ordinary stage, day and night, through Canada to Buffalo. This was the season for French gayety and resource to display themselves. No aid from foreign sources was needed to make the winter pass pleasantly. And who could surpass the French for parties, balls and merry-makings!

At these were gathered, especially, the young of both sexes, who kept up, until a late hour in the morning, that fascinating amusement of whose saltatory mazes a Frenchman never tires; and here were exchanged glances from those lustrous black eyes, so suited to brunette complexions, and which lighted up even the most ordinary face, like native diamonds, sparkling through their rusty covering. And, indeed, the demoiselles were not to be despised for graces of face and figure; for though the men mostly had long, thin visages, scarcely in keeping with their fun-loving propensities, the girls were both plump and handsome.

During the period of depression which followed the speculations of 1836, when a general stagnation and gloom overspread the whole land, there was no lack of French gayety. In the winter of 1841, when times were at their worst, this was manifested, even to an unusual degree, in numerous balls and other social gatherings. With a characteristic tinge of superstition, the French considered this unusual gayety ominous of approaching war, or other calamity, and that they were impelled to it by some secret and uncontrollable impulse. Perhaps philosophy may find a more reasonable solution. I relate the fact only.

Sundays, as in all Roman Catholic countries, were holidays, and were improved as such to much greater extent among the Canadians of half, or even quarter of a century ago, than now, among their descendants. Possibly they were spent quite as innocently, though more noise and hilarity prevailed. The parents and daughters of the family travelled to church in sober jog-trot style enough, in carts drawn by a single pony. But the young men went mounted on their nags, and returned in the grand style, racing, with whoop and hurrah!

In winter these races were exchanged for trotting-matches on the ice, in their light, home-made carry-alls. Long and eager were the contests for superior speed and skill. No docks and piers then interfered with this winter use of the river, which was thus improved, from the very heart of the city, down to and up the Rouge. Many noted trotters and pacers are still to be found among the keen, little, rugged breed of Canadian horses. The example has not been lost upon the bloods of the modern city, famous yet for fast nags and fast men.

A season of great excitement to the early settlers was that of the white-fishing, which was confined to the late fall months, commencing about the middle of October, and continuing until very cold weather. Seines only were used, and a feature in the river landscape, as numerous and almost as striking as the windmills, were the reels, the platform and the fish-houses which pertained to the business.

This season was looked forward to with great interest and pleasure, and was one of feasting and merriment, for the fish were as abundant and cheap as the flesh was admirable ; and for cooking these, as well as most other natural products of river and forest, none could excel the French. Although few engaged in the business—for the market was limited—almost every farm front was available. And truly it was an interesting and inspiriting spectacle ;—the boats leaving the shore with the nets coiled on the stern, as the men pulled up the stream, until, reaching the channel bank, the net was dropped and the boat rowed rapidly back to the land,— the floats following in a graceful curved line : while often a song kept time to the oars. Then as both ends were drawn briskly in, to see the beautifully white and silvery bodies glancing through the water, and finally tossed, all glowing and active, on the beach ! White-fishing is still pursued on the river, but the old-fashioned reel is to be seen in but one place within the limits of the extended modern city,—a place famous still for its fortunate ground,—the Loranger farm.*

I cannot omit to mention a commendable trait in the French character,—their early and sincere attachment to the United States, and her republican institutions. To be known as a Frenchman was to be known as a patriot; and in the times which tried men's souls—and few parts of our country had more varied and bitter experience—the Frenchman was always our reliable and

---

* Now for many years docked and abandoned to business uses.

active ally; cool and unflinching in danger; shrewd and watchful when caution was most needed. If a man was wanted for a dangerous enterprise, it was a Frenchman who was chosen.

Few now survive of the old habitants who were interested and intelligent witnesses of General Hull's surrender of the fort of Detroit, and with it of the whole territory of the North-west, to the British arms; and the rapid succession of events has almost crowded out the recollection. But when I first came to reside here, the feeling of indignation was still fresh and warm, though more than twenty years had elapsed since that event. And it would have been a vain attempt to convince one of those who witnessed and entered into the scenes and feelings of those times, that the act was one of mere timidity and weakness, and not of downright treason.

Among the many interesting reminiscences of that period which have been collected and published in newspapers from time to time by an honored citizen and friend (now, alas! departed—Judge Witherell), I am pleased to find honorable mention of Captain Whittemore Knaggs, the patentee of the old farm to whose proprietorship I had the honor to succeed. As the record is illustrative of my theme, I make no apology for copying the following anecdote of my predecessor in the now peaceful homestead:

"Captain Knaggs was a firm and unflinching patriot, in times when patriotism was in demand,—during the war of 1812. He was one of the Indian interpreters; spoke freely six or seven of their languages, besides the English and the French, and possessed great influence with several warlike tribes. On the surrender of Detroit to the enemy he was, by the British commandant, ordered to leave the country, and did so, of course, but joined the first corps of our army that advanced towards this frontier. He acted as guide to the division under General Winchester, and was at the fatal and bloody defeat of our troops at the Raisin. The British Indians discovered him after the surrender, and determined to kill him. There happened to be present, among the enemy, an Indian whom Knaggs had often befriended in former years; this Indian resolved to save him at every hazard, but the savages would not listen to him; they were not yet fully gorged with blood. Nothing daunted, however, the brave red warrior placed himself between Knaggs and his foes, and for some time kept them off; they pressed on, however, and, as a last resort, the brave fellow seized Knaggs around the waist, kept his own body between him and the enemy, and kept whirling around, and so prevented the oft-repeated blows of the tomahawk and war-club from taking effect on the victim's head, until he succeeded in getting him in the midst of a number of horses that were harnessed together. Here they struck under at his legs, and over their backs at his head; he, however, avoided the blows, till a British officer interposed and saved him. After escaping innumerable dangers and death, from the white and red warriors, he departed this life in peace, about 1827.

"On the day of the surrender of this post, Knaggs' dwelling was sacked by the savages; his furniture hewed and hacked to pieces, and all that was valuable to Indians was carried off. Mr. Knaggs had succeeded in saving a few blankets, and they had many wild ponies in the bush. During the year succeeding the surrender, in 1812, and while Knaggs was yet absent, very many of our people, soldiers and citizens, were brought in as prisoners by the

Indians, from the frontiers of Ohio, etc. Poor creatures were they, some wounded, many sickly, and all nearly naked, bare-headed and barefooted, the personification of misery and want,—compelled to follow their savage captors around the streets, and to sleep on the bare ground, in their smoky and filthy tents, or under the open sky.

"The compassion of our citizens was deeply excited, and every effort was made in the power of a plundered and impoverished people to ransom the suffering captives. Mrs. Knaggs, among others, parted with horses, blankets, and nearly everything that she had saved from the pillage of her home, to purchase the freedom of the prisoners."

The mother of Captain Knaggs, a lady eighty years of age, was compelled to ride from Monroe to Detroit, on a traineau, on the ice, thinly clad, in the most severe winter weather. When asked why she did not freeze, she replied, "My spunk kept me warm."

I do not mean to say that there were no exceptions to patriotic conduct among the French. During the war of 1812 there were some who were suspected, and not without reason, of giving aid and comfort to the enemy. These excused their conduct on the pretence of fear of the Indians, who, especially after the defeat at the Raisin, were patrolling the country, in hostile bands, and committing many savage atrocities.

James, a brother of Captain Whittemore Knaggs, resided at the Raisin. Some of his neighbors were strongly suspected of favoring the British, if not of consorting with them and their Indian allies. Against these the indignation of James was aroused, and he did not hesitate at open accusation. A Mr. Lasselle was one of the supposed culprits, and though he declared that his adhesion to the enemy was only feigned, for the protection of his family, James Knaggs would by no means admit the justice of his plea. Meeting him some time after the massacre, Lasselle offered his hand, which Knaggs scornfully refused, saying, "I don't shake hands with traitors."

James was at the battle of the Thames. He saw the shot fired by which Tecumseh was killed, and was one of two Frenchmen who brought off Colonel Johnson, wounded, from the field.

Among a people so circumstanced as were the early settlers on these Straits, it may be imagined that schools did not receive a large degree of patronage. Few children learned to read and write; but the catechism was taught by the priests, and the pious art of telling their beads.

At every few miles was to be seen the little chapel, surmounted by bell and cross, and sometimes a tin cock; and in the open space in front was often erected a tall wooden cross, which on Corpus Christi and other festival days was crowned with flowers, and became the goal of a long procession of the young people.

But, though good Catholics, the Canadians were not bigots. Their religion was simple as their tastes, and suited to the light-hearted gayety that was so prominent a characteristic. I speak in the past tense, because within the last quarter of a century many changes have taken place, mainly through the disturbing elements that have poured in around them.

In spite of defective education, such is the native force of the French character that I have known, among the present generation, many a hard-working and successful farmer, and an industrious and really accomplished mechanic, not one of whom could read or write.

I should do injustice also to the merits of our old habitants if the conclusion was left to be drawn from the above observations, that neglect of education was universal. This was not the case. There were schools at Detroit, besides the Sunday-schools, in the olden times; and the labors of good Father Richard, in this direction, were appreciated, and are well remembered by many still living among us.

The very Rev. Gabriel Richard, for many years a priest in this community, had the entire respect, confidence and affection of the whole people, and was the first representative to Congress from the Territory of Michigan. At the commencement of the present century there were schools under his encouragement, if not due to his efforts, not only in the town of Detroit, but at Grand Marais, at Springwells, and at the River Huron. At "Spring Hill"—a mile below the town—Père Richard had established, not only an academy, but a printing-press. It was the first one that was set up in the territory, and here was published the first book printed in the Northwest.

In regard to these schools, the following pertinent facts are gathered from a quaint memorial, addressed by the reverend father to the then legislative authority of Michigan. It bears date Oct. 18, N. S., 1808.

We learn from it, that "three of these schools are kept by the natives of the country, of whom tow [*sic*], under the direction of the subscriber, have learned the first rudiments of English and Latin languages, and some principles of Algebra and Geometry, so far as to the measurement of the figures engraved on the tomb of the immortal Archimides." Also, that in the Academy at Detroit "there are better than thirty young girls who are taught, as at Spring Hill, reading, writing, arithmetic, knitting, sewing, spinning, etc. In these two schools there are already three dozen of spinning-wheels and one loom, on which four pieces of linen or woollen cloth have been made this last spring or summer." I note this for the benefit of modern schools for young ladies, where the piano is so often thumped. It is pleasant to know that the ears of our neighbors of a century ago were more agreeably entertained with the music of the spinning-wheel.

At this same Academy of Spring Hill—the memorialist goes on to say—"the number of the scholars has been augmented by four young Indians, headed by an old matron, their grandmother, of the Pottawatamies tribe. Five or six more are expected to arrive every moment."

We are also told, that "to encourage the young Students by the allowment of pleasure and amusement," he had sent "orders to New York for a spinning-machine of about one hundred spindles, an air-pump, an electrical apparatus, etc.," and "a few colors for dyeing the stuff already made or to be made in his Academy." Take note of that, ye modern educators, who are in pursuit of sources of "pleasure and amusement" for the young people!

As a further memento of those times I add—*verbatim et literatim*—the concluding appeal of the Memorialist, asking that "for the encouragement of Litterature & Useful arts, to be taught in the same Academies, one of the 4 Lotteries authorised by the Hon. Leg. on the 9th of 7ber, 1806, may be left to the management of the subscriber, on conditions that may appear just & reasonable to the Board."

A word about the *language* used by the French Canadian. It is generally believed that this has become so corrupted from the pure Parisian as to constitute a patois, so abominable as to be with difficulty understood by one skilled in the standard tongue of the Academy. The truth is, this so-called *patois* is the old French tongue, continued almost unchanged, like the manners and habits of those who use it; while the language of cultivated France has undergone many modifications.

It is satisfactory to find these observations upon the French character confirmed by an early authority. Charlevoix, who was at Quebec in 1720, says: "The Creoles of Canada draw in with their native breath an air of freedom, which renders them very agreeable in the commerce of life. And nowhere in the world is our language spoken in greater purity. There is not even the smallest foreign accent in their pronunciation." He describes them also, as "gay and sprightly, rusticity being unknown, even in the remotest parts."

I have alluded to one trait, in which the French *emigrés* differed widely from the English and Spanish settlers in America,—their friendliness towards the aboriginal inhabitants. This kindly disposition was appreciated by the Indians; so that the two races, whenever they fairly understood each other, lived in peace together.

I am not aware that intermarriages were very frequent, or that this relationship was often entered into by the peasantry of this part of Canada. It was common enough at the remoter posts, down even to times within my personal knowledge. The Indian trader, whether

Frenchman, Scotsman or Yankee, prompted partly by interest, usually took to himself an Indian wife. At such places as Mackinaw and Sault Ste. Marie, half-breeds were quite numerous, as they had been at Detroit at an earlier day. The class known as voyageurs—the *coureurs de bois* of the older times—had become, to a very considerable extent, of mixed blood. The licentious lawlessness of those wild-wood rangers was not only well-known, but was a subject of much complaint at a very early day. Certain it is, that in many points there was greater assimilation between the natives and the people from France, than was the case with the emigrants from any other civilized country.

In several excursions which I made, between 1836 and 1840, in the wilderness portions of Michigan, and along the large streams and channels, it was not uncommon to find the solitary lodge of a Frenchman, with his squaw wife, and sometimes two wives, and a troop of half-breed children. They lived more like Indians than white people, associated chiefly with them, and depended upon fishing.

The class of men known as *coureurs de bois*, or voyageurs, was extinct at Detroit some time before my acquaintance began with the country and people. But at Mackinac and on Lake Superior these found somewhat of their old employment, and retained a good degree of their ancient character. They manned the "Mackinac barge" and the canoes of the fur traders that still plied along the northern waters of the Hudson's Bay Company.

A wild-looking set were these rangers of the woods and waters! The weirdness was often enhanced by the dash of Indian blood. Picturesque, too, they were, in their red flannel or leather shirts, and cloth caps of some gay color, finished to a point, which hung over on one side, with a depending tassel.

They had a genuine love for this occupation, and muscles that seemed never to tire at the paddle and oar. From dawn to sunset, with only a short interval, and sometimes no midday rest, they would ply these implements, causing the canoe or barge to fly through the water like a thing of life; but often contending against head-winds, and gaining but little progress in a day's rowing. But how sweet was the rest, when a favoring breeze sprung up, enabling the little craft to carry sail. Then in came the oars, and down lopped each mother's son, and in a few minutes was in the enjoyment of a sound snooze.

The morning and evening meal consisted, almost invariably, and from choice, of *bouillon*,—a soup made from beans, peas, or hulled corn, with a piece of pork boiled in it, and hard-bread or sea-biscuit. To the Northern voyageurs, rations were generally served out of one quart of hulled corn and half a pint of bear's grease or oil, this being the daily and only food. The traveller, Henry, says (1776): "A bushel of hulled corn with two pounds of fat is reckoned to be a month's subsistence. No other allowance is made, of any kind, not even salt, and bread is never thought of. The difficulty which would belong to an attempt to reconcile any other men than Canadians to this fare seems to secure to them and their employees the monopoly of the fur-trade." As late as the end of the last century, Detroit was one of the principal depots for provisions, and fitting out for the Indian trade; and here, particularly, the corn was prepared, hulled, boiled, and mixed with fat, for the voyageurs.

After supper, pipes were lighted, and, seated on logs or squatted around the camp-fire, they chatted until bed-time. This came early and required little preparation. To wrap a blanket around the person, placing coat or shoe-packs beneath the head, and a little greasy pillow—the only bed that was carried—constituted the whole ceremony; and speedy and sound was the sleep, beneath the watchful stars.

The labor of the oar was relieved by songs, to which each stroke kept time, with added vigor. The poet Moore has well caught the spirit of the voyageurs' melodious chant, in his "Boat-Song upon the St. Lawrence." But to appreciate its wild sweetness one should listen to the melody, as it wings its way over the waters, softened by distance, yet every measured cadence falling distinct upon the ear.

These songs are usually half ballad or ditty, and love, of course, the main theme. They express the natural feelings of a people little governed by the restraints of civilization. Here is a specimen, which I have preserved. The words were sung by one of our party, and all joined in the chorus.

LA JEUNE SOPHIE.

La jeune Sophie
Chantait l'autre jour,
  Son echo lui repetè,
Que non pas d'amour
N'est pas de bon jour.

Je suis jeune et belle,
  Je vieux mé engagé
Un amant fidele,
  Je suis jeune, etc.

Mais ce vous etre belle,
  Ce n'est pas de jour;
Ce n'est que vos yeaux
  Qui bris à la chandelle.
  Mais ce vous, etc.

Unisons ensemble,—
  Son cour et le mien,—
Pourquoi tant le defendre,
  Puis qu'il s'amaient bien?
  Unisons, etc.

Point temps de badinage,
　Envers mon amant,
Car il est jaloux :
　Tout lui port embrage.
　　Point temps, etc.

La jeune Sophie,
Chantant l'autre jour, etc.
[Repeat.]

Sometimes the *bon vivant* is predominant, as in the following rude song:

Mon pere a fait bati maison,
　Ha, ha, ha, frit à l'huile,
Sont trois charpentiers qui là font,
　Fritaine, friton, fritou, poilon,
　Ha, ha, ha, frit à l'huile,
　Frit au beurre à l'ognon.

Sont trois charpentiers qui la font,
　Ha, ha, ha, frit à l'huile,
Qu' apporte tu dans ton giron ?
　Fritaine, friton, fritou, poilon,
　Ha, ha, ha, frit à l'huile.

Qu' apporte tu dans ton giron ?
　Ha, ha, ha, frit à l'huile,
C'est un pâté de trois pigeons,
　Fritaine, friton, fritou, poilon,
　Ha, ha, ha, etc.

C'est un pâté de trois pigeons,
　Ha, ha, ha, frit à l'huile,
Assieds-toi et le mangeons.
　Fritaine, friton, fritou, poilon,
　Ha, ha, ha, frit à l'huile,
　Frit au beurre et à l'ognon, etc., etc.

These boat-songs were often heard upon our river, and were very plaintive. In the calm of evening, when sounds are heard with greater distinctness, and the harsher notes are toned down and absorbed in the prevailing melody, it was sweet, from my vine-mantled porch, to hear the blended sounds of song and oar,

"By distance mellowed. o'er the waters sweep."

To my half-dreaming fancy, at such times, they have assumed a poetic, if not a supernatural character, wafting me into elf-land, on wings of linked sweetness.

> " Some spirit of the air has waked the string;
> 'Tis now a seraph bold, with touch of fire,
> And now the brush of fancy's frolic wing."

At other times these sounds harmonize with scenes that are still more inspiring. Seldom have I witnessed a more animating spectacle than that of a large canoe, belonging to the Hudson's Bay Company, manned by a dozen voyageurs,—the company's agents seated in the centre,—propelled with magic velocity, as if instinct with life, every paddle keeping time to the chorus that rang far and wide over the waters!

But times have changed, and with them have passed from our midst the voyageur and his song. French gayety is rapidly ebbing into more sober channels. Even the priests have set their faces against balls and merry-makings!

As I call up these reminiscences, with the same noble river in my view, I listen in vain for the melodies which were once the prelude to many joyous hours of early manhood. But instead, my ear is larumed by the shriek of the steam whistle and the laborious snort of the propeller.

All announce that on these shores and waters the age of the practical, hard-working, money-getting Yankee is upon us; and that the careless, laughter-loving Frenchman's day is over!

THE NAMING OF LAKE STE. CLAIRE.

On the 12th August, 1879, at GROSSE POINTE, where the Lake Ste. Claire begins to narrow into the Straits, or River Detroit, a celebration took place. The occasion was the Second Centennial anniversary of the discovery of the lake, and the bestowal of its name, by Robert Cavelier, Sieur de la Salle, commander of the "Griffin," the first sailing vessel that ascended the lakes.

The programme of the exercises contained a wood-cut of the "Griffin," from a sketch by his Honor, Judge James V. Campbell, and an announcement as follows:

Regatta, with Aquatic sports; Music; Prayer by Father De Brouex, in French; Historical Address, by Bela Hubbard; Song, "Men of ye Olden Time," by D. B. Duffield, Esq.; Poem, "Legend of L'Anse Creuse," by Hon. J. V. Campbell; Brief Addresses; Music; Fireworks.

All which came off duly and pleasantly, under the skilful leadership of Hon. G. V. N. Lothrop, president of the day.

The Address was as follows:

THE NAMING OF LAKE STE. CLAIRE.

HISTORICAL ADDRESS.

IT is good for us to look back into the past. The custom of celebrating the anniversaries of events that have had important influence upon a nation's history, or the welfare of mankind, is justly honored in the observance. That which we are met to commemorate has remained unhonored for 200 years. Yet two centuries ago to-day occurred an event which has mightily influenced the destinies of our race and proved an epoch in the history of this continent! It was the launching at Niagara and the arrival at this Point of a little vessel—not so large as many of our pleasure yachts—but the precursor of a long line of craft, of every size and character, which, passing through these waters, has swollen into a commerce that has become the wonder of the world.

I have undertaken to relate the story of this achievement and of the naming of Lake Ste. Claire, in the default of those whose superior local knowledge and research would have entertained us with "Outlines" of far greater interest and value. I propose to engraft upon the story of the "Griffin" some memories of the extraordinary man with whom the conception originated.

Of all whose names are associated with enterprise and discovery in New France, the Sieur de la Salle is the most illustrious. The history of his various undertakings is drawn mainly from the writings of Hennepin,

Joliet and Membré, and the details have been collected into a fascinating volume by Parkman. I trust that a brief recital will not be uninteresting. He was of an honorable family, a burger of Rouen, where he was born in 1643, and named Robert Cavelier, better known as the Sieur de la Salle, from the name of his estate near Rouen. He was educated among the Jesuits, but, preferring science to theology, and being of a daring spirit and eager for adventure, he sailed for Canada, that paradise of adventure, being then twenty-three years of age.

According to an unpublished memoir, we first find him, in 1669, making his way with a Seneca guide to the Ohio, which he descended as far as the rapids at Louisville. Here, abandoned by his men, he retraced his steps alone. The following year, according to the same authority, embarking in a canoe on Lake Erie, he reached the Straits of Detroit, coasted Lakes Huron and Michigan, and descended the Mississippi to the 35th degree of latitude. Assured that the Father of Rivers discharged not into the Gulf of California, as had until then been supposed, but into that of Mexico, he returned to seek means for more extended exploration. Unfortunately, La Salle's journals, and a map which he is said to have made, and which existed in 1756, are lost. If the accounts be correct, these would have given to him and the first knowledge of the Ohio, if not of the Mississippi.

It is certainly known that the latter stream was explored in 1673 by Father Jacques Marquette, accompanied by Louis Joliet, an adventurous merchant, and the subsequent associate of La Salle. These did not, however, go far enough to solve the problem of its terminus.

That these straits were visited by the white races at a much earlier period is certain of history. The route of the French from the St. Lawrence to their missions and trading-posts on the upper lakes, via the Ottawa, being the most direct route, Champlain himself had in 1611 and 1612 ascended that river to Lake Huron. Thence he visited the country of the ⟨...⟩ near Saginaw Bay, returning by way of the straits to Lake Erie, as is shown by his book published in Paris in 1632. Accompanying La Salle's first expedition (1669) were two priests of the order of Sulpitians, Dollier and Galinée, who, on arriving at Niagara, were diverted from their purpose and resolved to carry their spiritual succor to the Pottawattomies of the upper lakes. After various misadventures, in one of which they lost a great part of their baggage in the waters of Lake Erie—a mishap they attributed to the anger of the devil— they reached the Detroit in the spring of 1670. Of it they relate: "At the end of the lake we found a very remarkable place, in great veneration among all the savages of these regions because of an idol of stone which nature has formed there, to which they say they owe the good fortune of their navigation on Lake Erie, and which they propitiate with presents of skins, provisions, etc." The stone was liberally painted and bore a rude resemblance to humanity. The priests convinced that this was the devil, to whom they ascribed the shipwreck. The relation proceeds: "I leave you to think whether we avenged on this idol which the Iroquois had greatly recommended us to honor, the loss of our chapel. We also attributed to it the scarcity of provisions we had been in up to this time. In fine, there was not a person whose hatred it had not incurred."

The priest tells us that he consecrated one of his axes to break this stone god; then "having lashed two canoes together, we carried the fragments to the middle of the river, so that no one should hear of it again." "God," he says, "immediately rewarded us for this good action, for we killed the same day a buck and a bear."

This place being, as the narrative tells us, "full of the lodges of those who had come to render their homage to this stone," it seems incredible that such a deed could be done in the very presence of its savage worshippers, if it were indeed a manitou. Whether the savages were restrained by the audacity of the act, or the huge proportions of one of the reverend friars, or whether they attached less importance to the "idol" than these zealous iconoclasts supposed, does not appear. Sacred stones were not uncommon in these parts. I have seen several such altars, sometimes in the most wild and lonely situations, invariably covered with bits of tobacco and other petty gifts, which cost little sacrifice.

Several years had passed since these adventures, but La Salle had lost neither energy nor purpose. Means only were lacking. But he had rich relatives, and he was aided, so far as authority could go, by the most energetic and astute governor that had yet administered the affairs of Canada. Together they planned a post on Lake Ontario, far beyond the settlements of the St. Lawrence, which might overawe the Iroquois and turn to France the stream of wealth that was inuring to the Dutch and English from the fur trade. Twice La Salle visited France, where his influence at court obtained for him permission to pursue his plans at his own expense for five years. He received from the king a patent of nobility and a grant in seigniory of Fort Frontenac, as the new post was called.

But the ardent nature of the man was not content with the prospect of fortune now secured. To him it was only a base for operations of vaster extent and bolder enterprise. The object which he had in view was most comprehensive. If the project of a passage to China, across the continent, proved delusive, he would anticipate the Spaniards and the English in their occupation of the great West. He would colonize it with Frenchmen, develop its resources, make friends of the Indian tribes, and, by controlling the mouth of the Mississippi, secure an outlet for a vast trade in the future. As necessary to his scheme he proposed to build a vessel for the navigation of the lakes, above the Niagara, where only canoes had been seen before, sufficiently large to carry the material needed for so vast an enterprise. In the corps organized for this expedition were two noted men, afterwards famous in Canadian annals. Henry De Tonty, his lieutenant, was a young Italian officer who had lost a hand in the Sicilian wars, and whom political troubles had driven to the New World. For the lost member he had substituted one of iron, which gained him the sobriquet of the "iron hand." It was symbolic of his indomitable character. The other adventurous spirit was the bold, audacious, and hardy friar, Père Louis Hennepin, who had more taste for wild and romantic travel than for the spiritual part of his mission. He became the historian of the expedition, but is too little trustworthy, and is inclined to magnify his own exploits at the expense of others of greater merit.

The place where was built the first vessel that sailed the upper lakes is the mouth of a small stream, the Cayuga, about six miles above the cataract, on the west side of Niagara River. Hennepin says: "Most of the Iroquois were gone to wage war on the other side of Lake Erie," so, though exposed to occasional alarms, the party were in little danger. Two Mohegan hunters prepared lodges and supplied game. The vessel was finished early in the spring of 1679. She was, according to Hennepin's first account, of about forty-five tons burden. He afterwards reports it as sixty tons, which is much more probable, considering the number of men and munitions she carried. Accompanying Hennepin's volume is an engraving representing her in an unfinished state. The drawing made by Judge Campbell and printed on the programme of to-day's exercises, gives a clear idea of its character. It was a two-masted schooner, but of a fashion peculiar to that day, having double decks, and a high poop projected over the stern, where was the main cabin, and over this rose another and smaller cabin, doubtless for the use of the commander. The stern was thus carried up, broad and straight, to considerable height. Bulwarks protected the quarter deck. She bore on her prow a huge figure, skilfully carved, in imitation of an heraldic monster—the arms of Count Frontenac—"and above it an eagle." This, in the representation, adorns the top of the stern. La Salle bore no good-will to the Jesuits, who hated him, and he often boasted that he would make the "Griffin" fly above the ravens, meaning that he would triumph over the blackcoats. The ship "carried five small cannon, three of which were brass, and three harquebusses, and the rest of the ship had the same ornaments as men-of-war use to have." "It might have been called," adds the historiographer, "a moving fortress." In fine, it "was well equipped with sails, masts, and all other things necessary for navigation," besides arms, provisions, and merchandise.

The previous autumn La Salle had sent fifteen men up the lakes to trade for furs, and open his way to the Illinois. He also despatched Tonty to the mouth of the strait to intercept these should they be returning. Then with much difficulty the vessel was urged up the two and one-half leagues that remained between the building site and

THE "GRIFFIN."

the lake. On the 7th of August the thirty-four voyageurs embarked, spread their canvas to a favoring breeze, and having sung Te Deum, set forth on their voyage. The ship proved a good sailer. On the 11th they entered "a strait thirty leagues long and one broad," called in the language of the French, "the Detroit," where they were joined by Tonty, and the next day reached the beautiful expanse which spreads before us.

Tradition says that on reaching the lake they were wind-bound for several days, and this is rendered probable by the fact that they did not reach Lake Huron until the 23d. Here, too, let us stop, and inquire whence was derived the name which the lake bears. On Champlain's map (1632) no name appears. Sanson's map, published officially 1656, calls it "the lake of salt waters;" Huron being designated at that period as "le mer douce," or the fresh-water sea. Galinee, the hero of the stone idol, who passed here nine years before, says, "We saw no mark of salt in this lake." The notion probably originated from the brackish springs which exist at the mouth of the Clinton River. Hennepin tells us that "the Iroquois who pass over it frequently, when upon their warlike designs, call it Otsi-Keta." It bore, also, according to Judge Campbell, the Indian names of Kandekie and Ganatchio. Many suppose that the lake was called after Patrick St. Clair, who was lieutenant-governor at Mackinaw in 1783. But this is altogether too modern.

It was a custom of French voyageurs in new regions to bestow upon any prominent feature of the landscape the name of the saint to whom the day of the discovery was dedicated in the church calendar. There was a saint who bore the present modernized name, and who was one of the headless saints, a martyr to his virtue, but his calendar day is November. The saint whose name was really bestowed, and whose day is August 12, is the female "Sainte Claire," the foundress of the order of Franciscan nuns of the thirteenth century, known as "Poor Claires." Clara d'Assisi was the beautiful daughter of a nobleman of great wealth, who early dedicated herself to a religious life and went to St. Francis to ask for advice.

On Palm Sunday she went to church with her family dressed in rich attire, where St. Francis cut off her long hair with his own hands and threw over her the coarse penitential robes of the order. She entered the convent of San Damiano in spite of the opposition of her family and friends. It is related of her that on one occasion, when the Saracens came to ravage the convent, she arose from her bed, where she had been long confined, and placing the pyx, which contained the host, upon the threshold, she kneeled down and began to sing, whereupon the infidels threw down their arms and fled. Sancta Clara is a favorite saint all over Europe, and her fame in the New World ought not to be spoiled—like the record of the dead in a battle gazette—by a misspelt name!

The interest of the subject will, I know, with my present auditors, pardon the introduction of a few further researches into the history of the Lady Claire. She was one of the most celebrated foundresses of orders in the Roman church. Besides the Clarisses, instituted in 1212, she is said to have founded the Capucines, the Annonciades, the Cordolieres or Gray Sisters, the Nuns of the Ave Marie and of the Conception, and the Recolletes. At a time when all the communities were extorting from the popes the authorization to possess property, she solicited from Innocent IV., in favor of her order of Franciscans, the privilege of perpetual poverty! F. Way, in his work on Rome, published in 1875, says: "Sancta Clara has her tomb at the Minerva, and she dwelt between the Pantheon and the Thermæ of Agrippa. The tenement she occupied at the time of her decease still exists, but is not well known. In a little triangular place on or near Via Tor. Argentina, lodged the first convent of the Clarisses. If, crossing the gateway, you turn to the left of the court, you will face two windows of a slightly raised ground floor. It was there Innocent IV. visited her, and there on the 12th August, 1253, listening to the reading of the Passion, in the midst of her weeping nuns, died the first abbess of the Clarisses and the founder of 4000 religious houses."

We are not told with what imposing ceremonies the christening was performed, but surely some inspiration was derived from the beautiful scenes of nature through which the voyageurs had just passed, which then surrounded them, and which to our eyes this day are no less lovely and inspiring. The natural beauty of the region lying between lakes Erie and Huron had been recorded by all the early travellers, with words of admiration. Many of the islands were low, and some of the river margins scarcely above the water. But all was green and peaceful. Dark forests extended to the river edge, and many a tall monarch of the wood waved its gigantic arms over the brink, and was reflected in a glassy surface which no tide or flood ever disturbed. The marshes were luxuriant with wild rice, that furnished a sumptuous repast to a great variety of birds and water fowl, and even a welcome supply to the Indians. Occasional villages and bark wigwams enlivened the shore, surrounded with gardens and corn fields, and the most elevated points were crowned with burial mounds. Most of the shores had high banks and were covered with timber. Especial notice is bestowed upon Grosse Isle, and forest-crowned Isle au Cochon—Belle Isle—lay like an emerald gem, in its setting of bright waters.

The choniclers all allude to the abundance of wild game and fruits. There were " apples as large as the

Pommes d'Api," or Lady Apples, and nuts "like moderate sized oranges." La Hontan says " the pears are good but rare." The apples were probably crabs, though one writer speaks of the trees as set methodically; but who can tell us what were the pears? Can it be that the famous French pear trees, whose origin no man living knows, existed here as natives at that day? The beauties of the passage filled our voyageurs with rapturous delight. Hennepin records the loveliness of the shores, the prairies, and the forests. The "Griffin" was covered with game and fruits which had been gathered in great abundance and with little effort. The fruit consisted of chestnuts, walnuts, and butternuts, apples, pears, plums, and grapes; the game of deer and many smaller animals, and flocks of swans, ducks, and turkeys, and they had feasted on the meat of a bear they had killed. The Father adds, "They who shall have the happiness some day to inhabit this pleasant and fertile country will remember their obligation to those who first showed them the way."

The chronicles are silent as to Indian settlements on the Straits, which is not singular, considering that they seldom recorded such things unless there was special occasion. The white occupation followed closely upon this period. A fort was established, as we know, near where Port Huron now is, in 1687; and it would appear from a memoir of the Sieur de Tonty, then on his way down from the Illinois, that something of the kind existed in the same year between lakes Erie and St. Claire. He says: "We came on the 19th of May to Fort Detroit. We made some canoes of elm, and I sent one of them to Fort St. Joseph on the high ground above Detroit, thirty leagues from where we were, to give the Sieur du Leet (who commanded there) information of my arrival." Twenty-two years after the visit of the "Griffin" the first colonization was begun in this region, at the place which now monopolizes the name of "Detroit."

Le Détroit, or the Straits — under which name the French included the entire passage between lakes Erie and Huron—was visited by Charlevoix in 1720, who thus records his opinion of the country. "Above the Isle of Sainte Claire the Detroit widens and forms a lake, which has received its name from the island, or which has given its name to the latter. It is about six leagues long by as many wide in some places. This is pronounced the most beautiful part of Canada, and truly, judging by appearances, Nature has refused it nothing which can constitute a charming country; low hills, prairies, plains, old forests, streams, springs, rivers, all are so good of their kind, and so happily assorted, that one knows nothing further to be desired. The lands are of admirable fertility. The islands seem to have been placed with a view to charm the senses. The river and the lake are full of fish, the air pure, and the climate temperate and very healthy."

The many beautiful homes we see around us to-day show how amply these favorable judgments of the early chroniclers have been confirmed and illustrated by those to whom the inheritance has fallen.

I shall follow very cursorily in the path of La Salle and his party. The "Griffin," which hitherto had been favored with prosperous winds, encountered off Saginaw Bay a furious storm, which sorely tried the skill and courage of the voyageurs. Nor did it calm until they had called upon St. Anthony of Padua—the patron of mariners—to whom, says Membré, "they made a vow, which delivered them by a kind of miracle." Hennepin narrates that during the height of the gale "everybody fell on his knees to say his prayers and prepare for death, except our pilot, whom we could never oblige to pray, and he did nothing all the while but curse and swear against M. de La Salle, who had brought him thither to perish in a nasty lake and lose the glory he had acquired by his long and happy navigation of the ocean." At length, escaped the tempest, they reached Point St. Ignace, the centre of the Jesuit missions and the Indian trade.

A very slight sketch must here suffice us of the further fortunes of La Salle; and the fate of the "Griffin" will command our interest. Brave, adventurous and successful as were the early explorers of New France, there was but small recognition of their services, either by the Government at home or in the New World. A deep jealousy of La Salle's designs pervaded the fur traders as well as the Jesuits, and made them hostile to his enterprise, since it threatened injury to their private gains. Had Jesuit and Recollet, merchant and officer, constituted a band of brothers, all would have gone well for France in the New World. Unhappily it was far otherwise. The clashings of interest could never be reconciled, and it often happened that the meetings of white men in the far wilderness were those of enemies in disguise. Of the fifteen men sent out by La Salle the year before, a few who remained faithful had collected at Green Bay a store of furs, which he resolved to send back with the vessel to satisfy his creditors, while he, with his stores, his Mohegan, and his three friars, should continue up Lake Michigan. After completing her errand the "Griffin" was to return to St. Joseph, where a fort should be built, and preparations made for the descent of the Mississippi.

But the "Griffin" was never heard from again. Whether she foundered or was burned by the Ottawas is not known. La Salle believed she was treacherously sunk by the pilot to whom he had entrusted her. Whatever was her fate, the salt-water hero of the storm on Lake Huron was doomed to perish in "the nasty fresh water" which he so detested.

The loss was vital. Yet the brave-hearted cavalier, undeterred by a misfortune so great, pushed on to Illinois, where he built a fort. Leaving Tonty and Hennepin to occupy the fort, and in the midst of a savage winter, he made his way back on foot to his far distant Fort Frontenac. The path led through wilds unknown, across the Michigan peninsula. He crossed the Detroit on a raft, and almost alone, for his men were worn out, reached his seigniory. Thence he hurried to Montreal, giving no rest to his ardent spirits and iron nerve. Here the intelligence met him of the desertion of his men and the destruction of his fort on the Illinois. Tonty and Hennepin must be rescued. With their aid and with fresh supplies he might yet save the vessel, which was on the stocks, and make good the descent of the Mississippi. He returned to Ottawa and reached his destination, only to find a solitude. The dreaded Iroquois had driven off or murdered his friendly Illinois, the plain was strewn with mangled corpses, and no tidings could be learned of Tonty.

We are told of new schemes which now occupied his fertile brain, among which was that of a grand confederacy of the tribes against the common foe. We are told of the recovery of his two companions in the spring, with whom he paddled back to Fort Frontenac; of his commutation with his creditors, by the loss of half his seigniory, and of his third journey to Illinois to recover the lost ground. Abandoning the building of a vessel, and dragging their canoes on sledges, they embarked, and on the 6th of February, amid floating ice, issued forth on the majestic Mississippi. With his small party, and amid new and strange scenes, they reached the outlet of the great river, and on the 9th of April, 1682, La Salle planted his standard and took possession of Louisiana, " in the name of the most high, mighty, invincible, and victorious prince, Louis the Great, by the grace of God king of France and Navarre." What did not such zeal and enterprise deserve of his country, for which he had obtained an empire so boundless? But what availed this success to a prince who, though so " high and mighty," had not contributed a sou to the enterprise, and who could write thus to the governor of Canada: " I am convinced, like you, that the discovery of the Sieur de la Salle is very useless, and that such enterprises ought to be prevented in future, as they tend only to debauch the inhabitants by the hope of gain and to diminish the revenue from beaver skins!"

Need I recount how this great man, ignorant of the change in the Government and filled with bright visions of the future, retraced his steps to the Illinois, where his influence had assembled thousands of Indian warriors friendly to his cause, how that here he learned not only that the new governor, Le Barre, turned a deaf ear to his appeals, but that under a frivolous pretext he had seized and wasted his property and reduced him to poverty, and how nothing remained but for him to again cross the seas and lay his cause before his sovereign in person?

It must suffice me to say of this personal appeal to the throne that truth and eloquence once more gained for La Salle a just recognition of his great services. Having thus recovered his influence he was enabled to carry out a scheme worthy his character and fame,—the colonization of Louisiana. He was granted four vessels and one hundred soldiers, besides ship-builders, mechanics, and laborers, and many so-called "gentlemen of condition." Poor material these for a colony in the wilderness, but a more prudent addition was made in a number of girls, who joined the expedition with the prospect of becoming wives to the colonists. Alas, that of this well-concerted project we have to record only the most bitter failure! From lack of harmony between the leader and his captains, ignorance of the coast, or design on the part of the pilot, the fleet sailed past the mouths of the river, and in attempting to land the store-ship was wrecked, with the loss of most of her cargo. The naval commander spread his sails and returned to France, leaving on a wild and desolate shore a forlorn hope,—the infant colony who were to conquer for France a territory half as large as Europe. After a winter spent in vain attempts to find the fatal river a settlement was begun. But two years of suffering and disappointment reduced their number to less than one-fourth. La Salle now attempted to make his way, with a trusted few, across the country to the river and thence to Canada, to obtain succor for the colony. With this party were two men who had sworn vengeance upon their leader. On the morning of May 16, 1687, they killed his three servants, including his faithful Indian hunter, and as La Salle himself approached where the murderers lay, a bullet pierced his brain and he fell dead.

Thus perished at the age of forty-four years a man of whose like there have been few examples. In his active nature and determined energy a close resemblance may be found in our own youthful Houghton. He had spent twenty years in incessant activity, and in pursuit of his grand scheme, as he himself says, had "traversed more than 5000 leagues of new and unknown territory, among savage and cannibal nations, often on foot, through snow and water, without escort, without provisions, without bread, without wine, without recreation, and without repose." And now nothing remained of all his labors.

It would be too much to say that no selfish motive actuated him. He hoped to make for himself an abiding fame, and, doubtless, he looked for the time when wealth and power should reward his toils. But he was essentially a man whose heart was in the work of discovery, and in this field there is no brighter name in American annals.

It is for us, who share the benefit of his life, to perpetuate his memory. But where or how shall we erect his monument? A few years ago there was in the city of Detroit a street called by his name; a petty tribute, but even this has disappeared in the demand for a new nomenclature. Another street, recently opened in the western suburb, alone bears evidence of his honored memory. Let me add a suggestion. On the outer walls of the beautiful edifice which Detroit has erected as her hotel de ville, or city hall, are four niches designed for statues. They are now empty. Let them be filled with marble images of men whose names and fame are indissolubly associated with this region.

Foremost will be that of the Sieur de la Salle. An engraved portrait of him is given by Hennepin, from which his features may be modelled; and we have a sufficiently accurate description of his tall figure and manly and somewhat austere bearing. On the occasion of his visit with the "Griffin" he donned, when it seemed advisable to make some display, a scarlet coat with gold trimmings. The dress of a gentleman of that period in Canada is well known, and there should be no difficulty in sufficiently distinguishing him.

The other pedestals may be filled with men of noble fame, whom France gave to America, and who belong to us. I need only mention De la Motte Cadillac, the founder of Detroit,—a portrait of whom is known to have existed, for which search is being made, and (as Hon. Levi Bishop assures us) with promise of success. The devoted and self-sacrificing Jesuit, Père Marquette, than whom none is more deserving; and lastly, though of later time, the Catholic priest whom all loved, and who first represented this territory in Congress, Father Richard. Of him an excellent portrait is extant. The flowing yet diverse robes of the two priests will contrast strikingly with the rich official vestments of the nobleman and the courtier.

And now, as we look back upon the past that we have recalled, with its wild surroundings, its hopes, and its disappointments, and note the changes which two centuries have wrought, let us take heart, and hope that the future of this great country will be more glorious than the discoverer's wildest dreams!

LA SALLE.
(Statue—City Hall, Detroit, 1884.)

INDIANS IN MICHIGAN.

"During the course of a long life, in which I have made observations on public affairs, it has appeared to me that almost every war between the Indians and Whites has been occasioned by some injustice of the latter towards the former. It is indeed extremely imprudent in us to quarrel with them for their lands, as they are generally willing to sell, and sell such good bargains; and a war with them is so mischievous to us, in unsettling frequently a great part of our frontiers, and reducing the inhabitants to poverty and distress, and is besides so expensive, that it is much cheaper as well as honester to buy their lands than to take them by force."—*Letter of* BENJAMIN FRANKLIN, 1787.

INDIANS IN MICHIGAN.

THOUGH it is many years since the last individual has disappeared of the several Indian villages that, on the first establishment of the French, peopled the shores of the Detroit, there yet remain in Michigan small remnants of tribes belonging to several nations.

At the establishment of the present State Government, in 1836, the most numerous of these tribes or nations was the Chippewas,—or Ogibways, according to their language. They claimed a large portion of the country bordering upon Lake Superior, and were scattered through the valleys of the Grand and Saginaw rivers. There were small bands of Ottawas and Pottawatomies living upon reservations in the western part of the peninsula, upon and near Lake Michigan, and a small band of Sauks or Sacs (the tribe to which the celebrated war chief, Black Hawk, belonged) were settled upon a reservation on the Huron River.

A considerable portion of the upper peninsula of Michigan, when the writer first visited it, in 1840, was still unceded Indian territory.

In most of the Indian cessions to the United States reservations were made, at favorite points on the streams, of extent sufficient for the wants of the greatly reduced bands, or such portions of them as did not wish to remove to lands offered them by the Government, beyond the Mississippi. Of these, few now remain in Indian possession.

However just may be the complaints of injustice done to the aboriginal tribes of America, in the bargains so often made with them for the purchase of the lands held or claimed as theirs, it is gratifying to record, that no stigma attaches to any transactions of this nature within the limits of Michigan. Full compensation has been given in all cases. In the treaty made through Mr. Schoolcraft, as commissioner on the part of the United States, for the territory claimed by the Chippewas of Saginaw, the price paid was probably more than the Government will ever realize from the public sales of the lands ceded.

Though, with the exception of small reservations, all the lower peninsula had been ceded to the United States, there remained in 1837 a very considerable Indian population, residing in villages and small agricultural communities, at various points. These received annuities from the federal government, through Indian agents. Schools were also established among them, each community was provided with a blacksmith, maintained at the national expense, and considerable sums were yearly expended in the encouragement of agriculture. The entire Indian population of the State, at that time, was probably not less than 15,000.

In Clark's Gazetteer of Michigan, for 1863, are enumerated the following, as the entire Indian population:

	BANDS.	POP.
Chippewas of Lake Superior	7	1,004
Ottawas and Chippewas south of Lake Superior	49	4,826
Chippewas of Saginaw	13	1,632
Chippewas, Ottawas and Pottawatomies of southern counties	2	235
Pottawatomies of Huron	1	51
Totals	72	7,748

Among these are twenty-eight schools, supported by the federal government.

They have six smiths, and from fifteen to eighteen missionaries.

The Government pays annually:

In cash annuities, about	$40,000
In goods	3,000
For schools, smiths and agricultural purposes	20,000
For agencies	8,000
Total	$70,000

which amounts to more than nine dollars for each man, woman and child.

Yet all this provident care does not prevent their rapid diminution.

In the fall of 1837 I visited a village of the Chippewas of Saginaw. It was situated on the river Tittabawassee, sixteen miles above Saginaw City. The small-pox had lately visited the band, and the village was nearly deserted. It consisted of a few lodges only. These differed from any I had before seen; being built of strong poles, covered and lined with bark, and large enough to accommodate, after the native fashion, a family of ten to twenty persons. Several fields of maize, of perhaps twenty acres each, constituted the cultivation. These were ploughed and planted with regularity, showing a good degree of agricultural improvement.

That dire disease, small-pox, unknown to the Indians before the coming of the whites, and, next to "fire water," their most fatal gift, had made cruel havoc among this band, and nearly annihilated it. It was said, that out of five or six hundred, who composed the band, not more than a third were left.

Being desirous to obtain a canoe belonging to the chief, I went, late in the evening, with an interpreter, to his lodge. This old chief was named Ba-mos-éya (Dried-in-the-Sun), and was called by the whites the "pox-marked chief." We sat with him an hour, though he and his family had gone to rest some time before. He seemed glad of the interruption, for the desolation of his band had made the old man lonely. Two of his three wives had died, and his lodge—about sixteen feet square—was occupied by him, with his remaining wife, and a large family of children. He sat upon the bed in his blanket, naked to the waist, and talked with much energy on the subject nearest his heart for half an hour, during which we did not interrupt him. He told how a strong disease had attacked his little band, until one by one they dropped away, and dying families left their dead unburied, or covered with sand upon the beach.

What greatly increased their distress was the refusal of the Government agents to assist them. Through fear of the disease, they deserted the band in its utmost need, and when wholly unable to hunt, withholding the supplies so much needed, and which were due them by treaties, permitting the band to perish of sickness and starvation. To the shame of humanity, it is to be feared that this charge was too true.

This chief was not called to the treaty recently concluded at Detroit, where the lands of his tribe had been ceded away, and he was much dissatisfied in consequence, he and his band refusing to remove.

Altogether, this is the best-looking tribe I have seen in Michigan. Some of the girls have regular features, that even among white beauties would be esteemed handsome. Among these was a young granddaughter of old Bamoseya, a beautiful half-breed, with brilliant black eyes. Notwithstanding the pleasing poetic fictions of poets and painters, it is rare to find, among any of the Indian tribes of this region, the forms and features which, according to our ideas, constitute beauty.

Possibly the life of labor to which the squaws are subjected has helped to entail upon them some organic defects. In general the men have much the finest forms. Among the Chippewas, as well as the Pottawatomies and Ottawas, I have been struck with the many agile, lithe and manly figures.

The chief of a small band of Pottawatomies, whom I saw in Branch County, named Sauquoit, was a man of tall and elegant stature, and of an open, intelligent countenance. His dress, like that of most of his tribe, consisted of a few tattered garments of the white man, with cloth leggins, having a broad fringe at the sides, after the Indian fashion, and fitted tight to the limb.

There is in the Indian organization more of agility and grace than of strength. Of this I witnessed an instance among some young Ottawas and the young men of my party of whites. In a wrestling match the Indians were easily thrown, until they resorted to the stratagem of entirely stripping and greasing their bodies. In swiftness of foot they were more than a match for our men, though the wind and endurance of the latter were greater.

The love of the Indians for the "fire-water," and the ease with which they are enabled to procure it, through the cupidity of the whites, have ever proved one of the great obstacles to their civilization. The State and general governments have frequently passed laws to prevent the sale of ardent spirits to the Indians, and many attempts have been made to enforce them, but in this, as in most other cases, self-interest usually gets the better of good resolutions.

An anecdote in point was related to me by a merchant in one of our interior villages. At the time of my story he was a trader with the Indians, having his store at Jackson, from which, after the custom of the traders, he would send out runners to intercept the natives on their trail, and toll them to his store. "The sale of spirituous liquors was contrary to law, yet no one," said Mr. D——, "could deal with those thirsty souls, without supplying their taste for the dram. If they could not obtain it here, they would mount horses and go to Detroit for their trade, where whiskey could be got." So, when a trade was concluded, it was his custom to lock doors, and treat his customers to their favorite beverage, taking care that none should be seen drunk within village limits.

"There were only about twenty whites," said he, "with whom I traded, out of the whole county, but they were mostly 'church members,' and indignant at the merchants' reported dealing of spirits to the Indians." They assembled a county meeting on the subject, at which Mr. D—— was called to account. The trader, being thus summoned, appeared and made a speech in his vindication. He represented to the meeting, that, as the giving of liquors to the Indians was unlawful, he had never acknowledged, nor would he, that he had ever furnished it to them. "But," said he, "you very well know the impossibility of effecting a trade unless liquor comes from some quarter, and that if it is not forthcoming they will invariably trade elsewhere. It is therefore my opinion that somebody does furnish it, in order that their trade may be secured to us."

Whereupon an influential citizen arose, and moved that Mr. D—— be *required* to supply the Indians with as much liquor as he thinks necessary to retain their trade. The question being called for, notwithstanding so ludicrous an appeal, and so entirely at variance with the object of the meeting, after much awkward objection, was put to the county, and carried by acclamation!

Of the labors of the early Jesuit missionaries, among the Indians, in the far wildernesses of this region, few monuments remain. But that the results have, in some instances, been lasting, we have at least one interesting evidence.

In the summer of 1838 I had the pleasure of visiting several villages of Ottawas, about L'Arbre Croche and Traverse Bays, of Lake Michigan. They had here formed several agricultural communities, with a total population of more than one thousand souls. All around was uninhabited wilderness.

They dwelt in cabins built of logs, twenty to twenty-five feet square, and thatched on roof and walls with cedar bark, solidly constructed and comfortable.

The principal village, of about fifty cabins, was arranged in a regular street, sixty feet wide, the houses opposite each other, and from fifty to one hundred feet apart, and most of them had private yards, filled with currant bushes, and other shrubbery.

The internal appearance was equally neat. There were several apartments, and the walls were adorned with highly-colored pictures.

Upon the height, above the village, stood the Mission

Church, a building of considerable size, with the dwelling of the priest adjoining, and in front a large white cross.

The farm, on the upland, was worked in common, and fine crops of Indian corn and potatoes were growing.

The dress of these Indian communists consisted of a mixture of the white and Indian costumes; for with the savage the taste for leggins, and ornamental work in the native style, never yields to his progress in civilization.

This simple community was still far from any settlement of the white man, and it seemed as if here at least the first seeds of Christianity, planted by the zealous labors of the Jesuit fathers, among these children of the forest, had blossomed into a little flower of civilization and borne fruit.

It is probably two centuries since this germ was planted. More than a century ago the community was visited by the English trader, Alexander Henry (1761), and I quote his brief account, as showing how firmly rooted it then was.

"At the entrance of Lake Michigan, and at about twenty miles to the west of Fort Michilimackinaw, is the village of L'Arbre Croche, inhabited by a band of Ottawas, boasting of two hundred and fifty fighting men. This is the seat of the Jesuit mission of St. Ignace de Michilimackinac, and the people are partly baptized and partly not. The missionary resides on a farm attached to the mission, and situated between the village and the fort, both of which are under his care. The Ottawas of L'Arbre Croche, who, when compared with the Chippewas, appear to be much advanced in civilization, grow maize for the market of Michilimackinac, where this commodity is depended upon for provisioning the canoes."*

Some young men from this tribe, as well as the Chippewas, were sent to schools in the States, and received a liberal education. They were not behind white scholars in aptitude or capacity. I was acquainted with one who adopted the law for his profession, establishing himself, I believe, at Mackinac; and, although I am unable to aver that he was eminent as a lawyer, I do know that few surpassed him in refined eloquence.

Some of these educated Indians were unable to resist the charms with which the greenwood had impressed their youthful imaginations, and, after some years of trial, abandoned their civilization, and returned to the wild life of their ancestors.

POLICY OF THE GOVERNMENT TOWARDS THE INDIANS.

I would here say a few words in regard to the policy pursued by the United States Government towards the Indians. The difficulties in the way of doing them exact justice are very apparent. So little form of government exists among them; so limited, uncertain, and often feeble, is the authority of the chiefs, that the binding force of a treaty signed by those calling themselves such, is open to much doubt. It is not to be wondered at that these are often repudiated by large portions of tribes, which are supposed to be held by their obligations, and

---

* This once isolated Indian mission and flourishing settlement of Ottawas is now (1886) usurped by a white man's village—a well-frequented watering-place—where tasteful cottages are embowered amid the trees. Though the Catholic mission remains, most of the Indians have been removed to a "Reservation"; their communistic community broken up, and the farm abandoned to modern agriculture.

that, in fact, treaties are a very imperfect expression of the will of a people who recognize no law which is opposed to the independent judgment and consent of individuals.

Nor is it easy to ascertain the exact limits of Indian claims to title or occupancy, in the conflicting pretensions of different tribes.

But however ill defined these rights may be, the Indian is as jealous of any encroachment upon them, as civilized man is of any infringement of his claims.

Moreover, he sees himself continually being deprived of them. He sees mile after mile of territory, which was once the recognized land of his ancestors, and the hunting-grounds of his youth, in the remorseless grasp of another and hated race ; even the graves of his fathers—objects of veneration amounting to superstition—swept from him. He sees whole tribes of his kindred undergoing a gradual extinction,—a warning of his own fate. His means of subsistence are reduced ; the provisions and payments promised by treaty stipulations, and upon which he relied for alleviation of his growing wants, are fraudulently withheld, or misapplied. He knows no one to whom he can apply for redress, and his appeals, or claims to sympathy, are treated with contempt by the increasing bands of hardy settlers that are forming a cordon around his narrow possessions.

Can we wonder that he is often driven, in his ignorance and exasperation, to desperate methods of redress ; to secret and violent means of retaliation? That conflicts occur between individuals subjected to these grievances, enhanced by the irregular advances of the whites and the settlers on the frontiers, in which both parties are aggressors? That tribes band together in the vain effort to check the invasion, and to regain their ancient liberties?

History records with admiration the deeds of a Tell, a Leonidas, a Washington, in shaking off the yoke which tyranny had imposed upon a people. Shall we regard as less dignified, just and heroic, the efforts of a Philip, a Pontiac, and a Tecumseh, to restore to their people their ancient freedom? Shall we withhold our sympathy, because a wild and ignorant race are stimulated to occasional savage barbarities?

I am not one of those who see in the Indian only the being he has been painted by poetic minds. There is a halo of romantic light which rests upon his name and story, and lingers about his retreating form. It gives a glow to the colors with which the philanthropist and the poet love to illuminate his few hardy virtues, and invests them with many noble and heroic qualities.

The wildness and solitude of his abode; his simple and hospitable life; the expressive melody of his language; above all, the traditionary tales and stories of wild wanderings and savage feats, clothed with the imagery of imaginative and enthusiastic minds, and with the illusions of poetry, have served to convey many erroneous impressions. It is soothing to human pride to dwell upon uncultivated virtues, and to picture humanity clothed in so fair a garb by the hand of nature.

But, in truth, the virtues of the Indian are few and simple; his failings such as are little in accord with the standard of civilization.

The Indian in a state of nature is cruel and vindictive. He delights in war. His art is to take advantage of his adversary, by every species of deceit; to pursue him with relentless hatred; to waylay, and to murder him in the dead of night; exposing his own person as little as possible in open combat; and, if his victim be captured, to put an end to his miserable existence by lingering tortures. Revenge is a virtue to the savage mind. Even his generosity is often the offering of one who has little to give, and expects much in return.

Among them, woman—the pride of civilized life—is a drudge and a slave. At war with each other, the tribes have, even among themselves, little of fixed and recognized title to the lands they occupy. They wander like ships upon a desert ocean, leaving scarcely the trace of passing humanity; their meetings are more often the interchange of the war-whoop and the scalping-knife than the friendly greetings of brethren.

On the other hand, the superiority of man in his civilized state over the savage seems almost immeasurable. His physical strength and powers of endurance are increased, his intellectual faculties are more acute, and his capacity for advancement in the arts of life are far beyond that of the savage.

He is also a land worker. The territory which is required for the support of a single hunter will maintain a thousand agriculturists. He builds cities, and forms constituted governments.

His wants become commensurate with his enlarged capacities. Civilization has given him a far-reaching spirit of enterprise, which demands and must occupy a more extended field of operation. Confined to the narrow limits of primitive life, forbidden to exercise sovereignty beyond the little sphere of immediate necessity, if conflicting with savage claims, he must be doomed forever to repress those powers which, if left free to expand, would turn solitudes into cities, and convert the earth itself, and the ocean, into the magnificent domain of mind. No sublime applications of science would open the treasures locked up in the earth; the arts and the use of metals would be unknown; the laws of matter, now subservient to our use, would be mysteries; no commerce would whiten the sea, and carry from people to people, from clime to clime, the productions of far distant nations, and the discoveries of intellectual man. The command of Jehovah himself, to "multiply and replenish the earth, and subdue it," would be a dead letter on the Statute Book of Deity!

Such is the course of reasoning which has led the wisest of American statesmen, and the ablest of her jurists, to recognize in the Indian tribes—thinly scattered over an immense extent of territory—only a very qualified title to the soil. They hold, that to the civilized race belongs the right to extinguish the Indian title and occupancy, by purchase, or even by conquest; that the very existence of political societies involves permanent rights of property, and of sovereignty, over the soil, as against the feebly held and uncertain tenure of the savage; and that the peculiar character and habits of the Indian nations render them incapable of sustaining any other relations with the whites than that of dependence and pupilage.

Yet it is easy for the strong to make laws over the weak. To the credit of a Christian nation, the right thus laid down has been exercised by the United States to a very qualified extent. It has been their policy to treat the Indians as free and independent tribes, competent to act in a national character, and, within their own territories, owing no allegiance to the municipal laws of the whites. They have recognized the various tribes as treaty-making powers, and in the purchase of their lands it has been the aim to give just and fair equivalents.

An omniscient and wise providence has placed in our hands the fate of that unfortunate race. The history of the past tells in unmistakable language what is to be the final consummation: that the Indian is destined to fade before the Anglo-Saxon, until the now wild and warring tribes west of the Mississippi become as those who peopled the land east of that once mighty barrier, and who have perished before our eyes.

If such is to be their fate, before that event occurs we have our duty to perform. We can at least alleviate their downfall. We can exercise that justice which is the best prerogative of power.

The plan of collecting the scattered tribes into reserves, from which the evil influence of the whites shall be, as far as practicable, excluded, was no doubt the wisest that our fathers were able to devise. But the humanity of the Government has not controlled the action of individuals. Were these equally interested with the Government in carrying out its paternal measures, the success of the plan, in the increased happiness and prolonged existence of those it aims to protect, might be secured. But there are never wanting unprincipled and interested men, who excite evil passions, encourage rebellions, overreach in bargains, and rob the pensioners of their annual stipends. Nor can the Government always prevent iniquity in its agents, who have frequently and outrageously abused their trusts.

The system hitherto pursued, of Indian agencies,— mere political appointments, with whom the large opportunities for speculation and gain are the main inducement,—is most objectionable.

In many cases—eventually, in all—the duties of these agents may be more safely and wisely intrusted to commissioners from the tribes;—to men *selected by themselves*, of their own race, having education, authority, and the confidence of the red men. This would, at least, lift from us, to great extent, the responsibility of unfair dealing. It would bring the half-civilized tribes into nearer and more direct relationship to our Government. It would make their dependence less felt, and develop their capacity for self-government.

Nor has Congress shown that regard for the faith of the nation, pledged in the numerous Indian treaties, which is consistent with the good-will that originally inspired them. How many wars might have been avoided but for the neglect of Congress to pass the called for appropriations, and for the niggardly and dishonest withholding of supplies that were part of the contract.

Admitting that these wars have been provoked chiefly through the aggressions of white settlers, desperadoes and thieves, still how many a murderous outbreak would have been prevented had these unlawful acts been followed by prompt redress on the part of the Government. The law's delay, the false representations of interested parties, the insufficiency of our army, the race-hatred, and murders unavenged by the proper authorities, have often left the Indians no redress save a resort to their own code of vengeance.

And when treaties have been broken by the unauthorized acts of our own people what has the Government done? Instead of avenging the wrong, it has been but too ready to make new treaties, followed usually by removal to another reservation, only to be again broken in upon, and succeeded by another new settlement, always in favor of the whites, and in disregard of the interests of the weaker party.

There are scattered among us many Indian communities which have adopted an agricultural life, and the dress and mode of living of the whites. Many examples show that the Indian has more capacity and will for these influences than it is usual to credit to him. They encourage the belief that he is not averse to work, and to civilized requirements, if only sufficient incentive be set before him, and he can have assurance that his newly acquired privileges will be confirmed to him. But, driven from one settled home to another and unknown one at the caprice of his white neighbors, who crowd upon and covet his lands; subjected to the yielding impolicy of the Government; knowing how little dependence can be placed upon reiterated promises made to him in solemn treaties, and feeling that nothing is stable in his situation, is it strange that his advance in civilization is slow? Is it not rather strange that he has accomplished so much?

The experiment is yet almost untried of what may be accomplished by bringing this child of the forest under the operation of our laws, and endowing him with all the rights and privileges of citizenship. This will not be the work of a year, or of many years. Barbarian instincts cannot be subdued in a generation. There will be many failures, but the habit will be acquired, gradually but surely. Tribal systems will give place to forms of government better suited to the present condition of the tribes and to their future.

It is gratifying to know that the guaranteed rights of

the Indians are being more respected by those into whose hands are devolved the execution of the laws, and that the chief executive power is actively exerted in preventing individual encroachments. As a people, we are awaking to a clear sense of our duty. The Board of Indian Commissioners is faithfully urging upon Congress the fulfilment of obligations, and a more wise legislation. Their last report states, that the year 1884 has been for all the Indians one of peace and quiet; that there have been no outbreaks, no need of a "Peace Commission," but a year of steady progress in industry, in education, in material prosperity and in civilized habits.

Now let us take advantage of this better appreciation to do our whole duty. It seems to me that the wisdom of experience requires that we should abolish the old treaty system, which has so often proved a failure. Nevertheless, obligations already incurred should be sacredly fulfilled. If modification be desirable, it should be made in accordance with the wishes of the weaker party, not of those most clamorous for it.

As far and as fast as possible, and with their full connivance, the Indians should be brought into the same relations with the Government as ourselves, where tribes are so far advanced as to demand it. Land should be allotted to them in severalty rather than in common, so that no individual can be deprived of his land by unjust or mistaken action on the part of chiefs, whose authority is always doubtful, and of uncertain value. This plan has succeeded well where the people are fitted for it.

The tribes on the reservations should be induced to form communities, constituted, as nearly as may be, after our township, county and state governments. Encourage settled habits of cultivation of the soil, and raising of cattle. Give all needed facilities for education, and for forming industrial and civilized habits. Especially afford to the willing and industrious opportunity to acquire homesteads, securing to them such a title to the land they occupy that no power but their own can deprive them of it. As one tribe after another becomes prepared for it, admit them to the rights of citizenship, on a full equality in every respect with those who now enjoy its benefits.

But let the problem be worked out by the Indians themselves. Let citizenship be offered as a boon, to those only who are fitted for it and desire it. To this end instructions in the public schools, where young Indians are taught, should aim to educate teachers and to prepare the pupils—who are apt scholars—to understand the rights and duties of citizens.

I will not pretend to lay down the forms of law under which these results are to be attained, nor to predict the time when all will be accomplished. These must depend upon trial and experience. But let the end be ever held in view, and let the full, prompt and active protection of the law be afforded against whoever and whatever seeks to obstruct the laws, and to divert the nation from its just course.

Under wise regulations these advantages might be extended to all the tribes who come within our present agency system. Let them form a necessary part of that system. And instead of treating the Indian as a savage beast, to be kept under our civil and military control, lest he should break away and tear our people to pieces, let our people be taught to recognize him as having common privileges with ourselves; to direct his energies into the channels of law and of good government; to wean him, by encouragement and example, from habits of barbarism to industrial occupations.

It may be considered as certain, that the old system will not avail to save the perishing objects of its care from future misery and final extinction.

The wave of population has continued to flow westward, unchecked by the great Mississippi, and the large Indian reservations—already coveted and surrounded—are even now being broken in upon by the same insatiable race that has driven their occupants from the homes of their fathers, on the rivers which flow into the Atlantic.

Already, far beyond these "Indian Territories," Saxon energies have carried the arts of civilization and its ever unsatisfied demands along the shores of the Pacific, and into the strongholds of the Rocky Mountains. Even in the distant homes of the desert are occurring the same conflict of interests, with the same results which have attended our meetings and our progress hitherto.

When the last warring tribes shall have submitted to treaties, and been accorded the protection of territory set apart and solemnly guaranteed to their exclusive use, what will be in the end but the old story,—the influence of bad whites; encroachments—under various pretences, and with fair show—upon their lines and their privileges; robbery (under another name), by degrees, of their weak possessions; until they are exposed to all the evils from which they have fled.

It may be the inscrutable plan of Providence that this primitive race shall become extinct, and that civilized man, with his cultivated powers and larger means for carrying out the designs of the Creator in planting here a mighty nation, shall supply his place.

It is sad to think that, in a few years, will have utterly perished from the face of this goodly land every vestige of its former proprietors. Like the wild beasts which they hunted, *they*, too, pass from sight and from memory, leaving no memorials, except in the names which their poetic language has bestowed upon the natural features of their country. Powerful nations of antiquity have been overwhelmed in the desolating march of barbarous hordes, but the Indian has been swept by the advancing wave of civilization. No mighty monumental ruin, withstanding the desolations of time, and mantling with verdure in its decay, bears his history and his deeds to a future age. No customs or laws, which he originated, mingle the existence of the conquerors with the conquered. A few mounds of earth alone remain, evidence of his former being; and these the ploughshare will soon level with the surrounding fields.

Mindful of the mutability of fortune which may be in store for us, their now powerful successors, let us perform towards this perishing people the whole duty which our civilization and our Christianity require.

And if, finally, nothing can avert the threatened doom, but, like that now forgotten people whom their own has superseded, they also are destined to be extinguished; if, one by one, each remaining tribe must undergo the fate of the Delaware and the Mohegan; when some Uncas of the vanished race shall stand upon the lonely burial mound of his forefathers, to take his last survey of their once happy home, let him carry no reproach to the land of spirits, that anything has been neglected by us, consistent with the welfare of his race, or the preservation of our national honor.

THE MOUND-BUILDERS IN MICHIGAN.
PART I.

carrying out the designs of the Creator in planting here a mighty nation, shall supply his place.

> . . . . "Are they here—
> The dead of other days?—
> . . . . Let the mighty mounds
> That overlook the rivers, or that rise
> In the dim forest, crowded with old oaks,
> Answer. A race, that long has passed away,
> Built them;—a disciplined and populous race
> Heap'd, with long toil, the earth, while yet the Greek
> Was hewing the Pentelicus to forms
> Of symmetry, and rearing on its rock
> The glittering Parthenon. These ample fields
> Nourish'd their harvests."
>
> BRYANT.

THE MOUND-BUILDERS IN MICHIGAN.

PART I.—GENERAL CHARACTER AND DISTRIBUTION OF THE WORKS.

FEW works of a pre-historic people comparable to those found in Ohio, and elsewhere to the southward, occur in Michigan.

Some scattered earthworks are found, of whose origin and uses the tribes of Indians living here at the first advent of the white man had no knowledge. They are of far less extent than those of Ohio, and indicate a people of different customs.

Circular earthworks occur here and there, but they are of small size, and referable to a different purpose from the large circle-mounds of the Ohio. There are no truncated mounds, such as those found further south, and supposed to have constituted foundations or terraces for the dwellings of chiefs, or for religious edifices. No long earth-built ways, connecting the larger circles or squares, occur in Michigan. Nor are there any defensive works on so grand a scale as those in the Ohio Valley.

A few earth-mounds occur, some of which may be referred to a defensive purpose.

One of these is found—or was found, for the desolating plough has reigned rampant over it for the last thirty years—on the Clinton River, in Macomb County, and is thus described to me by Mr. J. E. Day, of Romeo. It lay

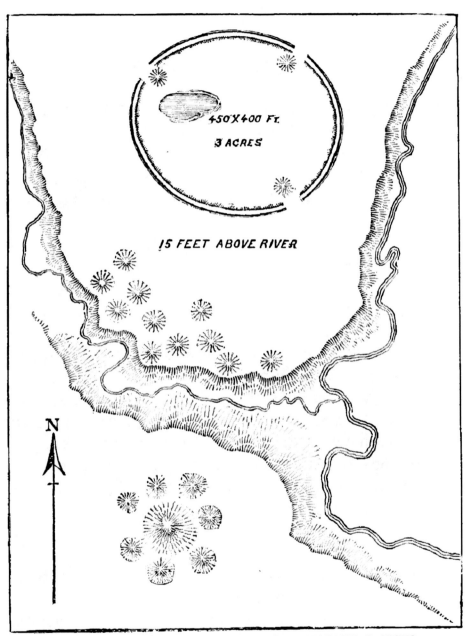

DIAGRAM OF ANCIENT EARTHWORKS, MACOMB COUNTY

between the north branch of Clinton River and a small spring tributary, and was about twenty rods distant from either stream, and on a plateau elevated fifteen feet above. It consisted of a nearly circular embankment four to five feet high, and enclosed about three acres. The diameters were 350 and 400 feet respectively. On the outer side was a wide ditch. There were three openings or gateways, each twenty feet wide, and protected within by a mound so placed as to shut off from without all view of the interior. A small lake within the enclosure supplied water to the garrison.

Between this "fort" and the smaller stream were a large number of tumuli, in an irregular cluster, each of which contained a single skeleton. A little below the junction of this stream with the Clinton was a very large tumulus, surrounded by seven smaller ones in a circle.

In situation and general character this work bears considerable analogy to the defensive works of Northern Ohio. The embankment may have been crowned with palisades, and the interior mounds may have served for observation, as well as defence, to a village within the circle. A large amount of broken pottery and other relics found in the vicinity seems to indicate a once numerous population. Nothing is known which would indicate a religious purpose, analogous to the so-called "sacred enclosures" of Ohio. In all the north-western portion of this county, extensive fields or gardens, in which the cultivation was in drills or rows, may still be distinctly traced.

Near the mouth of this river occurs another similar work, and of apparently a like defensive character.

Mr. Henry Little, in one of several papers on the Mounds, published in the Kalamazoo *Telegraph* in 1874, mentions an ancient work in Gilead, Branch County, which may with some probability be classed as defensive.

"It was an earth embankment, one end starting from the waters of a small lake, the other end coming around to the lake at a point considerably distant from the first. It enclosed an excellent spring of water."

He also describes an earthwork of this kind, and much more extensive, at Three Rivers, in St. Joseph County. "The Rocky River from the north, and Portage Creek from the north-east, unite their waters with the St. Joseph, but a few rods distant from each other, forming a tract of land in the shape of the letter V. About a mile north of this junction was an artificial earth embankment, about six feet high, stretching across the plain, from Rocky River to the Portage." This plain is elevated many feet above these streams, and with this triple defence a beleaguered army might here sustain itself with considerable confidence against the warfare of savage foes.

This defensive work has a peculiar interest, from its vicinity to those remarkable evidences of ancient labor, skill and taste, denominated the "garden beds," of which a description is given elsewhere.

Blois, in his Gazetteer, alludes to "forts of the square or rectangular kind," one of which "is said to be one or two miles below Marshall, one in town of Prairie-Ronde, and several on the Kalamazoo." It is to be regretted that no traces now remain of these structures.

On the banks of the St. Joseph River I remember to have seen, in 1837, a circular embankment of unknown origin. It was of small size, and so well defined that I could not pass it unnoticed. My recollection, however, does not enable me to give any very definite description.

Mr. Little, in the papers above referred to, mentions an antique work of very unusual form. Describing a tumulus on Climax Prairie, he adds, "South of the mound and in the edge of the timber, on the highest part of a hill or eminence, there was an *excavated ring*, which formed the whole of a perfect circle, and enclosed one and a half acres. The excavated hollow was about one rod wide at the bottom and between 2 and 3 feet deep. When first discovered, forty years ago, it was overgrown with large forest trees."

Circles of this kind are very rare. Some have been found in Ohio, and I remember seeing in Wisconsin an animal form made in *intaglio*, instead of relief.

The ring described by Mr. Little could not have had a military purpose, or pains would not have been taken to remove the earth, which, if thrown up as an embankment, would have assisted such an object.

A circular embankment occurs at Springwells, just below Fort Wayne. Of this I shall give a detailed description on a future page.

Some of the works above alluded to have a similar character to those small earthworks found in the vicinity of Lake Erie, on its south side, and extending into New York, which have been surveyed and described by Col. Charles Whittlesey. These consist of embankments with outer ditches, and are built across the necks of the uplands between ravines, thus aiding to render a small piece of land easily defended. Their purpose as works of defence cannot be mistaken.

These are all isolated instances of comparatively small defensive works, unconnected with each other, or with any plan or system, like those series of forts which are found in Ohio and which serve for the protection of a large district. It is probable they were temporary refuges, hastily erected against some sudden inroad. Possibly they were the last refuge of an agricultural people, like those who made the garden beds. This great emergency may have arisen when those barbarous hordes, who occasioned the final destruction or dispersion of the Mound-Builders of Ohio, turned their victorious arms upon the northern race of peaceful cultivators.

Of other kinds of relics of a past race Michigan has more abundant examples.

Tumuli or burial mounds, single and grouped, are very common in all parts of the peninsula. Many of these were in use by the Indian tribes inhabiting the country at its discovery and settlement by the whites, and some continued to be used for their ancient purposes for a long time afterward.

As I propose to describe with some particularity those which occur in the immediate vicinity of Detroit, I will content myself with alluding to a few only of special interest, elsewhere.

By far the finest group of mounds that has come to my knowledge occurs on the banks of Grand River, three miles south of Grand Rapids. They were still perfect when the writer had the satisfaction of seeing them in 1874.

The largest of these mounds has a diameter of 100 feet, and a height of 15 feet or more above the general surface. Close by are two others of nearly equal size, all very regular in shape and conical. They are in a line about 100 feet apart, and 500 feet from the river. Around them cluster seventeen smaller tumuli, without regular arrangement, and varying in height from eight to two feet. All are within an area of two and a half acres.

This group occupies the first terrace, which is overflowed in high water to the foot of the mounds. It lies in the shadow of the ancient, untrimmed forest, consisting principally of sugar maples. Trees were growing on the mounds of two to three feet diameter, and there were evidences of still older ones which have perished.

Seven of these tumuli were opened during the year preceding my visit, by Captain Coffinbury and others, and among them one of the largest. This was found to be wholly composed of the richest portions of the surrounding alluvial soil, differing in this respect from the others, which were composed of the gravel of the uplands. No relics were disclosed, except a copper awl. Patches of ochreous earth were met with, a bushel in a place, as though dumped from a basket. The absence of skeletons in this tumulus, and the red earth, together with ashes, mingled with comminuted bone, would imply that this mound was appropriated to such bodies only as were cremated.

Of the smaller mounds, six were opened. In all skeletons were found, generally one only in each, and all were so decayed that it was impossible to preserve them. They were of ordinary size, except one, which is pronounced gigantic, the proportions " indicating a stature of seven feet." All were in a sitting posture, and faced to different points.

With the bones were many relics, the lowest mound yielding the richest harvest. Besides the usual variety of stone arrow- and spear-heads, were several copper needles, and a copper axe, eight inches long by four wide, and one-fourth inch thick, quite smooth and perfect; several stone pipes and marine shells were also found. Four handsome pots constituted the most interesting discovery. These will be alluded to hereafter.

The spot occupied by this interesting group of tumuli, with its silent surroundings, lovely in its seclusion and grand with its overshadowing foliage, impressed my mind strongly with the poetical character of that race, who combined with the savage life such a sympathetic love of nature.

While certain tribes of the red man in historic times are known to have made frequent use for *intrusive* burial of mounds which they found in the land, it is the general opinion that the era of their original fabrication belongs to a more remote past. We can certainly point to an exception in this State.

On the beautiful prairie of White Pigeon, and near the village, I saw, many years ago, a tumulus of considerable size. It was found by the first whites who settled there in 1826, and tradition asserted that it enshrined the remains of a celebrated chief of the Pottawatomies who formerly occupied that part of the country, and who buried him there a century before the date of the white settlement. He was still held in such estimation that thousands of his tribe came annually to pay their tribute of respect at his grave, until the remnant were moved by the U. S. Government to Kansas, in 1841.

A different mode of entombing their great men was practised by the Indians inhabiting Western Michigan, in the early part of this century.

In 1837, I saw on the summit of a lofty bluff overlooking the river Kalamazoo, the grave of the renowned chief, Wacousta. He was placed in a sitting posture, and the body surrounded with a crib of logs, strongly put together, and entirely above ground. No attempt had been made at raising an earth mound. The skeleton was entire and still partially enveloped in its integuments.

Possibly this disposition may have been but temporary, with a view to removal of the bones, after the flesh had decomposed, to some general resting-place of the nation.

Among the mounds of the Mississippi Valley, and further south, are occasionally found some *built of stones*. An instance of a similar construction is reported to me by Mr. Day, of Romeo, associated with the ancient remains in Macomb County. He says: " In several places in this vicinity were found mounds made of stones, nicely piled up to a height of four to five feet, like a hay-cock. They were entirely alone, and more than a mile distant from the group of earth-mounds elsewhere mentioned."

One of these stone-mounds was opened forty years ago. " It was four feet in height and placed in a circular excavation of two feet depth by four feet diameter. The stones were nicely placed, and had been preserved in shape by a tree which grew on the summit, and threw its roots over the sides of the pile. The stones being removed, portions of a human skeleton were exhumed."

Piles of stone are mentioned by Mr. Schoolcraft as existing on the Island of Mackinac, and supposed by him to have been gathered by the ancient race for the purpose of clearing the land for cultivation. But, although ancient fields exist near, Mr. Day is certain that the stone piles mentioned by him were for a different purpose, and the discovery of the skeleton serves to confirm his opinion. My own theory is, that the stones were heaped about the body for protection, until the time should arrive for a general inhumation or "Feast of the dead,"—a custom which I shall notice presently.

The earth-tumuli in Michigan are nearly always found in some picturesque situation, on or near the banks of the larger streams, often on some promontory that commanded a lengthened prospect of the Indian's natural highway, and which was probably his favorite resort while living. But these places know him no more; his people have long ago departed; his history is lost to tradition, and even his tomb tells but an uncertain story of his former being.

> "Perhaps on banks of many a stream,
> Sloping beneath the day's warm beam,
> Tribes may have lived from sire to son,
> And down through generations run,
> Laying their bones within the mound
> Where all their gathered sires were found,
>   And yet the spot no sign disclose,—
> Save this rude mound,—that ever there
> The hum of men had filled the air,
>   And broke through Nature's wild repose."

These lines from "Ontwa," a poem by our distinguished townsman, the late Col. Henry Whiting, well illustrates the desolation which has fallen upon the race, whose sole monuments are mounds of earth.

The tumuli are monuments to the dead as well as graves. It is almost certain that one or more human skeletons will be found entombed, unless the bones of the occupants have perished through time, or from cremation. Original burials seem to have been made at or below the natural surface, and the bodies are found both in horizontal and sitting postures, and little regard seems to have been paid to the direction in which the face is turned. So unscientific has been the usual mode of unearthing these tombs, that the information they convey to us of the character of the ancient occupants, by cranium and other measurements, is far less definite and certain than could be desired. Amid the diversity of statement as to reported and actual finds, I think the conclusion may be drawn, so far as relates to the aboriginal Wolverines, that they closely resembled the historic races; although several very prognathous skulls and the "flattest tibia on record," found by Mr. H. Gillman in the mounds at Springwells, might seem to refer them to a lower type.

When mounds are opened in most cases, it is impossible to determine from the reports whether the skeletons found belong to original or intrusive burials. According to some accounts, the skeletons indicate a race of very inferior size; according to others, they show a race of giants. The elasticity of these ancient relics, to suit the zeal of the narrator, is truly wonderful. On one occasion I accompanied an old pioneer and worthy Judge to visit several mounds in Western Michigan. My guide gravely informed me that, twenty years before, he had dug from one of these mounds a skeleton which, when laid out upon the turf, measured eleven feet, eight and three-quarter inches, and the skull of which fitted entirely over the judicial head! The Cardiff Giant was a few inches longer than this, but as he was entirely of gypsum it was quite easy to fabricate any proportions which the gullibility of the public could swallow.

While the Michigan mounds contain the usual complement of stone axes, arrow-heads and spear-points, with knives and other implements of chert, it is a little singular that so few tools of copper have been found. Finds of this kind in Wisconsin have far exceeded those from our soils, and this would seem to indicate less acquaintance with the copper quarries of Lake Superior, on the part of the ancient inhabitants of our peninsula, than among the dwellers west of Lake Michigan. In connection with the copper axe mentioned as among the finds in the mounds at Grand Rapids, was some substance having the appearance of cloth, but too much decayed for preservation. Several copper axes from mounds in Iowa were found wrapped in a similar covering, which Dr. Farquharson pronounces to be cloth. Possibly a microscopic examination may prove that the Grand Rapids tool was similarly encased, showing both advance in the art of weaving and some especial reverence or consideration for the metal implement.

Among the relics found in the Grand Rapids mounds—and by no means uncommon in other tumuli—are marine shells. Some of these must have come from the Atlantic or the Gulf, while one is pronounced by Prof. Strong to be from the Pacific. They are interesting as showing the extended intercourse, and probably system of barter and exchange, practised by the unknown peoples. The Pacific coast shells had evidently served the purpose of vessels, the whorls being cut out and holes made for hanging. Shells similarly prepared were in use by the Southern Indians in the time of De Soto, for drinking-cups, as horns were used by our Saxon ancestors.

In pottery our mounds are quite rich. Some of the pots are at least fully equal to those of the bronze period in Europe. The four pots mentioned as disinterred at Grand Rapids were of very regular form ; one had a rim around the neck, from which the vessel, after a slight curve inwards, swelled into a bowl of uniform bulge.

The other three differed in this, that the bowl—round bottomed in all—was divided into four equal bulges. These were made more sharply protuberant by a smooth band, an inch wide, surrounding each, very accurately modelled and deeply impressed. On each side were ornaments of similar design. A smooth band encircled the neck, and the rim was adorned with cross-lines or hatching. The surface otherwise was covered with small indentations, the whole effect being quite tasteful.

Among the finds in Macomb County was a dish of an unusual size and form, and entire. It resembled the smaller half end of an egg-shell, and had a capacity of twelve to fifteen gallons. It was ornamented with figures of various kinds. Unfortunately this unique vase, on exposure, crumbled to pieces.

The pots found by Blois in the mound opened by him at Springwells in 1839 were generally too much broken to determine their shapes. They appeared to be in the form of a half egg, abruptly contracted toward the mouth, with a flaring brim, and of the capacity of one or two gallons. They were smooth on the inside but marked on the exterior with various fantastic figures.

By the side of each of the numerous skeletons found in what is known as the Carsten Mound, Springwells, lay a pot or urn, of which three only were obtained entire. Two of these were uncommonly fine specimens, in good preservation, and about a foot in height. The neck was about five inches wide, with a collar, below the rim, of two inches breadth. Below this the body swelled into a graceful curve, rounded at the base into a gourd form. The composition was clay, largely mixed with pounded stone, which contained much mica, and on the inside was black throughout. On the exterior

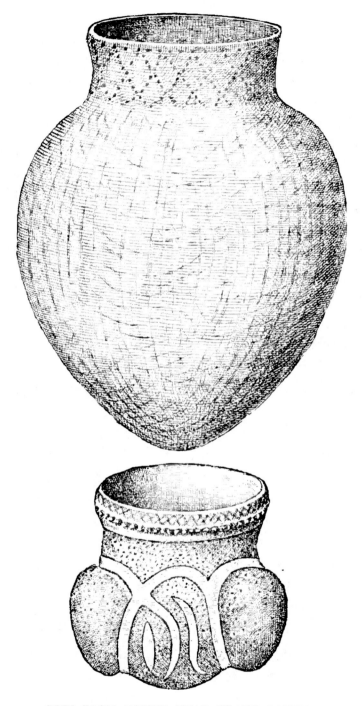

POTS FROM MOUND NEAR GRAND RAPIDS.

was a thin coating of reddish clay, quite distinct from the remainder. The fineness of the texture, combined with great lightness, was admirable. These vases were purchased by Mr. Gillman, and presented to the Archæological Museum at Cambridge, Mass.

The above describes but a few specimens of the many pots, found usually in fragments, in the mounds at Springwells and elsewhere. The composition and general character are much the same.

The art of the potter is so ancient and universal, and the character and forms of the utensils made of baked clay are so important, in a determination of the advance in culture of the people by whom they were fabricated, that more interest attaches to the remains of a perished race which show the state of the ceramic art among them, than to any other of the ordinary relics. The specimens from the Michigan mounds show a taste to appreciate, and an eye and hand capable of giving finish to articles of admirable form, symmetry and lightness, scarcely less perfect than if constructed on a potter's wheel.

Straight or zigzag lines occur on the coarsest specimens, and may betoken the first advance from the rudest savage ideas. But curved forms and figures are more pleasing to the cultivated eye, and imply a degree of æsthetic advancement. By some process differing from and less effective than the modern, an imperfect glazing was obtained, and the inner surfaces are often quite smooth and fine.

It is possible, though it seems hardly probable, that these pots were an importation from the South, the Indians of the Southern States, ancient and modern, being noted for the excellence and variety of their pottery.

That country furnished all the material desired,—colored clays, sea-shells, and micaceous rocks. Old kilns have been found in Georgia, and Adair suggests that the black color was owing to the smoke of the pitch pine used in the fires. The fact that in the better kinds of pottery found in the Northern mounds exactly the same materials combine, and the general resemblance of the ornamentation, may therefore warrant the conclusion that they were importations. This supposition, while it deprives the Northern Mound-Builders of the credit due to such skilful artisans, shows, at least, that the Northern peoples had the good taste to appreciate these beautiful and useful articles, and it conveys an enlarged idea of the extent of the traffic which existed in these ancient times, between the widely separated portions of the continent. The sea-shells tell the same story, and it is known that, even in modern times, the manufacture of stone implements, arrow-points, etc., was confined to a few skilled persons, and that such articles were transported all over the country, for purpose of sale and barter.

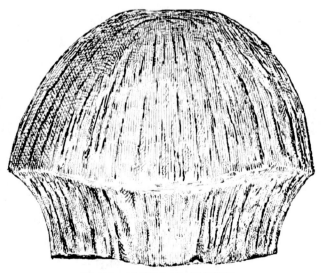

FROM MICHIGAN MOUND.

THE MOUND BUILDERS IN MICHIGAN.
PART II.

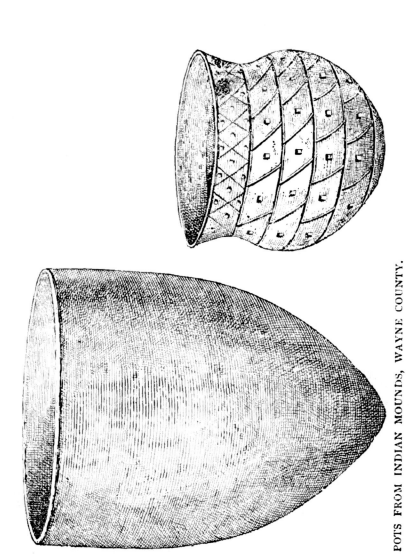

POTS FROM INDIAN MOUNDS, WAYNE COUNTY.

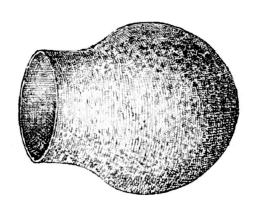

218

THE MOUND-BUILDERS IN MICHIGAN.

PART II.— INDIAN ANTIQUITIES AT SPRINGWELLS.

DURING the early French occupation of Detroit several Indian nations had settlements on the river banks, in the immediate vicinity. Conspicuous were the Hurons, Pottawatomies and Ottawas. They had villages strongly defended by stockades. They raised corn and many vegetables, in large quantities.

These incidents of history are recalled, because the fact of the considerable degree of settled and civilized habits attained by the Indian tribes of that day serves to throw some light upon those pre-historic antiquities whose origin and purposes are involved in so much obscurity.

When I came to Detroit, in 1835, many evidences were still existent of the old aboriginal occupation. It was hardly possible to dig a cellar or level a hillock without throwing out some memorial of the red races. Mingled with their half-decayed bones were pipes and other utensils of stone, broken pottery, ornaments of silver and copper, wampum-beads of curious workmanship, the arrow and tomahawk of the savage, and the figured cross of the missionary.

In striking relationship with the emblems of savage warfare it was not uncommon to find, "in one red burial blent," gun-barrels, sword-blades and cannon balls, mementos of the pale-faced warriors who strove on the same battlefields. But arrow- and spear-head, and other memorials of the savage—rude as were the artificers—are perfect as in the day when they left the hands that made them, while the implements of the civilized race are nearly perished with rust. Thus does the remote past outlive the present. The old alone is ever new, fresh and imperishable!

To unearth a human skeleton was a common occurrence. They were thrown out by spade and plough, and sometimes were seen protruding from the soil where the action of the waves had broken into the land.

Of several skulls thus obtained and in my possession, one is deserving of particular mention, from the fact that it is stained through with permanent colors of red and green. It was the custom among some tribes to paint the face of the dead with his war-colors, but it is not possible that these pigments, laid upon the skin, should have penetrated the bone. A close examination reveals the presence of a *belt* of color, extending around the head, on a line with the forehead, and my conjecture is, that the stain is a deposit from the oxidation of a copper band, placed about the temples. The colors are strong and penetrate the entire bone.

But more interesting memorials of a traditionary race were then extant. Allusion has already been made to tumuli at Springwells. A group of these existed on the river front of the Reeder farm. Just below the copper works the bank was very bold, and elevated about thirty feet above the water. On this bank were two mounds of conical form, of which one still existed at the time of my first visit, though injured by pilferers of Indian relics. It was then about ten feet in height, with a base diameter of forty feet. Large excavations were

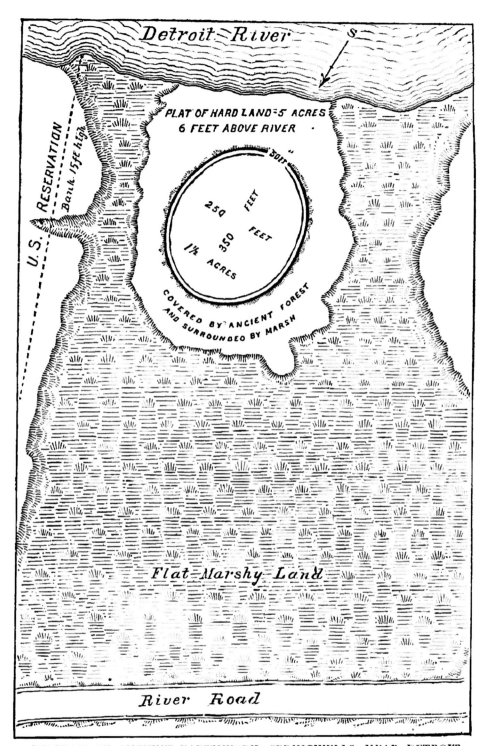

DIAGRAM OF ANCIENT EARTHWORK, SPRINGWELLS, NEAR DETROIT.

in progress for gravel, and for clay used in the manufacture of brick. These encroachments had destroyed one of the tumuli, and the whole have since disappeared.

On and around this spot, for the extent of an acre, were thickly strewn bones and broken pottery, mingled with shell beads, stone knives and arrow-points. Several rods below was a smaller tumulus in a field, then covered with forest. It did not exceed six feet in height, and is still in good preservation, within the grounds of the United States reservation.

In a "Gazetteer of the State of Michigan," published by John T. Blois, in 1839, is given an account of the opening of one of these mounds two years before, which has much interest.

The excavation was commenced on the top, and continued a depth of four feet below the base. The soil, like that of the surrounding country, was sand, but it exhibited a mixture of decomposed animal matter, and occasional fragments of bone, some of which had evidently undergone calcination. The first few feet revealed many human skeletons, laid in a promiscuous manner, with deposits of the usual utensils and implements, and with each were several pounds of a friable earth, resembling Spanish brown, but which colored red any object to which it was applied. About one foot from the base a stratum of charcoal, three inches thick, was penetrated. Immediately below this were found six human skeletons, lying in different parts of the mound. Each appeared to have been interred in a kneeling or sitting posture. The head was invariably turned toward the north; the body a little inclined backwards, and the hands supporting an earthen vessel, in the attitude of a person preparing to drink. Only the long bones and parts of the ribs and crania remained undecayed.

"The general contour of the cranium was different from what is commonly noticed in the present Indian races. The mouth large and broad, the face wide and short; the forehead exceedingly low and receding; the skull unusually thick; the volume of the brain quite small. It was judged that the stature of none exceeded five feet six inches."

Arrow-heads, pieces of hornstone and quartz, wrought and unwrought, of the rudest kind, but some forming very sharp cutting implements, were beside them. "No metal was discovered, but the oxide or rust of iron was traced in the shape of a vessel, holding some two or three gallons, which proved it to have been of iron. By the side of one was found the remains of an uncommonly large, white marine shell."

Great numbers of beads, in cylindrical form, and made of similar shell, were found. Some had been strung, others lay upon different parts of the body, and six were found enclosed in the mouth. The vessels were of the capacity of one or two gallons.

The most remarkable feature of this find is the presence of an oxide of iron, supposed to represent a vessel of that metal. It suggests a very difficult subject of inquiry, for if these bodies really belonged to the pre-historic race, as every other circumstance would imply, then are we in conflict with the apparently well founded opinion that the art of smelting metals, either iron or copper, was unknown to that early race. Iron is very perishable, and would probably be wholly consumed by rust, long before human bones deposited at that remote era would have crumbled away.

In a letter from Mr. Blois written me in 1877, he confirms his statement made in 1839, regarding the supposed iron vessel, by the recollection of Mr. H. Ransom, who was present. He says he had "broken one side of the top before he noticed anything peculiar. He then scraped the sand from the hollow interior, but there was not sufficient strength in it to hold together." The appearance, he adds, was certainly that of indurated oxide of iron, and yet the circumstance seems to him incredible.

The story of the use of these mounds by the native tribes to a quite recent date, for intrusive burial, is very interesting.

General Cass said that bodies were brought here from great distances, and were even preserved frozen during the winter, in order that they might be interred in these favorite mausolea.

The Hon. B. F. H. Witherell, in a paper read in 1858 before the Historical Society of Michigan, stated, that in his childhood he had seen the children of the wilderness deposit the remains of their departed friends in the bosom of one of these mounds. "They scooped out a shallow grave in the centre of the top, and, after covering the body with sand brought from the neighboring bank, the friends of the dead man went into the river and waded about in a zigzag course for some time, until the spirit had departed on its long journey. The object of this custom was, that the spirit might not be able to follow the tracks in the sand." According to a common superstition, the soul of the deceased lingered for several days, unwilling to quit his earthly belongings, and probably this artifice was required to compel him to set forth on his spirit travel. As a ghost cannot cross water, the above plan was resorted to, in order that he might lose sight of friends who would have otherwise attracted him to stay too long.

"This sand hill was a favorite camping-ground with all the Western tribes, in their annual migration from their far off homes on the banks of the Mississippi, the shores of Lake Superior, and the rivers and lakes of the western forests, to receive from the Indian agent at Malden the annuities so liberally furnished them by the British Government. At different times the Sacs, Sioux, Foxes, Winnebagoes, Menominees, Iowas, Wyandots, Pottawatomies, Chippewas, Tawas and other tribes congregated at this favorite spot, and made night hideous with their discordant yells. Here they held their war and medicine dances. Their music was the monotonous sound of the rude drum, beaten with unvarying stroke, frequently all night long. It was done to drive the evil spirit off, and sometimes indicated that a warrior was laid in his grave."

This practice on the part of the British Government was continued down to 1836, and I have seen the river alive with canoes of these various tribes, as late as the second year of my residence in Springwells.

The general level of the land in the vicinity of Detroit is varied, over a considerable portion of the town of Springwells, by ridges of sand and gravel. They mark the shores or water-lines of the ancient lake or ocean, at different epochs. These elevated places were often chosen by the natives for sepulchral purposes. Until recently it was not known that any portion of these was artificial.

In the year 1870, in digging away a section from one of these ridges, on land of Mr. J. H. Carstens, opposite Fort Wayne, one of the ancient tombs was disturbed, and the skeletons of fourteen bodies disinterred. They were in the usual contracted posture, and beside the head of each was an earthen crock. Two of these, which were quite perfect, were the vases described in a former page, and now in the Archæological Museum at Cambridge.

Among a large number of arrow-points and other articles common to the mounds were several lance-heads of unusual size and beauty. They were of milk-white quartz, about 7 inches long by 3 wide, and very finely and evenly serrated.

Among the relics was a long needle of copper, and a necklace of copper beads, but no vestige of iron.

There was the usual report of big bones. In this case the large individual measured seven and a half feet in height!

The original surface of the ground was about fifteen feet above the general level, and consisted of drift gravel, overlaid by yellow sand. The bodies were found at a depth of six or seven feet from this original surface, and were, of course, interred in these deep graves before the tumulus, which was only three or four feet high, was heaped above.

About half a mile below the group of Springwells tumuli already mentioned, is a small circular earthwork, of the kind alluded to at the beginning of these observations upon the Indian antiquities of Michigan.

It consists of a low embankment, of an oval form, enclosing about one and a half acres. The longest axis is 320 feet, the shortest 250 feet, to centre of embankment. The latter is about twelve feet wide at base, and about two feet in height. The ditch from which the earth was taken is about eight feet wide, and mostly on the outer side, but is in some places on the inner side, as though this had been a matter of indifference. At the south end, toward the river, and about 100 feet distant, is an opening or gateway, 50 feet wide.

The accompanying sketch will give a clearer idea of the situation. It is upon a small area of land, about 500 feet long, and as many wide, which rises gently from the river to the height of about six feet. No attempt seems to have been made to level the surface within the enclosure.

This tract of firm land is surrounded by a morass, or open wet prairie, which upon the north and west sides is several hundred feet wide. Upon the east this marsh narrows to a neck about 100 feet wide, which separates the hard-land tract from a ridge of some fifteen feet elevation. There are traces of what appear to have once been two parallel embankments, a few feet apart, which crossed the neck of marsh, in a direct line towards the circular "fort," if such it may be called.

Of the purpose for which this work was constructed, we are left to conjecture. It would hardly seem to have answered that of a fortification, as it is overlooked by the higher land on the east, within the distance of an arrow cast. There are no traces of a stockade, such as have been found with similar structures in Western New York, and attributed to the Iroquois. The width of the gateway, and the absence of any protective mound within, and the irregular character of the ditch hardly accord with the supposition that it was a military work. It might have served as a place of security for the women and children, while the warriors were upon a warpath, or been thrown up in some sudden emergency.

There is nothing to indicate that the enclosure surrounded a village, and neither the ancient nor modern races are supposed to have had herds of domesticated animals, requiring the protection of corrals. Yet the regularity of the work marks it as one of studied design.

When this interesting relic first came to my knowledge, half a century ago, it was in the midst of a dense forest and thicket, shrouded from any observation but that of an antiquary, and cut off from roads and settlements by the morass. Many generations had risen and passed away since the dusky forms of its artificers were consigned to the neighboring tumuli, and antique oaks and rambling grape-vines—its sole occupants—silently told the story of the years that had gone by.

I shall close these remarks with some account of the great mound near the junction of the river Rouge with the Detroit, at Del Rey, three miles below the city.

Ever since the settlement of the country this mound has been a well-known and conspicuous feature. To the old French habitants it was also known that it had been used by the Indians as a burial-place. Yet its true character seems never to have been fully appreciated, and the interest which attaches to it may warrant me in occupying some further pages in its description.

For nearly half a century, portion after portion has been dug away and removed, by wagon load and boat load, and little notice taken of its contents, until now it is but a miniature of its former self. Mr. Bourdeno, who has lived in the vicinity for more than sixty years, says the mound originally extended from its present limits westerly fully 500 feet, to where a bend in the Rouge brings that river close to the highway. The mound or hill was then 700 or 800 feet long, 400 feet wide, and not less than forty feet high. The south side bordered close on the river for its whole length. It was symmetrical in form, and the slopes were about as steep as the sand, of which most of it was composed, could be retained. Not only has it been reduced more than half the entire length, but more than half also of its width on the river side. Little of the original shape now remains, and the present extreme height nowhere exceeds thirty feet above the stream.

But little examination is needed to show that some part at least of the elevation is natural, for a stratum of gravel appears below ten or more feet of sand, which evidently belongs to the drift that has left many similar deposits over this region. A portion of the overlying sand may be ascribed to the same source, but I think the fact will be made evident that a considerable part of the original, and even of the present elevation, is artificial.

The situation is such as would be chosen by the Mound-Builders, over all others, for a resting-place and monument to their dead. It is most picturesque. At the base, circling nearly two sides of the mound, lay the deep waters of the river Rouge. Beyond stretched a field of natural meadow, to the river Detroit, half a mile distant, and visible for many miles of its course. To the south and west were seen Grosse Isle and the channel leading past Malden to Lake Erie. Above stretched the straits, as far as the site of the city, while northward the view commands many miles of rolling country. The tumulus must have been visible from a great distance, in every direction.

Much as has been lost by the wanton destruction of this instructive monument, enough is disclosed to show that this huge mound has been the memorial of many

THE GREAT MOUND AT RIVER ROUGE.

interesting and marvellous events. From the immense number of skeletons found within it, and the mode of their occurrence, there can be little doubt that it was one of these national sepulchres of the Hurons, and other Algonquin tribes, where were deposited the remains of their dead, that had been carefully kept for the purpose, until the flesh had disappeared, and the proper season had arrived for the great "Festival of the dead."

This was attended, amid the general gathering of the tribes, with many ceremonies, to which I shall only briefly allude. The festival has been so well described in the 15th Canto of *Teuch-sa-Grondie*, by our lamented townsman, Levi Bishop, that I refer the curious to that poem for its full illustration.

Until this ceremony had taken place the spirits of the dead were supposed to wander restlessly about, as did the unburied Romans on the borders of the Styx.

> "Departed spirits linger still,—
> Their vacant place in cabin fill;
> Awaiting for the festal day,
> To speed them on their destined way,—
> To final home,—to land afar—
> To land beyond the evening star."

When the appointed time has arrived

> "—the recent dead
> Are lifted from their temporary bed,
> The relics—shapeless forms, in swift decay,
> The mouldy bones, without the lifeless clay,
> Of both the sexes, and of young and old;
> The child, the lover, sachem, chieftain bold,—
> A frightful throng, a melancholy train,
> Come forth their final resting-place to gain."

The dismal process of cleansing the bones—the exposure of the remains to the view of mourning friends—the decoration in the richest furs—the display of gifts destined for sacrifice,—the procession—the harangue—the dance—the games—the feast—the solemn song, broken at intervals by the long-measured, dreary funeral wail, simulating voices of disembodied souls, winging their way to the land of spirits,—the promiscuous casting of the remains into one general pit, amid "a weeping, shrieking, howling concourse" of guests and mourners, gathered from the whole nation, all illuminated by the midnight glare of blazing torches and camp-fires, constituted a scene unique as it was solemn and awful; one of those mysteries of the past that is never to return.

> "Two fathoms deep the burial pit,
> And twice two ample fathoms wide;
> A circle that might well admit
> A thousand bodies, side by side."

The Jesuit Relations of 1636 tell us of a place of this kind set apart among the Hurons in Canada, before their fatal dispersion by the Iroquois, where they were accustomed to inter their dead in one common sepulchre, heaping above them the funeral mound. This ceremony took place once in ten or twelve years.*

That the river Rouge mound was of this character there is much cumulative evidence to prove. Mr. Bourdeno has seen hundreds of skeletons removed in the digging down of the hill. He says that in some parts there seems to have been a "cellar," which was filled with bones, mingled indiscriminately.

---

* It is matter of history that a portion of this nation, which escaped the massacre on Lake Huron, fled to and settled below Detroit, where they were known as Wyandots.

Squire Ludlow, an old resident, also gives similar accounts of the number of skeletons disinterred. His statement goes further, as to their immense quantities, much of which he collected and buried elsewhere. Thousands of fragments of human bones still lie bleaching on the sand, mingled with sherds of pottery and other relics.

Powerful as is the interest which attaches to this hill of the dead from this proof of its character, it presents other points of interest.

It affords certain evidence that *cremation* was practised by the Mound-Builders of this region. It was also, in all probability, a sacred or "altar" mound. In the account given me by Bourdeno he states, that in other parts of the mound than those containing the "cellars," much charcoal and ashes were found, mingled with burned bones. With these were many pieces of large pots, but all were broken. The latter fact is consonant with the theory of cremation, for on these occasions the relics, instead of being buried whole with the dead, as in ordinary cases, were thrown upon the burning pile, and of course suffered partial destruction.

Another phase in the history of this mound is related by Bourdeno, viz., that in Pontiac's time, and before the fatal ambuscade at Bloody Run, there occurred at this place a massacre of British soldiers by the Indians, and that the dead were buried in this mound. I am not aware that history alludes to this event, but the fact that many bodies of white soldiers have been interred in the hill is evident, from the character of the skulls found in a certain part of it, and from the attendant relics, such as pieces of scabbards, buttons and other portions of military equipment, which have escaped decay.

During old territorial times the mound was made to

subserve the living. A house was erected on the summit, near the east end, which was at first a trading-post for the Indians. It has been gone many years,—all except a large quantity of bricks and mortar, and other rubbish. The relic-hunter finds over the whole surface a curious intermingling of the old and the new;—glass, pieces of crockery, iron and other articles of modern housekeeping are in close communion with flint implements, antique pot-sherds, and Indian trinkets, and with bits of brass and iron that once belonged to the accoutrements of the British soldier.

Desirous of more fully determining the true character of the mound, a few years ago I proceeded, in company with Messrs. Henry Gillman and H. G. Hubbard, to a practical investigation.

Having determined, as nearly as possible, the central axis of the original mound, we proceeded to open a trench near to it, and through the highest part now remaining, a portion of which seemed to have been undisturbed and was still covered with sod.

This trench was commenced on the river side, near the top, six feet wide and five deep, and was continued northerly for the distance of ten feet before anything appeared to reward the labor, except an English half-penny of George III., and a United States cent of 1829. These were found about four feet below the surface of the digging. We then struck a skull. This was dug carefully around, and the skeleton exposed. It lay with the head to the east, and was so doubled together and crushed, that the whole occupied a space not more than two feet long by four inches thick.

It had evidently originally been placed in a sitting posture. The skull was so much flattened and decayed as to render it impossible to determine the shape or size. The ribs and most of the vertebræ and smaller bones had perished, but the larger bones of the arms and legs were sufficiently perfect to be removed. The flattening of the tibia, first pointed out by Mr. Gillman as characteristic of the most ancient human remains in this region, was very observable.

On the south side of the head was a small pot, composed of baked clay, which was also so flattened and decayed that it could be removed only in fragments. This skeleton was only three feet below the surface, but how many feet had been originally heaped over it it was impossible to say.

To the west, and about two feet from the above and one foot deeper, was a mass apparently composed of burned human remains. It formed a dark, reddish soil, several inches thick, and quite hard and compact. It occupied a space two feet by one and a half, and four inches thick. Close to this were a few unburned portions of a skeleton, and a perfectly formed greenstone "celt."

At about the same distance from the skeleton first mentioned, and a foot lower down, was another mass of cinders. Still deeper, and at a foot remove to the west, was another mass of considerably larger extent, and a foot thick.

Among these masses of compacted cinder were several large nodules of irregular form, and of a yellowish-red color, which seemed held together by a cement of iron rust. Nothing, however, beyond this indicated that these might once have composed vessels of iron. The lowest of the compacted masses was five feet beneath the present surface. That they consisted in part of burned human bones there could be no doubt, and they establish the fact of cremation beyond question.

In excavating another trench at a lower part of the mound, we came, at a depth of two feet, upon what appeared, from its color and character, to have at one period constituted the original surface. A few inches below this was disclosed a stratum of black earth, composed of cinders and burned bones, the extent of which was traced at several points, and found to constitute a bed not less than twenty feet square. On the disturbed surface was found a spot covered with broken fragments of clay. This, as the matrix is entirely sand, may be presumed to be an artificial deposit. It may have formed part of an "altar," or clay hearth, such as are pointed out by Squier in his so-called "Altar Mounds" of Ohio.

Continuing the excavations beneath the sodded portion of the mound, at three feet from the surface we uncovered numerous skeletons. They were disposed irregularly, as though hastily buried. The skulls and some of the bones were in tolerably perfect preservation. Quite a number were those of babes. Some of the crania were shattered, as if from heavy blows. Two of them exhibited a round hole at the apex, made by some sharp instrument after death. The rimming is plainly visible, and the holes are about half an inch diameter.

We now sunk a shaft or well into the sand at the place where the hard, cemented masses were discovered. This was continued to the depth of eight feet, and here were found numerous nodules or lumps of a white substance, which proved to be disintegrated bone. These continued in considerable numbers through the succeeding three feet, when the digging was discontinued. How much lower still these singular masses continue was left undetermined.

There was no appearance of the sand having ever been disturbed, yet the presence of these bones made evident either that interments had taken place at this great depth of more than ten feet, or that the earth had accumulated since the deposition. It is entirely improbable that any of the Indian races buried their dead in graves of that extreme depth, for no such custom is known. And as these occur immediately below the undoubted Indian remains first mentioned, it is apparent that interments took place during long intervals of time, the earth heaped above the first being a foundation for a new interment, bodies being sometimes buried entire and sometimes burned, the remains being covered, like the others, with a fresh deposit of sand. Thus year by year, and cycle by cycle, the mound grew in height and proportions.

Since the discovery of the two perforated skulls others have come to light, similarly treated, elsewhere in the State. The condition of these crania indicates that they are comparatively modern. For what purpose were these perforations? A suggestion has been made, and it accords with the known anxieties of the Indian, that the holes were for giving more speedy release to the spirit from its earthly tenement. Another supposition is of a very practical kind, that they were intended as a means of suspending the skull in view of the friends of the deceased, until the time of the great festival of inhumation.

We must regard this great mound—now being so ruthlessly destroyed—as a vast necropolis, containing the dead of many centuries, belonging both to the prehistoric past and to our modern era.

In this beautiful spot the red man of all those departed

eras, perhaps from many now forgotten nations, desired to make his final rest after the toils and pleasures of life were ended, and to be gathered to his fathers in the place where reposed the bones of generations gone before. To his limited comprehension this tumulus of sand was stable as an Egyptian pyramid, for it was secured by religious veneration.

Many a time had his canoe paused at this place, and landing, he had ascended the ancient mound, while his eye roamed over the wide expanse of river and marsh and land in search of friendly forms, or, it may be, of parties of his foes, creeping stealthily along its sandy shores. Here, as tradition tells, the great Pontiac resorted—that stern, uncompromising foe of the Anglo-Saxon. Where but upon the graves of their ancestors, could he so worthily arouse the hearts of the living to resist their oppressors? And here, when hope had perished, may this savage hero have come to muse upon the past and its faded glories. What shades would throng around him if each skeleton form of the thousands that lay below could answer to his summons!

> "From graves forgotten stretch their dusty hands,
> And hold in mortmain still their old estates."

Within even the brief period of the ascendency of the Anglo-Saxon in this region, how much of the past has been forgotten! Who can tell the story of that fierce struggle which took place on this spot, when the two races that in life had been so distinct and hostile, mingled together in death in a common mausoleum, that covered alike their bones and their animosities?

And now, how changed the scene! The same noble river, in undeviating flood, rolls its waters to the lake, but the canoe of the red man has given place to the winged barks of commerce, the barge and the steamer. The protecting forests have been superseded by cultivated farms and village streets, and smoking factories. In the distance rise to view the spires and buildings of a proud and prosperous city. The whoop of the savage and his funeral howl are supplanted by the hum of an untiring, practical industry.

Still, as of old, the warm sunshine rests upon this spot; the sparkling waters lave its base; the winds blow over it from the not distant lake, scattering the dust that once animated human forms. But the beings these cheered in the olden time have all perished from the land; their history is but a fading dream, and the proud pile which they created to immortalize their memory has nearly disappeared, and will soon have vanished altogether, in the progress of an unheeding and remorseless civilization.

ANCIENT GARDEN BEDS OF MICHIGAN.

ANCIENT GARDEN BEDS OF MICHIGAN.*

A CLASS of works of the Mound-Builders exists in Michigan, of unknown age and origin, which have received the name of "Garden-Beds."

An unusual importance attaches to these remains of a lost race, from the fact that they have been almost entirely overlooked by archæologists, and that of those which were so numerous and prominent forty, or even thirty years ago, nearly every trace has disappeared. For any knowledge beyond the scanty details hitherto recorded we are forced to rely upon the recollections of the "oldest inhabitants." We know how uncertain this reliance often is, and were it otherwise, we cannot but recognize the rapidity with which we are losing our hold of this kind of testimony, and the very brief period at which it must cease altogether.

The earliest mention of these relics which I find is by Haven, in his "Archæology of the United States." It is the report of Verandrier, who, with several French associates, explored this region before 1748. He found in the western wilderness "large tracts free from wood, many of which are everywhere covered with furrows, as if they had formerly been ploughed and sown."

Schoolcraft was the first to give to the world any accu-

---

*Read before the State Pioneer Society, February 7, 1877, and published in the *American Antiquarian*.

rate and systematic account of these "furrows." Indeed, he is the only author of note who honors this interesting class of the works of the Mound-Builders with more than the most meagre mention. Observations were made by him as early as 1827. He gives figures of two kinds of beds, and he records the fact, that "the garden-beds, and not the mounds, form the most prominent, and, by far, the most striking and characteristic antiquarian monuments of this district of country."

Another writer of early date, still resident of our State, John T. Blois, published, in 1839, in his "Gazetteer of Michigan," a detailed description, with a diagram, of one kind of the beds.

No mention is made of these remains by Priest or by Baldwin. Foster devotes to them less than a single page of his voluminous work, and only says, in effect, that "they certainly indicate a methodical cultivation which was not practised by the red man."

Dr. Lapham describes a few of this kind of remains which were found upon the western shore of Lake Michigan, as "consisting of low parallel ridges, as if corn had been planted in drills. They average four feet in width, and twenty-five of them have been counted in the space of one hundred feet."

Yet these relics constitute a unique feature in the antiquities of our country. They are of especial interest to us, from the fact that they were not only the most prominent of our antiquities, but, with the exception referred to in Wisconsin, they are confined to our State.

Some investigations, by no means thorough, enable me to define more accurately and fully than has been heretofore done the different kinds of these beds, which I shall attempt to classify, according to the most reliable information obtained. But I must first define their situation, extent and character.

The so-called "Garden-Beds" were found in the valleys of the St. Joseph and Grand rivers, where they occupied the most fertile of the prairie land and burr-oak plains, principally in the counties of St. Joseph, Cass and Kalamazoo.

They consist of raised patches of ground, separated by sunken paths, and were generally arranged in plats or blocks of parallel beds. These varied in dimensions, being from five to sixteen feet in width, in length from twelve to more than one hundred feet, and in height six to eighteen inches.

The tough sod of the prairie had preserved very sharply all the outlines. According to the universal testimony, these beds were laid out and fashioned with a skill, order and symmetry which distinguished them from the ordinary operations of agriculture, and were combined with some peculiar features that belong to no recognized system of horticultural art.

In the midst of diversity, sufficient uniformity is discoverable to enable me to group the beds and gardens, as in the following

CLASSIFICATION:

1. Wide convex beds, in parallel rows, without paths, composing independent plats. (Width of beds, 12 feet; paths, none; length, 74 to 115 feet.) Fig. 1.
2. Wide convex beds, in parallel rows, separated by paths of same width, in independent plats. (Width of bed, 12 to 16 feet; paths same; length, 74 to 132 feet.) Fig. 2.
3. Wide and parallel beds, separated by narrow paths,

arranged in a series of plats longitudinal to each other. (Width of beds, 14 feet; paths, 2 feet; length, 100 feet.) Fig. 3.

4. Long and narrow beds, separated by narrower paths and arranged in a series of longitudinal plats, each plat divided from the next by semi-circular heads. (Width of beds, 5 feet; paths, 1½ feet; length, 100 feet; height, 18 inches.) Fig. 4.

5. Parallel beds, arranged in plats similar to class 4, but divided by circular heads. (Width of beds, 6 feet; paths, 4 feet; length, 12 to 40 feet; height, 18 inches.) Fig. 5.

6. Parallel beds, of varying widths and lengths, separated by narrow paths, and arranged in plats of two or more at right angles N. and S., E. and W., to the plats adjacent. (Width of beds, 5 to 14 feet; paths, 1 to 2 feet; length, 12 to 30 feet; height, 8 inches.) Figures *a*, *b* and *c*, are varieties. Fig. 6.

7. Parallel beds, of uniform width and length, with narrow paths, arranged in plats or blocks, and single beds, at varying angles. (Width of beds, 6 feet; paths, 2 feet; length, about 30 feet; height, 10 to 12 inches.) Fig. 7.

8. Wheel-shaped plats, consisting of a circular bed, with beds of uniform shape and size radiating therefrom, all separated by narrow paths. (Width of beds, 6 to 20 feet; paths, 1 foot; length, 14 to 20 feet.) Fig. 8.

I present diagrams of each of these classes or kinds of beds. Of these only those numbered 1, 2 and 4 have ever before been delineated, to my knowledge. (See figures 1 to 8, pages 257–261.) Nos. 3 and 5 are *described* by Schoolcraft and Blois, while the others are *figured* as well—1 and 2 by Schoolcraft and 4 by Blois. No. 3, according to the latter, consists of five plats, each 100 feet long, 20 beds in each plat. Schoolcraft does not give the exact localities, and I am unable to state whether beds of the same class have been noticed by other observers. As to their extent, his language is, " The beds are of various sizes, covering generally from 20 to 100 acres." Some are reported to embrace even 300 acres. *Plats* of beds are undoubtedly here referred to.

Of the plat figured by Blois (No. 4), the writer says: " They are found a short distance from Three Rivers, on one side of an oval prairie, surrounded by burr-oak plains. The prairie contains three hundred acres. The garden is judged to be half a mile in length by one-third in breadth, containing about one hundred acres, regularly laid out in beds running north and south, in the form of parallelograms, five feet in width and one hundred in length, and eighteen inches deep." The distinctive peculiarity of these beds is what Blois calls the " semilunar" head, at the extremity of each bed, separated from them by a path as represented.

Class 6, so far as my own inquiries warrant, represents the form and arrangement which is most common, viz.: that of a series of parallel beds formed into blocks of two or more, alternating with other similar blocks placed at right angles to them. (See figures *a, b* and *c*.) The prevailing width of the bed is five or six feet, and that of the paths one and a half to two feet. The length of the plats or blocks varies, the average being about twenty feet. Gardens of this kind were found by the early settlers at Schoolcraft, the burr-oak plains at Kalamazoo, Toland's prairie, Prairie-Ronde, and elsewhere.

Mr. Henry Little says, that in 1831 they were very numerous on the plains where now stands the village of Kalamazoo; and south of the mound, eight or ten acres were entirely covered by them.

Mr. E. Laken Brown confirms this account, and says they reminded him of old New England gardens, being very regular and even, and the beds five feet by twelve or fourteen feet. In 1832 the outlines were very distinct, and the burr-oak trees on them as large as any in the vicinity. Mr. A. T. Prouty concurs as to the extent covered, but thinks the beds were six feet wide by twenty-five to forty long. On the farm of J. T. Cobb, section 7, town of Schoolcraft, the beds were quite numerous as late as 1860. There must have been 15 acres of them on his land. The "sets" would average five or six beds each. Neighbors put the number of acres covered with them in 1830, within the space of a mile, at one hundred.

Fig. 6-b, of class 6, is from a drawing by James R. Cumings, of Galesburg, of a garden in which the beds are of more than usual diversity in width and length. H. M. Shafter and Roswell Ransom, old settlers, say that three or four acres on the edge of the prairie, at this place, were covered with the beds. On the farm of the latter in the town of Comstock, of one hundred acres, there were not less than ten acres of beds, six feet by twenty-five to forty, arranged in alternate blocks, having a north-and-south and east-and-west direction.

Fig. 6-c, is from a drawing by Mr. Shafter.

The series represented by *Class 7* (fig. 7) were found at Prairie-Ronde. They are platted and described to me by Messrs. Cobb and Prouty. They differ from the more ordinary form of No. 6, in the arrangement of the blocks or sets of beds, which is here not at right angles, but at *various and irregular* angles, also in the single beds outlying. The number of beds in each block is also greater than usual.

Class 8 is established on the authority of Henry Little and A. T. Prouty, of Kalamazoo. The figure delineated is from the descriptions and dimensions given by the former. The diameter of the circular bed and the length of the radiating ones are each twenty-five to thirty feet. The latter describes two of similar design, but of smaller dimensions, the centre bed being only six feet in diameter, and the radiating ones twenty feet. All occurred at Kalamazoo, and in immediate association with the other forms of beds at that place, represented generally by Class 6.

There is reason for supposing that there may have existed another class of beds, differing altogether from any I have represented, from expressions used by both Schoolcraft and Blois. The former speaks of "enigmatical plats of variously shaped beds;" and further, "nearly all the lines of each area or sub-area of beds are rectangular and parallel. Others admit of half circles and *variously curved* beds, with avenues, and are *differently grouped* and disposed."

The latter says, the beds "appear in *various fanciful shapes*." Some are laid off in rectilineal and curvilineal figures, either distinct or *combined in a fantastic* manner, in parterres and scolloped work, with alleys between, and apparently ample walks leading in different directions."

This language is too vague to enable me to construct a diagram, nor have I any confirmation to offer from other sources. The reputation of the writers will not allow us to consider the descriptions fanciful, but it is possible to suppose they were misled by the representations of others.

Were these vegetable gardens? To answer this question, we must proceed according to the doctrine of probabilities. All opinions seem to agree, that these relics denote *some species of cultivation;* and that they are very different from those left by the field culture of any known tribes of Indians. Nor do we find any similar remains in connection with the works of the Mound-Builders, which exist, on so extensive a scale, through the valley of the Mississippi River, although those unknown builders were undoubtedly an agricultural people.

The principal crop of the Indians is maize, and this was never cultivated by them in *rows*, but in *hills*, often large but always disposed in a very irregular manner. As little do these beds resemble the deserted fields of *modern agriculture*. On the other hand, the resemblance of many of the plats to the well-laid out *garden beds* of our own day is very striking; while the curvilinear forms suggest analogies quite as strong to the modern "*pleasure garden.*"

The nearest approach to anything resembling horticultural operations among Indian tribes, within the historic period, is noticed by Jones, who refers to a practice, among some of the southern Indians, of setting apart separate pieces of ground for each family. This author quotes from Captain Ribault's "Discovery of Terra Florida," published in London, 1563. "They labor and till the ground, sowing the fields with a grain called *Mahis*, whereof they make their meal, and in their gardens they plant beans, gourds, cucumbers, citrons, peas, and many other fruits and roots unknown to us. Their spades and mattocks are made of wood, so well and fitly as is possible."

In the St. Joseph Valley I learned of numerous places, widely apart, where the labor and skill of our ancient horticulturists were apparent in small gardens, *laid out in different styles*, and with an eye to the picturesque; as if each family had not only its separate garden patch, but had used it for the display of its own peculiar taste.

Historians tell us of the Aztecs, that they had gardens in which were cultivated various plants, for medicinal uses, as well as for ornament. Was there something analogous to this in the Michigan Nation? Did the latter also have *botanical gardens?* May we accord to this unknown people a considerable advance in *science*, in addition to a cultivated taste, and an eye for symmetry and beauty, which is without precedent among the prehistoric people of this continent, north of Mexico?

These extensive indications of ancient culture necessarily imply a *settled* and *populous* community. We are led, therefore, to look for other evidences of the numbers and character of the people who made them. But here an extraordinary fact presents itself; such evidences are almost wanting! The testimony of nearly every one whom I have consulted—men who were among the first of the white race to break up the sod, that for ages had consecrated these old garden lands—agrees in the fact, that almost none of the usual aboriginal relics were found; no pottery; no spear- and arrow-heads; no implements of stone; not even the omnipresent pipe. Tumuli, or burial mounds of the red man, are not uncommon, though not numerous, in Western Michigan, but have no recognized association with the garden race.

Upon the St. Joseph and Colorado rivers, and in the town of Prairie-Ronde, exist several small circular and rectangular embankments, resembling the lesser works of the Mound-Builders so numerous in Ohio. But no connection can be traced between these detached earthworks and the garden-beds. None of them seem to have been the bases of buildings, nor do they give indication of any religious origin or rites. There are no traces of dwellings, and the soil which has so sacredly preserved the labor of its occupants, discloses not even their bones!

At Three Rivers, and in Gilead, Branch County, are some ancient embankments, which are probably referable to this people, and may pass for works of defence. That at the first named place was notably extensive. It consisted only of an earth embankment, about six feet in height, extending between two forks of a river, a mile apart. It thus enclosed a large area, and with a sufficient garrison might have withstood the siege of a large army of barbarous warriors.

It seems strange, indeed, that these garden beds, suggestive as they are, should be the only memorials of a race which has left such an evidence of civilized advancement, and was worthy of more enduring monuments! We may reasonably conclude, that they were a people of *peaceable disposition*, of *laborious habits*, and of æsthetic if not *scientific tastes;* that they lived in simple and *patriarchal* style, subsisting on the fruits of the earth, rather than of the chase. Their dwellings and their tools were of *wood*, and have perished. This simple record of their character and labors is all, it may be, we can ever know.

But is this *all?* May we not form some reasonable

conjecture as to the *period in which these gardeners lived?*

A fact mentioned by Dr. Lapham furnishes a species of evidence, as to the *relative* antiquity of the garden beds of Wisconsin, as compared with the animal mounds. They were found overlying the latter; from which he infers, of course, a more recent origin. We may also suppose a considerably *more recent* age, since it is not likely that the race could have thus encroached upon the works of another, until long after these had been abandoned, and their religious or other significance forgotten.

The date of the abandonment of the beds may be approximately fixed, by the *age of the trees* found growing upon them. One of these mentioned by Schoolcraft, cut down in 1837, had 335 cortical layers. This carries the period back as far as 1502, or some years prior to the discovery of this country by the French. How long these labors were abandoned before this tree commenced its growth may not be susceptible of proof. Early French explorers do not appear to have been interested in the question, and it does not seem to me necessary to go further back than the three centuries during which that tree flourished, for a period quite long enough to have crumbled into indistinguishable dust every trace of wooden dwellings and implements, as well as of the bodies of their fabricators, if the latter received only simple earth burial.

At the time of the arrival of the French the country was in possession of Algonquin tribes, who emigrated from the St. Lawrence about the middle of the 16th century. They were ignorant of the authors of these works, and were not more advanced in the arts of culture than the other known tribes.

It is probable that the few defensive works I have mentioned were erected by this settled and peaceful race of gardeners, as places of temporary refuge for the women and children, against the raids of the warlike tribes living eastward of them. The larger one may have served for the general defence in a time of sudden and great emergency. It is probable that on some such occasion they were surprised by their savage and relentless foes, and were overwhelmed, scattered or exterminated.

Most of the facts I have been able to present are gathered, in large part, from the memories—of course not always exact or reliable—of early settlers, and after modern culture had for many years obliterated the old.

It is perhaps useless to regret that these most interesting and unique relics of a lost people have so completely perished, through the greed of the dominant race; or that they could not have received, while they yet remained, the more exact and scientific scrutiny which is now being applied to the antiquities of our land. Much that might then have been cleared up, must now remain forever involved in mystery, or be left to conjecture.

In September, 1885, the writer visited the region of the ancient garden beds, in hopes of being so fortunate as to find some remaining. He did discover, near Schoolcraft, on a plat of land which had been recently cleared of its timber, a few traces of beds, belonging to a set, most of which had been broken up by the plough.

Four or five beds could be distinctly traced, for the distance of some ten to fifteen feet. The remainder of their lengths, said to be some twenty to thirty feet, had been obliterated by cultivation. Each bed had a width of about ten feet from centre to centre of the intervening paths. The latter had apparently a width of two or three feet, but it was impossible to define the exact outlines.

After much inquiry I could learn of no other place in or near Prairie-Ronde, or the plains of St. Joseph and Kalamazoo counties, where any traces of the old garden beds remained.

Mr. Cobb informed me that about 1859 he endeavored to preserve portions of a set of these beds, which were well covered by tough, protective prairie sod. But when the white grub took possession of the turf thereabouts his ancient garden reserve did not escape. In a year or two the hogs, in their search for the grub, had so rooted and marred the outlines that he ploughed the beds up.

I found many old residents who well remembered the garden plats as they appeared a half century ago, and all concurred in the admiration excited by their peculiar character and the perfection of their preservation. Mr. Cobb says, he often took his friends to see his " ancient garden," counted the beds, and speculated upon their object. The *set* of beds, which is shown only partially in his sketch (Fig. 7), contained thirteen beds, and was the largest of the sets. The others averaged five or six beds each.

All concurred, too, as to the great extent of land, amounting to several hundred acres, covered, wholly or partially, by the beds, chiefly upon the northern edge of the prairie. That all visible evidence of their existence should have so completely disappeared is not surprising to any one who notes their situation, upon the richest portions of the mixed prairies and plains. The lands most esteemed by the garden race were those which first attracted the modern farmer. These lands still constitute fields as beautiful as the eye can anywhere rest upon, and in a region second in loveliness to no other part of our country. The wants of the early settler almost preclude any care for the preservation of what was regarded as mere curiosities. Even when spared from the plough, and left to the care of nature, the absence of the annual fires, which had prevented the growth of timber; the roots of trees upheaving the beds; the decay of fallen timber; the hummocks caused by upturned roots; the destruction of the turf by the forest growth, and by cattle and hogs, all tend to deface the beds, and leave them to be reduced to the general level by the elements. Under these circumstances, a few years even would suffice to obliterate outlines which had remained almost unaltered for centuries.

Fig. 1.

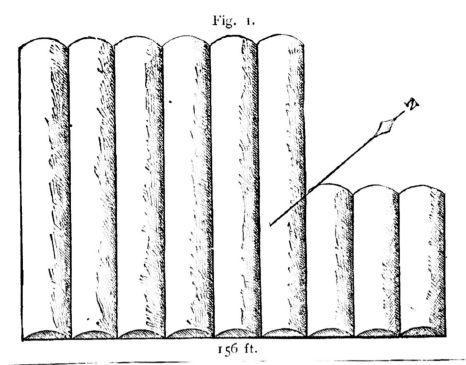

156 ft.

Fig. 2.

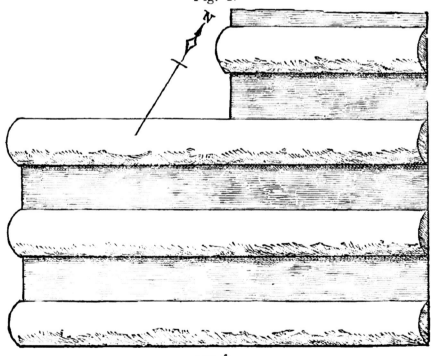

132 ft.

ANCIENT GARDEN BEDS, GRAND RIVER VALLEY, MICHIGAN.
(SCHOOLCRAFT.)

Fig. 3.

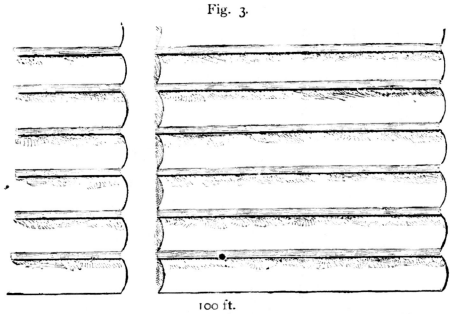

100 ft.
GARDEN PLATS, ST. JOSEPH RIVER VALLEY. (SCHOOLCRAFT.)

Fig. 4.

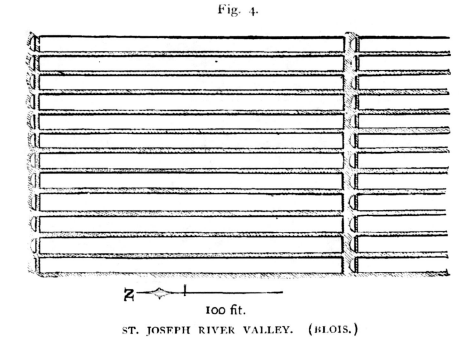

100 fit.
ST. JOSEPH RIVER VALLEY. (BLOIS.)

Fig. 5.

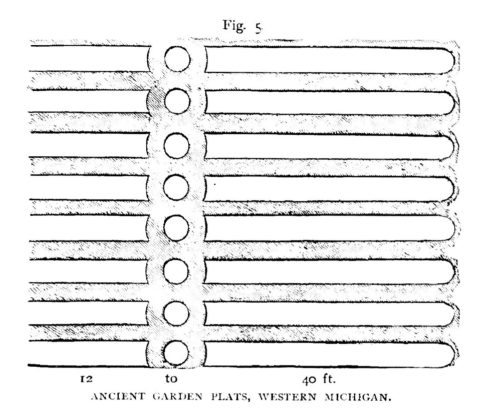

12 to 40 ft.
ANCIENT GARDEN PLATS, WESTERN MICHIGAN.

Fig. 6.

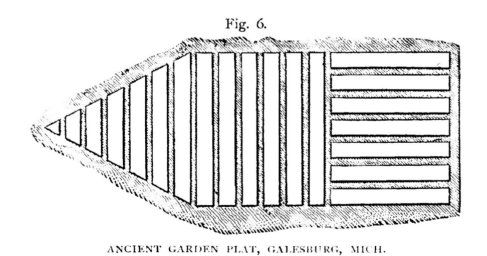

ANCIENT GARDEN PLAT, GALESBURG, MICH.

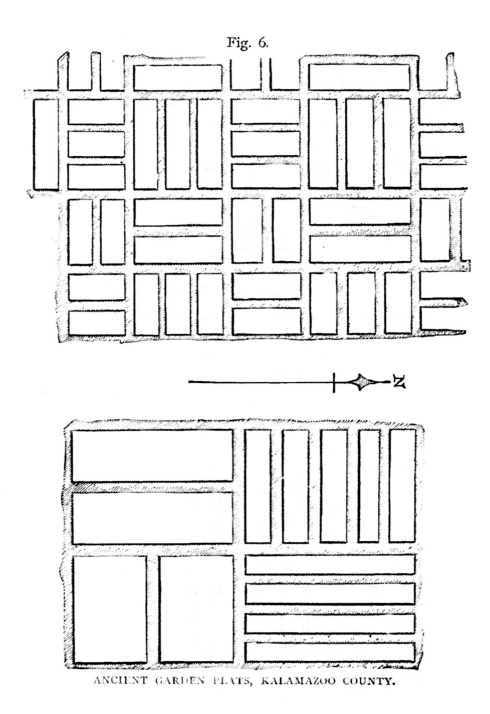

ANCIENT GARDEN PLATS, KALAMAZOO COUNTY.

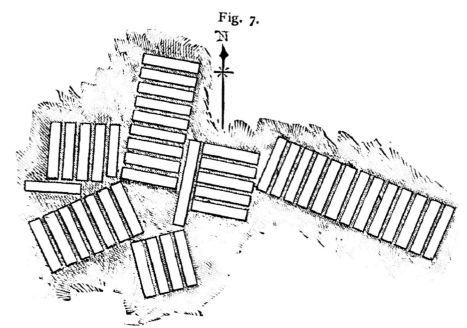

ANCIENT GARDEN PLATS, PRAIRIE-RONDE, MICH.

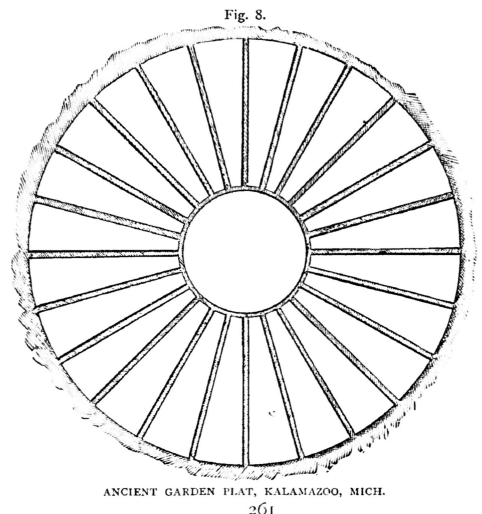

ANCIENT GARDEN PLAT, KALAMAZOO, MICH.

FISH AND FISHING.

"*Piscator.* I hope I may take as great a liberty to blame any man, and laugh at him too, let him be never so grave, that hath not heard what anglers can say in the justification of their art and recreation; which I may again tell you, is so full of pleasure that we need not borrow their thoughts, to think ourselves happy."

* * * * * * * * *

" But the poor fish have enemies enough, besides such unnatural fishermen; (natural enemies) against all which any honest man may make a just quarrel—but I will not; I will leave them to be quarrelled with and killed by others: for I am not of a cruel nature, I love to kill nothing but fish."—IZAAK WALTON, *Complete Angler.*

FISH AND FISHING.

SPRINGWELLS, ——, 1841.

DEAR TOM:—What you ask of me will, I fear, prove in the recording of less interest than you are pleased to anticipate. Nevertheless you stimulate me to the attempt.

I confess to but little of the zeal of honest Izaak Walton, and accomplish scarcely any exploits in the piscatory line. Nor have we any rippling brooks, whose active inhabitants, brilliant and shy, call forth the highest exercise of the art. But our clear and rapid river abounds in excellent fish, of many noted kinds. To manage the pole and line, however it may require some skill, seems to me but a lazy sport, in our broad stream, compared with the ways and means for ensnaring the shy denizens of the smaller water courses. Unfortunately there is not a trout brook, that is, a stream containing real "brook trout," in the whole peninsula.

In admitting this I derogate nothing from the purity of our waters. No element can be more fresh and limpid than that which flows in such immense volume directly before me. Neither have we the eel, which delights in sluggish and muddy waters: none have been found above the falls of Niagara. The moment the Straits of Mackinaw are crossed the brook trout is found in abundance, in all the rills of the upper peninsula. Some other reason exists for the absence of this fish from the lower streams than the character of their waters, for all these, as well as the interior lakes that exist so numerously in Michigan, abound in the same kinds of fish as are found in the Eastern States. And we have in the "grayling" of our peninsula as gamy a fish, as brilliant in color and of as handsome form, and as delicate in the eating, as the true brook trout. Many sportsmen, as well as gourmands, indeed, give him the preference.

I have two prosaic methods of capturing some of our finest Detroit River fish, which involve little trouble and no waste of time. One is by "night lines." A strong cord is needed, with large hook and sinker, and the best bait is pork. This line is fastened, at one end, to the shore, and is carried out at evening to the distance of several rods by boat, or is thrown by force of arm as far out as possible. It sinks to the bottom and remains until morning, when it is drawn in, and usually affords me the satisfaction of taking off a large pike or pickerel, or a black bass. Sometimes, it is true, my reasonable expectations are disappointed, by a huge cat-head or a dog-fish. Such are generally thrown away as worthless, but having learned the secret of cooking properly, they prove to be no despicable food. So you see "all is fish that comes to my net." In fact, French cookery can accomplish almost any wonder, from making palatable a roasted gull to a savory muskrat stew!

A more ingenious and even a more profitable and easy mode of fishing was suggested by the cove, which sets up from the river across my claim. As soon as the ice breaks up in the spring, fish from the river, in pursuit of early worms and insects, enter the cove and work their way up the current, until it loses itself in the meadows. Boys hunt them in these shallows, whence they are frequently unable to retrace their course. I have overtaken accidentally and killed with an axe a very large fish, as I was traversing the fields.

The road from my house to the fields crosses this cove, leaving a narrow channel, which is bridged. On the upper side of the bridge has been constructed a trap, or "fyke." It consists of a box formed of strips of boards, so nailed as to permit free passage to the water, but not to a fish of a size worth detaining. This box, which is about four feet square, is firmly fixed by stakes, and occupies half the width of the channel. The other half is obstructed by stakes, so driven as to divert the fish in their progress up the current, towards the box. The latter has a wide opening on the bridge side, to which are nailed laths or small strips converging to near the centre, on the plan of the old-fashioned wire mouse trap.

By this simple contrivance do we manage to secure many a fine fat pickerel, and I have known the water absolutely black with the multitude of fish caught in a single day. Later in the season the run of the better kinds ceases, and bull-heads are almost the only sort that enter. Fish are taken from the trap by means of a small scoop-net. The slender long-nosed pike (*Esox reticulatus*), here called pickerel, is often a foot and a half in length, and furnishes a good meal.

Another curious mode of fishing is sometimes practised here, and which, to me, was entirely novel. The fish that frequent my pond have a habit of basking near the surface, where they lie perfectly still for a long time enjoying the superior warmth; for it seems that even creatures whose veins are not chilled by the icy touch of winter derive pleasure from the warm rays of the life-giving sun. The snake loves the heated dust of the road-way. Frogs, turtles, and indeed all amphibious and cold-blooded animals, indulge in the same kind of enjoyment.

While thus taking their ease, and apparently in a quiet sleep, along the shore glides an artful rogue of a boy. With cautious movement—for a fish, be it remembered, sleeps with both eyes open—he brings to the level of his shoulder, what! a fowling-piece! Bang!—the fish is seen floating on its side. He is not killed, only stunned. Quick now, or the prey escapes. Here, Veto, the pond is too muddy for any limbs but yours. The dog too must be expeditious, otherwise the prey recovers his momently lost faculties, and in the twinkling of an eye (canine or human, of course, not fish) is off to deeper water.

But all this is small game, merely boy's play, compared with the catching of white-fish (*Coregonus albus*). All the world is now familiar with this lustrous and exquisite fish, with which our strait and lakes abound, and which has come to be an important article of commerce.

In our river they are taken only with seines or dragnets, in the spring and fall. The latter is the season of the great run, and commences with the approach of cold weather in October, lasting until nearly winter. Several of these fishing-grounds are in my vicinity; and many a time have I watched the boats as they pull up the stream,—a song keeping time to the oars—drop the net, and row rapidly back to the shore. Here both ends are drawn in by a horse-windlass, the bag of the net soon appearing, distended with the shining captives. These are thrown into a pile, from which the finest and largest may be selected at five to ten cents apiece.

The largest and best white-fish are taken further up

the lakes, the ordinary weight of those from our river being about four or five pounds. In lakes Huron and Michigan they average five or six pounds, and in Lake Superior attain to ten pounds, and even more. The largest I ever saw was estimated to weigh twelve to fifteen pounds, and had been pulled ashore by an otter out of the cold waters of our great lake. The creature made off on the approach of our boat, relinquishing his prey to our superior claims—the right of the strongest.

The seine, of course, catches all kinds of fish that come within its sweep, and are not too small to escape through its two-and-a-half-inch meshes. Among these is occasionally a huge sturgeon, often of forty pounds weight. And more rarely that prince of a fish and delicate *bonne bouche*, the muskallonge (*Esox estor.*—Cuv.). The latter is also taken by hook and line in our river and in Lake Ste. Claire.

Another fish of the salmon family is caught in great numbers in the lakes above, and is an article of commerce only second in importance to the white-fish—the salmon trout (*Salmo amethystus*). It is much larger than its white cousin, attaining to forty pounds. Though a hard fleshed and admirable fish, it lacks the delicate flavor which makes the white-fish so dainty a dish for the epicure.

There is a secret about this matter of flavor which not every cook knows, though Indians and Frenchmen well understand it. On my first visit to the "Sault," our party were invited to the house of an Indian trader, to dine. Our host, a Scotsman, had been many years on the frontier, and had fallen into the fashion of the country and the times, and taken unto himself an Indian wife.

It was his squaw who cooked our meal, and who waited

on us at the table, not presuming to sit or eat with us. I observed that immediately after our arrival our host sent out to the shore of the rapids for a white-fish, and having procured the largest and finest male specimen, that had just been drawn out of the foaming waters, it was at once dressed, broiled and served up. "Twenty minutes ago exactly," said our entertainer, as he divided a steaming portion to each guest, "this fish was enjoying his native element. Had he been half an hour dead no understanding gourmand would have thought him worthy of his table. He must be eaten while the flesh is hard, for it softens immediately with keeping. The flesh of the trout is harder and will keep longer."

Another fish familiar to me, and esteemed by the ichthyophagist, is caught in limited quantities, and only in Lake Superior,—the siskiwit. It is much too oily to be eaten fresh, being a mere mass of fat, but is good salted and smoked, and in this state resembles a very fat mackerel. Lake Superior furnishes another white-fish, of the genus Corygonus, which far exceeds in size the river species. It is caught with gill-nets, at a depth of from six to sixty fathoms, and has been known to attain the weight of forty-five pounds! The scales on throat and belly are tinged a rusty red. Otherwise, except in its enormous protuberance, it resembles the common white-fish. Like most overgrown things, it is coarse in flesh.

Before concluding my "angling" experiences, I must relate a yet more novel method of fish capture, of which I was witness, "et quorum pars fui," in one of my wanderings upon our great inland waters. Our party, landing at a rocky island in Lake Huron, came suddenly upon a shoal of fish, that were gambolling in the light surf that broke among the boulders which lined the shore. They were not porpoises, as you might suppose had it been an ocean shore, but sturgeon, better known in a distant part of the country as "Albany beef." So engaged were they in their sport as to be unconscious of our presence, while we stripped and waded in among them. We thus succeeded in nabbing several with our hands alone, and after a pretty hard tussle one fine fellow was safely landed. It kept our larder in beef and chicken for several days.

On the flats of Lake Ste. Claire a novel scene may be witnessed from a boat floating over the shallows: namely, sturgeon in the act of *pumping*. This is their mode of supplying themselves with craw-fish. These burrow in the sand, leaving holes behind them. Here the fish stations himself, with his mouth over the hole, and by a strong effort of suction produces a current in the water, which is drawn violently into his mouth. Considerable sand accompanies, which is ejected by the gills, and settles in piles or ridges on either side. Whether or not the crawfish comes out from his retreat to see what all the commotion is about, or whether he comes because he cannot help it, certain it is that up he comes, the torrent carrying him directly into the mouth of the wily fish; but he does not pass out through the gills.

I was once party to an easy kind of fish capture among the hollows, in the rocky bed of a small rapid stream on Lake Superior. Numbers of suckers were resting in these hollows, in the attempt to make their way up the ascent. We caught and threw many ashore with our hands. But they paid only in the sport, as they were poor eating.

There are other modes of catching the white and other fish of commerce of our waters besides the seine, and much controversy has arisen among fishermen as to the respective merits and demerits of the different methods.

At the Falls of St. Mary both white-fish and salmon trout are taken by the Indians with scoop-nets, as also with the spear, in the very midst of the foaming rapids, where the fish are temporarily stopped in their upward passage. It is a very exciting spectacle to see numbers of bark canoes darting, light as feathers, in the boiling eddies, at the foot of the great "leap," an Indian controlling its dexterous movements with a long pole, while another stands at the bow, with spear, or scoop, at the end of another pole, watching the finny prey. In winter, trout are caught here by hook and line, dropped through holes in the ice; but the white-fish never, or seldom—for the fact *is* vouched for,—bites at the hook.

Another mode of catching white-fish, which has increased greatly within the past few years, and in many localities almost superseded the seine, is by the trap or pound-net. This consists of a net called the "lead," having meshes of five inches from knot to knot, which is fastened at one end to the shore and reaches into deeper water, where it joins another net, called the "pot." The latter has meshes of only half the size of the first, the object of the lead being to divert the fish, from their passage along the shallow grounds, into the trap or pot.

The vast increase of our fisheries during the last ten years, and the repeated observations of intelligent fishermen, as well as of a few scientific observers, have elicited many curious facts in the life history of the white-fish, which are of great interest.

The following facts seem to be well established:

The white-fish is short lived, and of very rapid growth,

maturing the second year, and ending its life with the third.

The spawn is deposited in the fall (October and November), in shallow water, and the hatching takes place in the spring, or first month of summer, according to locality.

Soon after hatching, the young fry withdraw into deep, cold water, where they remain until the summer of the following year.

They then commence their return to the hatching grounds, for the purpose of spawning. And it is well attested,—incredible as the fact may seem,—that during the three months succeeding, or between June and September, they increase in size from about two and a half ounces to from four to nine or ten pounds weight. In other words, from mere minnows of one year they attain maturity.

Early in the summer of the third year they retire again into deep waters, and are seen no more. The white-fish is a bottom-feeder, and lives upon the young, or aquatic larvæ of the ephemera, which are found in the river mud.

These fish do not migrate, as was formerly supposed, from the lower to the higher lakes, the superior size of those found in the latter being due to the local breed, and not to age. Fish of the same locality are of remarkably uniform size.

During the summer months, it will be observed, the fish of the second year are making their way up from the deep waters to the spawning grounds, while the old fishes are returning to the deep water to die. The fishing season is therefore confined to the spring and fall,—

from the time the ice leaves until about the middle of June, and from September to the end of November.

At these seasons only full-grown fish are liable to be taken.

It is contended by advocates of the exclusive use of the seine that the stock of fish is being needlessly diminished by the use of the pound, which takes the fish indiscriminately, the small with the large, whole schools being taken at once.

On the other hand, it is maintained that the pound-net cannot so operate, for the reason that the minnows and half-grown fish escape through the meshes of the lead. And further, that by the constant capture of the sturgeon and long-lived fishes of the sucker tribe, which live upon the spawn of the white-fish, the annual stock of the latter is on the increase wherever these nets are in constant use.

It is also said that it is impossible to diminish the number, no matter how many are taken, because only those are caught which have matured and never propagate again. Some further time and observation must yet be had before these questions can be fully settled.

It is remarkable that the spawning season of the white-fish, unlike that of most other fishes, should be in the fall. Still more remarkable is the extraordinarily rapid growth, from a minnow of two or three ounces to a full-grown adult, in the short space of less than three months. It is probable that much of the delicacy of flavor of this celebrated fish is due to this rapid growth.

There is a notion among fishermen—who have, usually, numerous offspring,—that the prolific qualities of this fish are bestowed upon its consumers. Whatever of truth there may be in this tradition, certainly the great fish-eating locality, Mackinaw, bears a charmed reputation, as a favorable resort for ladies who desire an increase of their families.

Schoolcraft hints at this quality, in the following lines from his poem, "The White-fish":

> "And oft the sweet morsel up-poised on the knife,
> Excites a bland smile from the blooming young wife;
> Nor dreams she a sea-fish one moment compares,
> But is thinking the while not of fish but of heirs."

The trade in the white-fish has been steadily on the increase, and has become a very important and profitable one to our State.

The first fishery from which any export was made was that of Mr. Barnabus Campau, on Belle Isle (late Isle au Cochon of the French), in 1825, but the trade continued small and unprofitable until the tide of emigration set in, about ten years later. From that time the fisheries, which had been confined to Detroit River, gradually extended to the lake borders, and during the present year two schooners have been hauled around the rapids into Lake Superior, to assist in bringing this fine product of that noble lake into the market.

Sincerely Yours.

Since the above was written, forty years ago, fisheries have not only been largely extended, but stringent laws have been enacted for their regulation. Active measures are also being taken by both the general and State governments, for stocking our streams and lakes with young fry, artificially hatched, of the kinds most suitable.

In 1841 about 30,000 barrels of white-fish only were

packed annually. Probably not less than 50,000 are now sold annually by Detroit merchants alone.

In 1868 half a million of white-fish were captured by Detroit River fisheries, as many as 20,000 being sometimes secured in a single haul of the seine.

Though the fishing season proper is in the spring and fall, modern luxury, at the time when this note is being recorded, has invented methods for bringing to our tables at all times of the year this estimable food. Not only are the finer sorts brought from the cold waters of the upper lakes, packed in ice, and with their firmness and delicacy little impaired, but they are transported in the same frozen condition to the most distant markets.

In 1855, Mr. George Clark, of Detroit, inaugurated a method of impounding the fish, at the time of the fall fishing, by dragging them by means of the nets into large pens, where they are kept alive and sound for the winter supply. There is a very large demand, and the trade is carried on in Detroit chiefly. Probably not less than half a million are sent from here annually, the produce of these winter pens.

How well I remember the time when the fishing season —at which time alone could this dainty fare be obtained —was looked forward to by the old residents with pleasure and impatience, and one of the hardships of a removal to other parts of the country was experienced in the longing after this favorite dish. Now this "deer of the lakes"—par excellence—is not only universally known, but is procurable cheaply, at all seasons, both fresh and salted, from the lakes to the Gulf, and from the Mississippi to Cape Cod. It has even overleaped these bounds, and is shipped direct to Liverpool.

But this constant drain has of late years, in spite of all

precautions, tended to constantly diminish the annual catch. The gill-net has superseded the seine, necessity having withdrawn the operations into deeper waters. The greed of trade outruns all sober precautions. And it is to be feared that the time is rapidly approaching when the inhabitants of our lakes and rivers, like the wild animals which were once so abundant and are now so few, will be in like manner exterminated, and this great industry of Michigan will cease to be remunerative.

BIRDS OF MY NEIGHBORHOOD.

' He therefore makes all birds of every sort
  Free of his farm, with promise to respect
  Their several kinds alike, and equally protect."
                                        DRYDEN.

BIRDS OF MY NEIGHBORHOOD.

SPRINGWELLS, ——, 1850.

DEAR TOM:—You ask me for some account of the feathered inhabiters of my neighborhood. As the meagre notes you received from me a long time ago about the fishes seem to have pleased you, I willingly comply, promising only that you must not expect from me the language of a naturalist.

One of our earliest looked-for indications of the return of spring is the flight of aquatic birds. Our position on the great chain of lakes gives unusual facilities for observing these migrations.

The breaking up of the ice does not always indicate the final departure of winter, for it often happens many times during that season that our river is entirely free from ice, and so also in great part the lakes. But the migrations of water fowl to points above, are a certain forerunner of the final dissolution of the icy bands. "One swallow does not make a summer," nor is it certain that the warm breezes of spring will surely follow the first flocks of wild ducks. But as their course is northward, and their object the breeding grounds, the sway of winter must be broken to enable them to accomplish what they are in search of. The commencement of their flights usually is early in March, but this depends upon the character of the season.

Wild geese are less numerous than the ducks. They number about twenty in a flock, and always fly with military precision. They range themselves along two sides of a triangle, so as to constitute a wedge, and cleave the air with greater facility. A general or leader always precedes, and they obey the democratic doctrine of rotation in office, the rear being allowed at intervals to overtake the van and change with it.

Ducks are not of so orderly a disposition, but migrate in more straggling bodies. They fly with necks stretched out in a straight line with the body, and feet drawn up, so as to offer least resistance to the air; and it is astonishing how rapidly they cut their liquid way, and how long sustained is their flight.

Swans are less often seen, but I find mention in my note-books of their appearance March 31, 1836, and in other years. Capt. Luther Harvey, of Monroe, tells me they were formerly quite numerous in the bays of the lakes. I do not think that either swans or geese now alight in our river. Ducks frequent the bays and indentures of the stream in great numbers, even in the vicinity of settlements, but where they are a good musket-shot from shore, though out of reach of the current. Here they swim about and dive at a generally safe distance from sportsmen, who watch for such stragglers as are tempted by the facilities for feeding to approach nearer. The sportsman often hides successfully behind some object on the shore, where, protected from observation, he is enabled to make game of many unwary ones. Among these birds are some teals. These are so watchful and lively as to dive at the flash, and thus escape even the well-aimed ball.

One of my sporting neighbors practises a mode of deception which is new to me. In the early spring, when ice is floating down in large, irregular masses from the lakes above, dotting the whole surface of the water, he converts his canoe into a mimic cake of ice by stretching a sheet over the front. Ensconced behind this, he floats down along with the moving masses, and is often enabled to get into the very midst of a flock before they have warning of the trick.

During a cold winter many years ago, the French and half-breeds of Presque Isle found geese so frozen to the ice that they caught them in great numbers. Thirty or forty years ago, I am told, ducks were so numerous in Maumee Bay, and so fat on the wild rice, that they were speared by thousands.

Capt. Luther Harvey relates that in the early days, soon after the war of 1812, swans and brants occasionally visited the marshes at the west end of Lake Erie. One day a pair of brants came to his farm and settled down among his geese, where they remained for two weeks, and until they were shot by a boy. They became so tame that he could approach them within twenty feet. They partook of the corn distributed to the other fowls, eyeing him suspiciously and keeping a little off, but not flying away. They were beautiful birds, slenderer than the geese, white, with black on ends of tail and wings, and a black spot on the shoulder. From the description I conclude that they were the white brant, or snow-goose (*Anser hyperboreus*), a rarer bird than the common brant (which is gray), and whose breeding-grounds are well up to the Arctic seas.

Of the large family of Natatores the wide, encircling waters of our peninsula furnish a greater number of species than any other portion of our continent. Specimens of most of them are in the State collection at the University of Michigan, deposited by the zoologists of the Natural History Survey, under Dr. Houghton.

Among them is the celebrated canvas-back duck, so much sought by epicures, and fully equal to those which feed upon the wild celery of the Chesapeake. Detroit markets are well stocked with water fowl in great variety during the season. They get very fat in the fall on the wild rice that abounds hereabouts, but their numbers are rapidly diminishing.

How different the life of these wild fowl from that of the domesticated kinds. The latter seldom range far from the hand that feeds them, and seek the protection of man. They have become essentially a *land* bird, living as much on shore as on the water, even when they have free access to pond or river. Wild ducks, on the contrary, with few exceptions, do not visit the land except for incubation, feeding and sleeping on the wave. The domestic bird will not fly many rods without seeking rest; the wild makes continuous journeys of many hundred miles. Yet tame ducks are sometimes enticed to join the flocks of their wild brethren. In fact, this happened with me so frequently some years ago, that I was forced to abandon the attempt to keep ducks in my pond. The near and open connection with the river, and the rice and other food with which it abounded, tempted the wild birds to resort thither, and the acquaintance which they formed with my domestic species proved too strong for the hitherto good habits of the latter. Having tasted the sweets of the wild liberty of their ancestors, they deserted me, never to return.

Among the winged frequenters of our river, the gull lives even more exclusively upon this element, alighting always in the water, as do many of the ocean birds. Indeed, the sea-gull is not an uncommon visitor of its lake cousins, among whom its larger size and brilliant white plumage render it conspicuous. I am not aware of any land resort the gulls have in these parts, but on Lake Superior and Thunder Bay of Lake Huron I have seen isolated rocks—their breeding-places—covered with them in countless numbers, and the young are easily caught.

The great Northern loon was formerly a frequenter of our river, but is now seldom seen here. It is still common in the small lakes and rivers distant from settlements, where I have often heard his cry in the cool of evening. What a weird, wild, lonely cry it is! It may be near or far off, you cannot tell which. But the bird is very wild and difficult of approach.

Of other birds that move in flocks during the spring season, we have our share of those two distinguished game birds, pigeons and quails. The former never appear in this locality in such prodigious numbers as in territories further west, but they come in little squads numerous enough to afford excellent sport, and the markets are amply supplied during their short stay.

Quails abide with us during nearly the whole year, and visit familiarly our fields and homesteads. They are so tame as to allow man to approach within a very few feet, and it is an amusement to listen to their answer to calls made in imitation of their peculiar whistle. Their song consists of two or three clear whistling notes in rapid succession, the last a little prolonged and on a higher key. One comes suddenly upon a bevy of quails in a morning walk over the fields or along the roads, when they will start up, almost from under your feet, with a sharp whirr of the wings and scuttle away in a low flight to a little further distance, perhaps to a neighboring fence, whence they can watch and form an opinion of the intruder. Pretty things they are, round, plump, and very toothsome when made acquainted with griddle and toast. Detroit journals of May, 1839, mention the phenomenon of a sudden, uncommon abundance of these birds in this neighborhood. So great were the numbers, and so fearless were they of man, that many were knocked down in the streets with clubs and canes.

Yet though such close attendants of field and home, quails are not easily tamed, and when caged retain to the last much of their native wildness and impatience of restraint. Even when hatched under a hen it has been found impossible to domesticate them.

Of all the birds that visit us in flocks we love least to see the blackbirds,—those arrant thieves, that steal our corn and oats so pertinaciously. The river marshes afford such congenial habitats for these birds that their numbers scarcely diminish, notwithstanding the havoc made among them by the guns of boys and outraged farmers.

They congregate by thousands in these river borders and coves, where they find a favorite food in the wild rice (*Zizania aquatica*). The cove or pond near my farmhouse, covering an area of some two or three acres, is nearly every season filled with this plant, and is often black with the birds. On firing, or throwing a stone into their ranks, they rise in dense flocks, with a loud rushing sound, fly a short distance, wheel about, and again settle to their repast; or they collect in dense, black masses in a neighboring tree. Here they hold council over their misdeeds, or rather, it is probable, over the unauthorized insult to which, in their opinion, they have been subjected. The chatter is loud and incessant.

Woe betide our corn and grain fields, when sufficiently advanced to tempt these voracious marauders! Scarecrows are of temporary avail, but suspicion soon turns to contempt. Then shot-guns again give temporary relief, which lasts no longer than one can afford to hold patient watch.

As they are not game birds, sportsmen do not thin their ranks to supply the luxuries of the table. Yet they are eaten, and I can testify from experience that " four-and-twenty blackbirds baked in a pie" are no mean "dish to set before a king." At any rate, a sovereign Frenchman does not despise it. They are also "a dainty dish" to another epicurean animal, the omnivorous hog. Often have my hogs enjoyed a rare treat, as I rambled, gun in hand, about my orchard bordering the pond, the hogs following and devouring the birds which I brought to the ground.

The blackbirds come early, and are the last to depart, the sexes taking their departure in separate bands. There are two species, the males of one being distinguishable by their red wing-covers. When congregated to talk over the question of departure they are very loquacious, the subject being discussed over and over again, with as much noise and confusion, but in a more friendly spirit, than attends many of *our* deliberative assemblies.

Their gay, sociable, chatty dispositions are qualities not to be despised among the boon companions of our fields and river-side, and offer some amends for the mischief they do us. We know too that, like most of our birds, they are insectivorous, their food consisting of grubs, caterpillars, moths and beetles, as well as grain, and we may well believe that the mischief they accomplish is more than compensated by habits and virtues of which we take little note.

Wild turkeys were among the game birds of our neighborhood until the extension of the clearings drove them to more distant retreats. But even yet they occasionally approach the settlements. Recently a flock of them came into a piece of my enclosed woodland, a quarter of a mile only from the house. Here I would gladly have left them undisturbed, but they were discovered by prying hunters, shot at, and driven away. Guns are becoming the terror and nuisance of our neighborhood.

The wild turkey is considered one of the wildest of forest game, being much more difficult to get a shot at than a deer. Yet I not unfrequently flush them in my woodland rides. On one such occasion I came suddenly upon a hen turkey with a brood of young. The old bird flew upon a fallen tree, bristling its feathers at me in great rage, while the chicks dispersed and sought the cover of the nearest leaves and underwood. It was her mode of distracting my attention from her young. Springing at once from my horse, I without difficulty caught two of the little ones, carried them away in my pocket, and made an acceptable present of them to one of my young friends.

A gentleman living in one of the interior counties of the State, but little settled, vouches to me for the following fact, as showing how readily the wild bird may become a subject of domestication. A neighbor woman kept domestic fowls, and throwing corn to them daily, gradually decoyed a wild turkey into her yard. Associating with the domestic brood, and finding what an easy life they led, he became at length so tame that she actually caught and took possession of him. Whether he continued to live like a prince, or went to her pot, I did not learn, or have forgotten.

Hawks and owls are among the birds of prey that make frequent visits to my poultry yard. The latter are seldom seen, as they avoid the light of day. The former are very bold in their approaches, and will allow a man to come within a few feet, if he have no gun. They are quick to learn the meaning of this subtle weapon. They are often conspicuous objects, as perched upon a tree in the fields, or upon a post of the fence, they audaciously survey the neighborhood, and calculate the chances of an attempt at robbery. Though these fellows have little to recommend them, in public estimation, except their fearlessness, I would willingly allow free license to enjoy their observations, and follow unmolested the life that nature has taught, but that some unusually bold and successful raid raises my resentment, followed by retaliation. I once shot one that had been thus depredating, breaking his wing, so that he could not fly. On my coming up he made no attempt at escape, and as I held him up by the wings, his large open beak, black, piercing eyes, and strong hooked claws gave him a very formidable appearance. There was a contempt of danger and a valor in the stern, restless eye, which followed my motions, that displayed the indomitable spirit of an Indian warrior, who may aptly be likened to a bird of prey; untamable as the wild eagle of the mountain, and scorning the hand of mercy. I hung him up, in terror to the winged robbers of my cornfield.

Did I not, thoughtlessly, by this very act—making even of his dead body a useful friend—acknowledge this creature's claim to protection? How many of these lesser thieves may he not have captured. How many mice and other cunning depredators may he not have destroyed, as his common and daily food, for every chicken which he occasionally regaled upon? Nature is full of compensations, and did man better heed her lessons, he would find that many a creature he ruthlessly seeks to exterminate is one of his chiefest benefactors.

Quite a variety of birds make their abode with us throughout the winter; so that our fields and woods are far from cheerless, from the absence of animated life, during that cold season.

The blue jay is a very constant attendant throughout the year, never leaving us for milder climes. But he is by no means so familiar as the robin, his actions showing rather a contempt for man, as an order of animals beneath his notice. Nevertheless when snow covers the earth, and food is difficult to find, he will approach nearer the mansion, searching for such crumbs as may be thrown out. But he generally keeps aloof, and is more attracted by the grassy spots, bare of snow, about the roots of trees. A gay and handsome bird he is, with his soldier-like, clean, blue-and-white uniform and feathery crest; but his shrill voice has not even the music of the fife in it.

Woodpeckers remain with us long in the autumn, and several kinds throughout the winter.

Flocks of snow-birds—buntings—are visitants, but only occasional, through the winter, and usually as attendants upon a snow-storm. They are very sprightly and sociable, and of course are very cheering companions for sharp atmospheres and wintry blasts. They are the only non-resident birds that visit us only in the winter. Coming when other guests have deserted, they are like the memories of sunny days, that cheer the heart in the winter of life.

Robins have been reported as seen in my woods in the middle of December. There is a vulgar belief that during mild days they come out of the reeds and marshes, where they have winter habitats. It is certain that they put in an appearance here early in March but so do the bluebirds, which are well-known birds of passage. There can be little doubt that a few individual robins do occasionally remain all winter in our neighborhood, sheltering themselves in the dense woods and swales. Occasionally they leave their retreats so early in the spring, deceived by a passing mildness, that they are frozen to death by a sudden wintry turn.

Our spring is made gay with the beautiful plumage of many birds, as well as by their songs. Those early and familiar favorites, the blue and yellow birds, and the orioles, never fail to be with us at this hopeful season, in great numbers; cheering us with their notes of gladness, and, like winged flowers, anticipating the blossoms that shall soon clothe the garden and orchard with tints rivalling their own.

The bluebird is one of the earliest harbingers of spring, arriving early in March and remaining until November. His services, too, are of a very practical kind, for he devours multitudes of noxious insects, and never, that I can discover, plunders the fruit.

The still more brilliant scarlet tanager is a more shy and unfrequent visitor, and arrives later from his congenial South. He delights, here at the North, to veil his beauties in the deeper woods. But his first compliments are paid nevertheless to the homestead; where he flashes through the shrubbery like a glancing flame. He soon retires to the thick woods, to bring up his family, and very early takes his departure. He belongs to a Brazilian family, and perhaps has not yet acquainted himself sufficiently with our harsh Northern tongue to become familiar.

Another handsome bird is very common here, and he is among the most persistent of the winged thieves that prey upon our fruit. This is the cedar-bird, known also as the cherry-bird, from his remarkable fondness for cherries, which he devours in great quantities. I am willing to believe that even he repays the injury he does us, and possibly earns his guerdon by clearing the trees of canker-worms and insects that hide beneath the bark. His dress is very neat, and the French call him by the name of Récollet, from the color of his crest, which resembles the hood of that religious order, once so numerous in the New World.

I have recently had the opportunity of a very interesting subject of study,—the habits of wild birds domesticated. An ingenious brother has constructed a mammoth cage, which he has filled with "many birds of various kinds." It is wonderful to see how well they agree, only now and then one being found that is quarrelsome or of an ugly disposition. Of this sort was a blackbird, who rapaciously snatched food from the other tenants, always greedy and careless of the rights and comforts of others. So neither in his wild nor domestic state does he make himself a favorite. He had a way of amusing himself that was in keeping with his character,— that of plucking the feathers off the breasts of his companions. In this manner he completely stripped a large chicken that had been confined to the cage for a few days.

A little Java sparrow affords much amusement, by a particular friendship he has formed with the robins. These birds are several times larger than he, but stand somewhat in awe of him. It is his custom to shelter himself from the cold at night by making use of the warmth of their bodies. This use is, in fact, somewhat compulsory, and is obtained by stratagem. He does it by hugging closely up to one of the robins; the pressure forcing the bird to raise and extend a leg, in order to preserve his balance. The sparrow seizes this chance to slip in between the legs, and thus secures a warm downy covering for his bed. If unsuccessful in this expedient, he contrives by the use of his wings to get into his favorite position; for he is a determined little fellow, and does not readily abandon his undertakings. This sparrow is a very grave-looking bird, notwithstanding his facetious tricks. He has brilliant stripes of white under each ear, which look like shirt-collars, and a very large prominent bill, like the red Roman nose of a free liver. We name him the "Bachelor."

Most of the birds in this cage have been brought up together from the callow stage, and have become very familiar with each other. A male oriole and a female canary, being mateless, entered into a "civil contract," and proceeded very diligently to build a nest. But the robins did not approve the match, and tore the nest to pieces as fast as it was constructed, scattering the materials about the cage.

How strong the breeding instinct is was shown on another occasion, among the canaries. A pair had constructed a nest in their breeding cage, but from some cause failed to raise a brood. A friend having accidentally found a nest of yellow birds of unfledged young, took two of them and dropped them into the empty nest. They were first espied by the male canary, who, after eyeing them awhile curiously, gave place to the female. She, with a motherly tenderness, at once accepted the gift, and thenceforth the happy pair adopted the little foundlings, and reared them to maturity, with many demonstrations of pleasure and affection.

Most of the birds are made very tame by handling. This is particularly the case with the thrushes; but they lose this tameness to man when kept confined to the cage. They also lose the power or inclination to sing when together. An indigo bird, a famous songster when in his solitary cage, so lost his vocal power, after a few weeks' intercourse with the birds, that it became necessary, after separating him, to set before him the example of the best vocalist among the canaries, before he recovered his lost art.

Some time ago a large green parrot was added to our feathered family. He is a good talker, and amuses us with some extraordinary exhibitions of the faculty of speech and of mimicry. Like other individuals of this loquacious species, he pronounces quite plainly such familiar words and sentences as "Good-by," "Polly wants a cracker," etc. But what is more astonishing is the ease with which, like a child, he catches and imitates sounds heard for the first time. He soon learned to repeat the names of every member of the family, including the servants. These he often rouses from the kitchen by loudly calling their names. Sometimes he varies his tones, from those of an old person to those of a child, with marvellous accuracy.

He is fond of holding with himself long imaginary conversations. In these he will seem to ask questions, to reply, and to dispute, deny and recriminate; now in the gruff voice of a man, and now in the finer tones of a woman, getting quite warm in his earnestness.

During this harangue few words may be distinctly uttered, but the whole has the character of a conversation indistinctly heard, or which is listened to without taking note of the language used. In what fish-market this Billingsgate was learned we do not know. The persons from whom the bird was purchased had emigrated, and from the frequent use of the word "California," by the bird, it is probable they had gone to that country, and possibly the journey had been preceded by long, and perhaps angry, discussions on the subject.

A gentleman resident in the city is owner of a parrot, of the African gray species, which is quite remarkable for his intelligent use of language. When his master comes home the bird recognizes his step, and calls out to him, "How do you do, old boy?" Being answered, "Pretty well," his response is, "All right." On his master's leaving the house he salutes him with, "Good-by, old boy,—come and kiss me good-by." This bird also calls by name every member of the family.

The speech of the parrot is ventriloquial. There appears to be no motion of the beak or tongue, while a very perspicuous motion is observable in the throat. Indeed, the labial sounds are as distinctly articulated as any other, which would be a phenomenon indeed, if performed by a bird's beak. The curious orifice at the root of the latter may have something to do with this faculty, but I am not learned on the subject.

Truly Yours.

THE BIRDS, FURTHER CONSIDERED.

"——nor these alone, whose notes
Nice fingered art must emulate in vain,
But cawing rooks, and kites that swim sublime,
In still repeated circles, screaming loud,
The jay, the pie, and e'en the boding owl,
That hails the rising moon, have charms for me."
COWPER.

THE BIRDS, FURTHER CONSIDERED.

I WOULD supplement the foregoing account of my earlier experiences by a few more items, and a little further chat about the birds of my neighborhood.

Mr. J. S. Tibbits, in a paper read before our Wayne County Pioneer Society, in 1874, alluding to the first settlement of the country, mentions among "the birds common in those early days," the eagle, turkey-buzzard, raven, hawk, owl, crow, turkey, partridge, duck, and wild goose. He says, "The turkey-buzzard, which is seldom or never seen now, was common then. The crow did not make its appearance till a number of years after the first settlements were made."

I have several times, in years gone, seen the bald eagle, perched upon some tree on the banks, or sailing over the Lake Ste. Claire. The buzzard must have betaken himself to other latitudes for some good reason, known best to himself, before my arrival in 1835. With the crow (*Corvus Americanus*) I made better acquaintance. This bird, cousin-german to the blackbirds mentioned in the foregoing letter, is of much larger size, but of like social disposition. On my first coming to this county I was informed that the large, dusky birds seen occasionally high in air were *ravens*, and that the true crow was not found here. Yet I was aware at that time, that great precautions were used by farmers in the State of New York to protect their corn from the depredations of crows. The *Genesee Farmer* of 1867 says, "It is little more than twenty years since the first crow crossed the Genesee River, westerly." The first appearance of crows in this neighborhood, that I have noted, was in the autumn of 1858. So it must have taken about a decade for their journey westward, from the Niagara to the Detroit, supposing they came from that quarter.

An entry in my journal of November 12, 1858, states, "For a week past, large quantities of crows have made their appearance, coming over the river, from Canada, each morning, and returning about sunset. They are in thousands, and wing their way in a narrow track that passes nearly over my homestead. They fly at great height generally, but sometimes descend within rifle distance. They croak but little, and seem to be on business. Last evening the number was unusually large, and I observed that their point of departure seemed to be the oak grove in the rear of and not far from my house." I must here state that my residence is no longer upon the river, but about half a mile back, and nearer the woods.

The evening was clear and moonlit, and I walked out into the grove, about nine o'clock, guided by the noise. There I found that several thousand birds had taken roost in the tallest trees. Something of importance was on their minds, for they kept up an incessant chatter, not their usual formal *caw*. A portion would now and then rise on the wing, in a flock, wheel around, and alight on a neighboring tree, all within a small circle. It was like the swarming of bees. Their notes were more varied than I had ever before heard. Besides the common caw would be an occasional chuckling sound, or warble, and now and then some words resembling "get out"; whether this was addressed to me or to some offender among their own community, I could not tell. At times the mingling voices made a medley resembling the concert of frogs. They seemed to be in 'high feather'; which is probably their term for enjoyment. In the morning all were gone.

Their diurnal passage of the river this year continued for several weeks, but the same roosting-places were not always selected. I have noted their re-appearance in the winters of 1861 and 1862, and of 1864 and 1865. In November, 1865, I again noticed their passage overhead, crossing into Canada at sunrise, and returning to our side at night.

The *Detroit Free Press* of March 21, 1867, notices the advent of crows for the two weeks past, in unprecedented numbers, making in clouds for some rendezvous on the Canada side, and says a gentleman counted two thousand in two hours.

My notes of March, 1869, thus again alludes to the return of the crows,—an event always of peculiar interest to me: " For several days we have noticed unusual numbers flying overhead. Last evening about five o'clock they began coming in flocks of several thousand, and settled down in the pine grove of my neighbor, where they remained all night. The pines were thickly planted and were about twenty feet high. About five o'clock the next morning they were astir, and for some fifteen minutes before their departure completed their toilettes amid an incessant uproar, and were off for breakfast. This evening at the same hour they again commenced their visitation, coming from the south and south-west, in long straggling files. All came to the pine grove, as before, flying quite low, but after settling there for about a half hour, changed their minds as to their night's quarters, and the main body rose and moved off to the tall trees on the outskirt of my woods. Here they clustered on the tops, in black masses. These occasionally rose, and after sailing about settled again on the trees. Deputation after deputation continued to arrive, and all made for the pines, but finding their associates gone, they also steered their course to join the main body. About six o'clock all had assembled. Their united deliberations now resulted in a resolution to return to the pines, where they settled down, apparently for the night, the taller trees in my adjoining grounds being occupied by sentries. Suddenly some roving mischief-maker let off a gun into their ranks. All now rose, and with angry clamor departed for the taller trees of my woodland. Not one remained. Half an hour later another gun frighted them from this roost, and compelled a retreat to a more distant camp. Here, as darkness fell, I made them a visit. Several trees were filled with them, in black clusters. Their object seemed to be rather the holding of a council than for a night's repose. Certainly their whole time was occupied in talking, and the clamor at times was overpowering. At length a pause occurred in the general debate. One or two only continued to hold forth; after awhile others would break in and interrupt the orators. Now the whole assembly felt authorized to express their sentiments, which they did not fail to do, with the utmost vociferation. The excitement would have done credit to a political caucus.

On this occasion, as I had observed on a former one, every few minutes a portion of the assembly rose, wheeled around in a large circle, and returned to their places. While this movement was taking place the tumult ceased, or fell to an occasional caw; when all were again together, the chatter once more became incessant. The noise occasioned by the mingling of so many throats bore little resemblance to the harsh croak with which these birds accompany their flight by day. It was more like the hum of a multitude of human voices; it was difficult to resist the impression that such voices were really aiding the din. Several inferior animals also found imitators; I could distinctly recognize the mew of the cat and the chirrup of the squirrel.

My appearance created some distrust, which was not to be wondered at, after the affair of the guns. When I moved into sight from behind a tree the conversation ceased. After a little while a few voices began a kind of inquiring note, very plaintive and low; doubtless asking my motive, and deprecating hostility. Frequently an entire cessation took place in the debate—a silent deliberation—during which, for one or two minutes, no sound was heard, except the flapping of wings in the efforts of the birds to keep their places on the limbs, from which broken pieces were continually dropping. Though tolerant of my presence, the assembly did not seem disposed to admit me to their councils. I have no doubt that the subjects discussed were of the utmost importance, and I would gladly have reported the speeches for the *Free Press*, had they furnished me an interpreter.

For several succeeding nights the crows, to the great delight of my family, continued their visits to the pines, or to the taller trees in my grounds, but they held no more mass meetings. I hoped that these trees would form for them a secure retreat, and that the frequenters might become half domesticated, like the rooks of England. But some sporting characters again brought their ill-timed guns upon them, killed many, and drove the rest away, and they have gone to quarters unknown.

What these creatures find to subsist upon, in quantity

sufficient for such numbers, is a mystery. They are supposed by some to consume the acorns, of which there is great abundance, but I have never observed them at this work, nor have I ever heard any blame attached to the crows, as depredators upon the corn and grain fields, in this State. They are naturally carnivorous, and consume grubs, the larvæ of beetles and insects; perhaps also mice. Thus they are of real service to the farmer. These sources of supply being cut off in the cold season, it is said that they resort to carrion. But how they manage to find sufficient of this, or any other food, to sustain life in winter is unexplained. A mile or more back from the river are several slaughter-houses, and in the fall crows may be seen, at almost all hours, in their vicinity. Garbage and the carcasses of animals, that are often exposed in the fields, without the city, may also attract them. But why their so regular transits of the river I have not been able to discover.

On the occasion of their visits to this vicinity, in the winter of 1864-5, there was an enclosed lot near my residence, which had been recently manured with garbage from the slaughter-houses. The crows were attracted to this lot, and for many days settled there in considerable squads. They ranged themselves about the heaps, as I have often seen turkey-buzzards do, apparently satisfied to be near such food, but though I watched them often, I never once saw any engaged in eating. Late in the afternoons these settled upon the pines before mentioned, where they kept noisy council until far into the evening, when all returned into Canada. Unless they live upon smell, as the fairies do, they must find their chief subsistence somewhere in Her Majesty's dominions.

The crow is one of the few birds that are attendants

upon civilization, continuing about the settlements of man all the year. His resemblance to the rooks of Old England, who make their nests under the protection of lordly mansions, and roam undisturbed meadow and cornfield, gives to our bird additional interest. I must however tell the whole truth, and am compelled to admit that these black friends of mine were detected by a neighbor depredating upon his young chickens. I was incredulous, until convinced by the contents of the stomach. A few days afterwards a young crow fell into my hands, and I confined him in a cage in my orchard. Here he was visited by the parent bird, who was actually seen carrying to her captive child portions of the body of a chicken. After these disclosures I no longer felt disposed to give the crow such free title as before. At the same time I remember in their favor that they destroy cutworms and many things injurious to man, and are perhaps, to a certain degree, scavengers. I will not therefore withdraw my protection, because of their occasional theft of things that we value.

Finally, I love the crow for the independence of his character. He keeps aloof from the servile throngs that crowd around the habitations of men. Like the latter, he has his parliaments, but he keeps his own counsel, and cares nothing for those who differ from him.

> " He sees that this great roundabout,
> The world, with all its motley rout,
> Church, army, physic, law,
> Its customs and its businesses,
> Is no concern at all of his,
> And says—what says he?—caw!" *

---

* Cowper.

I much regret that wild turkeys have now been all driven from this region by hunters. It has always seemed to me that this bird would be our country's much more appropriate emblem than the eagle. It certainly represents our land better, and the national character as it should be. The turkey was once common over all the United States, and is peculiar to North America. The eagle is found all over the world, and is peculiar to no one country. It was the national bird of ancient Rome, and is now of the almost equally extended empire of Russia, as well as of other lesser States. The eagle is a bird of prey, does no service to man, nor does it possess any noble qualities that compensate for the cruelty and rapacity which are its nature. It is the inferior in courage of many birds of far less pretension. It is a selfish bird, living for himself and by himself alone. The turkey loves society and friendship; he is devoted to his clan, who consort together in deliberative assemblies, and act with that common consent which is the basis of democratic government. The turkey lives only on the fruits of the earth, wherein he appropriately symbolizes the agricultural character of our people. Even in the whiteness and sweetness of its flesh, it is significant of the good things in store for the citizens of a mild, paternal government, that does not thrive by the woes of others. It is a proud bird, too, as conscious of its merits, and in the lustre and beauty of its plumage yields the palm to no feathered creature. Those who see his form only among the stuffed specimens of a museum have but a very imperfect idea of the matchless beauty, the blended shades and hues, and the noble bearing of the wild bird in his prime, and in his native haunts.

It may be objected that so timid a creature does not

represent the bold and active element of national character. But why should ferocity be paramount to the peaceful qualities? To be bold in defence of its rights, and in its protecting care over its offspring, but not aggressive upon the rights of others; to be diligent in the useful, and not disregardful of the ornamental, are qualities which are paramount in the turkey. They are worthy of any creature, and would befit the character of a just nation.

We have had enough of "spread-eagle" boasting over our country's greatness and glory. That kind of vanity has been humbled, and it would be well if, with the emblem, it was repudiated altogether. Franklin, philosopher as well as statesman, saw the inappropriateness of the eagle as the emblem of his country, and proposed the rattlesnake—an exclusively American animal, and who always gives warning before he strikes. But a reptile has not sufficient dignity for so important a purpose. The turkey equally is exclusively American, and, while he combines, in the highest degree, the useful and the beautiful, is free from any of those qualities which in a people cast a stain upon the national honor.

Of birds of America that collect in large flocks none exceed in marvellous numbers the pigeon. Most persons have heard about the immense roosts of this bird in some of the sparsely settled portions of the West, and it has been well known for years that they had one of their favorite roosting-places in this State. But the great pigeon-roost of 1874, in Benzie County, so far transcends any other of which I ever read or heard, that I cannot forbear transcribing for this chapter some graphic portions of a letter to the New York *World*, by a correspondent from Frankfort, Michigan, dated June 25, 1874. He says:

"The number of the birds this spring has exceeded even anything recorded in the traditions of hunters and oldest inhabitants. The miraculous flight of quails that fell by the camp of the Israelites, a day's journey on this side and a day's journey on the other side, and two cubits high upon the face of the earth, is as nothing to the 'Betsey River nesting.' Imagine if you can a tract of land about sixteen miles long and three wide, where every bough is occupied by a dozen nests and a hundred birds; where the air whirrs from dawn till dark with ceaseless wings; where the flights that settle cover square acres with a living carpet; where from 250 to 400 men have for six weeks or more been engaged in trapping and killing without cessation, and yet not made the numbers appreciably less; imagine 50 square miles of pigeons, and that is the scene. Almost daily armies of re-enforcements fly northward from far-away Kentucky and Missouri, the beat of whose wings and whose countless numbers obscure the sky, and emit a hollow roar, as if a tornado or thunder-storm were approaching.

"There are three regular 'flights' a day—two 'tom flights' and one 'hen flight!' At early dawn the male birds set out, flying to the east and north to seek a breakfast of seeds and berries, 10, 20, or 50 miles away, and by six or half-past six the sky is black with the departing birds. They tower up in great armies to a considerable height, each sheet of birds—sheet is the word that best describes them—wavering a moment like the needle of the compass when disturbed, then taking flight in the appointed direction, with a unanimity and evenness of speed that would make one believe that every bird was animated by the same impulse at the same instant. An hour later not a bird is to be seen, but toward 8 o'clock the rush of the returning armies is heard. Squadron after squadron arrives, cleaving the air with unwearied wing and unfailing sense, fluttering, wheeling and descending, each division over its own district, each bird over the nest of its faithful mate. As 'tom' after 'tom' returns to take his trick at the domestic helm, 'hen' after 'hen' rises upward, and the armies of the Amazons go out to the East and North. Towards 9 o'clock the scene is indescribable. It is a very atmosphere of wings; earth and forest have been converted into feathers, and the eye gazes down vistas of pigeons to far horizons of squab pies and *salmis de tourtes sauvages*.

"By and by the last female departs, and the meek males remain incubating with a faithfulness and amenability to domestic discipline that would delight the sternest unfeathered sister. In the middle of the afternoon the hens return and the toms depart to make an evening of it, returning before or about sunset. The late birds, who stay out till dusk, having apparently the latch-key to their several nests, seem bothered and fly very low, sweeping along the ground till they get their bearings.

"Then begins such a slaughter as marked the *coup d'état*. Poles and clubs are the weapons, and at every sweep a dozen birds, brained, crippled or maimed, tumble to the earth. Scarcely less simple and efficient is the practice of raking them down at night with poles, from the lower branches where they roost. The foxes and, later, the hogs fatten on the ungathered hecatombs that are left dead or to die in the grass. . . ." The writer, after detailing other and the principal modes of capturing this game, adds: "The New York State Sportsmen's Association has taken 40,000 or 45,000 live birds from Frankfort, and Fisher & Sons as many more, alive and dead, and as for small dealers, it is impossible to say how many hundreds of barrels and coops they sent away weekly."

Whether the lesser song birds favor this neighborhood in any unusual degree I am unable to say, nor will I undertake any extended mention of these universal favorites of the wood, field and door-yard; which would swell my meagre notes into a treatise. Only let it be understood, that the little I do say falls very far below the standard of their merit and the admiration they excite.

It is certain that we have occasionally song birds of more Southern habits. Possibly the extraordinary heat which sometimes attends our summers, and the increased number of insects then called forth, but more the charm of our Northern woods and waters, are the prevailing inducements to these extended journeys.

Among these Southern guests is the well-known mocking-bird (*Orpheus polyglottus*), which is seen, though but rarely, in this State. The powers of our Northern, or "French mocking-bird," more commonly known as the brown thrush or thrasher, and ferruginous thrush (*Orpheus rufus*), certainly compare most favorably with those of his Southern cousin, and are not appreciated to the extent, it seems to me, which they deserve. There is among naturalists some difference of opinion, whether this bird is an imitator, or his song native and only varied. The latter is the generally received conclusion. It may seem strange there should be any difficulty in determining the fact. The natural song of this thrush is so near an approach to the cries of many animals, and even the voice of man, and so many changes are rung by different individuals or by the same at different times, that it is not easy to distinguish between what is native and what is acquired. I believe that he is a born mimic, as well as somewhat of a joker.

His notes are exceedingly joyous and playful, and full of a sort of contemptuous triumph, as though he sought to flout the rest of the world. May is his nuptial month, and it is at this period he most delights us with his varied melody and wild song. The nesting is done in some low, sweet copse, hidden closely from the eye of man, but he lauds himself in the full sight of day. In the early morning and evening particularly he makes the grove vocal, and drowns the song of other birds. Mounting the topmost spray of the tallest tree in the vicinity of his lowly home, he glances proudly around, and pours out his feelings in a strain somewhat like this,—" chick, chick, chick, —look here, look here! wheu . . . . u,—what, what, you did, you did,—tewee, tewee, (a soft treble)—where, where, where! whi-r-r-e-e, (a whistle)—wh-i-r-r . . . . up. See here, see here,—ho! who are ye? who are ye?"

Going out one morning at sunrise I was greeted in this manner: "What, what! Up so early? up so early! Whew! ha, ha, ha, ha,—go to bed again—to bed again. You will? you will? ha, ha, wh-e-w!" All the while I could not catch sight of the saucy rascal, who from a lofty, but leafy tree top thus jeered over my head at lazy man, who spends in sluggard slumber those precious hours of early day which are the very carnival time of these happy songsters.

This kind of rhapsody is continued many minutes—sometimes a full half hour—at a stretch. Then he quits, only to find a new station and renew his wild refrain. As soon as the young are hatched the cares of family are a sad drawback to his gayety; superseded, perhaps, by a deeper joy. At least his glad strains are heard at long intervals, and are only feebly renewed until the next nuptial season. But even this short season of song establishes for this mock-bird of the North a place in our homage second to no other of our American choristers. He is more than the rival of the Southern mocking-bird.

During the summer he is a frequent visitor to my lawn, on the lookout for worms. Here he hops about, almost as familiarly as the robins, contrasting with their plump, well-to-do, cheery air his more slender and graceful figure and quaker suit of sober brown. Though easily tamed, he loses taste for his ambitious performances when caged. The Southern bird, on the contrary, is very socially inclined, whether he be free or caged, and has a natural tendency to domestication.

I will barely mention one other bird which is named among our mockers—the cat-bird (*Orpheus carolinensis*). Aside from its harsh *mew* and other discordant notes, it has a peculiarly sweet, low song of its own, which few who note its harsh cry are aware of.

Birds, unfortunately, have often found their worst enemy in man, though it is to be hoped that time has nearly gone by. Game laws are now common in most of the States, regulating by legal enactment the seasons when, and the kinds of birds that may be killed for food or sport. At last, Michigan has gone further still in the right direction, by a law which prohibits *at all times* the destruction of "song birds." If all cultivators of the soil, as well as all lovers of birds, will be convinced of the wisdom of this law and will see it enforced, we shall soon have full light on the mooted question, how far the little plunderers of our grain and fruits are our real friends. In this matter the Germans have shown much practical wisdom, their laws affording protection to nearly all the species of birds common to that country, and leaving no useful bird outlawed.

Almost all birds are known to be insectivorous, and in by far the larger number their chief food is animal and not vegetable. If the records of those investigators who pretend to accurate computations of the amount that birds consume are reliable, it is almost incredible the number of insect pests which are thus got rid of. It defies calculation. We have statements like these: A family of jays, with five young, requires for its commissariat, in a season of one hundred days, 20,000 insects; 'Bradley, an English writer, mentions watching a nest of birds and discovering that 500 caterpillars were consumed in one day;' the titmouse or chicadee is computed to destroy over 200,000 eggs alone of noxious insects in a year.

Birds get at insects that man, with all his arts of destruction, cannot reach; on the topmost boughs—the under side of leaves—in the crevices of bark—within the tree itself—beneath the surface of the soil. If those who kill birds that they chance to find in their grain fields or fruit gardens will examine their crops, it will generally be found that worms, insects and larvæ constitute the principal contents, greatly predominating over the vegetable portions. With few exceptions the young of all birds are fed with this kind of animal food. Robins and thrushes, who make so free with some of our fruits, certainly do not make these their chief food even at such times. The whole summer long they are busily consuming our insect foes, and when we see them upon our lawns they are always diligently occupied in searching for and tugging at the worms which infest the roots of grasses.

Dr. Trimble has devoted an active life to the discovery

of the means of getting rid of the curculios and other insects that are so destructive to fruits. Hear what he says of the cedar-bird, that persistent plunderer of our finest cherries, and who receives no mercy at the hands of fruit lovers. "The cedar-bird, though it is a great consumer of cherries and berries, feeds as freely on insects. Canker-worms, beetles and other insects, injurious to the foliage of fruit and shade trees, are devoured in vast numbers by these birds. I have found as many as thirty-six young canker-worms in the stomach of one, and I have known companies of these birds come after a species of canker-worm on a cherry tree several times every day for two weeks during the last summer; and when I saw them afterwards feeding upon the cherries, I felt that they had saved the crop and were entitled to a part of it."

But while our song birds sometimes receive legal protection against wholesale slaughter, other kinds, which do not come under that appellation, are left without the pale. The popular voice condemns the crow and the blackbird. Legislatures have even offered rewards for their destruction, together with woodpeckers and other birds that are generally supposed to be injurious to the crops; and the whole family of hawks find in man a most inveterate enemy. This discrimination is hardly fair to the poor beings that suffer from it, and its wisdom is at least very doubtful.

The food of these, as of most birds, is almost exclusively animal. Naturalists who have studied the habits and examined the stomachs and crops, speak in their favor, as the friends rather than the enemies of man,—even those most proscribed by him. They are proved to be more destructive to the pests of the planter than to his fruits and seeds. Their structure, too, confirms this judgment. I think it a safe *rule* that birds of all kinds are of greater benefit than injury to man, and are entitled to his protection, until experience shall have conclusively shown the contrary.

Audubon defends the crow, which, he says, " devours myriads of grubs every day in the year, that might lay waste the farmer's fields ; it destroys quadrupeds innumerable, every one of which is an enemy to his poultry and his flocks. "

Insects have been found to increase in proportion as birds have been proscribed by public opinion and by law ; so that, in some instances, counter legislation has become necessary. This was the case with the rook in England —a bird whose habits resemble those of our crow. Now he enjoys protection from the law, and is everywhere the welcome guest of the people. Let such as condemn the birds which they sometimes see eating their corn or fruits, read " The Birds of Killingworth." Longfellow's poem is no mere poetic fiction, but illustrates a truth which will soon come home to all who, in the spirit of the old Spaniards, cut down their trees, because they harbored the birds that consume their grain. Even in this country, and near home, we have had examples of this kind of wisdom. I trust to see Michigan— already in many things in the van of public opinion—so amend her law as to include under its protection all the birds that now suffer unjustly from its real or implied proscription. But still more, I trust to the advance of an enlightened public opinion, and therefore throw in my mite towards a just decision.

In our plea for the birds shall we make an exception of the European sparrow? Imported into New York City some twenty-five years ago, it is said they cleared the trees in the parks of caterpillars that had long greatly infested them. I have felt disposed to question the fact, from my observations here. They had full opportunity to do the same service to my linden trees, but did not. They must have found America a congenial home, for they have spread with wonderful rapidity, until now few parts of the country are without them. Wherever these saucy little fellows appear they take undisputed possession, driving out other birds, and asserting their superior claims with mettlesome vivacity. They enliven the city streets with their pert ways. They would leave the farmer no grain to harvest, if it were not that they prefer city life to country. No one seems to know whether they have any good to balance their evil qualities, and public opinion universally condemns them. I am happily able to give one recent and notable instance of their insectivorous habit. During the year 1885, the seventeen-year locusts made their appearance in some of their old haunts, and, among other places, in the vicinity of Washington. A scientific gentleman there watched the proceedings of the sparrows. He saw that they devoured the insects voraciously, and at first whole. After awhile, finding the supply so considerable, they satisfied themselves with the bodies only, rejecting the wings and legs. But the numbers being great and the birds satiated, they began to content themselves with the heads only. In this way they succeeded in clearing the whole district of a pest that certainly would have proved a much more formidable enemy than its destroyers.

Much as we see of the birds, and many as are the beautiful things told about them by such admirers as Audubon, Wilson, and a host of lesser lovers, there is still enough that is unknown in their history to arouse the interest of fresh observers. Could we, like Prince Ahmed, of the fairy tale, understand the language of these beings of the air, how much would their song and twitter convey to us of the hidden mysteries of their lives!

We know little about their courtships, the tender communications of the married and the parental pair, perhaps of their lovers' quarrels. For, though patterns of conjugal fidelity, there are exceptions to the rule, and known instances of jealousy and of unfaithfulness. Have they Caudles among them too? How do they decide in selecting sites for their nests? We know that many days of anxious search and inquiry are often consumed in this business, and that individuals of the same species do not follow an unvarying instinct. Which of the lovers yields to the other, when there is difference of opinion? We will presume that the gallantry of the husband abandons the decision to his chosen mate, else why are these questions so readily settled and with so little debate? Does the married pair continue faithful to their early love, during all the seasons that follow, and do they always return—we know many do—to the same nests? How are their deliberations conducted and decisions arrived at, when, contemplating their long journeys, they hold council together? What unknown law or instinct regulates these migrations, and "guides through the pathless air their certain flight?" Have they a correcter prescience than we, wise men, of the future, of coming storms, of earlier or later renewals of the spring? Will they not some time impart to us this secret and important knowledge?

It may be that man is debarred from this kind of insight until he shall return to the innocence of that happy era of which the poet tells us:

> "When time was young,
> And birds conversed as well as sung;"

when their conversation—he means to say—was understood by human ears; for even now they talk, and very volubly, with each other. And even now we are on the road to a more perfect knowledge, and have learned enough of their language and ways to stimulate further inquiries and keep alive enthusiasm.

It is wonderful how easily most birds may be tamed. Whether or not those about my home, protected by the law of the place, acknowledge more emphatically the fact that they have here a safe asylum, certain it is that they are very fearless and almost domesticated. Cherries and favorite fruits suffer more, in consequence, but such thefts are richly compensated by the crowd of songsters that charm us with their thousand winning ways.

Even old birds are easily caught, and it is almost a daily occurrence, during the breeding season, that half-fledged youngsters are brought into the house by some of the family, fed and nursed for a few days, and sent forth into their own world again. Almost any young bird will scarcely make the attempt to escape after being held a few minutes in the hand, his feathers stroked, and food given him. A five-minutes petting makes him one of us. The old birds are naturally more wary, but let suspicion once be removed, and they are readily brought to recognize human kindness.

A male of that shy family, the cherry-bird, was captured in my grounds, on the very scene of his pilferings. It was found that he had been wounded, though slightly, yet in such a manner that one wing had become glued to his side by the dried gore, and was useless. He was taken in charge by a lady of the household, bathed with warm water, and fed with a few worms. He was at once reconciled to his captor, ate ravenously the congenial food, sipped water from his nurse's mouth, and sat upon her finger, as familiarly as if they had been acquainted for months, instead of minutes.

The result of this kind and brief attention exhibits in a remarkable manner the readiness with which gratitude may be awakened in the bird breast. The lady friend after her nursing care, took him to the balcony of an open window where the sun was shining, to dry his drenched feathers. Here she began tossing him on her finger and fluttering his wings. The impulse of his suddenly regained powers of flight was too strong to be resisted, and the bird made speedy use of his wings to fly to a neighboring tree. There he sat a few moments, trimming himself; then, as if conscious of the French leave he had taken, he flew back to his protector, alighted on her shoulder, and put his beak to her face, as if in penitence for his forgetfulness; but upon her attempting to enter the house, he again made his adieu and disappeared. But gratitude was not yet expended. The next day, as his nurse stood in the window, he came and alighted on the balcony, almost within reach, but he would not permit nearer approach; his old wariness was returning, and on the attempt being made to capture him, took his departure and was seen no more.

Every one loves the birds, but it is only one who truly loves and revels in country pleasures that appreciates to the full this source of enjoyment. Birds are the earliest acquaintances that greet us in the spring, when no feeling heart can resist their nuptial notes of gladness. They continue to haunt our homes, and flit about our gardens and copses, still uttering their songs, in somewhat soberer strains, during the long days of summer; and some remain to cheer that bleak season, when so much of nature is dormant, becoming more familiar with us as they more need our care.

Wherever heard or seen, they communicate to our bosoms the joy which inspires their songs, and they teach us heedful lessons of conjugal love and domestic felicity. How large a share indeed of the charm of rural life is due to the birds!

FOUR-FOOTED INHABITANTS.

"Himself to Nature's heart so near
That all her voices in his ear
Of beast or bird had meanings clear."
                                        WHITTIER.

"I think every family should have a dog (or a cat or a parrot); it is like having a perpetual baby; it is the plaything and crony of the whole house. It keeps them all young."—Dr. JOHN BROWN.

FOUR-FOOTED INHABITANTS.

SPRINGWELLS, ——, 1851.

DEAR TOM :—I am not a naturalist, but am by no means indifferent to the brute creation around me, and such facts and observations as I have garnered, in this my distant home, are heartily at your service.

Beasts of prey have been far from numerous in this neighborhood for many years. Yet we hear occasionally of their depredations. There are in this county swamps which are the resort of bears, and from which they sometimes emerge upon the settlements, stealing a pig or two.

The Detroit journals once in a while give, for the morning entertainment of their readers, accounts of the marauding exploits of these animals, within five or six miles of the city.

In 1839, during a night which I passed at the village of New Port, on St. Clair River, several bears visited the place, their tracks being plainly visible in the streets the next morning. They are still quite common about the remoter settlements.

While encamped in the woods of Michigan, at many places I have heard "the wolf's long howl," but never caught a sight of the "varmints." Large bounties offered by most of the counties for their scalps have so reduced their numbers, that, except in the extreme settlements, we seldom hear of any depredations committed by them. Sheep in the vicinity of our towns suffer more from dogs than from their wilder cousins.

Another of the disturbing cries of the remoter forests is that of the lynx. It is so like the voice of a man that I have been deceived by it, while following a newly blazed township line, and made frequent rests, answering back, under the impression that some man had lost his way, and was endeavoring to overtake me. The animal was indeed following our trail, stopping and uttering his cries at each pausing place, attracted probably by the scent of the provender we carried in our knapsacks.

Such fierce brutes as panthers and catamounts are but little known in Michigan, even in the wilder portions of the upper peninsula. As to still fiercer brutes, every schoolboy knows that the poet Campbell had no zoological authority for his line:

"On Erie's banks where *tigers* steal along."

Unless *panthers* were intended, this is rather a strain even upon the poetic license.

In my experience of many nights passed in the solitudes of Lake Superior, my camp was never disturbed by the presence of wild animals, nor suffered from their thefts; which is more than I can say for the lords of creation, white or red.

In the fall of 1850, while at Yankee-Springs, in Barry Co., a hunter brought into the village a wild-cat which he had just shot. It measured three feet from snout to end of tail! The animal measured in height, standing, eighteen inches. Color of back a dark gray; belly and thighs spotted, like a lynx. Its resemblance to the domestic cat is most striking, particularly in the face, but the tail of the wild animal is very dissimilar, being only three inches in length. The man said he shot it on the openings, a mile from the village; that being intent upon a deer, he at first supposed the catamount to be a rabbit. The cat was hunting mice, and was equally oblivious of the man's presence.

The wolverene, which has given a pseudonym to the inhabitants of Michigan, might on that account be supposed to abound in the State. But the fact is, the animal is extremely rare. It may have been, and probably was, once numerous, since the beaver and muskrat, which are its prey, abounded in our rivers and marshes.

Not long ago I saw the stuffed skin of a wolverene at a fur store in Detroit. It was considered a great curiosity, on account of the rarity of this fierce quadruped. Some of the oldest inhabitants, even that old fur-trader, James Abbott, had never before seen one. This skin, which was brought from Lake Superior, measured, from snout to extremity of tail, 3 feet 10 inches; the tail being about 8 inches and very bushy. The hair is coarse, but long and brushy, like that of a bear. Indeed, the resemblance to that animal is quite close in some particulars. Its color is mottled brown and black, with a patch of white under throat and breast. The claws are long, sharp, and much hooked, the legs stout and hairy down to the claws, like those of a bear, and the hind feet, like the bear's, are plantigrade. The snout appears to be long and tapering, but from the imperfect manner in which this specimen was preserved, this feature could not be accurately determined. I have been told by an Indian that it climbs trees as the bear does, which from the similarity of its structure seems probable.

Though not large, this beast is very formidable; its great strength and ferocity making it a terror to animals larger than itself. It is known to the French voyageurs as the *carcajou*,—probably a corruption of its Indian name.

Among predatory animals, the fox had not been entirely extirpated from these parts at the time of my first residence. I saw in 1836, in the sandy lands at Springwells, several fox holes, and could hear the bark of the inmates, but sly Reynard kept himself concealed. The holes were a curiosity, being large enough almost to admit a man, and running to a considerable distance, judging from the large heaps of sand collected about the mouth. Master John, one of my young neighbors, who showed them to me, thinks they all terminate in an extensive apartment,—the social parlor of the clan.

Quite recently a red fox established a hiding-place under the portico of my house, from whence he made sundry destructive raids into the hen-roosts.

Among the rarest of animals sought for their fur is the silver-gray fox. Its skin commands a high price, and is said to be particularly esteemed by the nobility of Russia. I saw recently the skin of one of those foxes, caught in Michigan. Its gray fur is tipped or, as it were, frosted with white, like frozen vapor, an appearance both unique and beautiful.

Of the smaller animals that make inroads upon our poultry, the skunk is one of the most numerous and troublesome. It is by no means so cunning as the fox, and if found at a distance from its retreat is easily killed. I will not say *caught*, for direful consequences frequently attend even the operation of killing. Without seeking them, the inmates of the mansion have but too often an all-pervading notice of their presence near the premises. The house dog sometimes encounters one, and in consequence his approach to the family must be tabooed for several days. The horses not unfrequently come from the stable strongly redolent of a perfume which is neither musk nor ottar of roses.

But they are a beautiful animal, and might be pardoned the moral pollution of their thieving habits if they would refrain from tainting the physical atmosphere. I once came upon a family of young ones, which had crept out of a hole beneath an out-house. They were mostly white, and playful as kittens, rolling themselves together in such a complicated way, that, like the Dutchman's frisky pig, it was impossible to count them. Although the fur is coarse, I once received from an Indian a tobacco-pouch made of the skin of this creature, which was deservedly prized for its beauty. I have been told of Frenchmen who domesticate the animal, as they do a cat, in their household, and who know how to extract the odorous sack.

These are among our pests. I am pleased, on the contrary, with the presence of those little depredators, the squirrels, and will not allow them to be shot—if I can help it—on my grounds. One of the pleasures of the country consists in watching the habits of animals, and the squirrel tribe is so lively and graceful, that his winning ways atone for all his petty thefts from the field and corn-crib. Gladly would I domesticate him—a not difficult task—if dogs, boys and guns could be kept at a respectful distance. He shall be free, so long as I have sway, to come and go, to hibernate on my premises, to glean the nut trees, and of course to lay up stores of acorns.

But though dogs may be taught to respect these wards of their master, not so the cat. A colony of the little red squirrel, which had become quite tame, and amused us with their lively gambols from tree to tree, just in front of the house, were all murdered by a mere kitten,—a famous mouser and bird-catcher, who in turn suffered the penalty, but only too late.

The little red squirrel is the most abundant, but we are visited also by the larger gray-and-black species, and the fox squirrel. All these would become frequent and well-contented visitors in my grounds if they could be protected from lawless sportsmen.

It is only in recent years that the *flying* squirrel has come to my knowledge as an inhabitant of my premises.

My first discovery connected with them was the finding of several holes in a poplar tree, about fifteen feet from the ground, and seeing a small animal issue from one. Each of these holes was about an inch diameter, and as exactly circular as if smoothly bored with an auger.

Running to the top of the tree the creature made a spring into the air, and spreading its webs,—which are wings in the same sense as a bat's,—reached another tree fully a hundred feet distant. Its flight was not horizontal, but in a descending line, which bore it to the tree at only a few feet above the ground. The animal does not merely spread its membranous sides, but has a balancing motion, like that of birds sailing through the air, which no doubt greatly assists to sustain it, and its progress may fairly be called a flight. It evidently has some command of its *wings*, beyond that of a mere parachute, for I observed that when a few feet from the tree, instead of continuing its direct course, which would have carried it to the ground, it changed the direction to that of an upward curve, alighting on the tree.

About two years ago I fixed up a bird-house in a small tree, where it was sharply contended for, and finally taken possession of by a pair of bluebirds. After the first year I observed that birds no longer frequented it, and on getting up to investigate, out rushed a flying squirrel, which immediately, as is its wont, ascended the highest branch, and thence took flight. This adoption of an abode so near my own would have been a very pleasing incident, but for the fact that these little animals seldom make their appearance by day, coming out only after nightfall, so that their acquaintance is rare and unsatisfactory.

I have discovered one other nut-collector in our neighborhood. While chopping one winter day in the woods, I found in a hollow tree a nest of deer-mice. They were snugly housed in various soft materials, and had an entrance just large enough for their purpose, at the height of two feet from the ground. It was small enough to exclude their enemies, the black squirrels, who—the thieving rogues—I very much fear help to maintain themselves during the winter by depredating upon their weaker neighbors. Cruel as we may sometimes deem it, the law of the strongest is nature's law:

> "——the simple plan,
> That he should take who has the power,
> And he should keep who can."

In the wild state, almost universally, one half of life is spent in providing for self-gratification, and the other in self-preservation against natural enemies.

Just over this nest were found two quarts of peeled acorns, with a large quantity of beach-nuts and seeds. These little creatures, it seems, by no means lie dormant through the long, cold winter. They are a harmless animal, never found except in the forest.

The American deer formerly abounded in these parts,

and is still hunted and killed in considerable numbers not many miles from the city. Settlements have now excluded them from this vicinity. In the early days of my residence here it was not an uncommon thing to find them in the woods that bordered the clearings, within sight of the dwellings along the river road. I have seen one in full day making his way down a lane which led from the woods to a pond on my farm, probably attracted by the water. He had almost reached it, when, catching sight of my terrible self, he turned and bounded back to his covert. I was reminded of Campbell's description, in "Gertrude of Wyoming":

"The wild deer arched his neck from glades, and then
He sought his woods and wilderness again."

In my first drive through the oak-openings of our peninsula, which I recall with infinite delight, frequent glimpses of deer were caught, through the open park-like timber. Sometimes they would come out and stand in the road, curiosity for awhile overcoming their natural timidity.

During my horseback rides it has several times happened that I came upon deer standing with the cattle, near a farmer's homestead. They seem to have no fear of these domesticated animals, nor of the horse, and they evidently did not notice the rider, until close upon them, when they instantly turned and fled. That 'the fear and the dread of man' has been impressed 'upon every beast of the field' since the days of Adam is no compliment to man. It would not have been so, but for the discovery of his duplicity and cunning.

The deer is so readily domesticated that it would be easy to stock every farm or gentleman's grounds with them, as is so largely done in Europe. But a gamekeeper would be necessary, and so near as this is to a considerable city, the case is difficult. I made the experiment with several that had been reared from fawns, two of which were with me for two years, and until the buck's horns had sprouted several inches. They roamed at large through a woodland pasture of some 20 acres. This was enclosed by a six-foot picket fence, with a light wire railing next the grounds, and provided in winter with a warm shelter for the night. But boys or men, dogs and guns, caused the loss of all of them, much to the regret of the children, for they become very tame, and delight to be petted. The bucks are sometimes saucy, and a little dangerous to timid children. They will not attack a courageous boy, but beat down and strike with their hoofs one who runs from them.

I must mention that one of the deer, frightened out of the enclosure, which they could jump in a moment of terror, swam the river,—a mile to the Canadian shore,—whence he was returned to me, after a long time.

In woods frequented by deer, it is quite common to find their horns, which are shed every year. These have been found pierced through the trunks of trees. I have several times seen sections of trees preserved as curiosities, in which the horn appeared with its root on one side and the tip projecting on the other. It is commonly believed that the animal has forcibly driven this weapon through the wood. Such a feat is impossible. The probability is, that, in the effort to disencumber himself of his horns, the buck rubbed them so hard against a sapling as to break through the bark, and wedge the tree firmly between the antlers. These remain fixed, and the wood grows over them.

Sometimes the antlers of two deer are found interlocked. I have seen a pair so firmly wedged together that they could not be separated. In this situation they were found in the forest, with the skeletons of their owners. Either in play or fight they had intertwined their horns, and unable to part them had thus perished. Probably they were engaged in fierce combat. And what a weird thought, that a blow aimed in mutual hate should have linked two foes together, and made them in their unhappy fate inseparable.

Elks and moose deer are still found in the northern and little settled portions of our lower peninsula, where I have seen the tracks of both, and procured the meat of the former, which I thought superior to venison.

A few years ago, an unusual spectacle appeared in our city streets: a fine male elk, harnessed to a sleigh, and drawing two men. His owner was a farmer near Detroit. The poor animal seemed to submit very unwillingly to this slavery, and panted much after a drive of four miles.

The same day a Mormon exhibited here, from Salt Lake, two female elks. They were beautiful animals, and though bearing a general resemblance to the red deer, had a camel-like crook to the neck, and were quite shaggy. Their color was gray, with light cream-colored rumps; tail very short; the head beautiful, with fine pointed nose, and lively, good-natured eyes, very black.

Of the small and common fur-bearing animals, the muskrat still remains with us in considerable numbers, making every season his house of reeds and mud in my pond and in the marshes which margin the river, at and about the mouth of the Rouge. When the winter frosts have cut down the rushes and wild rice, these houses become very picturesque objects, rising several feet above the water, and looking like hay-cocks.

That ingenious animal, the beaver, once so numerous in this part of the country, is exterminated. But he has left many traces of his former labors in the beaver-dams, still visible about the interior marshes, and in which the logs and sticks that composed their foundation are still to be found, deeply covered with soil. Though I have never met with the living animal, I have several times seen trees that had been recently cut down by them, along our Northern streams. The marks show that quite large chips were cut out by their powerful teeth, and the stump is left with a cone-shaped top.

Truly Yours.

SPRINGWELLS.

DEAR TOM:—Perhaps it will interest you if I follow up my epistle of last week with an equally voluminous one on the traits of domestic animals. These are a source of great amusement to me, in town or country. But in the latter, as there is more freedom, opportunities for observing them are greater.

Everybody in the country keeps one or more dogs. Every Canuck, it is well known, keeps five. The first which acknowledged me master was of the "bull" variety and aptly named *Veto*. He received his cognomen with his puppyhood, about the time of President Jackson's famous bank veto, but he earned it afterwards by his Jacksonian qualities and boldness in my service.

For several years my farm was greatly pestered with ponies of the little Canadian breed, owned by some of my neighbors, but running at large. These were branded with their owner's initials or mark, which was all the evidence of ownership ever exhibited, until they were transferred by sale into other hands. They received no care whatever, were neither housed nor fed through the long, cold winters, but browsed and foraged for themselves, and contrived to "make by hook or crook a decent living."

Of course there were many days when they must either starve or steal, and as no merely lawful fence could restrain the strongest ones, they lived by depredation. Most of the land of their owners was still in a state of nature. Mine had a more extended cultivation, stretching back a long distance between woods belonging to my neighbors. To keep out these marauders was practically impossible. To impound them, or take the law in the case, was difficult and costly, and besides brought on disagreeable quarrels. Yet a tame acquiescence in the injury could not be thought of.

These ponies would scour along the road, and down the lane, like a troop of fiends, making night hideous, break down my fences, visit my barn and stacks, and paw up my grass, which they bit to the very roots. Going forth in the morning I would find a troop of horse in possession.

In this extremity, Veto stood me in good stead. He was large and powerful. He would seize a horse by the nose, and maintain his grip until the terrified animal was fairly out of the pasture and thrown to the ground. I have known a powerful horse leap a fence, with the dog hanging to his nose by the teeth, and refusing to let go his hold. Cattle sometimes entered the field by the gap which the horses had made. These Veto would seize, sometimes by the tail, and suffer himself to be dragged to the extremity of the enclosure.

One of my own cows once came near being the victim of his fierce attacks. Her face had by some means become plastered with mud, and as she was entering the open gate with the others, at nightfall, was not recognized by the watchful dog. He sprang furiously forward and was on the point of seizing her by the nose, when he discovered the mistake. It was curious to see his look of mortification as he slunk away, ashamed of having committed such a blunder.

Having attempted in vain to procure a law passed at town-meeting, restraining horses from being free commoners,—this Canadian custom being even yet too strong for modern innovation,—I became at times sufficiently exasperated to use my gun, and sting the robbers with fine shot. One day I was going to the woods, my gun loaded by chance with buckshot. Finding the meadow full of ponies, now grown so prudent as to keep well out of range of dog and small shot, I was tempted to fire at a white mare, who with her colt was a chief sinner. Both were touched pretty severely. On my return the colt was found dead, and the dam, tamed by her loss, stood mourning over him, and permitted my approach. Though I had convinced myself that the act was justifiable, on witnessing the result I felt it to be cruel. It was indeed piteous to witness the affection of the mother, herself wounded, and moaning over her offspring. I felt the pity of mutilating these fine animals, who are not to blame for the neglect of their owners. I could not repeat the harsh remedy.

Early one January morning, I found my farmer driving ponies out of the meadow, and resolved to secure some of them, with intent to advertise and claim damages. This was no easy matter. With the assistance of a third person we drove them into a smaller enclosure, where we noosed four by the feet, and secured them with rope halters. One, known to be the property of my next neighbor, was turned over to him. Two were black mares, and had to be halter-broken. They were mastered after some obstinate resistance. The remaining one was a fine young horse, full of fire and strength, that had never felt curb or halter. It may be supposed that he was not inclined to surrender. Driving him close to the fence, and there tying him by his noosed foot, we contrived to fasten a rope to his head. With these double means of restraint, four persons now undertook his conquest. His eyes flashed, and his nostrils dilated with fear. With sudden impulse he would bound almost away from our grasp. At last, exhausted with exertion and terror, he was dragged to the stable.

My triumph seemed complete, when the neighbor whose property I had suffered to escape came over on a tour of observation. He informed me that the spirited young animal was his property, the other two that of another French neighbor. Rubbing up the long hair, brands were discernible. He informed me further, being himself one of the appraisers, that my fence, though of extraordinary height and strength, did not conform, in some of the numerous requirements, to the fence law. So, fearful of a flaw in my case, and averse to altercation with neighbors, I gave the captured animals release. The remedial project consumed the day, the only profit being the sport which the occasion afforded.

Veto at length came to a violent end. After recovering from repeated shot wounds, doubtless revengefully inflicted, he at last succumbed, under the combined effects of wounds and poison.

"Doters upon dogs" would be delighted with *Medoc*, a dog purchased for me by a friend at Mackinac. He is of the breed much employed by the French at that place for draught purposes. On being admitted to my household he was deaf to all language addressed to him except French, but was obedient to orders delivered in the tongue with which he was familiar. A wagon and harness had been constructed with which he goes to market, drawing home the articles purchased. He has drawn in this way a barrel of flour from the store. When the load is heavy he does not refuse to pull, nor become cross and sullen, like uneducated dogs, but buckles down to the task like a well-bred draught horse, pulling stoutly over the hard places, and doing his utmost. He is of medium size only, not very stoutly built, of pure white, and has a tail not more than an inch long, the size natural to that breed.

A friend of mine is owner of a dog named *Dash*, noted not only for his precipitancy, but for a very capacious mouth. Of this open feature sundry anecdotes are related, not less curious than true, in convincing proof of which I submit the following:

This capacious mouth was twice put to singular use. A mouse had taken refuge in a closet, and Dash being called, soon cornered the varmint, and made at him so fiercely, with distended jaws, that the poor terrified creature, seeing no chance of escape, or mistaking the wide open mouth for a hole of refuge, or perhaps resorting to stratagem—if we may credit so much sagacity to a sorry mouse—leaped into the living sepulchre. Snap went the jaws: the prey was securely entrapped. But those prison doors could not remain long shut, and when they again opened, the mouse, seizing the opportunity, made good his escape.

On the other occasion referred to, a mouse had made his way into the store-chest of a boat, and the like refuge presenting itself, it leaped in, as did the other. But on this occasion the little animal, not discovering the nature of the trap, made its way directly down the dog's throat. No "presto change" ever created greater astonishment than did this sudden annihilation. Dash was not equal to the solving of the riddle, and his look of bewilderment, as he sought everywhere for the vanished game, was very amusing.

Another instance of the valuable purpose that a dog's capacious jaws subserved has come to my knowledge, although it did not occur under my own observation. It was told me on the best authority, and is a striking instance of the sagacity and devotion to his master's interests of the faithful animal whose actions I have been recording.

A family in C., New York State, kept a fine mastiff and a canary bird. One day the latter escaped from its cage, and, the window being open, flew out, and perched upon a shed in the rear of the house. Every effort was made by members of the family to secure the fugitive. He would not be caught, nor would he be enticed by food to enter his cage, nor by the artifice of a trap-cage and bird. After two days' useless efforts, the attempt was abandoned, and the bird given up for lost. In the evening of the second day, as the master was seated with friends in the parlor, the dog entered and approached him. By pressing against his legs he induced his master to notice him. The latter then rose from his seat, the dog continuing his demonstrations by leading towards the door.

Seeing that the animal was on an errand, the gentleman followed into another room, where hung the empty birdcage, towards which the dog's eyes and nose were directed. The master now perceived, for the first time, that something like a feather was sticking out of a corner of the creature's mouth. He took down the cage, and its door and the dog's mouth being opened simultaneously, out rushed the lost canary, from its new prison into the old one, uttering a loud and gleeful chirrup, which ended in a song the moment it reached the accustomed perch.

Before bringing this dog chat to an end, I must add a few parting words about one of the smallest of his kind, a little dwarfed specimen of a black-and-tan terrier, named *Pete*. We used to call him Melancholy Pete, for his misanthropic look and cynical disposition. Pete well understood his position as pet of the household, and considered the whole dignity of the family centred in his single small person. He became very angry when any meanly dressed person was admitted into the house, and if by chance such person came into the parlor his offended dignity drove him into the dark corner, from which he would not emerge for some time after the offending visitor had departed. The children amused themselves with his moroseness, pointing finger and making faces at him, which he resented with much surliness. He died finally of a broken heart, caused by the admission of another dog of the same species as a pet into the family. Poor sensitive Pete. How many ambitious lives, like thine, surrounded with every luxury, still fail of happiness!

After these "desultory dottings down upon dogs," you may be pleased with a few "cursory cogitations concerning cats."

I have to relate a singular incident illustrative of strong

natural affection in this much slandered animal. I must premise that at the time of the introduction of Medoc into the household, my domestic establishment was graced by two feline pets: Nora, a fine Angora cat, and her son Jose.

Medoc's disposition was by no means savage, but rather peaceable: but he could resent indignity. Nora, on the contrary, was fiercely hostile to the whole canine race, and would consent to no familiarity with them. Hitherto she had always succeeded in keeping every dog at a distance, and she commenced immediate war upon Medoc. His dogship at first submitted to her unfriendly demonstrations with exemplary patience, the only sign of resentment being a growl. Nora was implacable, and on a second occasion, when he entered her presence, flew at his face with her sharp claws. The dog, a little aroused, but still generous, seized her by the neck, and administered a gentle shake, by way of reproof. A third time puss repeated her offensive conduct, flying in his face, with the added insult of hissing and spitting at him. This was more than his wounded dignity could bear. "Three times and out" was Medoc's motto. He seized her in his strong jaws, but this time by the spine, and my beautiful Angora was dead in an instant.

Nora had shown great partiality to her son Jose, consenting for his sake, I believe, to the death of a recent litter, in order that her favorite of a year old might continue to nurse. Jose showed equal fondness. A grave was dug for the dead mother in the yard, where she was deposited with befitting solemnities, the kitten watching the proceeding. Jose then took possession of the grave, which no persuasion could induce him to quit. He refused all sustenance, was often seen scratching the earth, and was at length found dead upon the body of his mother,—an example of filial love very rare, and surpassing even that of a parent for its offspring.

I was afterwards possessor of a feline of the sterner sex, a fine large animal of pure white, who became a great favorite, and who was equally attached to me. He always came into the parlor to be petted or lie at my feet, when he heard my footsteps in the house, after out-door labor was over. During my temporary absences of several days, he would seize the occasion to absent himself on hunting expeditions, after ascertaining that I was not in the parlor at the usual time, but he always returned to greet me when I came back.

Tom would perform a number of tricks at my mandate, such as jumping through my arms, or over my head, and these he would do for no one else. One of his tricks was to feign death. At the word "die" he would lie perfectly still, and suffer himself to be lifted and carried about, like a defunct, for the amusement of the company.

This cat had a brother of the same breed, and both were trained hunters. Tom and Jerry usually hunted in couples. Stealing forth together, one would tree the game, or keep it at bay, while the other "went in" and secured it. This proceeding they would change about, so as to give each an equal opportunity of indulging in the pleasanter part of the performance.

Poor Tom died of an asthma. He was accustomed to be fed by one of the ladies of the family, to whom, next after myself, he was most attached. During his sickness he slept in her room, upon a bed prepared for him, and she alone administered his medicines. One day his nurse discovered him lying upon her own bed, and scolded him somewhat sharply. Tom immediately left her room, turning at the door and hissing, and would never again be induced to return, nor would he, in his peevish resentment, permit any further acts of kindness on the part of his former friend. He retired to a lonely room, where a few days afterwards he was found dead. Alas! loving, but too sensitive Tom!

Domestic animals—the dog, for instance—often exhibit a horror of music, but I can testify to a contrary taste in a cat.

My family had been frequently awakened in the night by the tones of a piano in measured cadence sounding, sometimes passing through all the notes of the gamut, from bass to treble. It was some time before this musical ghost was laid. This was effected by the discovery that the piano was sometimes carelessly left open, after the evening hymn, and that on these occasions puss improved her opportunity for practising. She did so by walking forwards and backwards over the keys, evidently greatly relishing the harmony,

"In linked sweetness long drawn out."

Powers of fascination have been ascribed to the cat, in common with the snake, but the fact has been disputed. I was witness to an occurrence which seemed to me confirmatory of its truth.

Sitting under my porch one day, my attention was attracted by an incessant chirping. I soon discovered a small bird, hopping continually from branch to branch of a tree, ten feet or more from the ground. Casting my eyes below they fell upon my domestic tabby, sitting composedly on the grass, and apparently not noticing the bird. I could not determine whether or not the chirp was a cry of distress, but the poor little bird seemed to be under some spell, for each time he hopped lower, and still lower, and at last down to the ground. In an instant puss sprang and seized upon the prize thus offered up, a voluntary victim.

Doubtless you, in common with many of my friends, some of whom I know to be lovers of pets, can relate anecdotes quite as curious as any of these. I record them as among the treasured recollections of early and happy days, amid quiet enjoyments and in rural pleasures passed.

Your true friend.

WILD ANIMALS OF MICHIGAN.

"When we discovered this vast continent it was full of wild beasts. A handful of Frenchmen has made them almost entirely disappear in less than an age, and there are some the species of which is entirely destroyed. They killed the elks and moose-deer merely for the pleasure of killing them, and to show their dexterity."—CHARLEVOIX, 1721.

WILD ANIMALS OF MICHIGAN.

TO render this subject more complete, I append to the foregoing letters some later and more systematic observations.

The diversity of climate of the United States affords to mammalian life a large range, compared with Europe. And in this respect no portion of our country of equal extent is more favorable than our peninsulas of mingled prairie, oak-openings and timbered lands, and giving the advantages of a softened lake climate on the south, with that of a more cold and broken country on the north.

Our existing mammalia include only three orders. *Rapacia*, *Rodentia* and *Ruminantia*, unless we may claim a *Marsupial*—the Opossum. This animal, I have been informed, once existed in or not far from this neighborhood, but I will not vouch for the fact.

With all our vast extent of sea-like waters, neither any of the whale kind (*Cetacæ*) nor of the seal kind (*Phocidæ*) visit our fresh-water seas.

Among the Carnivora, or Rapacia, in the family *Vespertilionidæ*, we have several species of Bats. But, excepting the common bat (*Vespertilio novaboracensis*) and the little brown bat (*V. subulatus*) I am not familiar with them.

The family *Sorecidæ*, or Shrews, which belongs both to the Old World and the New, has two species in Michigan, of the genus Sorex,—*S. platyrhinus* and *S. talpoides*.

The Moles, family *Talpidæ*, abound in every part of

North America. In our State, in genus Scalops, are the prairie mole (*S. argentatus*) and the common mole (*S. aquaticus*), that so persistently burrows beneath the sod and the walks, in pursuit of worms. Genus Condylura includes the star-nosed mole (*C. cristata*), which is more rare.

Of the family *Ursidæ* Michigan has, in common with the northern portion of the Union, the Black Bear, Racoon, Badger, and Wolverene; though these have all nearly disappeared from this neighborhood.

That bears had not all been exterminated from this part of the State down to a recent date is apparent from an item which appeared in the *Detroit Free Press*, in 1871.

A resident of Springwells, named Tyrell, brought into the city the skin of a bear, shot near Algonac, on St. Clair River, where he had been hunting, about which he had a story to tell.

Just at dark he had traced the animal into a swamp, but concluded to wait until morning before coming to close quarters. He had just made his way to dry land when two bears appeared on the ridge, two rods in front of him. Levelling his rifle he fired, and the next moment both animals were coming down upon him at full speed. There was no time for reloading. The hunter dropped his gun, and made for a scrub-oak, which he reached barely in time to swing himself by a limb out of reach. He worked his way through the thick branches, as high as the tree would bear him, about fifteen feet, and through the gloom could discern the bears snuffing at the base. One of them was not long in attempting a closer acquaintance, but on getting up half the distance to the hunter found his way impeded by the thick limbs, and dropped to the ground. Repeating his efforts, the hunter struck a match and dropped it on bruin's head, which frighted him back again. This trick was repeated at every fresh attempt of the animal to climb the tree, and was every time successful.

The animals ceased their efforts to climb, but remained so long pacing and growling around, that Tyrell did not dare to come down, but remained the entire night in his perilous and uncomfortable position, battling with the sleepy god. He says he would rather ride from Detroit to Buffalo, astride the walking-beam of a steam-boat, than do it again. When, stiff and sore, the next morning he ventured down, the welcome sight met his eye, of a bear lying dead, the blood on ground and leaves showing that he had bled to death. His companion was not visible. The hide was on exhibition for some time at the Central Depot.

The Wolverene (*Gulo luscus*), belonging to the family *Mustelidæ*, is now very rarely found. Michigan is about its southern limit. As this almost extinct animal has given to our State its slang name, some interest attaches to it which it would not otherwise possess. From his resemblance to the bear this animal has been placed by some authorities among the *Ursidæ*.

Having given some description of the wolverene in a preceding letter, I will only now add that considering his mischievous and destructive disposition, he looks quite meek. The head is almost sheep-like. Are we to infer that the people of the Wolverene State are very lamb-like to outward appearance, but very dangerous to meddle with?

In the same family we possess the Skunk, Mink, Marten, Fisher, and Weasel. I am not sure whether the

American Sable (*Mustela martes*) exists within our borders, but it is presumable that it once did so, its habitat being the wooded districts of this zone. It is a beautiful animal, and its extermination is due to the qualities of its fur, which is very highly valued.

Of the family *Lutidæ*, our northern waters still retain that sagacious animal, the Otter (*Lutra Canadensis*). Its fur, once valued next to that of the beaver, is now rare.

Some years ago Mr. L. B. Smith, of Detroit, purchased in Gratiot Co. a tame otter, of which I copy the following notice; " He was captured by an Indian when only about a week old, and has become as tame as a house-cat. He is of dark brown color, two feet in length from his nose to the tip of his tail, and lives principally on bread-and-milk and fresh meat, but whenever opportunity is given will catch fish, of which he is extremely fond. When sleeping (which he does the greater portion of the day), he lies curled up, with his tail between his fore paws and the extreme end in his mouth. The odd little creature has always exhibited a remarkable fondness for babies, and whenever brought into the presence of one is restless and intractable until permitted to fondle it, and no amount of coaxing can induce him to quit its presence. When grieved he sets up a shrill piping, not unlike that of a young chicken, but when particularly delighted emits a cachinatory sound, closely resembling the laugh of a human being. He has been taught to follow his master, and to perform several interesting tricks."

Of the *Canidæ*, or Dog family, are still found within the State the Wolf, gray and white (*Canis occidentalis*),—though in greatly reduced numbers,—also the black or dusky wolf, though the latter is very rare; we have also the common or Red Fox (*Vulpes fulvus*), and the Silver-gray Fox,—a rare variety.

The Detroit papers in 1871 gave accounts of the exploits of three Detroit hunters in the woods of Northern Michigan, bringing into town from Gladwin County among their trophies seventy-five wolf skins. These they captured by means of a wolf trap on a wholesale scale. It consisted of a two-story cabin, in the lower story of which, on two sides, were large doors, so constructed as to be drawn up and let down at the will of those above. For bait, old broken-down horses were used, as this kind of varmint likes its prey living.

When several wolves were thus decoyed into the house, the doors were let down and they were entrapped. Then by taking up a board in the floor the hunters were enabled to shoot the imprisoned animals. When this trick failed, a horse was tied to a tree in the woods, where the wolves, on coming to their prey, were exposed to their ambushed enemies. Generally one horse stood for eight wolves, before the poor beast finally gave up the ghost.

The *Free Press* of the previous year tells the story of a Canadian family coming to this city from Ottawa, and having in lieu of the family mastiff a large gray wolf. He was only half civilized, and so cross as to call for frequent beating from his owner. Whether or not this was the best way to civilize him may be doubted.

Belonging to the family *Felidæ* is the Panther (*Felis concolor*), under its various names of Cougar, American lion and Catamount. It is common to the whole of North America. In spite of its size, which exceeds that of the largest dog, and its big appellations, it is not at all a ferocious animal. The Lynx (*F. lyncus*) is also a timid animal.

Not so the Wild-cat (*F. rufus*), which is a hard and bold fighter, and an annoying depredator.

I give, again from the *Free Press* of 1871, the following account of a fight with wild-cats, which happened in Wayne County:

George B. Morris had on exhibition (Aug. 31, 1871) at the Campus Martius the paws of two wild-cats, and stated that he and two other farmers had a very exciting time in making their capture.

For three or four months farmers living in Brownstown and Huron townships had been very much annoyed by the two animals, who inhabited a swamp, or at least made it a place of refuge. The beasts had created considerable havoc among young lambs and sheep, and had been pursued many times by hunters, but always made their escape into the swamp. One evening, while a farmer named Mead was at the barn, one of the cats had the audacity to enter a hen-coop, not twenty feet from the door, and was not driven from her prey until Mead had wounded her with a pitchfork. Securing Morris and another neighbor, the three cleaned up their guns, and determined to devote a day to hunting down the troublesome visitant. They were under the impression at the time that it was a half-grown panther, Mead having never seen a wild-cat. At daylight the men mounted their horses, and rode to the swamp, having each a dog along. For several hours they beat about the place, without discovering any signs. At length one of the dogs, which had been prospecting in the swamp, set up a fearful yelling and howling, and came to the men with his back well scratched up. The other dogs made for the spot, and drove the cat out of the swamp, and up a tree, where she was despatched by a rifle shot. The farmers had no idea of the presence of another. They were seated under a tree, enjoying a cold bite, when a male cat, considerably larger than the one slain, came out of the swamp, and attacked a dog, which was lapping water at a small pond. In a second, hair was flying like thistledown in a gale, and the other dogs joined in. In two minutes, and while the men were picking up their guns and running to the spot, one of the dogs was disabled by the cat, and the other two refused to close in again, running around in a circle. As the men came up the cat leaped for Mead, fastening to his leg, and the sudden attack threw him down. He tried to shoot but could not, and for some time his friends found no safe opportunity. At length one of them knocked the beast over with his gun and then shot him through, as he was returning to the attack. After receiving the shot he was still a match for both dogs, until shot through the head. The brute which attacked Mead tore his boot-leg into strips with his hind claws, and he was so bitten and clawed about the legs as to be unable to work for some time. It would have been more than a match for him alone.

Of the *Rodentia*, many little animals of the squirrel tribe—family *Sciuridæ*—abound in Michigan. Among the number are the Fox Squirrel (*Sciurus cinerius*), the Gray—often nearly black—(*S. migratorius*), the Red or Chickaree (*S. Hudsonius*), the Striped or Chipmuck (*Tamias striatus*), the Flying Squirrel (*Pteromys volucella*), and the striped Gopher (*Spermophilus tridecemlineatus*). I do not remember having seen the latter in this neighborhood, but in great numbers on the prairies and openings in the south and west parts of the State.

The little red squirrel has a wide range, and is a migrant, sometimes marching in large bodies, and swimming the streams. I remember hearing, many years ago, of a large migrating band, which swam the Niagara, from Canada into the State of New York, many perishing in the transit. The object, of course, is larger supplies of food, but the instinct is a curious one.

A gentleman told me he was once on Lake George, in the State of New York, rowing alone in a boat, when he espied a squirrel paddling his way towards shore. The rower held out an oar, which the little fellow accepted, ran up it and the arm which held it, and sat on his shoulder. From this position he soon decamped to the bow of the boat, where he remained some time. At length, thinking himself sufficiently rested, he again took to the water, but finding he had miscalculated his strength, he a second time accepted the proffered aid, and remained in the boat until it neared the land, when he sprang ashore and made off.

In the family *Arctomidæ*, the Woodchuck, Ground-hog, or Marmot, as it is differently called, is the only burrowing and hibernating animal which I recall. It was formerly numerous hereabouts.

In the family *Garbillidæ*, we have the Deer-mouse, (*Mirone Americana*); in the *Castoridæ*, the Beaver (*Castor Canadensis*), of which I propose to give some extended notice, in a separate paper.

I will here mention that a gigantic fossil species of the beaver, several times the size of C. Canadensis, has been discovered in New York and Michigan, in lacustrine deposits.

To the family of the *Hystricidæ* belongs the Porcupine, an inoffensive creature, common in all the Northern States, and very easily captured, as he makes no resistance. I have killed one that appeared in my path by striking him with my geological hammer. The spines are much used by the northern Indians, for ornamenting a variety of articles manufactured by them, for which purposes they stain them permanently with several bright colors.

The family *Muridæ* includes that pest, the Rat, several species of which, including the large wharf or Norway rat, were introduced into this country, that has opened so wide its gates to all the world, good and bad.

The black rat I have never seen, and am not aware that it is an inhabitant here. The common mouse (*Mus musculus*) is also an immigrant, but there are several others that are native, as the Jumping Mouse, the Beaver Mouse, the small prairie, or oak-opening mouse (*Hesperomys Michiganiensis*), and two species of *Arvicola*, or field mice.

To this family also belongs the Muskrat or Musquash (*Fiber zibethicus*). This animal is still numerous in the marshes of the Rouge and elsewhere, but much less so than formerly. Its range is as wide as that of the beaver.

One other family only belonging to this order, viz., *Laponidæ*, is known to me, but it is a very common one. It includes the American Gray Rabbit (*Lepus manus*), also the White Rabbit or Northern Hare (*L. Americanus*), found in the Northern States only. Though known in common parlance as rabbits, these are truly hares, and differ essentially from the European rabbit. The latter is a gregarious animal, inhabiting warrens. Our hares do not burrow, but hide under brush or long grass, where they make what are called "forms."

Before proceeding to a mention of our existing native animals belonging to the order Ruminantia, or those possessing more than two hoofs, I will refer to the extinct animals, belonging to the Pachydermata.

The genus *Elephas* includes the fossil elephant (*E. primigenius*), whose molars are found in the Salt Licks of Kentucky; none in this State that I know of. The teeth and bones of a similar quadruped, the Mastodon (*E. maximus*), have been discovered in this State, both in the eastern and western counties. Though fossil, it belongs to a recent geological period,—the drift, or glacial,—and it was possibly contemporaneous with savage man. Manufactured arrow-heads are said to have been found beneath the skeleton of a mastodon, in Missouri. I know of no complete skeleton in this State, that has been preserved.

It is probable that the Bison or Buffalo was a former inhabitant here. For it is matter of proof that they once roamed as far as the Atlantic coast, south of the lakes. None now exist east of the Mississippi, and, immense as their numbers were but a few years ago on our western plains, so great and wanton is the destruction that they are likely to suffer extinction, even within the life of the present generation.

The family *Cervidæ* includes the American deer, common from Canada to the Gulf of Mexico, and from the Atlantic to the Rocky Mountains. Yet it was not known in our upper peninsula, on Lake Superior, as late as 1840, nor until driven northward by the persecution of hunters.

The American elk (*Cervus Canadensis*), known also as the Wapiti, was once very numerous in this State, but is fast being killed, and is already very rare. It is a noble animal, and quite easy of domestication, as the incident alluded to in the foregoing letter is in proof.

It measures from seven to ten feet in length, and six feet in height. According to Audubon, the American elk is a foot higher in the shoulders than the European stag. The antlers are wondrously large, each main branch often three feet long. A specimen of the animal in the museum of the Detroit Scientific Association is seven feet in length, and the tail ridiculously small, only two and one-half inches long. The antlers of this specimen have a spread, from tip to tip, of four and one-half feet. The color on the sides is a light gray, nearly white, but on neck, belly and extremities a dark tawny red. The tail of the deer is much larger, and is beneath of a pure white, which is always exhibited when they are on the run.

The fine elk above alluded to is the property of the Audubon Club, of Detroit. It was presented to the club by General Custer, who shot it on the Yellowstone in 1873, and prepared the skin with his own hands.

In a letter to his wife, speaking of several heads of antelopes and other wild animals which he had prepared, the General says: "The ne plus ultra of all is the 'King of the Forest.' I have succeeded in preserving him entire,—antlers, head, neck, body, legs and hoofs,—in fine condition, so that he can be mounted, and look *exactly as in life*. The scientists informed me that there were but few specimens on this continent of elk preserved entire, and none so fine as mine. Had I saved the head and neck only, it was intended for you; but having it complete alters my intention, as it would require a room to contain it. So I have concluded, with your approval, to present it to the Audubon Club, in Detroit."

Another singular animal belonging to this order, and of the same genus with the deer, and a native of this State, is now nearly if not quite exterminated—the Moose (*Alce Americanus*). It is very wary, and is seldom caught sight of except by professional hunters. In size it exceeds the elk. The antlers are quite different, being palmated. They spread four feet, and the palm has been know to be thirty inches wide. The tongue used to be considered as great a delicacy as beaver's tail.

The *Portage-Lake Gazette*, of April, 1869, contains an item, headed, "Killing of the last Moose in Michigan," which I transfer in full.

"In the year 1847 there was a famous herd of wild moose living in the woods around the head of L'Anse Bay, but finally the herd were entrapped and all killed except one old leader stag, who broke away. For a year or two nothing was seen of him, but finally there came rumor of a gigantic moose, roaming the woods around the head of Torch Lake. This winter some Indians determined to catch him, and finding his track, gave him several lively chases, but until a week ago he always escaped. Then a half-breed, Peter Marksman, got after him, and there being a thick crust on the snow, the man could move about easily, while the sharp hoofs of the veteran moose broke through at every leap. Peter finally overtook him near Calumet Mine, and quickly closed his career with a rifle ball. He skinned him, cut up the flesh, brought it to town, and found a ready sale at fifty cents a pound, realizing over $300. The head was cut off and brought in. It alone gives token of the monstrous size of the animal. It measures 33 inches from tip of nose to crown of head, between the antlers. The nose measured 28 inches around. The nostrils, distended, each measured four inches diameter, and a large hand could be pushed up into them over a foot! The front of the under jaw has eight large cutting teeth, which bit against a tough semi-horny pad in the upper jaw, which has no cutting teeth. The head cut off entirely from the neck, and minus the tongue, weighs 78 pounds. Unfortunately it was killed at the season of the year when the head is shorn of its greatest beauty—the enormous antlers. The new ones were just rising, still encased in the skin, only making protuberances of four or five inches."

One other Ungulate—the Caribou of the early French settlers—(*Rangifer caribou*) was at one time an inhabitant of the northern portion of our State, but is now quite extinguished within our limits. It still exists north of Lake Superior.

In a paper read before the Detroit Pioneer Society, in 1874, by J. S. Tibbets, on wild animals of Wayne County, I find mentioned, as those mostly found here by the early settlers, the deer, bear, wolf, lynx, wild-cat, coon, badger, fisher, porcupine, woodchuck, rabbit, mink and weasel. He says the skunk and rat did not make their appearance in the rural districts for nearly ten years after the first settlements were made; wolves and bears were very numerous, and destructive to the few sheep and swine then in the country. He names as old residents now exterminated the lynx, badger and porcupine.

Mr. Tibbets mentions several methods then in vogue of trapping those destructive animals, wolves and bears. They were caught in traps and in dead-falls. A large pen was made with poles, and so constructed that it was narrowed up at the top, leaving an opening only a few feet square. This afforded an easy ingress for the hungry wolf, but an effectual barrier to his getting out.

A novel mode of trapping the bear proved quite successful. A hollow tree was selected, into which a hole was cut, some seven or eight feet from the ground, of a triangular shape, with the acute angle on the lower side, just large enough for bruin to squeeze his head through. Inside of the tree, a little below the hole, a piece of meat was suspended. Scenting the meat the bear would climb the tree, and in his efforts to reach the bait would get caught in the angle of the hole, from which it was impossible to extricate himself.

Many interesting facts might be introduced regarding the *Trade in Furs* of the animals of this country. But in view of the fact that these have now to be sought at a great distance,—the business of the trapper being at this time far removed from this vicinity,—I forbear to extend these observations.

I cannot, however, omit to state that Detroit, from its very first settlement, in 1701, has been one of the most noted markets for the collecting and sale of furs in the whole country. The Abbotts, Conants, Macks, Brewsters and Campaus, of half a century ago and more, are still well represented by modern dealers. One firm in especial—that of F. Buhl & Co.—has been doing business here since 1835.

Notwithstanding the steady diminution of furred animals, the trade is still very large, and furs continue to be exported from here to all the countries of Europe.

THE BEAVER.

IT is many years since that extraordinary animal, the beaver, disappeared from this State; extraordinary both in the constructive skill displayed by him, and in the results of his labors.

The beaver may well be considered the cause of the settlement of Canada. For among the fur-bearing animals which were the object of French enterprise in the New World, the beaver was by far the chief. So large, indeed, was the proportion, and so great the numbers, that beaver-skins became the medium of exchange employed in the Indian traffic, the prices of goods being so many beavers. It was, in Canada and the North-west, the representative product, as in Virginia *tobacco* was the currency of the country. The figure of the beaver constituted the armorial bearing of Quebec, Montreal, and other of the chief cities of Canadian trade, and it is still prominent in the escutcheon of Canada. The seal of New Netherlands, in the seventeenth century, bore the figure of a beaver, as is the case yet with some of the countries of Northern Europe.

The vast numbers of this animal and the ease with which they were captured seem to us at this day incredible.

Captain John Smith, who traded at the Isle of Shoals, on the New England coast, in 1614, says: "Whilst the sailors fished, myself, with eight others, ranged the coast in a small boat. We got for trifles near 11,000 beaver skins, 100 martens, and many others." Note the preponderance of beavers.

Vincent de St. Castin, who carried on an extensive trade at Penobscot Bay, says that 80,000 livres could be annually realized there out of the beaver trade.

Bryant, in his "History of the United States" (Vol. I.), says: "The beaver was to the first people of Massachusetts a better friend than the cod, though the cod hangs to this day in the State House at Boston as the emblem of its prosperity, while only here and there in the country lingers some dim tradition of the beaver, where an embankment across some secluded meadow suggests that a dam may once have been there."

But for the avarice of the fur traders, the beaver might still supply an article of export and of wealth to extensive tracts of unimproved lands in Michigan. In this neighborhood the traces of their former being are not only exceedingly numerous, but have an intimate relation to the topography of the country.

The region between Lake Erie and Saginaw was one of the great beaver trapping-grounds. The Huron, the Chippewas, the Ottawas, and even the Iroquois, from beyond Ontario, by turns sought this region in large parties for the capture of this game, from the earliest historic times. It is a region peculiarly adapted to the wants of this animal. To a great extent level, it is intersected by numerous water courses, which have but moderate flow. At the head-waters and small inlets of these streams the beaver established his colonies. Here he dammed the streams, setting back the water over the flat lands, and creating ponds, in which were his habitations. Not one or two, but a series of such dams were constructed along each stream, so that very extensive surfaces became thus covered permanently with the flood. The trees were killed, and the land converted into a chain of ponds and marshes, with intervening dry ridges. In time, by nature's recuperative process—the annual growth and decay of grasses and aquatic plants— these filled with muck or peat, with occasional deposits of bog lime, and the ponds and swales became dry again.

Illustrations of this beaver-made country are numerous enough in our immediate vicinity. In a semi-circle of twelve miles around Detroit, having the river for base, and embracing about 100,000 acres, fully one-fifth part consists of marshy tracts or prairies, which had their origin in the work of the beaver. A little further west, nearly one whole township, in Wayne County, is of this character.

The lands referable to this origin occupy not the lowest, but elevated and slightly rolling tracts. Numerous small streams have their sources in these prairies, or meander through them. These, flowing with little descent through the lower connecting levels, are ramified in every direction, and form a network or connected chain over the whole surface. Dry ridges intervene, mostly sandy, and producing a scattered growth of white and yellow oaks. The broader marshes, which often extend several miles, are occasionally varied by low islands, containing a heavy growth of timber.

These marshes have a soil of black muck and fibrous peat, averaging two or three feet in depth, and often much more. This is underlaid by clay, with a thin stratum of sand or gravel usually intervening. Wild hay and cranberries on the open portions constitute a natural product of considerable value; other portions being covered with tamarac trees.

The beaver-dams are still discernible. Their builders, so the Indians say, disappeared from all this region about the beginning of the present century.

Is there in nature another instance where the operations of a single animal have so changed the face of a country, over such extensive areas? For the region of which I treat is but a sample of many others, stretching through the border counties of Eastern Michigan, and about the tributaries of the Saginaw.

But even this large district only feebly represents the immense area on this continent whose character has been entirely changed through the operations of the beaver. A writer, speaking of the Hudson Bay Company's lands in Canada, says: "Nearly every stream between the Pembina and the Athabasca, with the single exception of the McLeod, has been destroyed by beavers, and nothing but vast pine swamps remain to mark their place."

Over all the southerly portion of this vast region the mighty labors of this active animal are now relics of the past. The beavers and Indian hunters and Canadian trappers have alike disappeared. Other furs, or substitutes for them, have superseded their value to the dealer, and the skins are but rarely met with in this whole region, which once yielded little other marketable product.

While the beaver is responsible for the flooding of such immense extent of lands once dry, the results are by no means an unmixed evil. The great accumulation of muck or peat may, with proper treatment, become the richest of soils. As prairies of the character described occupy summit levels, the practicability of drainage is at once established. Even the cutting through of an old dam—a day's work only, of one or two men—may be effectual to drain of its surplus surface waters several miles of country, and if this be followed up by ditches of sufficient depth and number to drain and dry the spongy peat, the wet prairie lands will, in time, become thoroughly tillable. Were as much attention paid to the proper methods of reclaiming these lands as is given to the improvement of other and dryer lands, these now unattractive regions would in time become the garden portions of our State.

The beaver is an eminently social creature. Its chief purpose in the building of its dams seems to be the creation of ponds suitable for its habitations. Usually twenty or thirty houses are assigned to a pond, one or two families occupying each, and they live in clans or societies.

It is probable that these ponds may also supply certain aquatic plants, specially liked as food, and they assist to float to their proper depositories the bark and branches of trees needed for the winter supplies.

As a builder and engineer the beaver exhibits a wonderful intelligence. Its dams are constructed of trees and sticks of timber, arranged with exact reference to peculiarities of situation and current, and filled in with stones and mud. They are often 100 feet and more long, and 10 feet thick at base, and become very solid and firm. I have seen along a stream stumps of trees that had been felled, as thick as a man's body.

This dam maintains the water at the level required for the houses, which are built one-third below the surface, dome-shaped, and with entrances both above and below the water. These houses are very strongly constructed of sticks and mud, several feet in thickness, and are plastered within and without with clay or mud, and they have within several stories. They are so strong as to be absolutely secure against the elements and all enemies, except man, whose ingenuity and cunning in ways of destruction alone exceed the sagacity of these poor animals in the defence of their possessions and lives.

The fondness of the beaver for the water is such as almost to constitute that its native element. In fact, its peculiar structure, its flat, scaly, fish-like tail, seems to exhibit it as a connecting link between the terrestrial and the aquatic.

Charlevoix says he found the beaver very good eating, and he adds, naïvely enough, "Besides, in respect of its tail, it is altogether a fish, having been judicially declared such by the faculty of medicine of Paris, in consequence of which declaration the faculty of theology have decided that it might be lawfully eaten on meagre days!"

The traveller, Henry, says the Indians considered beavers to have been "formerly a people endowed with speech, not less than with the noble faculties they possess. But the Great Spirit has taken this away from them, lest they should grow superior in understanding to mankind."

Indeed, the intelligence shown by this animal in the construction of its dams and houses is so striking that we are amply justified in attributing their acts fully as much to reason as to mere instinct. They know how to fell a tree in the proper direction, as readily as the most expert axeman. And they apparently consult together over the best mode of engineering their works. A distinguished engineer—Willard S. Pope—who saw these creatures at work in our Northern peninsula, relates that on one occasion, when in his engineering operations it became desirable to drain off the water from a beaver pond. Workmen were directed to cut a channel through the dam, which they did, lowering the water, to the great dissatisfaction of its owners, for, rising early the next morning, my narrator discovered an old beaver examining the place very carefully, where he was soon joined by others. The result of their consultation was favorable to the immediate restoration of the dam. This was accomplished, solidly and completely, the very next night, under the advice, no doubt, of their most experienced engineer.

The range of the beaver in North America is very wide, being as far north as 60° of latitude, or more, and as far south as 30°, though in greatly diminishing numbers. It is also an inhabitant of the whole of Europe and of Northern Asia.

The weight of our beaver is about 50 or 60 pounds. It differs from that of Europe, which is a burrowing animal, and not so distinguished for intelligence.

It is sad to reflect upon the breaking up of these sociable communities, once so numerous and happy. Our sympathies are aroused for the red man, when driven from his hunting-grounds; but the beavers were a settled race, owning the lands which they occupied, in a far more comprehensive sense than the roving Indian.

To the honor of the latter, their trappers never voluntarily destroyed whole settlements of beavers, but were at pains to preserve the colony, hunting them only every second year. But the emissaries of the fur-traders killed all they could find, leaving only a few chance survivors, to become solitary and miserable wanderers, where once their lives had been spent in social happiness. It is a relief to know that in most parts of the country their extinction has been so complete.

TREES,—THEIR RELATIONS TO US, ECONOMIC AND SCIENTIFIC.

" Serit arbores, quæ alteri seculo prosint."
        CICERO.

TREES,—THEIR RELATIONS TO US, ECONOMIC AND SCIENTIFIC.*

IN no one phenomenon has the century which rounds our national life been so marked, as in the attitude of our country towards its woodlands.

Over the whole central portion of the United States, a century ago, spread an unbroken forest, embracing a magnificent flora of deciduous trees, unsurpassed for size and variety by that of any territory of equal extent on the globe.

Southerly from this central region the deciduous trees mingled with and gave place to evergreens, live-oaks and pitch-pines.

Northerly this great forest region embraced, together with its deciduous trees, the stately white pine, and other coniferæ, as far as our northern boundary.

Along the Pacific slope a dense forest occupied Washington Territory, Oregon and California, consisting mostly of conifers.

Between these two regions stretched, with few exceptions, an almost treeless region, embracing nearly one-half the whole territory of the United States.

Nowhere in the Old World, from which had come the energetic races that were so soon to overrun these virgin forests, could the eye of man witness such a marvellous variety and immense growth of timber as shut in on the

---

*A lecture before the Detroit Scientific Association, 1877.

west the still struggling, but independent thirteen colonies. The large number of species, many of which were new to the botanist, the great size and height of many, and their dense growth, gave to the forests of the New World a solemn and majestic character which was the admiration and wonder of the Old World foresters.

According to the enumeration of its botanists, Great Britain contains 29 species of indigenous trees of 30 feet height and upwards; of which only 15 are classed as "large."

In France, authorities name 30 to 34 species. And Central Europe, from the Adriatic to the Baltic, and from France to Russia, contains about 60 species only.

Compare this meagre catalogue with that of America.

Gray enumerates in the states east of the Mississippi, and north of the Carolinas, 132 indigenous species which attain 30 feet in height.

New England has 80 to 85 species, of which about 60 reach a height of 50 feet.

The Middle States have over 100 species, of which about 60 reach 50 feet.

The North-west—Ohio to Minnesota—has about 110 species: of these 70 attain a height of 50 feet.

The South-east—from Virginia to Florida—is richest in species, having upwards of 150; 75 of which attain a height of 50 feet, or more.

On the authority of Prof. Brewer, the whole number of species of our native trees that attain to 30 feet and upwards in height is stated at above 300, or five times that of Europe; of these about 120 reach 50 feet.

So different an idea from that which we are accustomed to is current on the other side of the ocean, of what constitutes a "forest," that its expression may well cause a smile on the face of an American woodsman. This idea is well illustrated by Frank Buckland, in his " Log-book," in England.

"At one place the tourist asked, ' What do they call yon hills?'

"'Eh, but that's just a deer forest,' says the coachman.

"'Deer-forest,' said the tourist, 'but I see no trees.'

"'Trees,' said coachee, 'but, man, who ever heard of trees in a forest.'"

In this country that man would have been unable to see the forest, *for the trees.*

Yet to its first possessors, all this boundless natural wealth was thrown away. Everywhere the grand aim of the early settler was to get rid of the encumbrance. He must hew a way to his inheritance by bold strokes of the axe. The whole life of the hardy pioneer was a constant battle with these Titans of nature. To let in the sun upon his patch of culture was his first care, for upon the extent to which this was redeemed from the woodland depended the welfare of his family, and his prospects of future wealth.

Such sentiments as our great novelist puts so often into the mouth of Judge Temple, in condemnation of the general destruction of the forests, are indeed noble and prophetic, but it was well that they prevailed so little. Else agriculture would not so speedily have usurped the wilderness, bringing a thriving population and national prosperity.

But the century which has witnessed such a wonderful national progress did not pass without a change in the relationship of man to the trees.

The indiscriminate destruction of timber, without regard to the future, began at last to be felt, not only in increasing scarcity of supply, but in diminished value of the lands, and other attendant evils.

So great and indiscriminate has been this destruction, that already cause for a wide-spread alarm exists, lest our country be speedily reduced to the condition of many countries of the Eastern hemisphere. In many of the older states, where the supply at one time seemed exhaustless, there is now almost destitution of timber for the commonest needs. The destruction has amounted to absolute waste, and it has been going on in an increased ratio with the population.

When we look at the causes of this rapid diminution, it ceases to be a wonder. Let us examine these briefly.

With the enormous increase in the extent of cultivation has been coincident one of the earliest and largest demands upon our forests, viz., for *fencing* material.

Estimates differ as to the amount of wood consumed in fences, but all are large almost beyond belief of any one who has not well considered the subject. General Brisbin, an intelligent army officer, asserts,* "that the fences of the United States have cost more than the land, and are to-day the most valuable class of property in the country, except railroads and real estate in cities." Our fences are now valued at $1,800,000,000 and have required the clearing probably of 25,000,000 acres. To keep these in repair costs annually $100,000,000.

The timber which goes into *railroad ties* is also enormous. According to the same writer "the 71,000 miles of railroad in the United States have required in building 184,000,000 ties, and these have to be replaced every

---

* In an able letter to the New York *World*, 1875.

seven years." This annual supply is equivalent to not less than 2,000,000 cords of standing timber; so that, assuming the average yield per acre to be 50 cords, railroad ties destroy annually 40,000 acres of woodland.

The annual consumption of wood for *fuel* may be estimated at over 50,000,000 cords, causing a clearing of 600,000 acres. It took 10,000 acres of forest, in 1871, to supply Chicago with fuel for a single year. To this we must add the supply annually required for furnaces and manufactures of all kinds, which call for many thousand acres more.

The felling of forest in the process of *bringing new land under cultivation* is still going on, at a rate almost beyond computation. From 1860 to 1870 it is supposed that no less than 12,000,000 acres were thus destroyed, or 1,200,000 annually.

When we consider the great *lumber* interests of our country, the rate at which our woods are being felled, to supply the demand for pine and other timber used in the arts, almost staggers belief.

Michigan takes the lead of all the States. Her annual cut for the last ten years, as shown by reliable statistics, has been not far from 2,500,000,000 feet, board measure; equivalent to the removal of 33,000 acres of forest. With even no greater ratio of increase in the future, the next cycle of ten years will find little white pine timber left in this State.

Pennsylvania, New York and Wisconsin follow not far behind, and, taking into account the whole country, it is safe to set down the total annual consumption of manufactured lumber at not far below 20,000,000,000 feet; representing an annual clearing of 325,000 acres, or over 500 square miles.

The *Canadian Lumberman* gives some further items, showing where the wood goes.

"To make shoe pegs enough for American use consumes annually 100,000 cords of timber. Lasts and boot-trees take 500,000 cords of birch, beech and maple, and the handles of tools 500,000 more. To make our lucifer matches 300,000 cubic feet of the best pine are required every year. The baking of our bricks consumes 2,000,000 cords of wood, or what would cover with forest 55,000 acres of land. Telegraph poles represent 800,000 trees, and their annual repair about 300,000 more. Packing boxes cost, in 1874, $12,000,000, while the timber used each year in making wagons and agricultural implements is valued at more than $100,000,000."

To all these recurring causes of the destruction of our forests we must add *fires*, the *ravages of insects*, and other natural agencies; causes which are rapidly on the increase. The destruction by forest fires seems likely soon to equal all other causes, in our characteristic neglect of the proper remedies.

The total annual consumption of our forests from all these causes combined has been variously estimated at from 4,000,000 to 8,000,000 acres. Assuming the lowest estimate to be nearest the truth, and the annual increase to be ten per cent. only, it will require less than half another century to leave us treeless, unless planting on a large scale be resorted to. Wonderful progress indeed, but attended by what waste of this great natural store-house of wealth, and with how little prevision of the future!

I need not dwell upon the economical importance of this subject. When we consider how largely the wealth of the country consists in its woods, and how vastly the price of lumber of all kinds will be enhanced, so soon as we are reduced to grow our own forests, the results seem overwhelming.

There is another aspect of this subject which still more deeply concerns the national welfare, viz., the *relationship of trees to climate*.

There is not entire agreement among practical scientists, as to the effect of the removal of the forests upon the climate, and especially upon the rainfall. Without going into any discussion, I think the following propositions are well established, and of vital importance:

1st. That the temperature is *hotter in summer and colder in winter*, than when the country was covered with forest. This is a natural result of exposure of the soil to more active radiation, and consequent frost.

2d. The *winds have a more uninterrupted sweep*, and so the country is both dried up and refrigerated. Scarcely any influence is so deleterious to plant life as exposure to our severe westerly winds.

3d. The *rainfall* is either *less in amount*, or it is *less equally distributed* through the seasons, and its advantages to the soil and to plants are to a great degree lost.

It may be admitted that data are yet insufficient to determine the question, whether the removal of forest diminishes the actual amount of rainfall. The weight of testimony and philosophy tend to the latter conclusion. At least certain principles may be accepted as in harmony with the above propositions.

Trees are remarkable condensers of humidity, as may be seen from the drops which they precipitate during a fog, sometimes even producing rills of water. From this cause, and the shade which they afford to the ground, a more uniform degree of moisture is preserved in the atmosphere about them than in cleared lands.

Now, vapor pervading the atmosphere has a remarkable efficiency in preventing radiation of heat from the soil. Wherever the air is dry the thermometric range will be great. Tyndall says, "The removal for a single winter's night of the aqueous vapor from the atmosphere which covers England would be attended by the destruction of every plant which a freezing temperature could kill."

Observations made in Bavaria showed, that for the month of July the temperature at midday within the forest is 8° below that of the unwooded land, but at night it is 4.39° higher. During the night, the colder and denser air of the unwooded land passes into the forest, rises and is cooled, and during the day the contrary occurs. Thus a circulation is established which regulates the temperature.

By keeping up a cooler atmosphere over them than in the open ground, trees maintain the condition under which rain is precipitated by condensation. In open spaces the warmer ascending air tends to disperse the vapors which collect and are utilized by our woods and forest-covered hills. In this way the latter doubtless promote the frequency of showers, if they do not augment the total amount.

Finally, the presence of forest serves to retain the moisture that falls, as well as to diminish the evaporation from the soil. Thus the rains are allowed to soak into the soil, or to pass away gradually; which, falling upon open ground, are rapidly drained off into the dry water-courses, and occasion disastrous floods.

These propositions are so fully sustained by facts, all

over the world, and these have been so repeatedly brought to our notice, that I feel disposed to pass by any details. Yet I cannot forbear to fortify my position by referring to a few.

No one whose observations cover a quarter of a century can be unfamiliar with the fact, so frequently noticed, that the streams with which he was familiar in his boyhood have shrunken or dried up. Wherever the woods are cleared away to any considerable extent this effect invariably follows. Springs fail, water-courses become dry, or yield only a precarious and scanty supply compared with their former copiousness.

How different the aspect now of all the settled portions of our land from what it appeared to the eyes and was described in the relations of the earliest travellers.

> " Before these fields were shorn and tilled
>   Full to the brim our rivers flowed ;
> The melody of waters filled
>   The fresh and boundless wood ;
> And torrents dashed, and rivulets played,
> And fountains spouted in the shade."

In the desiccated county we now inhabit, how unreal seem these lines of our great poet, whose fourscore years have made him a faithful witness of the scenes he so graphically depicts?*

Droughts have become of frequent occurrence where they were seldom known while the greater portion of the country was covered with wood. They are now the rule in summer and autumn, rather than the exception. These are facts familiar to most of us. Our pastures dry up and are of little service for several weeks during the year. The more tender fruits, such as the peach,

---

* Bryant: died May, 1878.

cannot be successfully grown where they bore abundant crops some years ago. The grape mildews, or fails to ripen. Many of our most hardy trees and shrubs are killed, by the depth to which frost penetrates the soil. Wheat and other crops suffer from the same causes.

Should this state of things continue, and increase in the ratio of the past, another half-century will witness our land as unfruitful and barren as are those deserts of the Orient, now almost uninhabitable, which were once the homes of millions and the cradle of the human family.

The experience of the Old World should be a lesson to us. Says a writer in *Appleton's Journal* (A. B. Guernsey), "Palestine, when the Hebrews took possession of it, was a land of rivulets and fountains. In its palmy days the territory—not so large as Massachusetts—supported in plenty a population of at least five millions, where now not more than 250,000 find a scanty subsistence. Under the Roman rule it was still densely populated. But during the wars which followed the revolt under Vespasian and Titus, the Romans systematically cut down not merely the fruit trees, but the forests, and in the course of a few generations the greater part of the country was reduced to the almost waterless desert it now is. The channels of the rivulets still remain, but they are dry ravines, except directly after a rain, when they become roaring torrents; the only exception being those streams whose sources lie high up among the wooded heights of Lebanon."

"Greece tells the same story. In a large part of it the forests which once clothed the hill sides have long been destroyed; the famous fountains of antiquity now flow only in song, and rivers of historical renown are now but scanty brooks, which a child may ford."

"The African shores of the Mediterranean, long the granary of the Roman Empire, have from the same cause become not merely uninhabited, but practically uninhabitable, by any except nomads, wandering from one scanty fountain to another."

If the present physical condition of those classic lands belies the glowing descriptions of their fertility given by ancient geographers, what facts are within our more modern experience?

A recent traveller says (N. Y. *Herald* of Nov., 1872): "In Italy the modern clearing of the Apennines is universally believed to have altered the climate of the rich Po valley, where now the sirocco, unknown to the armies of ancient Rome, breathes its deadly breath of flame over that classic stream, in the territory of Parma."

The results of the clearing of the forests from the spurs and valleys of the Pyrenees, in Southern France, came to our ears last year, in reports of sudden and terrible inundations, which devastated whole provinces, sweeping many families, and indeed whole districts, with their herds, to destruction. The dry beds of ravines, that formerly were regular streams, became suddenly filled by rains of unusual copiousness, which rushed in headlong torrents towards the sea.

In Southern Russia, the winters are becoming colder every year, and the summers hotter, more dry and less fruitful, owing, as is clearly proved, to the destruction of the woods which formerly abounded. From the same cause streams are everywhere shallowing, not in Russia alone, but over Europe, so that many once navigable are no longer so.

Coming nearer home, we have similar reports from many islands of the West Indies. In the annual *Record of Science and Industry*, for 1874, Mr. Frederick Hubbard says, " Santa Cruz changed from fertility to barrenness by the diminution of the rainfall, owing to the removal of the forests. Streams fail, springs dry up, and cultivation has become impossible without constant irrigation.

" In the neighboring island of Porto Rico,- which is not so mountainous, the rain is abundant.

" The rainy seasons are a succession of sudden showers with hot sun at intervals. The opening of the soil to the vertical rays causes its rapid drying, and prevents the rain from sinking to the roots of plants.

" The small island of Curaçoa, in 1845, was almost a perfect desert, while, according to history, it had been a garden of fertility. The cause was the cutting down of the trees for export of timber. Almost within sight is the Spanish Main, covered with the rankest vegetation, over which the burdened clouds shower down abundant rain, while at Curaçoa fresh water is among the luxuries."

Another result of deforesting—as yet but little experienced in this country—is felt to baneful extent in those lands whose hills have long been stripped of their protective woods. I allude to the washing away and loss of fertile soil, in consequence of the absence of trees.

Sicily was once the garden of the Mediterranean, and its valleys are still fertile, but its hills, which were once so, are not only treeless, but so bare of soil as to render any attempt to renew their former condition almost hopeless. During my visit to the island, in the spring, after a year's drought, a violent rain-storm had converted the rills which descended from the slopes into the valleys into torrents. These carried with them all the loose materials into the larger streams, by which they were swept into the sea. As our train approached the coast, we found all the streams swollen, and the gullies so filled with the sudden flood, as to impede and endanger our progress. Looking towards the sea, far as the eye could reach, the waters were turbid with the spoils of the land. It seemed to my eyes that hundreds of acres of fertile soil had been carried off and lost by that single day's rain. How immense and irreparable the destruction resulting from the devastations of all the years that have passed since the hills were denuded of their forests!

If similar experiences in our own country have been less felt it is because the evil has not yet been so extended. But that like effects have followed like causes is notorious, as our agricultural interest universally has known, to its cost.

So widely felt are these evils, that legislatures, both national and state, have already been called upon to establish measures for the preservation of valuable timber, the restraining of waste, and for granting bounties upon the planting of trees.

It is a curious fact, which the contrasts of time set before our eyes in a new historic importance, that in our early colonial history, among the restrictions placed by the home government upon the industry of the colonists, none was considered more burdensome than that upon the cutting of timber. It was prominent among the causes of discontent which led to the American Revolution.

Sabine, in his "Loyalists of the Revolution," notices

among the restrictions upon lumbering in Maine, one which provided that all pine trees of the diameter of twenty-four inches, on lands not granted to private persons, should be reserved for masts for the royal navy, and that for the cutting down any such tree, without special leave, the offender should forfeit £100 sterling.

As we in Michigan look back to the times when the most valuable pine trees which graced the vacant United States lands were ruthlessly plundered, to no better result than the educating of communities of thieves, we may well wish that our Republican Government had displayed somewhat of the foresight and temper of the British king. In the light of our experience since we became a nation, how strange it appears, that a restriction upon the plundering propensities of the lumbermen of New England should be reckoned among the causes which led the way to our national independence!

Nevertheless the necessity was felt, even so early, of putting a stop to needless waste. We read that " att a meeting held this 29th day of April 1699, in Breuchlyn," Benjamin Vande Water, Joris Hanson and Jan Dorlant were chosen officers, to consider the " great inconvenience & lose " that the inhabitants suffered, because that unauthorized tradesmen " doe ffall & cutt the best trees and sully the best woods."

In some of the colonial grants of New York, more than 150 years ago, we find excellent provisions relating to precautions against fires in the woods.*

Congress also, at various times, from 1777 to 1827, passed acts looking to the preservation of timber for naval purposes, and to prevent poaching.

---

* Report of Commissioners on the Public Lands, to Congress, 1874.

Shall the sons be less wise than their sires? Though in many of the material resources and growth of the national life the infant of the past has become the strong man of to-day, yet as regards the reckless waste of *this* source of power we are still very far behind. A London writer, commenting upon the tremendous ravages of the settler's axe in America, compares the wholesale stripping of the Republic's soil of its timber to Delilah's robbing Samson of the secret of his strength.

In all the chief governments of Europe elaborate systems of forestry have long been established, to the end that the timber shall be saved from all unnecessary destruction, that it shall be allowed to grow in situations where experience has proved its importance in the amelioration of climate, and to ensure the planting of new forests.

In this country we have but recently awakened to the importance of considerations of this kind.

The American Association for the advancement of science, at its meeting of 1873, appointed a committee to memorialize Congress and the several State Legislatures "on the importance of promoting the cultivation of timber, and the preservation of forests, and to recommend such legislation as may be deemed proper for securing these objects." This resulted in the recommendation by the committee on the public lands, for the appointing of a "commission for inquiring into the destruction of forests, and the measures necessary for the preservation of timber."

Congress the same year passed an act "to encourage the growth of timber on the Western prairies." It granted for every acre planted out in trees, not more than twelve feet apart, a patent for sixteen acres. Under this liberal provision no less than 20,000,000 trees have been already planted on the hitherto treeless regions of Minnesota.

The subject was brought before our own State Legislature by a memorial from the State Board of Agriculture, referred to a special committee and reported upon by them, January, 1867.

This report, written by Prof. Kedzie, presented the facts of the injury to the agricultural, manufacturing and commercial interests of the State, resulting from the reckless and violent disturbance of her forest economy, in an impressive manner. Several remedies were suggested.

Among these was a proposition to exempt belts of timber of moderate width, running north and south, from all taxation.

Another forcible suggestion is to compel the fencing in of stock, by prohibiting their running at large, and thus make an immense saving by dispensing with the general fencing of farms.

A third measure is to encourage the planting of trees along the highways, by remitting to persons so planting part of their highway taxes.

Great difficulties surround this subject of legislative remedies, owing partly to a natural jealousy of any restriction upon liberty of action, in matters conceived to belong to the private judgment of the individual, and still more to the prevailing ignorance as to the proper method of planting and the care of trees.

In the States of Europe, and especially in Germany, forestry is a science, and there are schools for teaching it, and for educating young men to become capable members of a forest staff. Not alone are taught the practical branches, such as the best methods of planting, cutting, preservation against fire, etc., but also the diseases to which trees are subject, and their insect foes, and the remedies. All the minutiæ there practised may not be possible under our government, nor necessary for years to come, but certainly some system, more effectual than any yet adopted, is needed, and cannot be too soon applied.

Some permanent good might be accomplished by the appointment by the general government, and in each State, of a commissioner of forestry, with such powers and duties as our peculiar circumstances require. Under his direction commissioners of highways—who should be men of science and experience—may be employed to plant trees along the roads, taxing the expense upon the lands. Under such oversight the work would be done far more cheaply and well than is possible if left, as now, to individual caprice. Proper science would be exercised as to kind and number of trees, method of planting, distance apart, uniformity, etc., where now all is hap-hazard. In time our public roads would become embowered avenues, grateful alike to man and beast, belts of shelter to the enclosed lands from the blasting winds, as well as drifting snow and sands, and promoters of all kindly atmospheric influences.

The reckless slashing of timber as now practised, and which is the prime cause of our terrible forest fires, should be prevented by stringent laws and a watchful guardianship.

Another most serviceable State law would be one absolutely prohibiting the running at large of cattle and swine. As the only object of fences is to restrain cattle, what an enormous saving would be accomplished were fences to be universally dispensed with. It would equal annually the interest on the national debt, and would far exceed the cash value of all the horses and stock in the country. All this might be effected by the simple process of shutting in stock, instead of shutting them out! In Europe there are no cattle at large, and no fences. The custom is purely American, and its cost is only equalled by its folly.

In the once forest-covered regions of America, where the aim has so long been how soonest to get rid of the timber, men have hardly yet schooled their ideas up to the point of reversing their operations, and planting out new woodlands to take place of the old. But in the sparsely timbered and prairie portions, the planting of trees for timber, as well as for shelter, has for quite a number of years commanded the attention of land-owners and legislatures. Planting is now going on, on a large scale, in Nebraska, Minnesota, Iowa, and other of our Western States. These efforts, if continued with the zeal which now animates the people of those hitherto almost shelterless districts, bid far to soon reverse the old order of things, and transfer the forest region to the other side of the Mississippi.

I almost venture the prediction, that in another quarter of a century, the once densely wooded Eastern lands will be the treeless region, while the open and arid Western plains will be clothed with verdant forests, and, through their agency, be refreshed with more frequent showers, defended from the blighting winds, and blossom with unwonted fertility.

TREES, IN THEIR SOCIAL RELATIONS.

"O, hath the Dryad still a tongue
   In this ungenial clime?
Have sylvan spirits still a voice
   As in the classic prime—
To make the forest voluble,
   As in the olden time?"
Hood.

TREES, IN THEIR SOCIAL RELATIONS.

BEYOND the quality of utility, in its restricted sense, there is another view of our subject which I love to contemplate, and to which I ask your indulgent attention, namely, its æsthetic or social aspect.

To my mind, none of the productions of nature, next to a beautiful woman, equals in grace a well-developed tree. But to be thus developed, a tree, like the human form, must have full measure of light and liberty. It is not under the constraints of fashion that woman's form divine assumes its highest attractiveness; nor is it in the thick forest, which so thwarts the struggle for individual expansion, that we find in a tree its full expression of beauty. Its life must have a more free existence, a more liberal supply of the blessed sunshine and the fresh winds. It must have leave to strike its roots deeply and widely, and to spread abroad its branches as its nature prompts.

Of the natural forms even of our commonest trees, as well as of their amazing beauty and variety of feature, most people have little notion, who see them only as the artificially trained ornaments of the streets, or the crowded denizens of the woods.

Would many believe that the elm, that stately tree whose lofty head arches so high above its neighbors of the forest, inclines by the instinct of nature to rest its drooping limbs on its mother's bosom?

How many woodsmen recognize in the tulip-tree of

the lawn (*Liriodendron tulipifera*), with its wide-spread limbs, hidden by a drapery of leaves, and glowing with a profusion of magnolia-like blossoms, the tall white-wood of the forest, whose foliage and bloom are alike far beyond his vision? which

"——high up,
Opens in airs of June her multitude
Of golden chalices to humming birds,
And silken-winged insects of the sky."
BRYANT.

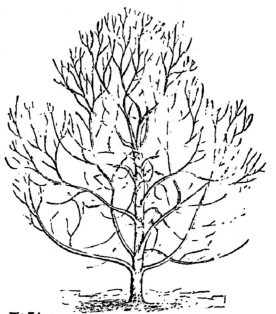

White wood   *Liriodendron tulip:*

The like tendency is true of the hickory, the maple, the linden, the sycamore, even the oak; trees more familiar to our eyes in the forms which art and constraint have given, than in their native characters.

Yet each species has its characteristic habit, so that their diversities and peculiarities are to the lover of nature a perpetual and delightful study. For this purpose the bleak season of winter, which has stripped off

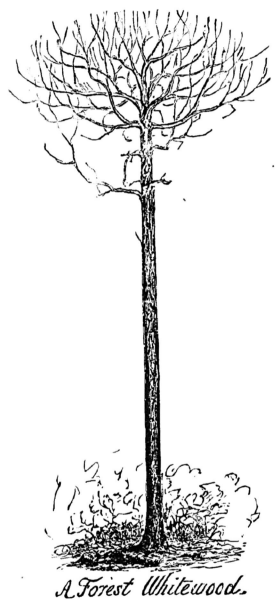

A Forest Whitewood.

the summer's drapery, offers peculiar advantages; as in Grecian art we are most delighted with the representation of the human form in its naked grace, strength and beauty of proportion.

> " With more than summer beauty fair,
>   The trees in winter garb are shown;
> What a rich halo melts in air,
>   Around the crystal branches thrown."
>
> ANDREW NORTON.

Maple — Acer rubrum

Let us direct our attention to the specific characters in a few of our common trees.

The Maples (*Acer*), in their several varieties, are perhaps the most acknowledged favorites of all the inhabitants of our forests. They are indeed among the finest of our round-headed trees, expressive of grace, rather than strength. Their limbs, left to their own free volition, are very evenly disposed and low growing. Beautiful in their clean-cut tracery against a winter sky, as in the delicate tints of spring, the dense drapery of summer, or the glowing hues of autumn.

The Ash (*Fraxinus Americanus*), is another round-headed tree of whose beauty our woods give little idea. It rivals the tulip tree in size, but its light-green, loosely-pinnated foliage is in strong contrast. It has a very compact head, and an air of easy but somewhat formal negligence.

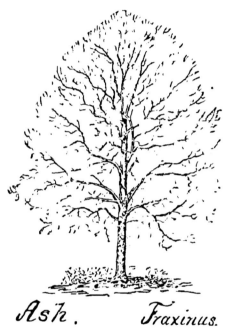

Ash. Fraxinus.

Another of our common trees, which in regularity of form nearly equals the maple, and surpasses it in the rich verdure of its large, heart-shaped leaves, is the Linden, Lime or Bass-wood (*Tilia*). It is comparatively in little esteem, but is deserving of greater popular favor. When permitted, its lower limbs sweep to the earth. Blossoming in mid-summer, at a time when most of our trees have passed the season of bloom, it fills the air with fragrance. To the bees

"A summer home of murmurous wings."

Our linden is less compact in form than the foreign species, but greatly its superior in foliage. As a street tree it is seldom seen with us, but abroad it is a favorite for avenues,—

"The broad ambrosial aisles of lofty limes,"

as the laureate describes them.

One of the most picturesque trees of our woodlands is the Sycamore, Plane-tree or Buttonwood (*Platanus*).

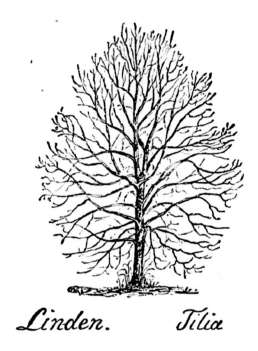

Linden.   Tilia

Its great size, the fantastic wildness with which it spreads abroad its speckled arms, its broad leaves, and its habit of shedding the outer bark in great scales, leaving the body a lustrous white, make it a very conspicuous object.

From the difficulty of working its twisted fibre, this tree is often left standing after its companions are felled, the solitary giant ghost of the clearings. The Oriental species, which closely resembles ours, was introduced into England about the middle of the sixteenth century, and is now a favorite tree for avenues throughout Europe, while it is seldom cultivated with us. Its size and ample shade made the plane-tree a favorite with the ancients. It was in academic groves, beneath

> "The pillar'd dusk of sounding sycamores,"

that the philosophers of old delivered their lessons of wisdom.

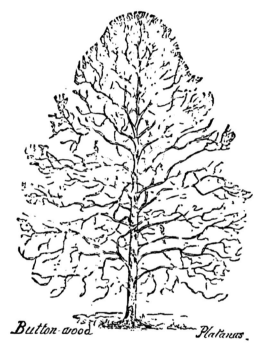
Button-wood. Platanus.

In the deep alluvion of our river bottoms this tree attains enormous size. I remember in my boyhood seeing a section of a sycamore brought from the valley of the Mohawk, near Utica, and converted into a travelling saloon. Its hollow interior was fitted up with the usual appurtenances of a grocery, including a stove, and a dozen persons found standing-room within. But my story is beaten by Pliny, who tells of a plane-tree in Lycia which measured eighty-one feet circumference.

In this tree Licinius, when consul, used to entertain dinner-parties.

Few trees are more strikingly beautiful in youth and grand in age than the Beech (*Fagus sylvestris*), with its wide-spreading, almost horizontal branches, its smooth bark, and its light-green, glossy and small but dense foliage. It is the very altar of love. Where but under

Beech. *Fagus Sylv.*

its shade has the traditionary sigh been so often heaved! Where have lovers so often delighted to exchange their vows, and on its

"————trunk's surviving frame
Carv'd many a long-forgotten name!"

Another most elegant tree of our northern woods is the Birch (*Betula*). The several kinds are among the earliest of our forest dwellers to put forth their foliage, delicate and drooping. The white birch, by its silvery bark, contrasts brilliantly with the dark evergreen forest, where it loves to dwell. It is also a favorite of the poets, and is not peculiar to America. Scott sings of climes

> "Where weeps the birch with silver bark,
> And long dishevelled hair."

Coleridge pronounces it the "lady of the woods." A larger species, peculiar to America, is well known in her aboriginal annals, from the use made of its bark in the

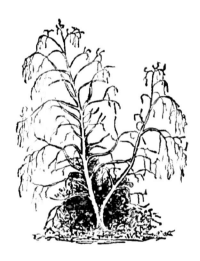

Birch. *Betula Popul^a*

construction of the light, elegant and serviceable Indian canoe.

Of all trees of temperate climes none equals in majesty the Oak (*Quercus*), the acknowledged king of the woods. In variety of kinds, if not in grandeur, this country exceeds all others. Micheaux enumerates forty indigenous species. Of these, at least half exist in this neighborhood.

The White Oak (*Q. alba*) attains the largest size and is truly a forest monarch. Some idea of the size attained by the white oak in the heavily-wooded tract about Detroit may be had from the dimensions of a stick of timber got out near Ecorse by one of our ship-builders. The trunk measured eighteen feet girth, and from it a single timber was squared to three feet diameter and

White Oak. *Quercus a.*

fifty-five feet length. An oak cut in my own woods, back of Detroit, whose circumference was fourteen feet, had a length of bole of sixty feet to the main fork, and a total length of one hundred and twenty feet. The annular layers showed it to be three hundred and sixty years old, or coeval with the discovery of America by Columbus!

The *Canada Lumberman* mentions a Red Oak (*Q. rubrum*), that was being made into beer barrels in 1881, which stood 135 feet from top to toe, its girth being 17 feet 9 inches, inside the bark. The stem was straight and branchless for 66 feet, and gave measurable timber 50 feet above that. Not a flaw nor rotten hole disfigured this magnificent specimen. Its age was calculated at 375 years.

The Walnuts(*Juglans*), including the Black walnut and the Butternut, have strong claims upon our social regard. Though resembling each other, the former is much the grander tree, its long pinnated leaves having greater ele-

Black Walnut Juglans

gance of form, and being more massively displayed. The green of the foliage is in fine contrast with the dark color of the trunk and branches.

In the strong, deep soils of Michigan this tree grows to an immense size. One near Kalamazoo—I hope it may be there still—measured, a few years ago, thirty-three feet circumference, at two feet from the ground.

The pleasing color of the walnut lumber, and the ease with which it may be wrought, cause it to be in deserved esteem for domestic architecture. But this appreciation is of modern growth. In a sparsely settled part of our State I once rested at a tavern where, to my surprise, the whole interior, even to the benches, was composed of these two costly walnuts. Their harmonious contrast produced a very pleasing effect. But their beauty and value were lost upon my landlord, for, perceiving my attention attracted to them, he remarked, in the way of

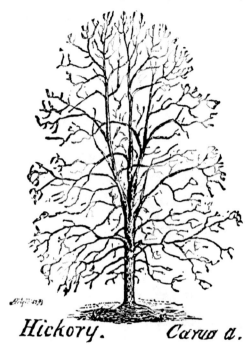

Hickory. *Carya a.*

apology, that he had been compelled to use these materials on account of the scarcity of pine in that region!

Allied to the walnuts, in our appreciation of their nutting qualities, are the Hickories (*Carya*). The variety known as shell-bark is equally worthy of admiration for its superb proportions. It is one of the round-headed trees, but possesses greater dignity than most of its class. It rises in successive stories, as it were, tower-like, while the limbs below sweep the earth; wearing in its grace a majesty that renders it an object worthy the eye of the landscape painter.

Another of our nut-producing trees, the Chestnut (*Castanea*), is equally worthy our notice for its picturesqueness. When growing upon the skirts of woods or on the

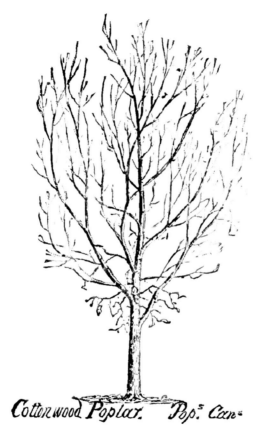
Cottonwood Poplar.   Pop.^s Can=

lawn, it forms a grandly spreading head, the lively green of its sharp-spined leaves being in pleasing contrast with the deeper tint of surrounding foliage. Whether in flower or fruit, it is a most striking object, a favorite for all time with poets and painters.

The American Poplars (*Populus*), though not favorites in landscape gardening, and of little value in the arts, are on many accounts worthy our regard. They are picturesque rather than graceful. The white bark of the common sort (*P. Canadensis*) gives variety and contrast to the wood-side, as the incessant motion of the leaves of the Aspen (*P. tremuloides*) gives animation. It is to be prized also for the earliness of its spring garb and tasselled flowers. Some of the species, as the Cottonwood, are among the largest of our Western trees, sturdy and majestic, while the Balsam has an element of the beautiful, in the droop of its spray.

Peperidge. — *Nyssa.*

Our Scientific Museum possesses two sections of a cottonwood, from Lapeer County, 7 and 5 feet diameter respectively. The tree was 140 feet high, 10 feet diameter at base, and three feet diameter at a height of 50 feet. Its annular rings number 188.

None of our native Willows (*Salix*) will compare in striking characteristics with those foreign sorts, the weeping and the golden. Nevertheless our willow is in certain situations full of a beauty of its own. It shows to best advantage skirting our rivers and ponds. Here

"——it dips
Its pendent boughs, stooping as if to drink."

The low-growing bushes display their long, lance-shaped leaves in star-like clusters, making a charming fringe to the water's edge.

"Eternal greens the mossy margins grace,
Watch'd by the sylvan genius of the place."

Young Peperidge.
age 20 years.

I would not fail to notice in this association of Northern trees, the Peperidge (*Nyssa*), a tree little known to fanciers, but of rare merit. It has a habit of disposing its limbs horizontally, this disposition being carried out even to the top, which is often flat, like a table. Its leaves, though small, are very green and glossy, and in autumn change to a brilliant purple and scarlet, making it one of the most striking objects at that gay season. Our Woodmere Cemetery has many fine native specimens.

In its combination of magnificence and grace no tree of our land equals the White Elm (*Ulmus Americana*). The European sort, though of grand proportion, is rigid, and lacks both the regularity of outline and droop of spray. This difference in character may be observed on Boston Common, where are rows of very perfect old English elms.

The habit of the American species is to divide into many branches, which, commencing at a few feet from the ground, rise at first in a compact body, and gradually curve outwards, the head forming an umbel, which terminates in clusters of long, pendent spray. These sway gracefully in the winds, and, if allowed to do so, will brush the earth with masses of small but thickly tufted leaves. In my admiration of this magnificent tree I would exclaim with Cowper,

"Could a mind imbued
With truth from Heaven, created thing adore,
I might with reverence kneel and worship thee,"

O thou American Elm!

The elm has this notable peculiarity, that it is alike graceful, whether allowed to spread freely, or so hemmed in as to cause it to branch at a great height from the ground.

It is pleasant to know that this beauty and magnificence do not pass generally unrecognized, as is testified by many fine specimens in private grounds, and along highways, gothic-arched, and by many of a past century, spared by the axe, and left to adorn the pastures through the Northern and Eastern States.

I recall an individual in this vicinity, well known for its magnificence,—the Lafferty elm. It was situated on the river road, in what was then part of the town of Springwells. It is known to have been planted a few years before the close of the last century, and was a striking example of the brief period required by the elm to produce a respectable shade. In 1864 the trunk measured, at four feet from the ground, ten feet circumference, which dimension it held to the commencement of

White Elm. *Ulmus Amere*

the limbs. At ten feet the stem parted into seven branches, each of which was in size a considerable tree. It stood within the fence, and its limbs extended across the road, a distance of more than fifty feet, so that the entire spread must have exceeded 100 feet. One by one its seven limbs were ruthlessly cut away by the axe, and finally the main trunk succumbed to the iron march of improvement. The tree was still in the vigor of three score years and ten, and might have continued for centuries, with increasing honors and usefulness, the glory of the neighborhood.

With a few words about the evergreen trees of our Northern forests I shall close these desultory sketches.

The world affords no timber more beautiful, as well as useful, than the pines, hemlocks, spruces and cedars that grow so luxuriantly in the northern portions of our State. What a majesty they add, not unmingled with awe, to the deep woodland. We recognize Milton's picture,—

> " Overhead upgrew
> Insuperable height of loftiest shade.
> Cedar and pine and fir, a sylvan scene,
> And as the ranks ascend, shade above shade,
> A woody theatre of stateliest view."

As we penetrate the profound depths, and listen to the murmurs—most musical, most melancholy—struck out by that grand old harper, the wind, from their branches, we catch the poet's enthusiasm,

> " Cover me, ye pines!
> Ye cedars, with innumerable boughs!"

To the more practical mind the consideration presents itself, how useful would be this density of foliage if transferred to the borders of our fields, as a shelter against the blighting winds.

Our White Pine (*Pinus strobus*)—the great tree of the timber district—lacks the sturdy aspect of the Scotch and Austrian, but is even more grandly majestic, and more regular in outline. Its foliage is of very pleasing green, unchanged by the severest winter.

Of the Hemlock (*Abies Canadensis*) it is safe to say, that it surpasses all the evergreens, as well for size as in the elegance of its feathery foliage and thick but slender spray. In the first few weeks of spring growth, the lighter tint of the new leaves, pendent from the ends of the branches like strings of emeralds, make it the jewelled queen of the arboretum. Yet this most graceful of evergreens is seldom seen in American lawns and dooryards, where foreign kinds are of common occurrence.

There is an old adage which says that " he who plants pears plants for his heirs," and many a man is restrained from setting out forest trees from the conviction that life is not long enough to enable him to enjoy their benefits. Now, aside from the fact that this is a selfish consideration, it is not true that most trees are of so slow growth. Some items may here be given from my limited experience.

In 1856 I transplanted into my grounds several trees of different kinds from the neighboring woods. Among these were an elm and a red maple. I measured these at intervals of ten years, with the following results: When planted each measured, at four feet from the ground, eight inches diameter. In 1866 the elm measured one foot six inches, the maple one foot ten inches. In 1876 the elm measured two feet, the maple two feet eight inches diameter.*

Thus each tree had in the first decade considerably more than doubled in diameter of trunk, and at the end of the second the elm had trebled, and the maple quadrupled the original girth. If we reduce the measurements to cubic contents we should find that each tree had increased in 20 years to more than 16 times its first bulk. In fact the maple nearly doubled in

---

* In 1886 the elm had increased to two feet five inches, and the maple to three feet three inches diameter.

size each year. The trees are now (1877) over 60 feet in height, and have a spread of limb fully as great. In each the lower branches bend quite to the earth, forming complete bowers.

This growth is by no means exceptional. That of smaller and younger trees far exceeds this, and I mention the instance rather to show with what rapidity a fine shade and ornament may be obtained for the dooryard, from one or two specimen trees only.

A dozen or more trees, planted on Vinewood Avenue, increased in eighteen years from about three inches diameter to an average of seventeen or eighteen inches; six times the original measurement, and thirty-six times the actual size.

All were excelled in rapidity of growth by a black walnut; a mere whip-stock when planted, but twenty years afterward a lofty tree, with a trunk four feet in circumference. Assuming its diameter when set to have been two inches, it had increased to sixty-four times its original size, trebling each year, and that, too, on a soil of light sand. How speedily at this rate may a forest be grown, and with what immense profit, within an ordinary lifetime.*

The planting of all our roadways is one of the readiest means of obtaining the results derived from the presence of trees, with the least expense or loss to cultivable land. By this means may be secured, at frequent intervals, belts for shelter to the fields, while a grateful shade is afforded to man and beast, and travel rendered a delight rather than a torture.

European travellers have noticed the little care taken

---

* This tree is now (1886) six feet circumference.

to preserve the finest specimens of our native trees in the country; while they speak with admiration of the pains taken to adorn our cities with handsome avenues. And here truly their social influence is widely felt.

> "But rising from the dust of busy streets
>   These forest children gladden many hearts;
> As some old friend their welcome presence greets
>   The toil-worn soul, and fresher life imparts.
> Their shade is doubly grateful when it lies
>   Above the glare which stifling walls throw back;
> Through quivering leaves we see the soft blue skies,
>   Then happier tread the dull, unvaried track."
>
> ALICE B. NEAL.

I have not yet noticed another aspect in which trees have their value, namely, as *scavengers of the atmosphere*.

But for them the air would become loaded with an injurious amount of carbonic acid, an element destructive to animal life. Especially in cities, and amid the settlements of man, is this protection desirable. The respiration of men and animals, the consumption of fuel, and other sources, pour into the atmosphere continually carbonic acid. Growing plants assimilate the carbon, replacing it with oxygen, the source of life and energy. This result the leaves accomplish; but the roots also have their part in the purifying process, by taking up the noxious products of fermentation with which the gutters are charged.

Paris is said now to have so large a number of parks, and its streets and boulevards are so profusely shaded with trees, that the death rate has been thereby reduced from one in 24 to one in 39.*

Where there is plenty of growing foliage there is no

---

* *Scientific Monthly*, April, 1875.

malaria. The project of Garibaldi to restore the deadly Campagna, by planting the rapid-growing eucalyptus, has been called wild, but it is entirely practical.

Can the laws be too cogent, not merely for the encouragement of planting, but in punishment for unnecessary destruction? Especially should the value and uses of trees be made to enter into the education of the rising generation.

Last spring I set out a row of 50 vigorous young saplings along a public street. Before the end of the season not one had escaped the knife or hatchet, all being injured and some killed. The act was undoubtedly one of youthful wantonness. But how much more appreciation is exhibited by boys of larger growth? Year by year our streets lose some of their finest ornaments, never to be regained. Many are suffered to be gnawed to death by horses. Some perish by the needless cutting off of roots by careless workmen, in the laying of walks and drains; others by rights heedlessly accorded to paving contractors, gas companies and others, for digging up the streets and walks at will, regardless of the trees.

There would even seem to be in some minds an innate hostility to these lovely products of Nature. I am disposed to think such are actuated by an instinct, legitimately descended from some ancestor who had reason for his hatred. For thus saith the poet,—

> "Indulgent Nature on each race bestows
> A secret instinct to discern its foes:
> The goose—a silly bird—still shuns the fox,
> Lambs fly from wolves, and sailors steer from rocks,
> The rogue a gallows as his fate foresees,
> And bears a like antipathy to trees."

Great men of all ages have loved trees, and have ever paid them a kind of devotion.

Alexander had his favorite among them, which, in moments of unambitious retirement, he treated with the endearment of a child.

The good Oberlin, whose moral instructions and paternal care over the flock of which he was pastor preserved among a people shut up in the fastnesses of Switzerland a character of piety and sober industry, while Europe was agitated with scenes of moral and civil discord, inculcated the raising of trees as a religious duty.

Many Eastern sages—among them the wise Zoroaster—made arboriculture a precept of religion.

In such estimation were trees held by many ancient legislators, that particular species were consecrated to the several divinities which the country worshipped. Under their hallowed shade were the national rites performed, and sacrifices to the deity accepted. In these sylvan retreats the gods condescended to hold intercourse with mortals.

The delicate fancies of the classic poets delighted to associate with the life of trees such imaginary forms as the elves, the dryads, the fawns, and other sylvan beings, whose lives were commensurate with that of the tree which each inhabited.

Though our purer faith has discarded such notions, the general advance of knowledge has given us even stronger ground for reverence and love. Botanical science has revealed so great a similarity between the vegetable and animal, that it is hard to tell where the one nature ends and the other begins. In fact, some vegetables possess a complexity and delicacy of organism, an exquisite adaptation of every part, and even a degree of instinct, which do not belong to the lower order of animals. So far, science confirms the imagination of the poet; for to her eye, as to his—though in a larger and better sense—the tree becomes a sentient being. It is but a step from this to a consciousness on its part of our care and homage.

When we transplant a sapling from the forest, and set it down in our own door-yard, it is as if we had tamed a wild animal, and made one more pet for our household. An untutored savage has been converted into a domestic, and become attached to us by a tie of relationship. Henceforth a new friend is added to our list, whose character is being yearly developed beneath our eyes.

Let Americans then cherish with pride the trees of their native land. While we look with rapture upon their grace of outline, the proud dignity of their rough bodies and lofty limbs, the rich green of their foliage in summer, or its rainbow beauty in autumn; while we enjoy their refreshing shade, and are made better by their companionship; above all when we go forth to

> "———rouse
> The wide old wood from his majestic rest,
> Summoning from the innumerable boughs
> The strange deep harmonies that haunt his breast,"

let it be a duty to see to their healthful preservation, to study their habits and virtues, and to encourage the public appreciation.

There is a moral to the fable of the dryads, for trees are the guardian genii of the places they inhabit. Associated with our earliest youth, they never cease to interest, while our sense of their benefits increases with advancing years. Though what we now plant may come to maturity only after we shall have ceased to behold them, we know that they will gladden the eyes even of our children's children, and that we leave behind us living monuments, that shall bear our memories to posterity when we are beneath the sod which they shadow and adorn.

CLIMATE OF DETROIT AND THE LAKE REGION.

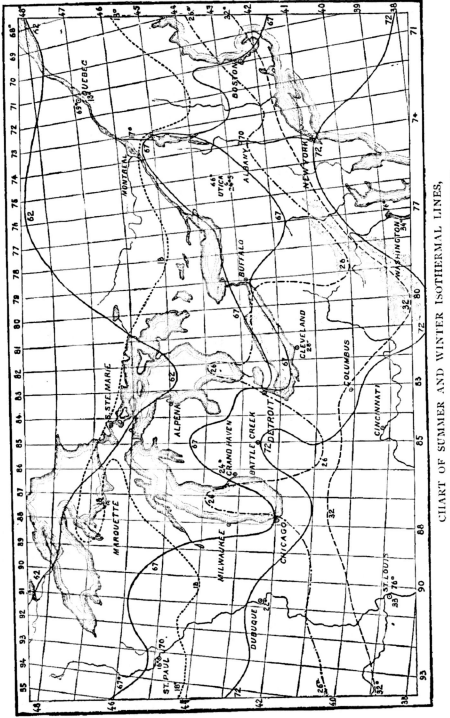

CHART OF SUMMER AND WINTER ISOTHERMAL LINES,
SHOWING THE INFLUENCE OF THE LAKES UPON THE TEMPERATURE.
(Full lines are Summer Isotherms; dotted lines are Winter Isotherms.)

CLIMATE OF DETROIT AND THE LAKE REGION.*

PART I.

WITHIN a few years the science of meteorology has made great progress under organized corps of observers. It is fair to state that while I make use of all the resources within my reach, in the preparation of this paper, its conclusions are based mainly upon independent observations, drawn from my records of the last thirty-nine years. Little of merit as these may claim, compared with the more strict deductions of the scientist, they may, like the observations of almost any lover of nature, serve to set facts in some new light, or new combination, and thus have a practical value.

That the immense bodies of water known as the Great Lakes affect the climate of this region is well known; but the nature and extent of their influence are yet but little familiar to the popular mind. Indeed, with all the advance in the science of weather, the data for scientific determinations have been and still are very scanty.

The controlling element in all climates is temperature. The direction and strength of winds, and the amount of moisture descending in rain, mist and snow, are sources of modification, or results, rather than chief causes. Though the temperature of any locality depends mainly upon general astronomical causes, felt all around the globe,

---

* Read before the Detroit Scientific Association, 1874.

it is also known that local causes have a very considerable share in the production of climate. Thus, the seasons on this continent differ greatly from those of the same latitudes in Europe, being hotter in summer and colder in winter. Our spring and autumn also differ from theirs in duration, and in other characteristics.

General facts like these I assume without going into the wide field of explanation. They and their causes are familiar to you.

I shall also assume as well known the fact that isothermal lines, or lines drawn through places of equal temperature over the United States, by no means conform to the latitude, but are deflected north or south by local causes, and that among these the Great Lakes have a prominent importance.

The winter isothermal lines are deflected northerly, and the summer lines southerly, in approaching these bodies of water. In other words, their vicinity is warmer in winter and cooler in summer than places in the same parallel removed from them, except in the immediate vicinity of the ocean.

These general facts I shall endeavor to render more clear by means of a chart. Instead of the usual method of delineating the isotherms in a regular series of degrees of temperature, I have taken only the means, in summer and in winter, of certain places specially important to my purpose, and carry the isotherms of these degrees across the region of the lakes, from the Atlantic to the Mississippi. For instance, Detroit has a mean summer temperature of 67 deg. and a mean winter temperature of 26 deg.*

---

* See Part II.—"Additional Observations"—for an increase in both summer and winter means, since the above was written.

Observers will notice the summer isothermal of 67 degrees, commencing at the sea-coast at Cape Cod. It passes a few miles up the coast and thence inland to a lower latitude in Central Massachusetts. From thence it rises rather suddenly into and along the Valley of Lake Champlain, almost to Quebec. Here it divides, passing southerly. One branch between Albany and Utica is carried into high lands of Pennsylvania, whence it rises again toward Buffalo, and west through Lake Erie. The other follows Montreal River and south shore of Lake Ontario and north shore of Lake Erie, uniting with the former at Detroit. From here it bears northerly into the Peninsula almost two degrees of latitude, until, feeling the cool waters of Lake Michigan, it loops suddenly down toward Chicago. Curving thence upward along the western coast, it leaves the lake at a point some miles north of Milwaukee, but at a lower point than on the eastern coast. Its course is now rapidly northward, until it reaches the parallel of 46 degrees, in longitude 95 degrees, a little north and west of St. Paul.

From the parallel of 42 deg. on the Atlantic it has passed through 4 deg. of latitude, or about 280 miles, in its approach to the Western plains. Over these, passing westward, it rises to a much higher parallel.

The cooling effect of the lakes upon the summer heat is here strikingly shown. Detroit has a lower mean summer temperature than Montreal and Quebec, although the latter is nearly five degrees further north.

St. Paul is hotter than Chicago, 3 deg. south.

The isothermal of the mean winter temperature of Detroit (26°) exhibits equal aberrations. Commencing at the sea-coast about latitude 43 deg., and coursing first south and then up the Hudson to Albany, it is thence pressed rapidly to the south and along the Alleghenies, down to the parallel of 40 deg. Thence it sweeps northerly to Buffalo, whence it passes west across Lake Erie, loops up into Lake Huron, down to Detroit, and thence rapidly south-west into Indiana. It thence again loops upward and far into Lake Michigan, sweeping the easterly coast. Turning sharply thence to Chicago it trends rapidly to the south-west, and strikes the Missouri at about the parallel of 40 deg.

From its lowest depression, at this point, to its highest, at the lakes, it has passed through four degrees of latitude, showing admirably the warming influence of the lakes upon the winter cold of this zone.

Let us now take a more northerly point and follow the isotherms of Sault St. Marie and Marquette, which have each a summer mean of 62 deg. and a winter of 18 deg.

You see by the chart how the summer mean of 62 deg. bends south from its high latitude, north of Quebec, well down into Lake Huron, and that passing thence into Lake Superior it trends still more rapidly to the north. Between the meridians of 70 deg. and 95 deg. it has ranged through 5 deg. of latitude, or 350 miles.

The winter mean of 18 deg. shows still more complicated irregularities, though not so wide a divergence. It has its most southerly deflections in Massachusetts and Minnesota, about latitude 44 deg., and its most northerly at the coast of Lake Superior, in latitude 47 deg., a range of 3 deg.

Take now some point south of Michigan, say the city of New York, which has a summer mean of 72 deg., and a winter of 31 deg.

The isotherm of 72 deg. follows down the Alleghenies as far south as the parallel of 38 deg. ; thence bears rapidly north-west to Dubuque, ranging through nearly five degrees of latitude. You cannot fail to observe how it loops up into the peninsula of Michigan as far north as Detroit, but bears away from the near vicinity of the lakes, where the summer means are cooler by 4 or 5 degs.

The winter isotherm of 32 degs., commencing at the sea-coast near New York, flanks the Alleghenies through several degrees of latitude, southerly, thence curves upwards towards the lakes, as far north as Columbus, Ohio, and thence again bends southerly, until it strikes the Missouri west of and about the latitude of St. Louis, a range of less than three degrees. Both these isotherms are too distant to be as much affected by the lakes as those first noticed.

These few observations perhaps sufficiently illustrate this part of our subject, though they by no means show all the divergences and irregularities to which many of the isothermals of this latitude are subject.

Our locality, though so greatly modified in several aspects of its climate by the presence of the Great Lakes, falls within the general system which prevails throughout the temperate zone on this continent.

It will be remembered that the lakes do not occupy valleys, as many suppose, nor do they fill gorges among mountains. On the contrary, there are no very elevated lands on or near their borders, but the region is rather a vast plain than a valley. The planes of ascent from their surface sare very moderate, the levels which separate the streams that discharge into the lakes from those which discharge into the Atlantic or Gulf of Mexico being broad and low, rather plateaus than hills.

Were these bodies of water dry land, of the same elevation, there would exist no conditions tending to deflect the isothermal lines from their regular curves from the great plains to the Atlantic. But so large a surface of water—warmer in winter and cooler in summer than the land—does very sensibly affect the temperature of the atmosphere which passes over them, and as temperature is the governing element of climate, the character of the season is essentially modified through their influence. The effect is to equalize the temperature over a considerable area, and to soften the extremes.

This modification of the climate may be made further apparent by a comparison of the *mean range of temperature of the months* for a series of years, at different posts of observation in this latitude.

Thus, while the mean temperature of the year does not vary greatly for the lake borders and places 500 miles distant, east and west, on the same parallel, the temperature at the latter falls to a lower mean in winter, or rises to a higher one in summer, or both. The mean of the year at Detroit and through New York and New England, on the same parallel (47 deg. to 48 deg.), differs only about one degree; but the mean range, that is, the increase from February, when the rising scale begins, until it commences to decline, in July, is at Albany and Amherst 4.5 deg. greater; the means rising from a range of 43 deg. during that period at Detroit, to 47.5 deg. at the other places.

Westward, this feature is still more conspicuous. At Battle Creek, due west from Detroit, and about equidistant from lakes Erie and Michigan, we find a mean range 10 deg. greater than in Detroit; the mean of the year being only a little more than 1 deg. higher. At Dubuque the difference is 12 deg. At St. Paul (2 deg. of latitude farther north) it is 16 deg. The mean of the year being at Dubuque 2 deg. higher, and at St. Paul 3 deg. lower than here, while the winter at Dubuque is 4 deg. colder, and the summer 4.5 deg. warmer than Detroit.

The mean temperature of each of the three winter months at Detroit is nearly the same, and varies but little from the general winter mean of 27 deg. At the other places named, on the same parallel, the lowest mean is not reached until some time in January; but the temperature begins to rise from that month onward, and merges more rapidly into the heats of summer.

The difference between the means of January and March at Detroit is 7 deg. At other places east, in the same latitude, it is 9 to 10 deg. The same difference is found at Battle Creek; scarcely less at Chicago; while at Dubuque it rises to 15 deg., and at St. Paul to 18 deg.

Equally marked is the rapid increase of temperature from March to May. At Detroit the advance does not exceed 22 deg. At Utica, Albany and Amherst it exceeds 25 deg. A like increase obtains at Battle Creek and Chicago, and at Dubuque and St. Paul it reaches 28 deg.

The maximum summer heat is attained in July in this latitude; the mean of that month being about 2 deg. above the summer mean at Detroit and eastward, and about 3 deg. at places westward.

Thence the decline into autumn is very gradual until September, the temperature of August corresponding nearly with the means of summer throughout (69 deg.), and that of September ranging from 6 deg. to 8 deg. below.

From September the decline is more rapid, but regular

to October, which represents the means of the autumn quite closely (50 deg).

The decline from the means of summer to those of autumn varies from 18 deg. to 20 deg., being a difference of about 2 deg. only for the different places named on this parallel. But the decline from autumn to winter, which is but 20 deg. at Lake Erie, ranges to 24 deg. at the interior stations east, and to 30 deg. at Dubuque, and at Battle Creek to 27 deg.

These results show the effect of the lakes, first, in a modification of the extremes, causing a difference of several degrees in the means of both summer and winter near their borders.

Second, in a prolongation of spring on the lake borders. Here the temperature of April represents nearly the mean of spring. At Battle Creek, April is about 4 deg. above the mean of spring, and at Dubuque April has nearly reached the mean of May at Detroit.

Third, in a prolongation of autumn or more gradual descent into winter. In December, places on this parallel in New York, Massachusetts and Central Michigan have reached the winter mean of Detroit, but still want two or three degrees of their own winter mean. Dubuque in December has reached a point 2 deg. lower than the winter mean of Detroit.

Fourth, in a modification of single extremes. The maximum noted by me in thirty years' observation, at and near Detroit, is 94 deg., the minimum —18 deg. Very rarely does the mercury fall below —10 deg. in any winter, the above extreme of —18 deg. having occurred only twice during the period.

During the same period in Central New York and

Massachusetts the maximum has reached above 100 deg. and the minimum −34 deg., the Detroit minimum of −18 deg. having occurred on an average once in every two winters.*

Such severe extremes are often sudden and very temporary, and afford little indication of the general character of the seasons. Nevertheless, they are an important element in our estimate, and often attest the capability, or otherwise, of any given climate for the growing of the more tender plants.

The character of our seasons as shown by these comparisons of temperature may be stated thus in general terms:

The winter of Detroit is warmer than that of places in the same latitude in Central New York, Massachusetts and Michigan, by at least two degrees, and 4.5 deg. warmer than the mean five hundred miles west.

Spring is 4 deg. colder than the central positions mentioned, and the increase from March to May is more gradual.

Summer is cooler than on the parallel east by 1 deg. to 2 deg.; than Central Michigan by 3 deg., and the more westerly positions by 4.5 deg.

Autumn is cooler by 1 deg. than the points east; by 2 deg. than Central Michigan, and by 4 deg. than the westerly posts; and the decline of heat is less rapid through the autumn months.

These favorable modifications of the prevailing climate of this region are still more strongly impressed on the eastern than the western borders of the lake, in consequence of the prevailing westerly winds, and the trib-

---

* But see Par. II.—

ute over the land the more equable temperature of the water.

The mean of summer at Grand Haven is 2 deg. lower, and that of winter 3 deg. higher than at Milwaukee. The summer temperature is also carried further on into the autumn, and the winter mean falls a month later.

Still more marked is the situation in regard to single extremes. It is claimed that the thermometer never falls below —16 deg. as an extreme at any point on the eastern shore of Lake Michigan (Winchell), even as far north as Traverse Bay, a latitude in which elsewhere, both east and west, the temperature has at periods of extreme cold fallen as low as —40 deg.

The wonderful advantages possessed by this favored coast of our peninsula are fast procuring for it an envied celebrity. It is destined to become the most noted fruit region of the United States, having all the advantages of the climate of the Ohio, the Missouri and California, without their drawbacks.

It will be seen that Detroit, though so favorably affected by the vicinity of the lakes, cannot claim all the extraordinary benefits they confer in so high a degree, and why the palm is borne from her by the locations on Lake Michigan and by the southern coast and the islands of Lake Erie.

That delicate foreigner, the peach, is with us liable to loss of the crop by May frosts, and even the tree itself often suffers from the winter extremes; but no such mishaps occur on the western coast of the peninsula. The native grape frequently suffers here, both in fruit and vine, but the crop almost never fails upon the islands in Lake Erie. These have a climate peculiarly favorable, both from the retarded spring and the prolonged autumn of their locality. In these respects they contrast most favorably with the much more southerly climates where the grape is cultivated.

An illustration of this came under my observation in the spring of 1860. Being at Lexington, Kentucky, on the night of the 25th of April, I was desirous to visit the most promising vineyard in that neighborhood, the vines of which were set full in fruit. The morning brought a black frost, and when I visited the yard not a bunch was found unspared; the whole crop was destroyed. Returning North, I reached Lake Erie on the 1st of May. There a winter temperature still reigned, and not a bud had put forth. In due time the island vines set fruit and produced an abundant crop.

The prevailing winds of this locality are in winter west, or those directions into which west enters. They vary from south-west to north-west, seldom east or south-east.

In spring, east and north-east winds prevail nearly half the time. They vary from east to west, and north-east to south, but seldom north-west. In some of the spring months, usually March or April, east and north-east winds are the prevailing ones. In others westerly.

In summer, south-west winds prevail, varying from south to west. East and west winds are frequent, but very few north-west or south-east.

In autumn, westerly winds are prevalent, varying to south-west and south, but a westerly direction enters into two-thirds of the winds of this season.

Taking the yearly average, probably two-thirds of the winds are south-west, west and north-west.

Light showers or falls of snow come with westerly winds, as also the summer thunder-storms, but the long rains and snow-storms are attended by an easterly wind. The severe and cold wind storms, however, are from the west, and it is from this direction that the winds come with greatest force, and we receive the storms that are so destructive to vessels on the lakes. This prevalence of surface winds from the west is only a necessary result of that majestic atmospheric current, which, in this temperate zone, is ever silently but unceasingly sweeping round the globe.

As the amount of precipitation of moisture, in the form of rain and snow, depends upon the vicinity of large water surfaces, it would naturally be supposed that the climate of Michigan should be a moist one. But the contrary is the case. In fact, the peninsula climate is exceedingly dry, if we consider the total amount of rainfall. The cause will be apparent when we consider the source from which our rains come, and the relation that subsists between the rainfall and the temperature.

The Gulf of Mexico undoubtedly furnishes the great source of supply to the atmosphere east of the plains. The vapor-laden trade winds, coming from the warm tropic seas, carry their volume of moisture over the Gulf States, where large quantities are precipitated. As it is borne further inland this supply meets the great current of south-westerly winds, and is carried north and east with a constantly diminishing amount of precipitation. From the gulf coast, where it is greatest, to the lakes, the rainfall has gradually diminished from the large mean annual amount of 60 inches to 28 inches.

The result would probably be quite uniform were there no diversities of surface to cause local differences.

The same effect is visible, to a less extent, along the

Atlantic coast, where the easterly winds contribute to the supply.

To a still less extent this effect is apparent in the vicinity of the lakes. The total rainfall is two to four inches greater in the interior of the peninsula than on the immediate borders.

The law which prevails in Europe, of an excess of precipitation upon the mountain summits and elevated plains, does not hold generally in the United States, where rather a contrary law obtains. The high plateaus —even the elevated chain of the Alleghenies—have less of both summer and annual precipitation than the lower lands on either side. Our peninsula, which is a plateau not exceeding 1000 feet above the ocean, is no exception to the rule.

This phenomenon is doubtless due to the lower temperature of the higher lands, during the season of greatest precipitation, and shows that general rather than local causes govern the rainfall throughout the whole country. The cooler summer atmosphere, which we have seen to be the effect of the near vicinity of the lakes, contributes to this result, and will explain in part, no doubt, the comparative dryness of the Michigan climate.

With the exception of the gulf coast this portion of the United States belongs to the great area of equally distributed rains, one that has no defined rainy seasons.

We have, consequently, no *periodic* rains, although the periods of most abundant rains are looked for quite regularly in the summer and the early autumn months. It is usual to expect the "equinoctial storm," as it is called, —a rainy period of several days,—about the end of September; but even this is quite uncertain, both as to its duration and even its occurrence.

During the heat of summer our rains occasionally assume a character suited to the tropical vehemence of the temperature, and pour down with great profusion though their duration is short.

A peculiar phenomenon of the rain storms in this locality is that they occur so frequently under the cool shades of the night, preceded and followed by cloudless days.

Although the amount of rainfall is so small in this district, I think it will be found, were the records sufficiently extended, that the *number of days* on which some rain or snow falls is as great as in more southerly districts, where the annual amount is twofold.

That our atmosphere is little, if at all, affected by the diffuse evaporation from the surrounding water surfaces is evident from its great clearness, the intense azure of its sky, and the brilliancy of its moonlight and star canopy.

The region of the lakes is noted also for its beautiful sunsets. In this, as well as in the transparency of its atmosphere, it excels the Eastern States, and more than rivals far-famed Southern Europe. Talk of the blue skies of Italy! We have more clear firmament, and of a deeper depth of blue, in one month than Italy in half the year.

To exhibit clearly our relation to the surrounding territory would require charts of the isohyetal lines. In the absence of these, a brief statement may serve to convey a proximate idea.

In broad terms, the area of 8 to 9 inches spring rainfall includes the whole Michigan peninsula. The central and western portions have nearly one inch more than the eastern, and at Mackinaw and St. Mary's the total has diminished to about 5 inches.

The area of 9 to 10 inches summer rainfall includes all the lakes and Lower Canada. There is but little variation throughout the peninsula; 9 inches representing fairly the eastern side, and 10 inches the central and western.

The autumn rainfall has about the same general average, but diminishes to about 8 inches at the north, or to the same mean as Wisconsin.

The average winter precipitation is about 5 inches; somewhat less on the east side of the State, and about one and a half inches more in the interior and west.

The total annual precipitation is 30 to 31 inches on the east side, increasing south and west to 34 inches, and diminishing to 25 inches at Mackinaw. The average for the whole peninsula is 33 inches.

Comparing these means with those which obtain at a small remove, we find that a summer rainfall of from ten to twelve inches (or two to three inches in excess of Detroit) crowds closely up lakes Michigan, Erie and Ontario, and sweeps over the lower half of Wisconsin, and as far north and west as St. Paul.

The winter precipitation increases rapidly as we advance south from Lake Erie, being fully seven inches through the north part of Ohio and Indiana (or two inches above the mean of Michigan), and increases to eleven inches at Cincinnati.

Proceeding south from Michigan the total annual precipitation increases at the rate of about three inches for every degree of latitude, to the Ohio River, where it is forty-eight inches, or fifteen inches more than the mean of Michigan.

At 95 deg. longitude the mean annual precipitation is about the same as at Detroit. But thence westward the diminution is rapid, and at the meridian of 100 deg. it is scarcely more than half that amount.

From the lakes to the Atlantic we find a gradual increase, from an annual mean of thirty-two inches to forty-four inches.

Thus notwithstanding our insular position, the climate of this region proves to be the dryest in the United States east of the headwaters of the Mississippi. But the rains are very equally distributed, through all but the winter months, which have only one-sixth of the entire precipitation. Crops, therefore, seldom suffer from the want of moisture, even in the dry periods.

South of the Ohio the winters have one-third of the whole precipitation—equal to that of the summer.

Having considered the character of the seasons and our relation to neighboring parts of the continent, as regards the average measures of precipitation, let us notice and compare the monthly fluctuations.*

At Detroit the smallest quantities fall in the months of December and February; the mean of thirty-eight years being 1.3 and 1.4 inches, respectively, and that of the three winter months being 1.7 inches.

From February to June appears a gradual increase, largest for March and April, when it rises to 2.9, the mean of the spring being 2.8 inches.

In June, which is the month of largest precipitation, there is an increase to 3.9 inches, the mean of the summer being 3.1. From June there is a falling off during the remaining summer months.

The mean for September rises to 3.3 inches, that of

---

* Comparing these measures with the "Table of Mean Temperature and Rainfall of the Seasons," given in the "Additional Observations," following this Essay, it will be seen that the figures above given require some modifications. These, however, do not affect the general deductions.

autumn being 2.4, and falls again through the remainder of the year.

These results show a tendency to two minima, in December and February, and to two maxima, in June and September.

The June freshet is looked for quite uniformly, and with more certainty than the floods which attend the melting of the snow in the spring, although the latter often exceed in temporary height and violence.

A table of the average precipitation for the seasons and months, for different places, from the Gulf to the coast of New England, exhibits very considerable contrasts. It would be interesting to examine them if we had the time.

For my present purpose I will advert to the fact only that there exists a general tendency to minima of precipitation about the middle or end of winter, and of maxima about midsummer.

Grouping the results, it may be stated that on or near the coast of New England the tendency is to one minimum in February of about three inches, and three maxima, in May four inches, August and November 4.5 to 4 inches.

Through Central New York one minimum, February, of 2 inches, and one maximum, June or July, 3.5 inches.

In the Lake region, west of Lake Erie, one minimum in February, of 1.4 inches, and one maximum in June, 3.5 inches.

In the Ohio Valley one minimum, January and February, of 3 inches, and one maximum about June, 4.5 inches.

On the Gulf coast two minima, April, 2 inches, and

November, 3 inches, and one maximum, in July, 6 to 8 inches.

The minimum of February at Detroit is less than one-twentieth, and the maximum of June nearly one-eighth of the whole average annual rainfall. In other words, the mean of February is 1.1 inch below the average mean of the months; that of June is one inch above the average mean.

On the diagram is shown the annual precipitation, running through the mean of the several months, at representative stations within the group referred to, including also the upper Mississippi. These few curved lines represent very closely, and as far as may be done from so few data, the rainfall through the year, over the whole United States, east of the great plains.

The remark is frequently made that our climate is undergoing a permanent change. Many think it is becoming drier, which is by some attributed to the destruction of the forests; according to others it is becoming permanently colder also.

These popular opinions suggest a very interesting inquiry. For the present it may be a sufficient answer that the statistics of the rainfall, as well as those of the temperature, do not verify such conclusions.

Throughout this region, from the Atlantic to the Mississippi, north of the Ohio, the fluctuations, both annual and for a series of years, are very great, and they show a tendency to an irregular *grouping* of years in which the rainfall is in excess, and of those in which it is in diminution of the mean. This is governed by no known or apparent law, and though in the main there is a general agreement throughout the region, yet considerable and

MONTHLY PRECIPITATION.—UNITED STATES. 437

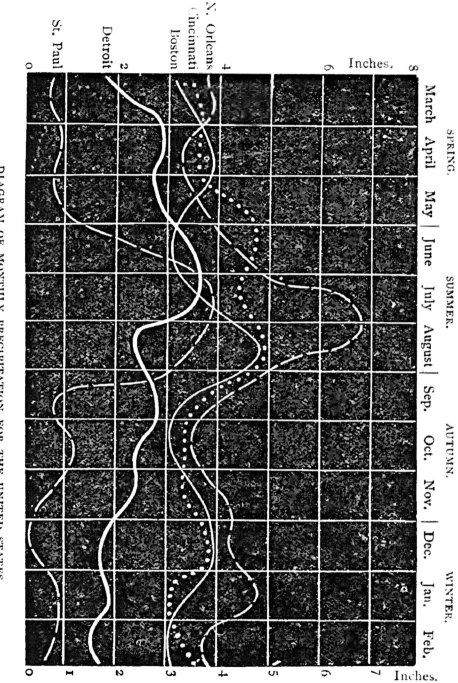

DIAGRAM OF MONTHLY PRECIPITATION FOR THE UNITED STATES.

remarkable differences occur, even at points not widely separated.*

Diagrams for all this region indicate an *average* increase of the rainfall from about 1837 until about 1862, and this fact contradicts the prevalent opinion of increasing dryness. Since that period a general decrease is observable in this region.

Within this first series of years occur one period of greatly diminished rainfall, common to the diagrams for New England, New York, Southern Michigan and Ohio, viz., from 1835 to 1845, averaging 10 to 15 per cent. below the mean for each district, and one period of increased rainfall, viz., from 1848 to 1862, which averages 10 to 20 per cent. above the mean.

Successive years, however, frequently show great irregularity in the amounts, sometimes falling from 20 to 30 per cent. above the mean of the place to as much below, within a period of two or three years, breaking in so violently upon the average as to render any generalization very difficult.

For the sake of comparison I select from each of the districts named three years of greatest and of least rainfall, and bring them together, exhibiting the percentage which each attains above and below the yearly mean of the district.

A comparison of these maxima and minima serves to show how extremely local are the causes of the differences; how small is the correspondence between the locations for the same years, while it does not indicate any decided differences in the variability in the different districts.

---

* See Part III.—"Periodical Changes," etc.—for more recent conclusions—1887.

A TABLE OF PERCENTAGES OF RAINFALL IN MAXIMUM AND MINIMUM YEARS.

	Years of greatest maximum.			Per cent. above mean.			Years of greatest minimum.			Per cent. below mean.		
New England Coast.......	1841	1850	1868	15	23	21	1837	1849	1856	15	12	12
New York	1842	1850	1857	12	17	20	1844	1856	1861	15	13	16
Southern Michigan........	1849	1855	1861	13	30?	26	1845	1850	1865	26	16	28
Ohio..........	1847	1855	1858	16	16	26	1838	1853	1856	23	16	28

The range at Detroit (between highest maximum and lowest minimum) is fully fifty-five per cent. of the annual mean, which does not differ greatly from that of the other districts, though in excess of the eastern ones, but at St. Paul the range is much greater. There the mean of the year is only twenty-five inches, while the range, in nineteen years' observation, is from forty-one to eighteen inches, or over 100 per cent.

The accompanying diagram will exhibit at a glance the annual fluctuations in the rainfall at Detroit since 1834. Each column represents the precipitation of the year, and the amount in inches is shown by the figures at the side. The curved line is an attempt at a generalization of the several means.*

To the facts we have been considering, and which have relation to our situation relative to the great sources of supply, as well as to the plateau character of the country, is due our comparative exemption from destructive flooding rains and deep snows. Neither the lakes nor the peninsula streams overflow their banks, causing such de-

---

* For this diagram see "Additional Observations"—Part II.—where the columns are extended to date, 1887.

vastations as are common in the States east and south of us. And in winter railroad trains are seldom blocked by snow, as frequently happens in this latitude.

The same cause which frees this locality from the inconveniences of deep snow also deprives us in many winters of sufficient snow for the ordinary winter sledding. The increased temperature, due to the extensive and open water surfaces around us, causes the snow to melt almost as it falls so that it seldom lasts long as a covering to the soil. The lower atmosphere, at such times, gathers increased humidity, which occasions a sensible chill, that is more uncomfortable in its effect than a steady cold below the freezing point.

Yet it is a noticeable fact that fogs are rare with us, at any season.

Our deepest snow and of longest continuance usually occurs in February, which is the month of greatest cold.*

The droughts which prevail, often disastrously, in autumn throughout Michigan are not peculiar to this district; although the less quantity of rain at that season, than falls over the country east and south, no doubt contributes to this result.

The still drier climate west of Lake Michigan, extending with increased severity to the great plains, exhibits this phenomenon in vastly enhanced proportions.

Yet to the same cause is due that peculiar and delightful phenomenon—the Indian summer—which is comparatively little known to the Atlantic States, but which constitutes so pleasing a feature in the lake region.

In a general survey of our seasons the winter at Detroit may, as a rule, be classed as " mild and open."

---

*The more extended observations—Part II.—show January to be the coldest month, by nearly one degree.

My notes show nearly two-thirds of the winters for the last thirty-eight years to be of this character. These kind of winters may be thus described: A temperature seldom below 0, and frequently above the freezing point; an average temperature 1 deg. above the winter mean of 27 deg.; a few weeks at most—often a few days only—of snow sufficient to make sleighing; many cloudless days, though the cloudy ones are in excess; constant alternations of frosty nights and days, with warm and damp or rainy ones, yet with a large number of days of clear, bracing atmosphere, when the thermometer falls below freezing at night and rises a little above it by day; prevailing west and south-west winds, an occasional storm that leaves its mantle of snow, followed almost immediately, or within a few days at most, by the prevailing openness.

As a rule, only the "cold" winters are snowy ones—winters whose temperature is 1 deg. or 2 deg. below the mean,—when it continues to freeze for several days successively. At such periods the local influences are overborne by the general causes which prevail in this latitude, and the cold storms, with their freight of heavy snows, sweep over and involve our district in the prevailing frigidity. At such times the ground freezes hard, if bare, to the depth of two or three feet. Streams are frozen over,—our broad river included,—and no longer lend their influence to soften the temperature. Winter gathers strength by its own progress, and forgets its ordinary relaxations.

Of the advance of spring-time my note-books furnish a few items which may serve for useful comparison with other localities.

The first of the forest trees to be animated by the genial breath are the poplar, willow, elm and maple. These are in flower from April 1 to 20, the average for the two latter being April 7. The earliest period on my records is in 1845, March 11.

Wild flowers make their appearance about the middle of April to 1st of May.

Those cultivated fruits, peach and cherry, come into bloom about a month later than the forest maple and elm,—20th of April to middle of May,—the average being May 8th. Pear and apple follow, 1st to 20th of May; average about May 12th.

The forests now begin to show a green tint, but the perfection of the leaf is not attained until late in June.

We have seen how much the heats of summer are moderated by our situation. Yet, notwithstanding, our climate, like that of the whole temperate zone, is one of fierce extremes; indeed, at times most fitfully intemperate, and making us acquainted, under the same sky, with the winter of the Arctic regions and the summer of the tropics. There are days in our short summers that fairly belong to the equator, which blaze and quiver with sunshine like a furnace, and when vegetable growth may actually be measured in its hourly increase.

There are days in our rigorous winters when the frosted air cuts like a knife, when storm so follows storm, in all the grandeur of the season, that for a time the landscape is obliterated, every familiar object buried out of sight beneath the congealed and hoary breath of the storm god.

"No cloud above, no earth below,
A universe of sky and snow."
WHITTIER.

But neither heated nor frozen "terms" ordinarily last many days at a time. Changes are sudden and violent, from one extreme of temperature to the opposite.

"Dry" seasons are often accompanied by flooding rains; frosts follow a period of hot days, and they have been known to occur—though very rarely, as in 1859—in every month of the year.

Between the spring and the autumn of our climate there is a striking contrast. For while the spring of the English poets, so familiar to our early literature,—breathing balm, and leading by slow gradations into summer,—scarcely exists here, where often winter lingers into May, and spring leaps at a bound into the arms of summer, or cheats us with successive storm, cold and wet, the autumn time is the most enjoyable of the year, and is in grateful contrast to the dull, wet season of Europe.

As a rule, our first two autumn months are pleasant, cool and dry, and sometimes this agreeable weather is protracted into the first month of winter. But this season, too, is changeable, and nearly one-fourth of the years on my calendar are classed as mild and wet or wet and cold.

This great and constantly recurring irregularity of the seasons gives disappointment to those who seek to form predictions of the weather, based upon observations of previous years.

My own notes are so general in character that they meet ill the strict demands of science. Yet some of the conclusions drawn from them may be worthy of record.

Winters which, in popular language, are called "mild and open," are ordinarily succeeded by "warm and early" springs, the proportion to those which are "cold and late" being about two to one.

Cold and snowy winters are certain to be followed by cold and backward springs. To this law my records show no exception.

Warm and pleasant summers, if succeeded by dry and pleasant autumns, are followed, as a rule (not without exceptions), by mild and open winters.

Cold summers and autumns are ordinarily succeeded by cold winters, the exceptions being as about one to two.

Warm and early springs are, as a rule, followed by warm and pleasant summers, the proportions of such to cold and wet summers being nearly four to one.

Cold and late springs, it may be expected, will be followed by cold or wet summers, but they are almost as frequently succeeded by warm and dry.

Though there is an approach to some measure of regularity in the character of the seasons for a succession or group of years, no certain law is apparent, but a warm or a cold, a wet or a dry year is likely to be succeeded by one or more of like character, before the character is reversed.

Upon the whole, notwithstanding the great range of climatic phenomena, and the extreme diversity of certain seasons and years, the observations of even the last thirty-nine years—short as is that period for scientific deductions—show our climate to be constant and uniform, returning always to the average standard of heat and moisture.

Popular opinion pronounces some extraordinary extreme to be "unprecedented" within the memory of that very unreliable character, "the oldest inhabitant." But science, from whose stern decrees there is no appeal, declares it to be but local and temporary, and part of those ever recurring features which, in the cycle of the years, only furnish proof of the stability and uniformity of nature.

In the natural divisions of the seasons another contrast appears between our climate and that of Europe, which, though less marked in the vicinity of the lakes, is yet a noted difference throughout the temperate zone of America.

The divisions of the calendar year appear much more arbitrary as applied to our circumstances, and show that they were meant for another hemisphere.

In attempting a classification better suited to our climate, if we define "winter" as the period of hard frosts and completely dormant vegetation, that season will embrace not merely a fourth part, but nearly half of the entire year, or from November to the middle of April inclusive, five and a half months.

If we call "spring" the period between the flowering of the earliest trees and shrubs or the first opening buds and the full development of the leaves, that season will have its average beginning about the middle of April and its end the middle of June, two months.

The reign of "summer," the season of the full perfection of vegetable growth, holds from the middle of June to the middle of September, three months.

"Autumn," the season of the ripening of the fruits of the earth and the gradual decadence of vegetable life, lasts from the middle of September to November, one and a half months.

In the more genial atmosphere of the lakes, as I have already noted, the autumnal season is often much more protracted, and cheats the colder months of a portion of their supremacy. The bland airs of the Indian summer help to prolong the illusion; but it is only an interloper, and, in general, by November the hard frosts have set in, and

"Winter comes to rule the varied year."

I cannot close these remarks without adverting to the substantial advantages which our climate possesses, especially that of the lake region, over most others on the globe.

If it is often excessive in its extremes, it has not the great daily range which in arid climates is so severely felt, causing a benumbing coldness to the nights after the oppressive heat of the day.

If we have sometimes droughts, to the injury of the crops, we have not those periodic seasons of completely dry weather, when no rain falls for many weeks, or even months; when vegetation can be sustained only by irrigation, and the atmosphere is charged with dust, features that so greatly detract from the excellences of California.

And if occasional drenching rains flood the growing crops, they bring at rare intervals to our doors only slight intimations of those deluges which deform the winters and the rainy seasons of the South and the Pacific coast, or which, in the hill countries, often fill the valleys with the débris of ruined homes.

If severe gales sometimes cause destruction among our lake craft, and even, though rarely, uproot our orchards, no tornado ever visits upon us its terrific fury, and our locality is remarkably free from the sudden and fierce storms which are an incident even close to our borders.*

The disagreeable features are but exceptions to the general rule of moderate but sufficient rains for all needs, equally distributed throughout the year; a summer temperature, which rapidly quickens into active life the hi-

---

*In 1875 Detroit was visited by a small cyclone, the only one known within the memory of the "oldest inhabitant."—1887.

bernating earth, and in its fervors gives to our zone some of the productive power of the tropics, enabling it to bring to perfection the bountiful maize and other tropical plants, and especially those various and valuable fruits that attain their perfection only in our clime—the apple, pear, peach, plum and grape.

> " Whatever fruits in different climes are found,
> That proudly rise or humbly seek the ground;
> Whatever blooms in torrid tracts appear,
> Whose bright succession decks the varied year;
> Whatever sweets salute the northern sky,
> With vernal lives that blossom but to die;
> These here disporting own the kindred soil."
>
> GOLDSMITH.

It must be acknowledged that our climate, like that of this continent generally, is a very trying one to the average American constitution. Its dryness and its frequent and excessive changes seem to sap from the body that juiciness of the blood which, under the moist and equable skies of England, blooms into ruddy complexions and swells into plump outlines.

Perhaps the climate is not alone responsible for the evil. Much is attributable to our mode of life; the incessant application to business, in the haste to be rich; or too much of indoor life and want of proper exercise in the open air. Our boys cannot be said to be pale and sickly, and they brave the weather in all its rudeness.

Though the climate of Detroit partakes of the general character, it does so to a modified degree. I believe it is admitted that our locality is remarkable for its healthfulness and freedom from endemic diseases. I put the question to our professional and well informed President,[*] whether Detroit is not even abominably healthy!

---

[*] Dr. Andrews.

Nature is full of compensations. The perpetual summer of torrid climes is enervating to mind and body. Even in our Southern States, agriculture, the basis of wealth, must be carried on by an inferior race.

Do the people who have been brought up in a clime where summer is eternal appreciate in their full measure those gifts of bountiful nature whose enjoyment is not enhanced by their occasional loss? Does the never-ending succession of flowers and fruits compensate for the absence of the "seasons," the return of spring, summer and autumn, after the dearth of winter; for that period of biting cold and storm without, and blazing hearths within,

"——king of intimate delights,
Fireside enjoyments, home-born happiness,"

enhancing even by its bitter contrast the enjoyableness and bloom of summer?

Where but in such a clime as ours, marked so emphatically by the revolutions of the seasons, with their cold and heat, and all their pleasing variety and change,

" Forever charming, and forever new,"

do the arts flourish best and man attain his highest perfection? Happy the land which enjoys the promise of spring and the realization of autumn; where the fruits of the earth are secured only by unremitting care and labor; where a frigid temperature strengthens those active energies that droop in a warmer clime; and where the glories of summer, being only an occasional gift, are more welcome from the contrast, and more thoroughly appreciated and enjoyed.

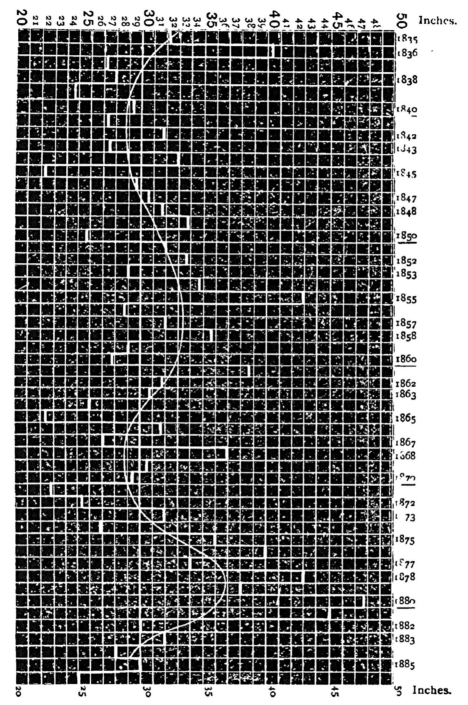

DIAGRAM SHOWING THE ANNUAL RAINFALL, DETROIT, 1835–1886.

CLIMATE OF DETROIT AND THE LAKE REGION.

Part II.—Additional Observations.

SINCE the foregoing essay on the climate of Detroit was written, ten years and more have passed. This considerable extension of the series available for scientific deduction enables me to supplement the first essay by some additional observations.

Attention is at once attracted to the very considerable increase in both the temperature and the rainfall during the last decade.

This increase, amounting to about one degree in the mean annual temperature, and to seven inches in the mean annual precipitation, brings up the mean temperature of the whole fifty-year series from 47°—the supposed standard in 1874—to 47.9° in 1886; and the mean of the rainfall from about 31 inches to 32 inches.

These facts serve to bring scientific observation into more confirmed opposition to the popular opinion, that our climate is becoming colder. They show, in fact, that Detroit has a somewhat warmer climate than has been generally accredited, and also a liability to greater extremes.

The diagram of the rainfall published with the above mentioned essay indicated for this region an average increase from about 1837 until 1862, and after that year a general decrease. As that record closed, in 1874, another period of increased precipitation had begun. It continued to 1881, culminating in 1880 in a register of 47.7 inches, the maximum of the entire semi-centennial series. Simultaneously, the mean annual temperature advanced, until it attained 51° in 1881 and 1882, or nearly the maximum of the whole series.

Since 1880 the columns of annual rainfall have diminished quite steadily, standing in 1884 at 28.2 inches, rising to 30 inches in 1885, and again falling to 25 inches in 1886.

The temperature has also fallen, and we seem to be once more on the downward scale. As even a half-century is an insufficient period to establish a certainly correct average, it is not at all improbable that the means as determined in 1874, of 30 to 31 inches annual rainfall, and 47° annual temperature, may approach more nearly the true standard than the higher means accorded by the half-century record. We are justified, however, in adopting the new means, which, being the results of the longest series possible, are at least likely to be substantially accurate.

Let us now inquire what changes, if any, the added years have brought to light in the *maxima* and *minima* of temperature.

The highest temperature noted up to 1874 was 98° and the lowest —18°. We must now concede to the record of extremes 100° maximum, and —20° minimum, the highest extreme having been reached in July, 1878, and the lowest in February, 1875. The minimum of —18° has been reached five times within the half-century, viz., in 1852, '57, '64, '73 and '79. That of —14° four times, —in 1855, '56, '59 and '67. That of —10° four times, —in 1860, '61, '66 and '72.

The maximum rainfall of 47.7 inches has been reached since 1874, as also the extremes of 45 inches, 43 inches, and 40 inches, within the same period; the year 1855 only, outside of this period, exhibiting so high an extreme as 43 inches. The three dryest years are 1845, '65 and '71, each having about 22 inches only.

From the means of the years let us proceed to those of the *Seasons,* as determined from the monthly means of the fifty-year period.

These I tabulate as follows:

TABLE OF MEAN TEMPERATURE AND RAINFALL OF THE SEASONS—1835 TO 1886.

WINTER.			SPRING.			SUMMER.			AUTUMN.			YEAR.	
	Temp., deg.	Rain, inch.		Temp., deg.	Rain, inch.		Temp., deg.	Rain, inch.		Temp., deg.	Rain, inch.	Temp., deg.	Rain, inch.
Dec.*	28	2	Mch.	33	2.6	June	67	3.5	Sep.	61.5	2.8		
Jan.	26.5	2	Apr.	45.5	2.5	July	71	3.5	Oct.	51	2.7		
Feb.	27.2	2	May	57	3.4	Aug.	69	2.5	Nov.	37.5	2.5		
Season	27.3	6		45.5	8.5		69	9.5		50	8	47.9	32

Of these means various combinations may be formed which, while curious in themselves, serve to show how equally distributed are the temperature means throughout the year, and also the relations which the several seasons bear to each other and to the year.

Thus as regards the *temperature,* the *means* of winter and summer combined (96.3°) correspond quite closely with those of spring and autumn, which are 1° only less (95.2°).*

Half the mean of each of these couples of seasons represents the mean temperature of the year. The mean of

---

* In making up the winter means of any year that of the December of the year preceding is used, so as to bring into the winter measures the months which are in juxtaposition.

spring is 2.7° below; while that of autumn is 2° above the yearly mean.

If we add together the means of any month with those of the months corresponding in place in the other seasons, we find their combined means to represent very nearly the annual mean. Thus, the means of December, March, June and September equal 47.4°; those of January, April, July and October equal 48.7°; those of February, May, August and November equal 47.7°.

The mean of winter a little exceeds half of the autumn mean, and equals one-seventh exactly the sum of the means of all the seasons. The mean of summer temperature is 36 per cent. of the sum of the seasons. That of autumn, 26 per cent.; that of spring, 23 per cent.; that of winter, 14 per cent.

Turning to the *rainfall*, the table shows that the spring and autumn means nearly equal each other; the former being 26 per cent., and the latter 25 per cent. of the annual precipitation. The summer rainfall is the largest, corresponding with the season of highest temperature, and is 30 per cent. of the entire precipitation. The winter precipitation is about two-thirds that of summer, being 19 per cent. of the yearly mean.

To these notes, showing the mean characters of our seasons, I add a table of seasonal fluctuations (see p. 456).

These figures show the extent of range, and consequent diversity of our seasons in different years.

The tables will prove useful for reference in the future consideration of our climatology.

The accompanying diagram of the *annual rainfall* for the semi-centennial period under review has been extended from the diagram first published with the essay of 1874.

TABLE OF SEASONAL FLUCTUATIONS,

SHOWING THE MAXIMA AND MINIMA OF THE MEANS OF TEMPERATURE AND RAINFALL; THE YEAR AND THE SEASON OF EACH.

SEASON.	YEAR.	TEMPERATURE DEGREES.			YEAR.	RAINFALL INCHES.		
		Max.	Min.	Range.		Max.	Min.	Range.
Winter	1882	38			1874	11.9		
	1875		19	19	1845		2.8	9.1
Spring	1846	50			1880	13.7		
	1837–38		40	10	1874		4.8	8.9
Summer	1868	79			1880	15.6		
	1836–42		64	15	1841		4.5	11.1
Autumn	1881	58			1881	13.7		
	1875		47	11	1871		1.6	12.1
50-year period	1869	52			1880	47.7		
	1857		43	9	1865		21.3	26.4

It may be noticed, in proof of the long period which is required to give accuracy to averages, that for the first half of this period, in fact down to 1874, the yearly precipitation but little exceeded a mean of 30 inches, while the last half shows a mean of 34 inches, and the last decade a mean of 37.5 inches. The mean of the whole period is found to be 32 inches.

To exhibit in another form and at a single glance the means of *annual temperature*, I subjoin a diagram corresponding to that of the rainfall. For more full comparison are added the means of summer and winter, and also the annual rainfall. With the aid of this diagram

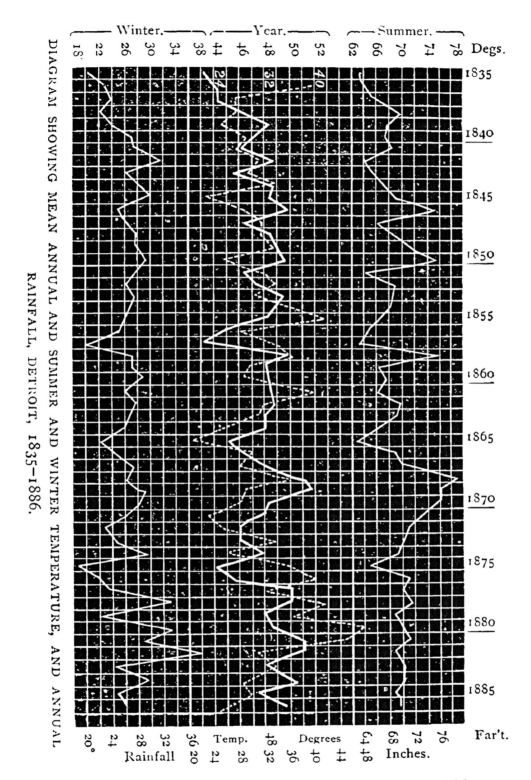

and our tabular statements, the relations of precipitation to temperature, and of the temperature of the seasons to each other, and to the year, may be readily seen.

The vertical lines represent the years, the horizontal lines the temperature means, and the rainfall. For the summer and winter temperature each horizontal line represents 2°. For those of the year each line represents 1°. For the rainfall (shown by dotted line) each horizontal line represents 2 inches.

Having laid before the reader a chart of the temperature and rainfall of the past half-century, we may inquire whether, out of the great and diverse fluctuations, it is possible to group the years into any marked series of dry and wet, warm and cold. Do the weather records sustain the old theory of the French habitants, that these changes follow a seven-year period?

For the sake of trial, I will here dispose the years since 1836 into groups of seven each, as in the following table:

NO.	GROUP.	TEMPERATURE — DEG.			RAINFALL — INCHES.		
		Mean.	Above normal	Below normal	Mean.	Above normal	Below normal
1	1837–43	46.5		1.4	28.2		3.8
2	1844–50	48.4	0.5		29.7		2.3
3	1851–57	46		1.9	33.5	1.5	
4	1858–64	48.6	0.5		32	0	0
5	1865–71	48.4	0.5		28.4		3.6
6	1872–78	47.8	0	0	35.	3	
7	1879–85	49.5	1.5		35.8	3.8	

We see from this table a disposition on the part of the temperature element to follow the supposed law for the first four periods; but the remaining three ignore it absolutely. On the part of the precipitation there appears no correspondence with any such law.

That there is a tendency to recurring periods of high and low, in both elements, we have seen. Can we arrange these into any system of grouping which shall show a correspondence between them,—a system that shall not be so broken in upon by violent and opposite extremes, in single years or in small groups of years, as to defy classification?

Both the temperature and the rainfall are susceptible of being grouped in periods of from ten to twelve years, showing a quite uniform recurrence of the same conditions. But after many attempts so to group these as to exhibit a correspondence between the two elements within the same intervals,—recurring periods common to each, —the task was found to be hopeless. But the investigation finally led me to a discovery of the true relation which exists between the two elements, and of the law which seems to govern. The results appeared to be of sufficient importance to be very fully set forth. This I have attempted in a separate essay, forming Part III. of these observations upon our climate, and to this the interested reader is referred.

But apart from periodical forms of change, how great have been the annual fluctuations! Extreme wet and extreme dry years are not always separated by considerable intervals, but the differences between contiguous years are often great. (See diagram of rainfall.)

Thus immediately succeeding 1844, with its rain column at 34 inches, followed one of the dryest, 1845, with its rainfall of only 22.5 inches. In the midst of the high rainfall period, during which, in 1855, the precipitation rose to 42.5 inches, the column fell the next year to 28.5 inches. During the long decline succeeding, the column dropped, in 1865, to 21.3 inches,—the lowest on my records. From this the recovery was gradual, to the next high culmination of 36 inches, in 1868. In 1871 the rainfall was again reduced to 22.6 inches, from which low point it mounted by regular gradations, to its extremest height, in 1880, of 47.7 inches.

These extremes indicate a total range of twenty-five inches, or more than three-fourths of the mean annual amount.

Fluctuations in the temperature exhibit a range considerably greater, from 76° in 1858—the highest summer mean—to 19° in 1875—the lowest winter mean; being a divergence of 57°, or a fifth more than the annual mean. The *mean* annual or periodical temperatures are, however, quite uniform, compared with those of the rainfall.

The decade of years that have been added to observation since my essay of 1874 serves to confirm the remark then made, as to the equal distribution of the rainfall throughout the seasons in this favored locality. And while no important differences are shown in regard to the means of the seasons, and their relations to places east and west of Detroit, as pointed out in my former remarks on "The Effect of the Lakes upon the Temperature," these are sufficient to modify in some particulars the comparisons then instituted, while they tend rather to confirm than diminish the favorable aspects.

Among sundry weather predicates, I there laid down the following:—"Cold and snowy winters are certain to be followed by cold and backward springs. To this law my records show no exception." The year 1884 would almost claim to be considered an exception to the rule,

But notwithstanding its continuance of cold and snow, the mean temperature of the winter (1883 and 1884) was 2° above the normal, while the spring was but 1.5° above. So the exception is apparent only. Continued observation has only served to confirm the law thus laid down.

It is a not uncommon remark, often heard at the close of a very severe winter, that the succeeding spring will be of an opposite character; the idea being that nature is bound to afford this result by way of compensation. But such criticism ignores the fact that nature takes her own time for her compensations, and seldom or never in the precise way, or at the exact time, which our imperfect faculties demand. In fact the case is exceptional in which an extreme year, whether of heat or cold, drought or wet, is immediately followed by one of a reverse character. But the change is sure to come. Man needs only to extend his observation, and to carefully treasure his facts, to find nature working by uniform and unerring laws. Nay more, that the hardships of her extremes are fully compensated by ever recurring benefits.

> "From seeming evil still educing good,
> And better thence again, and better still,
> In infinite progression."

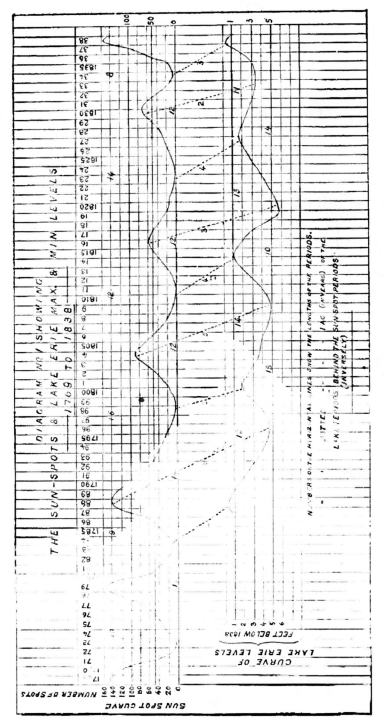

DIAGRAM NO. I, OF LAKE ERIE LEVELS AND THE SUN-SPOT CURVES. 1769—1838.

CLIMATE OF DETROIT AND THE LAKE REGION.

PART III.—PERIODICAL CHANGES IN THE LAKE LEVELS, RAINFALL, TEMPERATURE AND SUN-SPOTS; AND THEIR RELATIONS TO EACH OTHER.

CONNECTED with our considerations upon the climate is a subject which has excited great interest since the first settlement of the country, and about which much has been written, for the most part vaguely. I allude to the variations in the levels of the lake waters.

Many causes contribute to create a perpetual fluctuation, or rise and fall, in these inland seas.

First. A possible lunar tide; but so small and so broken in upon by greater causes as to be of very uncertain value.

Second. The winds, which often cause a difference in level of many feet; strong westerly winds causing a rise at one place, and easterly winds at another. These changes are irregular and transient, but often considerable in amount, ranging from two to five feet.

Third. Annual variation attendant upon the seasons and confined to the year. This kind of fluctuation is a winter and summer movement. The supply from streams and rains being wholly or partially checked in the cold season, the water is gradually drawn away, lowering the general level, which reaches its lowest ebb about January or February. As spring advances, with melting snows and increased rainfall, the waters rise gradually, and attain their greatest height in June or July. They then begin to fall again to their winter level. The extreme of this variation is about 2.30 feet, and is about the same in Lake Erie as in Detroit River.

Fourth. A rise and fall of the waters of the lakes and their connecting channels, extending through several years, and amounting to an extreme difference of five feet. Upon this kind of fluctuation Col. Chas. Whittlesey has bestowed the name of "secular variation."

The causes of this variation were long involved in much mystery. According to the old French tradition, it is independent of the seasons, and follows periodical intervals of seven years. To what extent these intervals of high and low water are regular in their recurrence, and how far they are connected with meteorological or astronomical causes, can be determined only after continuous and exact observations for a long series of years.

It is hardly more than a decade since the United States Signal Service has given scientific exactness to observations, and not over 30 years since thoroughly reliable statistics have been tabulated. Records of independent observers often differ widely, and though the writer has culled from different sources data sufficient to enable him to construct a diagram for this region, covering the past 50 years, and even more, many of these data are of uncertain value. For a period of 33 years, beginning with 1853, a record has been kept by the Detroit Water Board of the daily fluctuations in the level of the river, and partial records exist of other years since 1835.

In a comparison between the height of water in the river and the rainfall at Detroit, no conclusions drawn from these data will apply rigidly to the lakes above and below. The river levels are influenced not alone by the precipitation on its borders, but by the supply from above. Other causes contribute to its irregularities,— local rains, confined channel, rapid current. While a sudden increase in the precipitation will affect the broad surfaces of the lakes uniformly, a rise would take place at such times in the confined straits to a disproportionate extent. In discussing this so-called "secular" variation it becomes necessary to procure data from outside sources.

Milwaukee represents well Lake Michigan, and Cleveland, Lake Erie. Each is about half way between the head and foot of the lake upon which it is situated, and where the changes may fairly be considered as means of the whole. From Milwaukee I have a table of the rainfall from 1844 to 1886, and of the "secular" variations of Lake Michigan from 1859 to 1882. From Cleveland, of the rainfall from 1856 to 1886, and of the lake variations since 1859.

At each of these places the standard or plane of reference is the high water of 1838. The standard at Detroit is an arbitrary one, namely, the water-table at the Hydraulic Works. The mean of the last 50 years is five feet below that standard, and corresponds, as nearly as I can determine, to one foot below the *mean* of 1838, and two feet below the extreme of June of that year.

Of the fluctuations of the water prior to the period mentioned the only data are derived from the recollections of old settlers. These, though often indefinite and sometimes faulty, are yet of great value. Dr. Houghton, in his report of 1839, gives certain concordant statements of old inhabitants, going back as far as 1800. In a paper published in "Smithsonian Contributions," Vol.

XII., Col. Charles Whittlesey has collected items from all sources within his reach, going back as far as 1788. Vague as many of these details are, there is so much that is of definite value, that it seems to me possible to construct a curve of the levels of Lake Erie for the whole period, which should exhibit, with tolerable accuracy, the highest and lowest extremes at least. As I propose to use these aids in formulating certain conclusions, I ought here to give the reader opportunity to form his own judgment as to their value and authority.

To begin, it may be taken as universally admitted that the lakes were at a higher level in 1838 than at any known period before. In confirmation of this is the fact, among others, that forest trees of a century's growth and more were killed by the high water of that year. Two other eras of very high water are reported by tradition, the one in 1814–15, the other in 1788. Facts and comparisons reported render it nearly certain that at both these periods the levels attained to somewhere near the standard of 1838. At the former date much land and many buildings were submerged on the Detroit and St. Clair rivers. Many statements also bear upon the fact of high-water periods between the several dates mentioned. Dr. Houghton relates, on the authority of Col. Henry Whiting: "Old inhabitants agree that the water was very high in the years 1800 to 1802, roads along Detroit River being completely inundated, and even rendered impassable." And further, that in 1821 the river began to rise, "and in 1828 had again attained the elevation of 1815, submerging wharves that had been built in the interval; and it so remained until 1830."

As to low extremes, it seems well ascertained that the one of 1819–20 was the lowest known prior to 1841—

the low depression which succeeded the extreme elevation of 1838. Presumably it was the lowest known during the century. Old Frenchmen of Detroit had no tradition of a level below that of 1819. Statements regarding the stage of the water always make reference to the acknowledged highest and lowest years. Thus we are enabled to fix upon and determine with considerable exactness the relative values of other low periods. The water in 1796 was reported by lake captains to be universally low, and indicating a level five feet below the high extreme of 1838. From that year, they say, it rose rapidly, and continued to rise until 1800. Colonel Whittlesey says, "It was ascertained generally that the water was low in 1790, 1796, 1802 and 1810. Between February, 1819, and June, 1838, there was a continual rise, amounting to 6 feet 8 inches." Old settlers compare the low stage of 1802 with that of 1797. In 1806 it was reported at Cleveland lower than in 1801-2, and declining regularly to 1809-10. At this date it was reported nearly as low at Buffalo as in 1819. From 1828 it was reported as falling, and in 1833 was 3 feet 10 inches below June, 1838. From this year on we are able to trace the "secular" periods of lake and river with considerable accuracy; and data also exist in regard to other elements which it is proposed to include in our discussion. I give two diagrams, intended to exhibit graphically what is shown more in detail in the tables.

Diagram No. 1 (page 460) shows the curve of high and low water of Lake Erie, from 1788 to 1838, constructed in accordance with the above data. In connection with it is given the sun-spot curve, from 1769 to 1838, according to Wolf's tables, reference to which will be made hereafter.

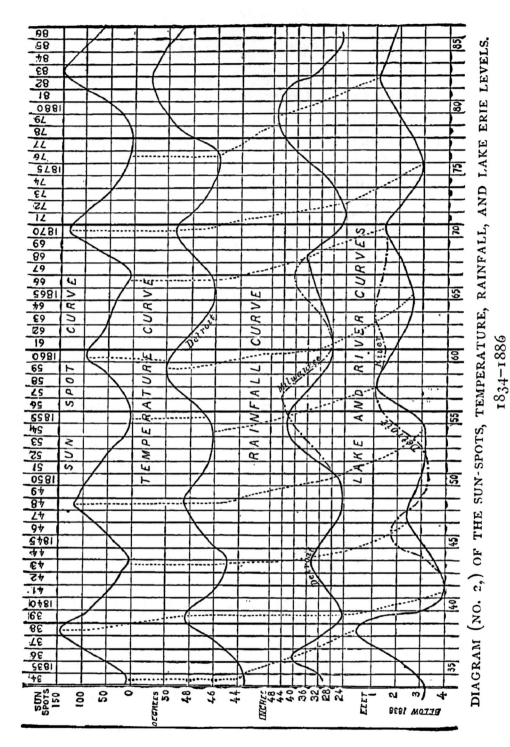

DIAGRAM (NO. 2,) OF THE SUN-SPOTS, TEMPERATURE, RAINFALL, AND LAKE ERIE LEVELS. 1834–1886

Diagram No. 2 (page 466) gives similar data for the term of years from 1834 to 1886, including, in addition to the curves of lake levels, those of the rainfall and of the temperature (registered at Detroit), and the sun-spots, according to Wolf's tables.

In these diagrams my endeavor has been to exhibit by curved lines the recurring maximum and minimum periods, eliminating intermediate and irregular fluctuations.

Confining our attention for the present to the curve of Rainfall (diagram No. 2), let us endeavor to ascertain whether among the many and often abrupt fluctuations it is possible to discover any periodicity.

The vertical columns represent years. In the portion devoted to the rainfall variations the horizontal lines represent the number of inches of annual precipitation.

It will be noted that the years 1836 and 1880 were times of excessive rainfall. Between these two extremes, and about equidistant, appears another strongly-marked period of excess, culminating in 1855. Again, between these three maxima are two lesser extremes, culminating in 1844 and 1868. Thus our curved line marks five periods of maximum rainfall.

Of low extremes we note four, which have their culminations in the years 1839, 1850, 1860 and 1871.

The intervals between extremes vary from 8 to 13 years, the general mean being 10.8 years.

Let us now compare with these curves, those immediately below, and which represent the periodic changes in the levels of Lake Erie during the half-century.

Here the horizontal lines represent the number of feet below the plane of 1838.

It requires but a glance at the diagram to show that

some relationship exists between the lake and rainfall periods. The first impression conveyed is that the curves are in opposition—that the high in one corresponds with the low in the other, and the reverse. But I think the true relation will be made to appear when we notice the important fact (which I endeavor to render more apparent by dotted lines), viz., that the water extremes lag behind the rainfall extremes,—following them at intervals from two to four years. Thus the seeming want of coincidence is reduced to harmony. It will also appear that the rainfall extremes are not only followed invariably by corresponding fluctuations in the water levels, but that these succeed each other in quite as marked and uniform periods.

The rainfall maxima of 1836, '44, '55, '68 and '80 have their corresponding extremes in the water maxima of 1838, '47, '58, '70 and '82,—the intervals or lag varying from two to three years. The rainfall minima of 1839, '50, '60, '72 and '84 have corresponding lake minima in 1841, '54, '65, and '75,—the intervals varying from two to four years. The mean lag is 2.8 years. The true relation—dependence—of the lake periodicities upon those of the rainfall is thus clearly shown.

It will be observed that I have chosen to consider the Lake Erie levels rather than those of Detroit River. I do so for the reason that the relation of the former to the precipitation are more simple and direct, and are not influenced by causes already pointed out (page 463), which tend to create irregularities in the river. A marked illustration is shown between the years 1859 and 1870,—where dotted lines represent the rainfall at Milwaukee, and the river levels as compared with those of Lake Erie, —of the effect of excess of precipitation on the lakes above, in keeping up the river to a disproportionate extent.

I do not consider it necessary to examine the various theories which have been broached from time to time, in explanation of the lake periodical fluctuations. Nor will I undertake to explain all the irregularities of the river and lake, which would demand many factors that are wanting to the present discussion. It will suffice if I have succeeded in making clear the relations which exist between the variations of the water levels and the rainfall, and in defining their periodicities. Probably few at this day would dispute the fact that the rise and fall, or "secular" variations, in the waters are dependent upon the rainfall. This is the first attempt, to my knowledge, at demonstration of their true relations.

Thus far I have not alluded to the important element of Temperature in its relation to rainfall. That an intimate relation exists is an admitted fact; it shall be my endeavor to show what this relation is.

In the portion of the diagram devoted to the Detroit temperature curve, the horizontal lines represent the degrees of mean annual temperature, which varies from 43°, the lowest, to 52°, the highest extreme. Considering temperature as a controlling element, we should expect to find a close correspondence between its curves and those of the rainfall. And we do so find, as is shown by the diagram. But, while the maxima and minima of the rainfall and the lake are directly as each other, we discover that those of the rainfall and the temperature are inverse to each other. For a full discussion of the relation between these two elements, no doubt we ought to take into account other important factors—barometric changes, winds, magnetic and other phenomena. The conclusions of this paper are deduced only from the data presented. Let us now compare the curves.

The *maximum* temperature periods of 1839, '48, '59, '70 and '82 at Detroit will correspond to the *minimum* rainfall periods of 1839, '50, '60, '72 and '84,—if we credit to the latter a lag or interval behind the temperature periods of naught to two years. The *minimum* temperature periods of 1835, '43, '54, '66 and '76 correspond to the *maximum* rainfall years 1836, '44, '55, '68 and '78 to '80, with a lag varying from one to four years; the mean of the lag being 1.8 years.

If this showing reverses the commonly received opinion that high temperature is followed by extreme rainfall, I can only say that the facts, as I find them, do not warrant any other conclusion. Let the reader attempt to connect either the maxima or the minima of the curve of temperature with the like periods of the rainfall, and he will find it necessary to admit intervals of from six to nine years, a conclusion which would be inconsistent with any influence whatever.

I now turn to another element, or phenomenon, which will be found to have an intimate bearing upon our investigation.

Recently, much speculation has been elicited by the ascertained periodicity of spots on the sun's disc. It is now an admitted fact that the increase and decrease of the spots affect the magnetic needle, and influence the earth's magnetic and electrical condition. The extent to which these affect the meteorology of our planet is a moot question with the learned on these subjects.

Some noted observers in Europe and India maintain

the theory of an influence exerted by the sun-spots upon the rainfall, and this directly as the number of the spots. In this lake region, attempts to establish or define these relations have been few and unsatisfactory. It will be my part to show that the sun-spots do decidedly influence the temperature, and indirectly the rainfall, and that the curves of temperature correspond directly with those of the sun-spots. This correspondence holds not only as regards the maxima and minima periods, but as to the general features of the two curves.

Wolf's tables of the sun-spots from 1769 to 1882 show ten periods of maxima, and as many of minima, the spots ranging from 0 in a minimum year to 150 in a maximum year. Of these periods, one-half are embraced within the sixty-six years from 1769 to 1834. For this cycle there are no reliable statistics of temperature and rainfall; so that my data are confined to the sun-spots and the lake periods, of which I present a tabular statement, as supplementary to Diagram No. 1.

Table No. 1 exhibits in groups :—

1. The years of maximum and minimum sun-spots from 1769 to 1834, according to Wolf's numbers,—the maxima and minima in separate columns.

2. The years of maximum and minimum levels of Lake Erie, which are given in feet and tenths below the plane of 1838,—the maxima and minima in separate columns.

3. The lag, or interval in time at which the periodic changes in the lake follow *inversely* those of the sun-spots. One column gives the number of years lag of the lake maxima behind the sun-spot minima; the other of the lake minima behind the sun maxima.

4. The sun and lake "*periods*." In one column are given the number of years between each maximum of

sun-spots and the next preceding maximum, and, alternately, the number of years between each minimum of spots and the preceding minimum. In the other column are given the like data for the lake periods.

TABLE NO. I.

MAXIMUM AND MINIMUM PERIODS OF SUN–SPOTS AND LAKE ERIE, 1769–1834.

Years.	Sun-spots + No.	Sun-spots − No.	Lake Erie Levels Below 1838 Feet & Tenths Plus	Lake Erie Levels Below 1838 Feet & Tenths Minus	Lag Lake + Behind Sun −	Lag Lake − Behind Sun +	Sun Years.	Lake Years.
1769	140							
1773		10						
1779	155						10	
1784		12					11	
1788	140		0.5		4		9	
1796				4.5		8		
1798		5					14	
1800			2		2			12
1804	85						16	
1809				5		5		13
1810		0					12	
1814			1		4			14
1816	55						12	
1819				6		3		10
1822		0					12	
1827			2		4			13
1830	75						14	
1833				3.5		2		14
1834		10						
Means			1.4	4.7	3.5	4.5	12.3	12.6

The phenomena which this table makes apparent are: First, that what I have called the *sun and lake periods* approximate in length, and the means of each are nearly identical,—12.3 and 12.6 years. Second, that the sun and lake periods are not synchronous, but that the changes in the lake follow at considerable distance (lag) behind the sun-spot times. Also that the lake maxima lag behind the sun-spot minima less than do the lake minima behind the sun-spot maxima; the means being respectively 3.5 and 4.5 years. That is to say, the waters fall more rapidly than they rise, by the mean of a year. We shall see presently how far these statements tally with the data drawn from fuller sources, for the half-century succeeding.

Let us now turn to Diagram No. 2, which exhibits the sun-spot curves from 1834 to 1884, paralleled with those of the temperature, the rainfall, and the lake.

We see five "periods" of sun-spot maxima, culminating in the years 1838, '48, '60, '70 and '82 or '83,—the number of spots at each varying from 95 to 150. And five of sun-spot minima—in the years 1834, '44, '56, '67 and '78, the spots in each varying from five to ten. The maximum periods recur at intervals of eight to twelve years—the mean being 10.6; the minimum periods at intervals of ten to twelve years,—the mean being 11 years. With the aid of the accompanying Table No. 2, we may proceed to compare results.

Table No. 2 aims to give in a succinct form all the data which our discussion requires. These are grouped in columns as follows:

The first group gives (in three columns) the sun-spot data, in the same manner as in Table No. 1, viz., the years of maxima and minima, the number of spots at each, and the lengths of the periods.

The second or temperature group gives (in two columns) for those years of maxima and minima which conform to the sun-spot maxima and minima, the degrees of temperature (the mean of the year at Detroit), and the lengths of the periods.

474   CLIMATE OF THE LAKE REGION.

TABLE NO. 2.

MAXIMUM AND MINIMUM PERIODS OF SUN-SPOTS, TEMPERATURE, RAINFALL AND WATER-LEVELS, 1834–1886.

Years.	Sun-Spots No. of Spots.	Sun-Spots Periods—Years	Temp. Detroit Degrees.	Temp. Detroit Periods.	Rainfall Detroit Inches.	Rainfall Detroit Periods.	Rainfall Detroit Lag behind Temperature	Rainfall Milwaukee Inches.	Rainfall Milwaukee Periods.	Rainfall Cleveland Inches.	Rainfall Cleveland Periods.	Water Levels Detroit River Feet below 1.8	Water Levels Detroit River Periods.	Water Levels Detroit River Lag behind Rainfall.	Water Levels Lake Erie Feet below 15.0	Water Levels Lake Erie Periods.	Water Levels Lake Erie Lag behind Rainfall.	L. Erie Lag Max. behind Sun Min.	L. Erie Lag Min. behind Sun Max.
1834	10?		43	13	40														
1835		8										0	11?	2	0	11	2	4	
1836	150		48.3	12	24	8?	1	25?				4.5	9	2	4	9	2		3
1837																			
1838																			
1839																			
1841	10	10	45	7	34	8	0												
1843																			
1844																			
1845	125	10	48.5	9			1	33	11			2	10	4	2.5	9	3	3.5	
1847																			
1848																			

TABLE NO. 2.   475

Year																			
1850											2		?						6
1854	10	12	47	11	26	11	1	26	11	2.5		3	4	13	4				
1855	5	12	48	11	43	11													
1856																			
1858	95		46	12	28	10	1	45	10	0.5	10	11	1.2	12	3	3		
1859																			
1860	9	11	49	11	36	13	2	24	10		11	11	2.5	11	3	3	4	
1861																			
1865			46	10	24	12	2	38	11	1.4	12	12						
1866	132													11		2		
1867																			
1868																			
1869		11			47	12	2	28	12	2.5	10	32	1.6	10	3	3		4
1870	5		51	10			4	48?	11			52						5
1872																			
1875																			
1876	160	13		12	25	14	4			1.5	14	26		12		2	4	
1878																			
1880																			
1881																			
1882																			
1883																			
1886																			
Means		10.8		11		11	1.8		10.9		11		1.5	10.9	3	2.7	3.5	4.5

The rainfall has three groups. The first gives for Detroit (in three columns) the maximum and minimum periods, the precipitation in inches at each, and the lag or interval at which each follows, inversely, behind those of the temperature. Like data are given for the rainfall at Milwaukee and at Cleveland, so far as I possess data, omitting the column of lag.

For the water levels there are two groups, each showing (in three separate columns) the periodicities, the measurements in feet and tenths below the plane of 1838, and the lag behind the rainfall at Detroit.

Lastly are given (as in Table No. 1) the lag of the lake behind the sun-spot periods,—lake maxima behind sun-spot minima, and the reverse.

My aim is to exhibit those fluctuations in the elements under discussion which conform to the sun-spot periodicities, according to the law which seems to govern, viz., temperature directly as the sun-spots; rainfall inversely as the temperature; lake levels directly as the rainfall, and the periodical changes in each, following uniformly those of the preceding or influencing element by a lag of short interval; and this increasing in length according to the remoteness from the original source of influence.

When we consider that the sun is itself the ultimate source of all our meteorological phenomena, the fact that the periods of greater and less energy indicated by spots on its disc have a well-marked relationship to the temperature and rainfall is not surprising. While there are many fluctuations for which no solution is attempted, it suffices if we are able to point out well-defined maxima and minima periodical fluctuations which conform to each other within small limitations.

The proof does not rest alone upon the Detroit observations. Though the rainfall at Milwaukee and Cleveland differs, often considerably, in times and amount, from the Detroit record, we find a close conformity in the periods. In fact, there is almost identity in the periodic means of all the elements contained in the table.

The two columns (on the right of the table) showing the lag of Lake Erie behind the sun-spots at each period, furnish a remarkable confirmation of the general conclusions. Comparing the two tables, it will be seen that the mean periodicity of the sun-spots is larger for the first half-century than for the last, by 1.7 years. Yet the same relation to the lake periods is maintained throughout both cycles. The lag for the maxima and for the minima periods is the same in both tables, the means being 3.5 years and 4.5 years respectively. This result is not merely remarkable ; it would be incomprehensible on any other theory than that here contended for. Its truth or fallacy the reader has the means of determining if he will closely study the details given in the table and the diagram.

Another feature of too much importance to escape attention is the difference in all the curves between the scales of increase and of decrease. This is shown by the diagram, and is computable from the tables. Thus, the times of increase in the sun-spot curve, from minima to maxima, are almost uniformly four years; those of decrease, or from maxima to minima, six to eight years. In the curve of the temperature these periodic times are slightly larger in the rising, and slightly less in the falling scale. The rainfall and the lake times are more irregular, and fall short of such uniform proportions. As regards the rainfall at Detroit the case seems to be reversed, the rising scale being accomplished in about seven years, and the falling in about four years. The "secular periods" of Lake Erie exhibit about equal scales. During the cycle from 1779 to 1834 there is closer correspondence between the lake and sun-spot times, the scales being about six years and seven years, respectively. Is it not possible that the traditional French weather-period of seven years connects itself with this recurrence of a period of about that length between one change and another?

Thus the cycle of change is "never ending, still begining." On its restless sea, man is tossed at the caprice of billows, whose wave-lengths are intervals of eleven years. The law of change runs through the scale from cold to warm in about four years, repeated after intervals of seven; and through warm to cold in seven years, repeated after intervals of four years. Meantime the changes from wet to dry are accomplished in equal times, but in reversed order, and after a delay of one or two years before the concord begins.

To sum up, it seems to me demonstrated, as regards this region:—

1. That the so-called "secular" changes in the levels of the river and lakes are dependent upon the rainfall.

2. That these changes in their maxima and minima fall behind the rainfall extremes in time, varying from two to three years.

3. That the times of maximum and minimum rainfall occur *inversely* as the temperature, and follow after, with mean intervals of one or two years.

4. That the times of maximum and minimum temperature occur *directly* as the sun-spots, with very small or no intervals.

5. That the times of high and low water of the lakes

and river follow behind the sun-spots, inversely, by a double lag,—of lake behind rainfall and of rainfall behind sun-spots,—the mean of both being four years.

6. That the periods of maximum and minimum sun-spots, temperature and rainfall have an intimate relation to each other, and that this relation appears in the respective periodicities, which differ but little, while the means are nearly identical.

7. That the scale of increase, or interval from minimum to maximum, of the sun-spots and the temperature is considerably shorter than the scale of decrease; the reverse being true as regards the rainfall. And thus the intervals between cold and warm years, and between dry and wet years, are less than those of the opposite conditions by about three years.

The question naturally arises, How far do the conclusions here recorded afford a foundation for forecasting the meteorology of the future?

If all the wave periods were of equal lengths and times, with sufficient allowance made for other factors not within our present discussion, we ought to do so with exactitude. But though our sovereign governor—the sun—exhibits a considerable degree of regularity in the increase and decrease of his spots, he has not as yet admitted us into the secret either of the cause or of the extent and frequency of his variations.

We have also seen that while the curves of temperature and rainfall are controlled by the sun-spot periods, their times of maxima and minima are not therefore synchronous. This is true to some extent as between the sun and the temperature, while those of the rainfall are not only inverse to, but lag behind, the temperature extremes, with varying times. There follows therefore a difference, both in the lengths and the times of the periodicities of each. Owing to this lag, and its variation in time of one to five years, it follows that when the temperature curve is at its maximum or its minimum, that of the rainfall is not necessarily at its lowest or its highest. In fact, such a conjunction may be brought about in the progress of time, that a wet period may correspond in time to a warm one, and *vice versa*, and yet the law of opposites continue absolutely persistent.

This observation applies with even greater force to the lake curves, the lag in which is uniformly greater than in those of precipitation. Thus it has happened three times within the last half-century that high water in Lake Erie has corresponded in time with a high sunspot period.

Another cause of lack of uniformity in the several curves is found in the difference—already alluded to—between the lengths of the rising and the falling sides. The result is a difference in the intervals between extreme cold and warm years, and extreme wet and dry ones, which would not be the case if the times of increase and decrease were equal.

We observe also, in noting the curves of temperature, as each approaches its low extreme, a sudden dropping of the temperature from a somewhat regular gradation, two to five degrees, during one, two or three years. And in the approach to maxima a rise nearly as precipitate. This has its parallel in the rainfall,—the precipitation experiencing a sudden increase in the high extremes of from four to thirteen inches, and during low extremes of from four to eight inches, within one or two years.

In these records of the past century, imperfect as they

are, will be found suggestions of more subtle and fundamental laws. The reader may notice a succession of three large sun-spot waves or periods followed by three lesser ones. They call to mind that succession of waves in the sea, called by sailors "the three sisters," and of the three-day weather period with which we are familiar. The conjecture may be warranted that we have here an indication of a major vibration of a six-period duration. It may be that all these cycles are but members of a grander whole, whose circles reach beyond our present ken, and to a perfect conception of which we may never attain, except perchance in that good time coming, when man's knowledge shall equal his aspirations. These considerations, and many more of which we are in ignorance, must enter into a calculation of the true horoscope of the future.

Nevertheless, we know that Nature governs by unvarying law. Assuming that her periodicities will bring about the same average results in the future as in the past half-century, I might undertake to be in some sort her interpreter of the coming events which cast their shadows before, along the pathway of a few unborn years; provided the same latitude be accorded me which was claimed by the old almanac-makers, to qualify the record with "about .... these .... days."

Premising that the sun-spot curve, which for five years had been on the rising scale, attained its maximum in 1883, we may infer that the temperature is now on its descending grade, and should reach its minimum by 1889 or 1890. The yearly mean, which for ten years past has maintained an unusually high degree, with small range, will fall rapidly five degrees or more. "Look out for ... cold .... weather .... about .... these .... years."

The rainfall, which, in accordance with its law of opposition and of lag, fell in 1886 to the low measure of 25 inches, is likely to continue small for a year or more to come. " Expect a .... period of drought .... about .... this.... time." The increasing precipitation following should reach its maximum about the beginning of the last cycle of the century, though the remaining years promise small precipitation. Maxima, or wet periods, seem also to be indicated for the years 1903 or '04, 1913 and 1924; and low, or dry periods, about 1895 or '96, 1909 and 1919 or '20.

Following these leads, lake and river levels will rise to their culminations, it is probable, about 1894, 1906, 1916, and 1927, and fall to low levels about 1888, 1899, 1912 or '13, and 1921. The depression of 1888 is likely to reach a lower stage than any experienced since 1841.

None need be surprised if the remaining years of the century witness disasters to the husbandman from drought and frosts, and to the business man from commercial disasters and stagnation in trade.

The new century, though opening with cold and wet, gives promise, in its first cycle, of returning general prosperity, inaugurated by abundant crops, and—if the nation be wise—by freer trade, restored commerce, satisfied wages, and solid wealth. Blessed be the sun-spots!

THE WINTER SEASON.

"Let Araby boast of her soft spicy gale,
  And Persia her breeze from the rose-scented vale;
  Let orange trees scatter in wildness their balm,
  Where sweet summer islands lie fragrant and calm;
  Give me the cold blast of my country again,
  Careering o'er snow-covered mountain and plain,
  And coming, though scentless, yet pure, to my breast,
  With vigor and health from the cloudless Nor'-West."
                                    Dr. J. K. Mitchell.

"All nature feels the renovating force
  Of winter; only to the thoughtless eye
  Is ruin seen."
                                    Thomson.

THE WINTER SEASON.

THE region bordering Detroit River and Lake Erie in its winter climate, exhibits signally the meliorating influence of large bodies of water. It experiences an exemption from the greater degree of cold which prevails in the same latitudes both east and west.

Some very cold days occur, when the mercury falls below zero of Fahrenheit. The lowest degree registered at Detroit during the last fifty years, from 1835 to 1886, is —20°. During the same cold storms in Central New York and New England it fell to —35° and —40°, and even lower on the Western plains.

A great depth of snow is also rare, and it is not uncommon to have none sufficient for sleighing during a whole winter, or, at most, for a few days only. At the same time large bodies of snow lie upon the ground in the central portions of this State, and through Canada and the Eastern States.

Ordinarily winter cold fairly sets in about the end of November, but frequently delays until December and even January. December often presents a succession of clear days, with a temperature below freezing at night, and rising a little above it during the day; a state of the atmosphere very exhilarating, and which tempts to out-of-door life and walking.

January is generally the coldest month, and the most snowy. Frequently snow falls in sufficient quantity or persistence for good sleighing only in the latter part of the month, continuing into the following month. By the middle of February it is usual for the snow to disappear for the remainder of the season.

Detroit River ordinarily is bridged with ice once or twice during the winter, for a few days at a time. And there have been seasons when teams have crossed on the ice for weeks together.

On the other hand, winters are not infrequent when the channel of the river has continued constantly open and free from ice, except occasional floating masses from the lakes above.

Generally this river is open to navigation a full month before the ice leaves the harbor of Buffalo, or there is passage for vessels through the Straits of Mackinaw. Whenever any of the harbors of Lake Erie are open it is a certainty that vessels may enter the harbor of Detroit.

The first approach of winter in this climate is almost always dismal. The frosty nights which precede would be pleasant enough if they did not always come a little too soon for our preparation, and when they are followed by cloudless days, as is generally the case, the cold is invigorating.

But the first snow is altogether another thing. November snows seldom lie long on the ground; the sun is still too powerful. They last, it may be, through one or two cold days, and then thaw into slush and mud. The atmosphere is then chilly and uncomfortable; the earth is wet and dirty. No word is too harsh to express the utter discomfort of such days, which have all the gloom of winter without any of its delights.

In our variable climate but little dependence can be placed on any long continuance of cold or heat. From the fall of the leaf we know that summer has ended. The hard frosts advertise the presence of winter, but after his first frowns he often treats us to a long holiday of genial smiles. Many days occur, even in midwinter, when the air is mild and balmy as in summer; when the frost has altogether left us; when even the mud is dried up, and the river, free from its icy chains, flows majestically; days as bland and invigorating to soul and body as it is possible to conceive. Such "spells" are very common indeed in this locality, where there is usually so little snow, or long continuance of extreme cold.

Whittier has well described this dream of summer in winter:

> "Bland as the morning breath of June
>   The south-west breezes play;
> And, through its haze, the winter noon
>   Seems warm as summer's day.
> The snow-plumed Angel of the North
>   Has dropp'd his icy spear;
> Again the mossy earth looks forth,
>   Again the streams gush clear."

The winter of 1837-38 was of this "open" and genial character. Navigation closed on the 8th of December, but so mild was the following January that steamers again made trips to Cleveland, and boats patrolled the river during the whole month.

The first two months of 1842 were still more remarkable for mildness, and this character of the winter prevailed, not only in the neighborhood of Detroit, but throughout the northerly part of the United States. It was accompanied with heavy and frequent rains, and consequent extensive freshets. The Buffalo *Journal* of Jan. 30, says, "For many days past the air has resembled that of April. Yesterday was as bright and balmy as those calm days of spring when all things animate are rejoicing; to-day a sad change to drizzling showers. Navigation of our lake continues perfectly open."

The papers of Rochester (N. Y.) tell of "grass-hoppers an inch long jumping about the gardens."

Here the mean temperature of the season was about 4° above the normal, of 27.3°. The maximum of both January and February was 56°, the minimum + 4° in February. The precipitation was a little below the winter average of 6 inches.

The winter of 1844–45 was of similar mildness. The lake harbors below were open, and steamers plied between Buffalo and Detroit every month. In this neighborhood the ground was bare of snow the entire winter, and the ice men were able to harvest only three inches thickness of ice from the river. The mean temperature of the season was 3° above the normal, and the precipitation 3 inches below. In the Eastern States, while the season was uncommonly mild, severe snow-storms occurred in February.

The winters of 1847–48 and of 1852–53, were also uncommonly mild and without snow. During the first, steamers made trips to Buffalo, and the Hudson River was open in February, 1853.

The winter of 1857–58 until February was yet more mild and open. From all parts of the country the report is "no snow, and an atmosphere like spring." On the last day of January violets were in bloom in my garden.

The winter of 1879-80 opened without frost and with heavy rains at night. On the morning of December 15, a light snow left its ermine mantle on tree and shrub,— a glorious spectacle. Snow continued to fall to six inches depth, and the thermometer fell to 12° and afterwards to —2°, which was the coldest of the winter. By New Year's day all snow had disappeared in the prevailing warm. Heavy rains fell early in the month, swelling the streams and demoralizing the roads. By the middle of the month the ground was bare, and so continued throughout that month and February.

The maximum temperature in January was 57°, minimum 19°; maximum temperature in February was 60°, minimum, 11°. The mean of the whole season was 30°, or 6° above the average; the precipitation 8.9 inches, or 3 inches above the average.

The winters so far alluded to would be considered in general language as "mild and open." Before proceeding to notice those of an opposite character, it may be well to see whether we can arrange the whole series into two classes, with reference to the controlling elements.

Many winters are so changeable, yet so near the average in temperature, that it is not easy to determine to which class they belong. But by arranging on one side those whose mean is considerably above, and on the other those which are below the winter mean of the series, with the aid of general memoranda, a tabular division may be made as below. In this table those years whose means vary but little from each other, and which are in immediate succession, are grouped together.

CLASSIFICATION OF OUR WINTERS, WITH REFERENCE TO TEMPERATURE.

YEAR.	WARM. Av. T. deg.	No. of years	YEAR.	COLD. Av. T. deg.	No. of years.
1837 to 1842.........	28	6	1836.............	23	1
1844–46.............	28	3	1843.............	26	1
1848................	28	1	1847.............	26	1
1850................	29	1	1849.............	26	1
1853................	27.3	1	1851–52..........	26	2
1858–60.............	27.5	3	1854–57..........	24.5	4
1862–63.............	27.5	2	1861.............	26	1
1869–71.............	27.3	3	1864–68..........	25	5
1874................	30	1	1872–73..........	24	2
1876................	31	1	1875.............	19	1
1878................	33	1	1877.............	24	1
1880–82.............	32.5	3	1879.............	22	1
1884................	29	1	1883.............	24	1
			1885.............	25	1
Range.... 5.5		27	Range.... 2.		23
Mean..... 29.2			Mean......24.4		

Mean of the whole series = 27.3°

Here we find that of the 50 winters since 1835, 27 may be classed as similar in character to those we above described as "warm," averaging about 2° of temperature above the normal; and that 23 may be classed as "cold," their temperature averaging 3° below the normal. The latter are universally followed by raw, cold and backward springs. In fact the succeeding March is often more in sympathy with winter than spring, and would find place with it if nature had the making of our calendar.

Let us now notice some of the winters which contrast with those we have described. The table shows how frequently (but not invariably), a mild and open winter is followed by a cold and stormy or snowy one.

Thus the winter which succeeded the mild one of 1842 was in striking contrast. Snow fell on Nov. 18, 1842, followed by a steady cold and successive snowfalls, which continued until April. Detroit River remained frozen nearly the whole winter, and teams crossed on the ice throughout March. With one week's exception, there was good sleighing in and about Detroit until the 8th of April. Lake Erie was so frozen over that teams are said to have crossed, throughout the winter, from various places on the south shore into Canada. It presented to view a great icy plain, from which no water could be seen. Large quantities of ice floated down the lake early in the season, became wedged in and froze, in many places probably in a solid mass to the bottom. Many thought this shallow lake was a mass of ice throughout. A Buffalo journal said that "on going out a mile from shore and cutting through the ice in three several places the result was, 28, 29½ and 31 inches of as solid and transparent an article as ever graced an ice-house."

The following March was practically a winter month and can be appropriately described only in this connection. It was noticeable for its unprecedented snowfalls throughout the United States.

On the 16th, snow fell in New York city to a depth of

18 inches. At Washington, D. C., railway trains were delayed a whole day by snow a foot in depth. Snow fell throughout South Carolina, and reached even New Orleans.

Through New York and the Eastern States the heavy foot of this wintry spring fell with tremendous weight. The storms seemed to rival those of Alpine regions. On the 18th of March the train of cars which left Albany for Boston, propelled by five locomotives, proceeded about three miles, when it encountered such a depth of compact snow that it was compelled to return.

On the next day the train which left Boston for Albany proceeded six miles, when it became fast in the snow, and the passengers left it and returned. In many places the snow drifted 15 feet. In one place, east of Utica, it is said to have been 40 feet deep.

A correspondent of the New York *American*, writing from Whitesboro, N. Y., under date of March 19, gives a graphic description of the state of things in that region: "On all sides of us, as far as the eye can penetrate, there is a desolating expanse of virgin snow. There is not a mountain around us that does not exhibit its towering masses of snow, shining like precious stones in the morning sun, and moulded into all the fantastic shapes that the wildest fancy can invent. The valley is full. Every road is embargoed. The Seneca turnpike, leading west from Utica, was open yesterday only a mile. The northern road, leading up over the hills through Trenton, is as unfurrowed by a track as the broad meadows on each side of it. In truth, the entire land from Albany to Buffalo is an *ocean of snow*. The railroads have lost their occupation!"

On the prairies west of Chicago trains were blocked

up by the snow many miles from the settlements, where they remained for several days. No help could reach them from any direction. The passengers subsisted on oysters and other stores found in the cars, and burned up seats and other portions of the cars for fuel.

The poets and story-tellers of Europe delight to give us exaggerated descriptions of winter in his fierce aspects; but such an exhibition of "the storms of wintry time," it is probable, never occur in the same zone in any other part of the world, except upon the high mountain tops of Alpine regions.

So protracted a winter could not be otherwise than fatally severe to cattle. In the inland parts of Michigan, snow lay for several months three or four feet deep on a level. Even in the woods about Detroit it was a foot in depth. It is very unusual for cattle to be deprived of grazing for so long a period. In the consequent failure of fodder many farmers cut down trees, upon which their "critters" browsed, and managed thus to support a meagre life. They perished by hundreds in all parts of the State. The same was the case in Northern Ohio. Many were killed "to save them."

Yet it was reported that at Sault Ste. Marie and other Northern places, the winter proved unusually mild and open. The Ohio River was navigable from the middle of February.

Cold and protracted as was this winter season, its mean was but little below the normal, and the lowest minimum was —6° in February.

Following the unusually open and mild winter of 1848, that of 1848–49 set in about Christmas, with snow, which continued throughout the season. In the interior of the State and in Ohio fruit trees were killed by the severity or long continuance of the cold; though the lowest of the thermometer was but—14° at Detroit, and the snow-fall was only two-thirds the winter average.

The winter of 1855-56 was a very severe one. The lowest degree noted here was —14°; but elsewhere in the State it fell to —24°. The usual January thaw did not occur, nor was there a day during that month when the snow melted, even in the sun. Cold continued throughout February, with good sleighing, and only a slight thaw. I find noted that I crossed on the ice to Canada, with hundreds of others, railway passengers, on the 15th of March; the ferry-boats being unable to force a passage.

Reports from all parts of the country indicated this winter as one of general and unusual severity. Snow fell throughout the Southern States, and ice formed at Mobile.

January, 1857, was remarkable for its extremity of cold all over the Union. On the 24th the thermometer indicated —40° in northern New England. In central New York—30°. In portions of Michigan —20°. At Detroit —18°. At New Orleans it stood at 28° for three days. A snow-storm occurred at the City of Mexico, lasting several hours,—a most unusual phenomenon. Early in February thaw set in, with heavy rains and melting of the snow, which flooded the country. This was followed by a second edition of winter, lasting, with frost and snow, almost into the summer months.

The winter of 1872-73, succeeding the cold and stormy one of '72, proved even more severe, though it followed immediately upon a genial summer and dry autumn. It set in during November, with considerable snow. During December there was no complete thaw. A fall of snow, of six inches, on the 20th, was followed by extreme cold. On the 21st, the thermometer indicated —14°, and on 22d, —18°. This cold spell was general over the United States. At the same period reports from Europe told of drenching rains, causing immense floods in Italy, Germany, France and England.

With us the abundance of snow made the holidays lively, but did not assist to supply the water famine. Cisterns were so low that many residents in the city suburbs were compelled to resort to the river. The drought was general over the State. The month closed with a foot of snow in the streets of Detroit.

Storms continued through January, with deeply drifted snows all over the Western States, broken only by a single day's thaw (16th), when rain fell in floods.

On January 23, 1873, set in one of the most violent snow-storms ever experienced here. It continued all day, with an easterly wind driving at the rate, apparently, of 40 or 50 miles an hour, with a blinding snow, which fell a foot in depth. Snow continued to fall at intervals the next day, but with less violent easterly wind. Intense cold followed. On 28th, my thermometer (Springwells) indicated —20°, but the Signal Service Office in Detroit, recorded only —12°.

February continued cold, with a few days of thaw, beginning on the 18th, which removed most of the snow from open grounds. On 23d, the mercury was again below zero, from St. Louis to Philadelphia.

The remainder of the month was more moderate, but March came in like a lion, with cold 5° below zero. Notwithstanding the continued and abundant snow, the winter precipitation, as determined by the Signal Service Station, was only four inches, or two-thirds the normal amount. The temperature mean was 25°, or two degrees below normal.

The winter of 1874-75 was extremely cold, having the lowest mean of any in my series, 19°. And very dry,—the precipitation being 3.3 inches only, or half the normal amount.

February was especially noted for its continued succession of cold waves, which were felt all over the United States, the Pacific Isles and Europe. The temperature fell to —20° at Detroit, and was below zero for fourteen days.

The winter of 1876-77 was of that peculiar character which refuses definite classification.

December was steadily cold, without thaw, except of a single day's duration, and sleighing was in perfection all the month. By the 20th the ice-houses were filled with transparent blocks, a foot and more in thickness.

The grounding of ice at the islands and shallows in the lower part of the river effected so complete a blockade, as to set back the water, for many days, to an unusual height at the wharves in the city, and so filled the whole channel with heavy ice as greatly to impede the passage of the ferry-boats. The railway-car ferries were on one occasion, for a whole day, embargoed in the middle of the stream, unable to advance or recede, the cars filled with anxious passengers. The lowest degree reached by the thermometer was —9°, but the mean of the month was 18.5°, or 11 degrees below the normal. The amount of snow-fall, converted to its liquid equivalent, was reported as 1.9 inches, which is above the average.

January was also of steady cold, the sleighing constant and good, without thaw until the 29th. The river remained frozen over, and the ice crops were never so abundant and fine. The lowest temperature was —5°, and the mean of the month, 20°. Precipitation, one and a quarter inches. Prevailing wind, south-west.

The thaw which began on the 29th January proved to be the precursor of a complete and most extraordinary change in the programme of the clerk of the weather. February was as sunny and warm as the two preceding months had been overcast and cold. A delightful temperature prevailed throughout the month, thawing by day and freezing by night, the snow gradually disappearing. Frost also left the earth, and the roads became uniformly hard and dry,—no mud, no ruts, no rain, no snow,—and nearly every day balmy and cloudless. The highest barometer, with least range, the highest temperature and highest means of both, for the last five years. The precipitation was almost too small to be registered (0.04 inches), and the wind, which continued to prevail from the south-west, had little velocity.

All this geniality was reversed by the spring which folowed; an account of which is reserved for my notes on that season.

The long continued, severe cold of the winter of 1884–85 is so fresh in the memory of all who undertake to read these minutes that I will make a brief allusion to it only. That winter is specially noticeable for the rapid succession of cold waves from the North-west, which involved in their widespread sweep the greater part of the United States, and were very remarkable.

But though the sensible cold was so severely felt, the actual mean temperature was but 2° below the normal. A low degree of temperature ran through the three months, the minima being respectively —6°, —17° and

—12°. The precipitation was normal, and the weather very changeable.

The advent of 1864 will be remembered for a very sudden and violent reversal of the temperature. Throughout December the weather had been mild, with but little frost, and the river contained only occasional masses of floating ice. The last day of the year was attended with rain, the wind being from the east and north-east. Late at night the wind shifted to west, bringing extreme cold. At 7 A.M. New Year's morning, the mercury indicated —5°. It continued to fall during the day, and at night stood at —20°, passing through sixty degrees in twenty-four hours; from the summer of the temperate zone to an arctic winter!

With us but little snow fell during this violent change. The day was clear, with a strong west wind, which at Buffalo raised the water of the lake twenty feet.

Westward the cold was preceded by a heavy snow-fall. The railways terminating at Chicago were reported stopped by snow. The mercury fell to —28½°. At St. Louis no trains arrived for two days, and the Mississippi was closed by ice. The storm extended as far north as Green Bay, and as far south as Kentucky. At Louisville the thermometer fell from 49° to —1°, and on New Year's day at 9 A.M. it had fallen as low as —19½°; a range of 68½°!

Much snow also fell in Maryland and along the upper Potomac, with a temperature much below zero, greatly to the distress of our army.

With the exception of this unprecedentedly cold storm, the season was in no respect abnormal. But my general notes of the remainder may be acceptable, as serving to exhibit the ordinary character of winter in this locality.

Jan. 5. Snow on the ground this morning about four inches, and being underlaid by a coat of ice, the sleighing is good. Wind continues westerly.

Jan. 6. Since 1st inst. the river has been frozen over, and is crossed daily on foot. The ferries continue their trips, but not with the usual regularity.

Jan. 12. Cold continues. Thermometer since 1st inst. has ranged between 10° and 20°, the sun shining out frequently. On the morning of the 9th it was at 0. Snow has disappeared from the streets and roads, by insensible evaporation, there having been no thaw. A little is still left in the woods. The river is being crossed above the ferry channels by sleighs, and an enterprising individual has avoided the license law by erecting a shanty on the ice, at the boundary line of the two nations, where "tangle-leg" and "complete disability" (the fashionable names for bad liquors) are dispensed to chilled passengers. Too many find themselves, literally and metaphorically—to use a slang phrase—"half-seas-over."

The Mississippi and Ohio are reported frozen over, and crossed by teams as far down as Cairo.

Jan. 18. A two days' thaw leaves the ground bare, but has not disturbed the thick-ribbed ice in the river. Since the 1st there has been more or less sleighing.

Jan. 25. A thaw has been in progress for three days past. This morning the broad expanse of the river is free from ice; even the floating cakes have disappeared. The sun rises clear and beautiful upon the plying ferry-boats, which are crossing in their usual tracks, as if no ice-bound surface had so lately barred their progress.

Jan. 27. A most lovely day, with clear, warm sun. Thermometer at midday 60°.

Feb. 16. Since last entry the weather has been mild, thawing during the day and scarcely freezing at night. The earth is bare, and frost is out in many places. Yesterday was bright and balmy as April. To-day Boreas descends upon us with bluster, and whirls the dust in eddies.

Feb. 17. A cold change, with slight flurry of snow. Thermometer at 7 A.M. —3°.

Feb. 18. Thermometer at 7 A.M. —0; at noon 10°. Roads are dry and good.

Feb. 29. Warmer. Thermometer at 7 A.M. 32°.

Feb. 29. The mild weather continues. Seldom frost, even at night. Thermometer ranges from 32° to 40°; days cloudy.

With the exception of the first ten days of January there has been no sleighing in this neighborhood, but in the interior and northerly parts of the peninsula the snow has been sufficient for sleighing during a considerable part of January and February.

The minimum temperature of February was —3°. The winds during January and February, west and west by south and by north, only three easterly, and for a short time.

It should be remembered that the Signal Service was not established at Detroit until 1871. Such phenomena as I have noted are now being recorded as well as traced to their sources, with a scientific accuracy and minuteness that will not be looked for in these general notes.

Snowy winters are of great advantage to our farmers and to those who make wood-craft an employment. "Timber" of all kinds is then best cut; the frozen, snow-covered earth facilitating the removal by sleds, from situations that are nearly or quite impracticable at other seasons.

Wood has become of a value for fuel undreamed of a few years ago, and is in so great demand that a large and profitable business is done, mostly by small farmers, who bring it to the city market from many miles, and from lands where a short period ago it was an incumbrance, to be got rid of by the usual wasteful process of wind-falling and burning. Fire-wood and timber are also cut and hauled to the river banks, from long distances, for removal by boats in the summer to the markets of Detroit, Chicago and other cities.

Within a few years an immense traffic has sprung up in staves, hoops, and other barrel material, in the heavily wooded districts along the river St. Clair, and elsewhere in our State and Canada. It employs many vessels, some of which are loaded from our wharves direct to Europe, through the Welland Canal and the St. Lawrence. The softer woods of Michigan forests have acquired a value for many purposes which they did not possess a few years ago. A winter of good sledding is of inestimable advantage, in the transsport of these forest products to the place of transshipment or manufacture. Though in consequence of the uncertain character of our winters, and of the increased distances of land transport, logs and timber are now, in many places, drawn out by tramroads, built for the purpose.

Among these occupations I need make only a bare allusion to the great pine lumber interest, and to the importance to it of winters of snow and ice.

A trip to the pine woods in winter will well repay any one who not only loves the forests at all seasons, even in

WINTER MORNING IN A MICHIGAN LUMBER CAMP.

the depth and gloom of the cold season, but who would witness an exhilarating spectacle of the triumphs of labor, and resolve the question, Whence come those immense piles of boards and lumber that are daily used by builders, in the infinite variety of structures, throughout our land.

Such an excursion I made into Sanilac County, during some pleasant days in February. A half-day's journey from Port Huron brought us into the heart of the pine district. Here the sleighing was superb, and the weather all that could be wished for wood travel.

A light snow had fallen the night before, and the earth was covered to the depth of a foot with a mantle of unsullied whiteness; in its crystalline purity a matchless creation! We passed through much pine, hemlock and beech forest. The new gift of the night rested on their limbs and foliage, so that they drooped under the load. What superb pictures they formed! the crests of pure white crowning, while they did not wholly conceal, the green foliage, and adding a pendent grace to their natural beauty. How admirably defined each bending bough, by contrast of its gleaming fringe with the dark shade beneath!

> "Every pine and fir and hemlock
> Wore ermine too dear for an earl,
> And the poorest twig on the elm tree
> Was ridged inch deep with pearl."
> LOWELL.

And if each individual tree was a beautiful object, what a magnificent spectacle their combination, as we entered a dense forest of these evergreens! The loftiest pines reared their heads one hundred and fifty feet above our own, crowned with their glittering diadems. Some of the hemlocks were but little less lofty; while the smaller trees and the underbrush formed a dense thicket, through which the eye could penetrate but a short distance. Much of the undergrowth consists of small beech trees, which retain their leaves through the winter, changed to delicate shades of brown.

All beneath—the soil and the fallen timber—reposed under the deep, fleecy coverlet. For three days no wind shook down the snow wreaths that the lightest touch of the limbs in passing sufficed to bring in showers upon our heads.

An orchard of fruit trees in full bloom may bear some comparison with these snow-blossomed evergreens, but it lacks the beauty of outline, the depth of foliage, and the majesty of proportion. If anything could add to the grandeur of a pine forest it is this crowning grace of winter. The sunny South, with its palms and its tropic scenes, has its own delights, but it cannot offer us such a gift as this.

To the man of robust health, whose blood circulates rapidly through his full veins, winter is a welcome season. Only the shivering invalid fails to appreciate its peculiar pleasures.

There is a keen sense of enjoyment which is known only in winter. The sharp frosty air imparts to the whole frame new life and vigor, and these react upon the soul. There is a wild delight in breasting the storm, as it howls along our pathway, the snow-flakes falling fast and thick, covering every familiar object, and imparting a new aspect to the face of nature. How lovely this spotless mantle in its purity, fit to be the gift from Heaven which it is! It is joy even to wade through its laborious depths.

See how the young people hail its coming! Hear their shouts of ecstasy, as they plunge into the drifts, or roll huge balls to build snow fortresses or mock statues, or hasten with their sleds to the hill-side! How their cheeks glow with the healthful excitement and the more impulsive life in the blood!

Now hurry out the sleighs! The jingling bells—"merry bells,"—the smooth, rapid motion, the absence of rumbling wheels and noise and jolts, and the fresh, bracing atmosphere, combine to create an enjoyment, a rapture which is felt only where King Winter reigns acknowledged. Farewell to mud, to dust and filth! Welcome the new creation, the soft robe, covering all earth's impurities; substituting for the faded garniture of summer an all-investing robe of celestial purity.

Well may the farmer rejoice, who looks only with practical eye upon the seasons as they change; for this snow-cover is the best manure for his fields, costing neither money nor cartage, and it is a shield of protection to all tender-rooted crops against the heaving frosts.

The trees, lately stripped of their dresses, have put on one which helps to relieve their barrenness. But are the naked trees shorn of their beauty, because divested of their summer clothing? On the contrary, at no time is their beauty of form so apparent. Compare the nude Apollo with the dressed statue of a modern hero! Every leafless tree has a character of its own, which is brought to view more distinctly when each limb and minute twig are printed upon the sky. It is a winter study full of instruction, and worthy an artist's eye, to note how different and how distinguishable are the various species, in those distinctive features of size, habit of growth, and arrangement of branches, which are more or less concealed by the summer drapery. There is a charm even in the disclosures which the fall of the leaf has made, of the deserted birds' nests, some pensile from the slender twig, some securely fixed in a crotch of the limbs. No landscape painter can be perfect in his art who has not studied—as how few do!—the trees in their winter anatomy, noted their blue shadows upon the snow, and the many other effects appreciated by the true student of nature, in this her sternest but most entrancing aspect.

Now stir the fire, and draw the shutters close, and wheel the sofa round. Let the wind whistle by or breathe its loud sough; let it bring King Frost and all the furies in its train. At this ample fireside we are safe from its chill blasts. Here all is warmth and light, and thoughtful life, in cheerful contrast to the scenes of cold, darkness and desolation without.

Gather around the parlor table, strewn with books, and littered with articles that instruct or amuse the varied members of the family. The long, long, delightful, social evening is before us; such an evening as only the season of short days and long nights can bring; such as is known only where Boreas reigns supreme. Who cares how fiercely the storm rages! Who cares what heaps of snow are piled up by the sweeping blasts! His fiercest howls only add a new sense of security and enjoyment to the winter fireside.

Little tired feet, that have been active all the afternoon, playing in the snow bank, or on the slippery ice, now rest in the genial warmth of the hearth, and after a brief hour of reading, or song, or game, drag themselves off to the welcome bed, leaving the older heads to their conversation, their papers or their books. Nowhere is the family tie so strong as by the winter fireside. Nowhere are the kindly feelings so aroused, not only for the happy group around, but for those destitute ones, who at this inclement period experience only its discomforts and its bitterness.

Be active, then, to relieve the distresses of the poor, ye who have such store of this world's comforts, as to convert its most drear and perishing season into one of amplest delight. Let the poor brutes, too, that are dependent on thee, receive a double share of care and solicitude, and let thy thanksgiving for bounties bestowed, and thy Christmas joy for Heaven's mercies to thee and thine, be expressed by renewed efforts to dispense the blessings thou hast so bountifully received.

SPRING-TIDE.

"So forth issew'd the seasons of the yeare:
 First, lusty Spring, all dight in leaves of flowres,
 That freshly budded and new bloomes did beare,
 In which a thousand birds had built their bowres,
 That severally sung to call forth paramours;
 And in his hand a iaelin he did beare,
 And on his head (as fit for warlike stoures)
 A gilt engraven morion he did weare;
 That as some did him love, so others did him feare."
                                                SPENSER.

SPRING-TIDE.

IN this uncertain climate the hopes of the eager watcher for spring are doomed to many and many a disappointment.

March is not continually given to bluster. Sometimes a succession of mild, sunny days, clinging to the very skirts of winter, will swell the earliest buds almost to bursting, and awaken the belief that the vernal season of the poets has really come. We join in his rapturous anticipations.

> "Soon o'er our heads blithe April airs shall sing,
> A thousand wild flowers round them shall unfold,
> The green buds glisten in the dews of Spring,
> And all be vernal rapture as of old."

Then winter again takes up the sceptre, which he had but laid aside for an idle nap, and rules with increased severity, as if to atone for the neglect, and cheat the poet of his prophecy. He dallies with March, and coquets with April, allowing to each intervals of favor, but unwilling to yield to the bland usurper his ill ruled and already broken kingdom. At last the milder power prevails; the enfeebled frost-monarch contenting himself with only occasional raids into his abandoned territories.

The struggle during March is often mixed and boisterous enough. Now it blows a tempest, now breathes a gentle calm; now freezes at zero, now thaws rapidly at summer heat. In the morning, snow; at night, a thunderstorm. Now wet, now dry; now sunshine, now cloud. Days that call a seraph down, but speed him back on the morrow to his more congenial heaven. Suppliant month, that invites the birds, and greets their opening music with piping winds and crackling frosts; that with soft breath dissolves the snows into rippling streams, but floods the land with water, embargoes it with mud, stiffens it with ice. Month full of promise, full of horror! All welcome thy coming, all rejoice at thy departure.

Yet how cheering to soul and body the first spring-like days,—and we always have some such in March, at farthest in April,—when the sun shines blandly; blustering Boreas has retired, exhausted by his late potent efforts; the soil reeks with the dissolving snows; the ditches are full of clear, running water, and little streamlets ramify over the land; fish run up from the river into the fields by these new channels; the birds, returning to their old haunts, by their first joyous notes bring back the memory of past sunny days; flocks of water-fowl wend their way up the river; pigeons fly in large numbers over our heads. If an occasional snow-bank hedges the fields, it is fast dissolving in the warm sun. In the river, masses of ice, which so lately formed a solid bridge, are broken into fragments, that rapidly disappear, softening, whitening, crumbling, and sinking or floating out of sight.

Attracted by the genial warmth everybody is out of doors; the fires are allowed to expire on the neglected hearth, and open doors permit the wind once more to circulate through the house. We tread again the long unused walks in the garden and shrubberies, in field and lawn, examine our cherished plants, to see whether the cold hand of winter has dealt kindly with them; while visions of bursting buds, of early flowers, and of the universal life and bounty of nature, come over our spirits, comforting as the visits of white-winged angels, and we live whole seasons in the swift memories and hopes of a single hour.

A succession of such sunny days in March, accompanied by powerful rains, and coming before the snows have lost much of their winter depth, is certain to create disastrous floods. I quote from my journal:

March 20, 1865. We have accounts of floods all over the Northern and Middle States. A larger quantity than usual of snow had been left by the retreating winter, and snow-storms were succeeded by heavy rains. The consequences have been tremendous. Streams have risen suddenly to a height not known for many years, covering miles of country, deluging cities as well as fields, carrying off houses, sheep, cattle and fences, sweeping away bridges, even of stone and iron, tearing away the banks of canals for miles, interrupting railway trains, the telegraph, and the roads, so that whole days have passed without intelligence between one part of the country and another that had been in daily, if not hourly communication. Millions of dollars in property are thus lost in a day.

Happily our neighborhood is but little subject to disasters from this cause, as it is seldom visited by a depth of snow sufficient to cause a deluge on this sudden "breaking up" of winter, and has no deep valleys to collect into vast bodies the accumulated waters.

Sometimes, nevertheless, the spring rains are so violent and copious as to cause destructive floods in this neighborhood. Such was the case in April, 1836, which was noted for a tremendous freshet, which destroyed roads and bridges, doing a large amount of damage, though little in comparison with the devastations occasioned by the flood of 1865, through New York and Pennsylvania.

Ordinarily, in this locality, the advance of spring is more slow and prolonged than it is a hundred miles to the west and north, where the transition from winter to summer takes place very frequently with scarcely an interval that is worthy the name of spring. Here the season is better characterized, though its natural limits are much shorter than in Europe. But many instances of such rapid transition are on my records.

The spring of 1841 followed a winter of little severity. Lake navigation opened unusually early—in April. March was rather mild, but with a mean temperature 3° below the normal, of 34°. The season proved cold and backward, retarded possibly by the presence of large bodies of ice floating off the Newfoundland coast, and even as far south as latitude 41°. April and May had each a mean temperature 4° or 5° below the normal (of 46° and 58° respectively).

There was much snow over the country throughout April, and ice formed at Washington on 3d May. Fruit trees were not in blossom until the 20th of that month, nor had the forests put forth scarcely a green leaf. On the 22d May, summer burst upon us in full glory. Fruit trees were in bloom, the forests quite green, and an almost summer foliage clothed many of the trees and shrubbery in the city yards. For several days successively the thermometer rose to 80° and above, during the afternoons. The summer following proved warm and dry.

The spring of 1844 afforded an instance of a very early as well as sudden advance of vegetation. The preceding winter was mild, without snow and with very little ice. March was also mild, and April had a mean temperature 8° above the normal. On the 11th of that month hardly a green leaf had appeared. Two days later gardens were quite green and many fruit trees in blossom. Frosts followed in May, and both spring and summer were very wet.

The opening of 1845 exhibited in a still stronger degree the contrasts which are so common between our spring seasons, and shows how extreme often is the diversity. The spring followed a winter of uncommon openness, which is described in my chapter on Winter. On 3d March steamers had commenced regular trips to ports on Lake Erie. Frost had left the ground for fully a week, and roads were quite dry. On the 11th, forest trees showed blossom, and vegetation began to advance. In a few days more farming and gardening operations were in vigorous progress. A week only of freezing weather occurred in March, although the mean temperature was below the normal. No untimely frosts subsequently marred the prospects of the year, which proved warm and dry.

The spring of 1855 followed a cold and snowy winter, protracted into April. On the 20th of that month the mercury leaped to 80°, giving a sudden start to vegetation, and bringing the elms and maples into blow. No such high temperature was experienced in May or June, and the summer was cold and wet.

The spring of 1857 was of a character still more

marked. An extremely cold and stormy winter, prolonged far beyond the ordinary period, chilled the lap of May. Until the last week of that month no influence of the spring was apparent. The last two days of May and first day of June were very warm, my Fahrenheit indicating 80° and 85°. Vegetation started with wonderful vigor, so that in three days, from the nakedness of winter every shrub and tree burst into leaf and blossom. A cool and moist summer succeeded.

Sudden changes in the opposite extreme are not infrequent in spring. That of 1862 succeeded a very mild and equable winter, whose temperature had at no time fallen below zero. During the latter half of April, the heat had been almost oppressive. On the 18th May, with a strong wind from the N. W., the temperature fell in two hours from almost summer heat to below 40°. Fruit trees had been in bloom for more than a week. This cold snap was followed by frosts which did much damage. The remainder of the year was pleasant and dry.

An equally violent change occurred in the spring of 1874, though following a winter which had been rather mild, with abundant snow. March came in decidedly lamb-like. Bluebirds, robins and song sparrows were around quite numerously as early as the 2d, and the month continued dry and of normal temperature to its close. The whole of April was dry, cold and blustering, with a mean temperature nine degrees below normal. Dry and cool weather accompanied sharp easterly winds until May 7. Then a sudden change occurred. A prevailing cold, which made overcoats desirable out of doors, and fires within, resolved itself into summer heat. On the 8th the mercury rose from a maximum of fifty-eight degrees and a minimum below freezing, of the previous day, to eighty degrees, which it maintained from noon till 5 P.M. On the 9th it rose to eighty-five degrees. On the 10th, to eighty-nine degrees. We experienced a heated term of six days' duration. Until the 8th of May no green thing was visible, except grass. During the day following many shrubs came into leaf. By the 10th, a general tint of green pervaded garden and forest. On the 12th I gathered a brilliant bouquet from my peach, apple, pear, cherry and plum trees. On the 15th came a welcome rain, with cooler temperature, followed by light frosts. The mean of the month was fifty-nine degrees, thirteen degrees above the normal! The succeeding summer was not an unusual one, either as to temperature or rainfall.

Other vicissitudes of spring-time deserve mention. Snow-storms late in April are not infrequent.

In 1854 a severe snow-storm set in on Good Friday, April 14th, lasting two days, the snow not disappearing until after Easter. This storm visited the Atlantic coast as far south as Virginia.

In 1856 snow also fell in April. The month of March was exceedingly cold, and the river froze so as to be crossed on the ice with teams on the 15th. A hard frost occurred on the 30th of May.

The cold and late spring of 1857 has been already alluded to. On the 20th of April a severe storm passed over the country, leaving snow three feet deep through portions of Western New York. The suspension bridge at Rochester was broken down by the weight.

Reports of travellers, and particularly English rural writers, have accustomed us to compare unfavorably the character of our spring with that of Europe. Its capriciousness is, however, not wholly unknown on the other side of the ocean, though it is there a less noted phenomenon. A writer in the *Spectator* repudiates the idea that the loveliness of the English spring is due to its gradual advance and lingering stay; he even lauds the season of 1875 for its very opposite character. He says: "It is the custom to talk of the beauty of an English May, but for seven years back, at least, May has been a work of shedding and of blight,—a shrinking of the spirit and wilting of the trees. In almost all English springs a large number of the leaves are crinkled by the frosts which succeed the first burst into leaf, and happy is the neighborhood in which a good proportion of the leaves are not blackened as well as shrunken, in consequence of the indomitable way in which winter keeps returning and returning upon us after he has made believe to go."

This is a species of blight unknown to us, even in our coldest or most capricious springs.

The spring of 1875 must have been imported from America. The *Spectator* says of it: "In England, almost for the first time within what is now a very considerable experience, the spring, long delayed, has come abruptly, with all the softness of an early summer, and yet with all the freshness of true spring. Not a single tree shows those powerful signs of pinched or blackened leaves due to the frosts which follow on soft weather. It is like the weather which the returning trade wind brings to the tropics when the rainy season is over, only without the midday glare, perfect in its freshness and softness."

"The only drawback"—the writer continues—"and it is so rare a phenomenon in England that it is hardly a drawback, is that there has been hardly any graduation visible in the leaf between the bud and the full bright green of early summer. A day's rainfall, and then the beeches and oaks and elms were all, as by one consent, in full dress at once."

This well describes *our* frequent experience, and surely it is a consolation, accompanying what we have considered a drawback, to know that it has its value and a peculiar beauty in foreign eyes.

One of the earliest indications of returning spring-time is the appearance of numerous flocks of wild ducks, geese and swans, proceeding to new quarters up the chain of rivers and lakes. This takes place in February and March, not often in the winter month, unless there is promise of a spring of unusual earliness. Sometimes the flight is deferred until as late as April, a late spring being always the accompaniment.

In the very cold and backward season of 1843, I observed them going northward in the latter week of March, and large flocks made their appearance, *returning upon their tracks*, on the third of the following month.

Robins and bluebirds, the earliest harbingers of spring among the songsters, always return to us in March, as early as the first week, if the season be mild and early, but they often delay their coming until the middle or end of the month, if the spring prove late and stormy. The yellow birds and the rest of the song tribe soon follow, until all the groves are vocal.

How few know fully what a day in spring is who have not been adventurous enough to rise with the dawn, and commence the day when the birds begin theirs. Let me describe a morning towards the end of May, when—I do solemnly aver—I tried the experiment.

The hour was three o'clock. Night yet held sway over the sleeping earth, and all was silent, with the hush that precedes the awakening. The moist air, loaded with the odor of innumerable blossoms, breathed around me a fragrance and freshness peculiar to the season and the hour. Soon the solitary note of a chanticleer—"the cock that is the trumpet to the morn"—broke the silence; another and another answered, until the welkin rang with their strains of rivalry. Dawn was but just visible, yet every cock for miles around " with his lofty and shrill-sounding throat," was chanting defiance to the rest of his sex, and arousing his feathered dames to the duties of the day. A flush of light brightens the eastern sky. It is the halo which precedes the chariot of Phœbus, attended by Aurora and the dancing hours.

Notice the clear distinction drawn in the sacred writings between those three periods of early day, "At dawn, at cock-crowing, and in the morning." A faint blush of light always precedes the awakening of the "bird of dawning," as his full chorus does the period when night fairly retreats before the "god of day."

To many it would be a new sensation to be up at dawn, or

> "At the cock crow,
> When the night is dying slowly
>   In the sky,
> And the sea looks calm and holy,
>   Waiting for the dawn
> Of the golden sun
>   Which draweth nigh.
> When the mists are on the valley, shading
>   The river chill,
> And the morning star is fading, fading,
>   Over the hill."

And now, while the mists are yet in the valley and on

the river, awakes the nuptial chorus of the birds. And what a concert it is! As if each little musician had aroused to a fresh sense of his happiness, and was striving to outdo all others in the expression of it. The whole air is vocal. The strains mingle in a confused medley, yet in perfect concord. Not one throat that ever poured a note is silent now. One after another takes up the strain, ever higher and higher, nearer and nearer, until the very heaven resounds, and " Earth rolls the rapturous hosanna round." If you would hear this sweet concert delay not until the sun is up, and not until the summer. It is the birds' epithalamium. Its set time is the dawn in spring.

Morning has now fairly broke, and human bipeds begin to arouse from their beds of slumber, awakened by the light. How pure and fresh the atmosphere is still; but the birds have finished their grand concert of thanksgiving, and are busy finding breakfast for themselves or for their little ones. To how many of us men does the day bring only care and wearying labor, without requital, and without the soothing influences of morning. The sun is in the heavens; the discordant sounds of busy life float upon the air; all is tumult upon the earth. Man's day has begun.

After the long deadness of winter, the first flowers which greet us in our country rambles have a peculiar attraction.

The most delicate among these, and one of the earliest, is the little spring beauty (*Claytonia Virginica*), very pure and lily-like. It grows low, with the violets, and loves to hide in the shadows and the fresh grass. Of the violets we have eight or ten species, of all shades, from blue to yellow and white. They have an associate in the anemone or wind flower, so called from its opening in the winds of spring. Our species (*nemerosa*) is a very modest flower, by no means so gorgeous as the several European kinds.

Early in May the "openings," or lightly timbered lands—which have so great extent on our peninsula, though but little in our immediate vicinity—are beautifully adorned.

Among the most conspicuous of the May gifts of Flora, besides those already named, is the bold Wake-robin, both white and pink; the Litchnidia, purple and fragrant; Bellwort, yellow with spiral petals; Crane's-bill, a crowfoot geranium, resembling a dwarf rose; the yellow Buttercup, of world-wide fame; the Lupine, purplish-blue; Lousewort, yellow and red; Vetch, a small purple-white blossom; the Lady's-slipper, or Cypripedium, yellow and mottled, worthy to fit the foot of Venus; Painted-cup, brilliant scarlet, in its colored bracts; Strawberry and Whortleberry, the latter quite elegant with its bell-shaped pink-and-white flower clusters.

These and many others are ever present and numerous. They love to associate in family groups, each kind excluding from its favorite locality all others, except a few solitary foreigners, who seem to be admitted by favor within the home circle. They occupy as partiality dictates, one tribe the undulating knolls, another the moist hollows. Some court the shade, others the fervid sun in the more open spaces, and all seem to set at defiance the withering fires that annually sweep these glades.

As a means of useful comparison, I add the periods of bloom of some spring flowers of this locality, as reported to me by a botanical friend.* Purple Spring Cress (*Cardamine purpurea*) is in flower by April 12, frequently; Spring Beauty by April 14; Marsh Marigold (*Caltha Palustris*), by April 16; Anemone, Ranunculus and Bloodroot (*Sanguinaria Canadensis*), by April 18; Liverwort (*Hepatica acretiloba*), as early often as the 10th of March.

Among plants coming into flower from the middle to the latter part of April are Blue Colosh (*Caulophyllum thalictroides*); several of the Violets (*Viola blanda, cucullata, sagitata, Mulenbergii and pubescens*), Shepherd's purse (*Capsella bursa-pastoris*); Ginseng (*Aralia trifolia*); the purple and white Trillium; Yellow Adder's-tongue (*Erythronium Americanum*); Dutchman's breeches (*Dicentra cucularia*) and the Sedge (*Carex Pennsylvania*).

So brilliant is the autumnal foliage in this climate, as quite to eclipse our notice of the leaf tints of spring. But these, if less brilliant, are scarcely less varied. Even the grass has in its young green blade a velvety softness which does not belong to summer. The stems of the willows, which are among the earliest of our shrubs to feel the enlivening influence of the vernal breath, assume a brighter yellow, red and green, according to their species, to which a liveliness is added by the young leaves that venture forth so early. The maples show blossoms of Indian red. The first leaves of apple-orchards have a somewhat brownish tinge of darker green than afterwards.

These lively tints of the fresh, young leaves contrast finely with the evergreens that deepen the green of their foliage with the advent of spring.

How refreshingly green is the grass, the first of the veg-

---

* Henry Gillman.

etable world to be stimulated into vigor by dissolving snows and April showers. How delicious to the sight is this soft carpet of green, while the trees are awaiting the warmer airs of June to put on " smiling nature's universal robe." What luxuriant beauty of the unsodded tropics can equal it!

A few general facts, drawn from my note-books, will serve further to illustrate the progress of our spring season.

The northward flight of ducks, geese and swans takes place in March, from the first to the end. Robins and bluebirds make their first appearance from March 1 to 20; the thrush, tanager, oriole and song-birds generally, seldom before April, and frequently not until May.

The first signs of vegetation among our common trees is seen in the blossoming of elms and maples, from March 10 to April 20, the average being April 10. The forests are green with the young leaf seldom before the latter part of April, the range being from April 1 to May 15, and they are seldom in *full* leaf before June.

The earliest fruit trees, as peach, cherry and plum, come into bloom from middle of April to middle of May, —a whole month's range, the average period being May 8. Apple and pear are a week later. Our large French pear trees are quite regular in their period, and are seldom full-crowned with their snowy blossoms earlier or later than May 20.

The latest spring frosts may occur from April to June.

I shall close these general observations upon our springs by quoting from my journals the weather notes of a single season, taken rather at random. Those of 1877 tolerably well represent the general average, the mean temperature of the three months being only a degree below the normal; that of March nearly 5° below, and of April 2° above.

The first two winter months which preceded were cold and snowy. But February (as we have seen in our notices of winters) was unusually mild and clear.

March 9. After several days of changeable and gusty weather, with winds from all quarters of the heavens, a storm set in yesterday, with fine snow and sleet, which has ended in a fall of 6 inches. Heavier snows are reported from the north and interior.

This evening (9th) an aurora was observed, lasting from 7.30 to 11.30 P.M. It consisted of a single stationary arch, without darting luminous beams.

20th. Since the 9th the ground has been covered with snow, and the sleighing good, though but little hard frost. This morning the trees were all mantled in thick hoar-frost, and presented a glorious appearance in the clear sun.

The snow soon began to thaw rapidly, and continued to soften through the day, although the heavens were covered with clouds after 10 A.M. About 6 P.M. the clouds deepened, a colder wind coming from the N.E., and snow began to fall. At the same time thunder was heard, and soon lightning began to play, very sharp thunder following at very short intervals. At every recurrence of the electric flash, the bell in the City Hall tower rang a loud, clear tone. Hail, snow and sleet fell in succession, and at 9 P.M. three inches of snow covered the ground.

The cause of this unusual phenomenon is thus explained by the Signal Service observer at Detroit (Van

Heusen): "For some ten days preceding the storm there had been a succession of mild polar waves, moving down from the N.W., and during the same period a warm current, highly charged with atmospheric electricity, moving from the S.W. These two currents, one of cold, dense, dry air, and containing a large amount of vapor, met somewhere in the neighborhood near the south-western portion of Minnesota. The warm air being lighter, ascended to the upper atmosphere, carrying with it the vast amount of electricity it contained. The cooler air clung to the surface of the earth, and this double current moved rapidly eastward, continuing on its course to the Atlantic seaboard, where its greatest violence was felt."

During March the prevailing wind was N.E. Highest temperature 50°, lowest —2°. Precipitation 5.43 inches. The number of days on which snow or rain fell was 23. Frosts on 1st and 20th insts.

April 18th. Thus far this month has been free from snow and severe cold. Frost did not fully leave the ground in shaded places before the middle of the month. No signs of vegetation, except flowering of the maples, until to-day, when, after a week's dry spell, rain has fallen, quite saturating the soil. *22d.*—The warm, sunny weather which followed has started the buds of early plants, and made the grass quite green. Crocuses and a few early garden flowers have been a week in bloom.

28th. Rain last night. The temperature continues very mild; buds are opening on the trees. Thermometer averages about 75° at noon. *30th.*—Vegetation is very backward, notwithstanding the mean temperature has been higher than for the last five years. The highest temperature in April, 75°; lowest, 20. Prevailing wind

N.E. Rainfall 3.27 inches. Much and thick ice still in the upper lake waters.

May 6th. No rain as yet, but cold, dry winds from easterly directions, with frosts every night until 4th. *11th.*—Cold and dry easterly winds continue, without rain sufficient to saturate the soil. Yet the forces of nature are at work visibly and daily in perfecting the leaf and blossom. The maples are coming into young leaf, and the horse-chestnuts are quite green. Currant bushes in flower; also cherry trees, but not the shad (*Mespilus*) nor the Judas-tree.

18th. Dry weather continued until 16th, when a very copious rain fell during the night and morning of 17th. This was followed by a great change in the temperature, which rose from about 70°—the highest heretofore—to 82° throughout most of the day on the 17th, and on the 18th to 88°, with a burning sun. Vegetation felt this extraordinary change most sensibly. The leaves of the maples and chestnuts, which three days ago were only one-fourth grown, are now of full size. The later trees, lindens, oaks and hickories are quite green; cherries, peaches and pears are in full blow, and the shad and Judas-tree nearly so. *20th.*—French pear trees in full blossom. The extreme dryness of the season has given cause for forest fires in Northern Michigan and in Wisconsin, and some of the Eastern States. In some instances much destruction has occurred.

The rainfall for May has been only 0.90 in. against 5.62 last year, and a normal precipitation of 3.4 inches. The mean temperature is the normal one of 57°, but the range has been considerable. Prevailing wind, S.W.

An aurora of unusual splendor occurred on the 28th,

a description of which I condense from the report of the Signal Service officer at Detroit:

"It consisted of three arches of light, one over the other, the last extending to the zenith. Slender, luminous beams of yellow and crimson followed, darting upward from the horizon, and waving like flame. These all grew more and more brilliant for an hour, when a complete corona of glory was formed. The spectacle was then most magnificent. The whole northern half of the heavens, to a point 10 degrees south of the zenith, was one mass of quivering flame, in which all the colors of the rainbow seemed blended. The rays of light arranged themselves in sinuous bands, like the undulations of a flag. At times these united to form a brilliant fringed curtain, whose folds were agitated by the wind in an immense variety of most graceful curves. After the formation of the corona, tremulous waves of light, in rapid succession, rolled upward, and travelled along the lines of the auroral arches. The southern sky was of inky blackness. After more than an hour the arches broke into segments, and the aurora disappeared."

OUR SUMMERS.

"From brightening fields of ether fair disclosed,
  Child of the sun, refulgent Summer comes,
  In pride of youth, and felt through Nature's depth:
  He comes attended by the sultry Hours,
  And ever fanning Breezes on his way."
                                    THOMSON.

OUR SUMMERS.

THE first of our summer months is undoubtedly with us one of the most enjoyable of the year. The labors of planting and preparing the soil for the long awaited vegetation are concluded; the dangers from frosts and blasting winds are over; we have a full realization of what the coming season of growth is to afford. Our keen sense of the change from the nakedness of winter to the greenness and bloom of nature is not yet blunted by long fruition. Nor have we yet been parched by the summer heats.

What a month of months is our Northern June! The trees lately so bare, or showing only the delicate tints of spring, have now perfected their foliage, and are fresh and lustrous as young brides adorned for their husbands. The evergreens are illuminating their sombre mourning suits with an embroidery of a new and lighter growth, that, like half-tints in a widow's weeds, betoken relief from the thraldom of sorrow, while they add enhanced beauty. How richly green the soft carpet that covers the ground! What land can compare with ours, at this season, for diversity of leaf and tint, and depth of color? Where is the tropical landscape that, with all its luxuriance, can compete with it, or that can compensate by its tangle and variety for the absence of turf? Trees and grass make a paradise of any Northern home, nor need we envy those sun-burned lands where that chief element of beauty—the greensward—is wanting.

Month of roses and of birds among the bowers! Month, too, of those luscious fruits, strawberries and cherries, which give us a foretaste of the bounties of summer, the first of that succession of delicious small fruits which no other clime produces in such exquisite perfection. Raspberries, currants, blackberries and whortleberries fill up the whole period until autumn, to be followed by the larger but equally characteristic fruits, pears, apples, plums, peaches and grapes. Short as our period of vegetation is, it more than rivals the tropics in the brief abundance, as well as exquisite flavor of its productions. The deep sleep of winter seems to be necessary to so brave an awakening. Nor is it in fruits alone that this climate so excels ; the round of vegetables also feels the superior influence, and gives us—happy dwellers in the temperate zone—what no other clime can furnish in perfection. I mention but one,—the lordly and incomparable "Indian corn." *Ab uno disce omnes !*

Sudden as is the transition of winter into summer, and short as that summer is, it is full of tropical character. Sometimes, for days together, the temperature exceeds that which is experienced under the equator. I have known persons born under the line, or accustomed to the sun of the West Indies, who complained of the oppressive heat of our Northern summer, and wished themselves escaped to the cooler airs of the tropics. At such periods vegetation is stimulated into excessive activity, and plants of a certain class are produced and ripen in an incredibly short time. An instance, universally known, is that American plant, the Maize, which comes to perfection even several degrees further north, while it refuses to grow with equal luxuriance in the extreme South. Allied to the sugar-cane, its rapid endogenous growth, its long sheathing leaves, tasselled top and silky ears, and its stately appearance, remind us of tropical productions. What a magnificent specimen of the grass kind it is! And the full corn in the ear,—how unspeakably superior to all other known grains! No wonder our Puritan ancestors, under the spell of this new-found wonder, lived and flourished on hasty-pudding. Or that Barlow, one of the earliest of our poets, should sing of the maize—

> "Thy constellation ruled my natal morn,
> And all my bones were made of Indian corn."

The daily extension of the blades of maize may be counted by inches, and on a still, warm summer night the crackling sounds of growth may be distinctly heard.

Still more astonishing is the rapidity with which the coarser vines, squash and pumpkin—natives, too, of America and its temperate clime — push themselves along; a foot in twenty-four hours being no uncommon growth during our torrid days! But the tropical character of our climate is perhaps better exhibited in the facility and perfection with which many trees and plants of really tropical origin, or closely allied to such, come to perfection in our latitude. I may instance the castor-bean among herbaceous plants, and the tulip-tree, the cucumber-magnolia and the pawpaw among trees.

Nor are other features wanting, to show how close is the communion we hold during our brief summers with those lands where summer is eternal. Usually our dry atmosphere causes the nights to be cool, and even cold, after a day of almost intolerable heat; but there are, not unfrequently, nights that in sultry fervor are truly tropical. Nights in which it is enjoyment to dispense with all the usual coverings.

Even the sounds are now tropical, and recall Humboldt's description of insect life in South America. The stridulous note of the Cicada is incessant. How few have ever seen these insects, or are familiar with their form and life, yet how they fill the whole palpitating air with the music of their love-notes. The melody comes to our ears, not in a continuous strain, but in a regular beat or throb, broken occasionally by a louder note, which rises above, and for a moment overpowers, the universal din.

About August the querulous Katy-dids add their voices, and distinct above other sounds fill the ear with their contentions. They do not scatter, like other *cicada*, but congregate in some favorite spot in the grove, where, undisturbed by a world full of wranglings of its own, they may dispute upon the great problem of their lives, still no nearer solution,—" Katy did, Katy did ; Katy did-e-nt." How well Holmes has written of them:

> " I love to hear thy gentle voice, wherever thou art hid,
> Thou testy little dogmatist, thou pretty Katy-did.
> I think there is a knot of you beneath yon hollow tree ;
> A knot of spinster Katy-dids,—do Katy-dids drink tea ?
>
> " Do tell me where did Katy live, and what did Katy do ?
> Was she so very fair and young, and yet so wicked too ?
> Did Katy love some naughty man, or kiss more cheeks than one ?
> I warrant Katy did no more than many a Kate has done."

What hosts of insects, brought to life by the heated atmosphere, have the night for their season of active existence and enjoyment. Only a part of animated nature sleeps through the hours of darkness. How little we, who slumber, know of the world that is abroad throughout the beautiful summer night.

There are "voices of the night" unsung by Longfellow. Some homely and familiar voices, scorned by the vulgar, but which to the ear attuned to a harmony untaught by human masters, are full of music.

From the marshy bayous of our river comes up at summer eventide the croak of frogs. A pleasing music is the nightly concert of these dwellers in the reeds and the shallow river-side. Was Pan their earliest instructor? First there is a rattling falsetto of small notes, varied by deep tones, like the heavy twang of a bass-viol. When one of these big-voiced fellows tunes up, another and sometimes a third strikes in, keeping up a simultaneous clangor, of about five seconds duration. Then succeeds an interval of silence,—a five-bar rest,—lasting fifteen or twenty seconds, when the leader again assumes his viol, and is assisted as before. These notes are heard a long way off. On still nights they are very distinctly heard from across the river, a full mile distant, a nightly challenge from the Canuck to his Yankee cousins over the way.

Though his praises are not sung by poets, and to many ears his notes are harsh, and suggestive of marsh and malaria, the association of the frog with the early summer, with plashing waters and dropping rains with the early cowslip, and the fresh grass in the moist meadow, make him a welcome attendant upon the season.

The note of the tree-frog is similar to that of his small brother of the marsh, and is loud and incessant throughout the night. These night voices do not assume a continuous strain, fatiguing to the ear, but occur with intervals of silence, like the measured breathings of a sleeping person, and consist with rhythmical harmony.

Another pleasing sound of the summer night is the sighing of the breeze in the tree-tops. It is like the rush of waves upon the beach, subsiding with the same gentle murmur, soothing in its crescendo and its fall.

Moonlight is a feature of the summer night, in the neighborhood of the lakes, which the peculiar clearness of the atmosphere renders exceedingly brilliant. Such nights can be thoroughly enjoyed only in the dewy freshness of the country, amid grass and shrubbery and fine old trees, where quiet reigns, and human sounds are banished.

Were we to analyze the nature of the charm which the moonlight has upon us, it would be found to be partly physical; the coolness, the quiet and the shade being soothing to all the senses. But the charm lies deeper than this. The landscape which we see by day is not the same as that seen under the canopy of night and her queen. The light which rests like a mantle on the earth is soft and silvery, unlike the dazzling glow of sunshine. Even in this feebler light shadows are more strongly drawn. The contrasts are deeper, from the absence of reflected light, which breaks up and diminishes the effect of shadows by day. Objects and their shadows are so nearly alike that they blend, the former seeming to be duplicated rather. The apparent size of objects is enlarged, which gives them a grander outline. A bush becomes a tree, and trees tower more majestically, for the glare of sunshine belittles. They loom like giants against the lower sky, and throw their dark shadows toward you, as if these were a part of themselves. Defects which are too apparent in the garish light that the sun throws upon all things, are hidden under Luna's tender sway. Tree and shrub assume greater perfectness of form. Her white beams glisten from every polished, upturned leaf, only to make deeper the contrast with the blackness beneath. Out of this depth of shadow the foliage appears larger and more abundant. As the eye cannot penetrate the gloom, the scanty arbor becomes a deeply covered bower. Imagination called into play pictures unreal beauties in the landscape.

A still greater charm of moonlight consists in the mystery with which nature is invested. The half known is always mysterious. The solemn stillness which prevails with the close of restless day, the myriad eyes that look down upon us from the firmament, the impotence of mortal vision to penetrate the half-revealed obscurity, the new and almost unknown kinds of animated beings which have their season of life in the absence of the sun, all tend to fill the soul with awe. Part of the mysterious charm of moonlight may be attributed to its moral influence. The sun is a male principle; it stimulates man to the active pursuit of business or pleasure, and arouses worldly ambition. The moon is a female power. She prompts to meditation, to religious feelings. We are nearer heaven by night than by day, whither our souls expand in the serene light of its apparent queen, or yield to the sweet influences of the Pleiades.

Excessive heats and droughts are by no means peculiar to this latitude in America, or characteristic of this region. Yet such periods are common, and are sometimes of many weeks' continuance.

Nor are these coincident with the hottest months. The "heated terms" occur usually in July and August; sometimes, but more rarely, in June and September; occasionally even in May, as in 1874. It is not uncommon for the thermometer to indicate 80° to 90° in the shade, for several days in succession, a powerful sun pouring down his unclouded rays upon the roasting earth, and producing an atmospheric condition more oppressive than the midday of the tropics. Should the air be still, it is possible for the night to take on a character hardly less endurable than the day. But such nights are happily rare.

It is often remarked that a "dry spell" is apt to occur at the season of the farmer's harvest. So, though the gathering in of the grain and hay is a most sweltering operation, it is the sort of weather to be prayed for at this particular juncture. We are also seldom without the mitigation of the life-giving westerly winds which, like "the good Doctor" of the West India Islands, serve to render the heat endurable, even under the temperature of 90 degrees. At these times the difference between the heated atmosphere of the city and that which prevails upon the river and in the environs is very noticeable, amounting to 8 or 10 degrees.

On such occasions all nature, animate and inanimate, succumbs to the dominion of Phœbus. The air quivers in the fervid beams which rest upon all exposed objects. The leaves hang indolently from the trees. The wise man seeks the shade, and even there finds no escape but in perfect rest.

> "Look forth upon the earth, her thousand plants
> Are smitten; even the dark, sun-loving maize
> Faints in the field beneath the torrid blaze;
> The herd beside the shaded fountain pants."

Blasts from an arctic winter seem then endurable in the comparison. Fortunately such terms are of short duration, three or four days at the most, and then the pendulum of the weather swings in the opposite direction, and sometimes causes us to wish the hot weather back again. Extremes of this kind are more severe away from the lakes and in latitudes still more northerly. I have experienced at Montreal heat more unendurable than any I ever felt at Detroit.

These periods of heat and drought often find sudden relief in summer storms.

Perhaps the day has been without a cloud, and while the earth is fairly staggering in the burning rays, suddenly black clouds gather in the western horizon. A sound is heard like the boom of a distant cannon. It is repeated at intervals, with growing distinctness. The clouds with their swift wings soon cover the heavens and obliterate the sun. Presently an angry flash portends the speedy onset of a tempest. The wind begins to roar and bend the trees, which sway wildly; dust flies in clouds before it, a few large drops fall; when suddenly down comes the watery tempest. It is not rain, but a cataract. A few moments suffice to convert the lately dry highways into streams, and torrents rush along the gutters. In a few minutes the storm has expended its fury, and ceases suddenly as it came. But what havoc has it occasioned, in gullies worn in the steep roadways, and in the growing and tender corn prostrated! Nevertheless it is a thankful gift to the parched earth, bestowing instant greenness and renewed life to nature, and freshness and purity to the atmosphere.

The amount of water which falls in these summer storms is seldom great, though copious for the time it lasts. In this respect it is in strong contrast with the rain-storms of the tropics, where the precipitation of a few hours sometimes equals that of the whole month in the temperate zone.

Rarely the storm visits us with a more terrible earnestness. The play of the lightning and the loud crash of the thunder—echoing peal on peal—which accompany the descending torrent are grand in the extreme, and appalling to the stoutest nerves. Fortunate if, while man escapes, some noble tree, the pride of the grove, is not rent and shattered by the bolt or the blast.

Happy, too, should this angry tempest be but the precursor of more gentle but copious showers that follow, assuring its benefaction. And what is more delightful than the soft patter of the rain upon the trees and grass when it comes in its kindly mood.

Perhaps all day long clouds have been giving promise of the much needed refreshment; but we get used to frequent disappointment in our climate, where it is a truthful maxim that "all signs fail in dry weather." All day long the struggle lasts between sun and cloud, but just at nightfall the latter prevails, and the increasing blackness gives welcome token of the promise about to be fulfilled.

Large but scattered drops, at first few and far between, descend as precursors of the more than golden shower. How deliciously soft and cool is the atmosphere! What an expectation pervades all nature! Then comes the rapid rainfall, making sweet music, as housetop and tree, dusty street and bending grass alike give forth a grateful murmur,

"Wakening each little leaf to sing."

Then when the clouds break, and the sun again asserts his predominance, though with gentle force, how joyous and fresh the earth he shines upon! How sparkle the myriad crystal drops, each a liquid lens, that hang on every branch and leaf and blade. No jewels of Golconda ever equalled the prismatic display. Each wet leaf is a mirror, reflecting the soft radiance. And see! above the new-born earth hangs the bow in the cloud; symbol of beauty, token of peace to men of violent mind. "Look upon the rainbow and praise Him that made it; very beautiful it is in the brightness thereof. It compasseth the heaven about with a glorious circle and the hands of the Most High have bended it."*

Sudden storms and high winds are universal phenomena, from which this region is by no means exempt. But though I have known the grain laid prostrate, and occasionally a tree overthrown or a limb torn off, it is not a little remarkable that during the entire period of my fifty-year records no storm of greater violence, or having the character of a tornado—with a single exception, which I shall notice hereafter—has occurred. Nor have I known, except rarely, a pane of glass broken by hail. Destructive gales and tornadoes are of no unusual occurrence in places not far removed, and we read with pain in the daily journals sad tales of the disasters attending them. The forests of this State record the passage in past times of terrific whirlwinds, in narrow, desolated tracts, sometimes of many miles in length; but, whatever may be the cause, the immediate vicinity of the lakes has happily claimed almost entire exemption.

The changeableness of our climate is sometimes uncomfortably illustrated in the rapid and great fall of the mercury, consequent upon a change of the wind, from south and west to north and east. On these occasions it is not uncommon to experience an extreme difference of temperature, within an hour or two. A person leaving his home in the morning, sweltering in a torrid

---

* Ecclesiasticus xliii., 11.

atmosphere, in his thinnest clothing, may return before night, shivering under a temperature fall of 40 degrees. A most untropical feature this, and no doubt quite prejudicial to health.

Fortunate it is if we escape a frost, even in midsummer, for if a dry air prevails this is possible in any month, from March to November. Frosts and dry weather accompany each other. My notes have entries like this: 1836, *May 8 to* 12.—Very warm and dry. Ther. has stood at 82° in the shade of my house, yet mornings are frequently accompanied by frost.

The year 1853 was remarkably dry and warm, the thermometer indicating 94° in June, and rising to 99° August 11 to 14. This heated term extended over the northern United States. On Aug. 28 a severe frost fell upon Central Michigan. For five months, ending Oct. 21, with the exception of a slight shower, there was not rain sufficient to lay the dust. Extensive fires spread through the woods and marshes. These will be specially noticed in treating of some of the features of our autumns.

In 1859, after an early spring, but dry, on the 11th and 12th June, severe frosts occurred, from Central New York to Iowa, and even as far south as Cincinnati. Maize and other tender crops were badly cut down, and fruit was injured. The latter part of June was continuously warm; but frosts again occurred July 4 and 5, though slight. The mercury, during the middle and latter parts of this month, rose to 94° in the city.

Aug. 28 and 29, again frosts occurred, searing tender plants. No rain had fallen for four months!

This year frosts occurred in every one of the twelve months. Only seven and a half inches of water fell during the summer months, and but 29 inches during the entire year. Such seasons are exceptional, and show that droughts and frosts are coincident phenomena.

The year 1858 furnished an example of a very warm summer, but one that was attended with abundant rains, and no frosts from April to October. As this year presents in its features a typical summer, or an average of more than half the summers of this locality, I quote from my journal somewhat in detail:

June 1 to 15.—Continued cool, with frequent and heavy rains, drenching the country and threatening destruction to the corn crop. These rains have extended over a large portion of the United States, since the 1st of May, embracing all the Middle States. At the south immense damage was occasioned by the breaking of levees on the Mississippi. A Pittsburg journal states that the average of observations gives about ten inches rainfall in May, and five inches to 12th June, or fifteen inches in forty-three days. I have no data for the amount which fell at Detroit.

From the middle to end of June, very warm and dry, with scarcely a shower. The mercury ranged from 80° to 95° nearly every day,—a heated term of very unusual length.

July 1 to 15.—Continues warm, but with some showers. Thermometer, at the city, often ninety degrees in the shade. At my house, exposed to the breezes from the river, and free from reflected heat, it has not been above 86°. Latter half of month very dry.

August set in with heavy rains, which continued at intervals until the 5th, fully saturating the earth, and producing immense growth of vines and vegetables.

Aug. 20.—The weather until to-day has been excessively warm. Highest of the thermometer at my house 85°. In the city it is reported at 98°.

This high temperature continued through September. Considerable sickness followed, from fevers, which assumed a typhoid character.

All the summer months of 1858 were above the normal temperature, and the mean was five degrees above. The rainfall was also in excess about 3.5 inches.

The years 1875 and 1878 I shall notice as examples of very changeable summers; of generally cool temperature, being each below the normal, but of excessive rainfall.

The spring of 1875 had been very cold and dry, with frosts down to 10th of May, when a sudden rise took place to 84°, succeeded again by cold weather. The early part of June was dry. By the middle of that month the foliage of trees was mostly fully grown. The latter part brought excessive rains, with moderate temperature, rising once to 90°.

On June 28 occurred a most unusual phenomenon for this region. Following the clearing up of a rain-storm, a tornado struck the north-western suburbs of Detroit, demolishing twenty-one cottages, and destroying two lives. No such occurrence has been known here before or since, during my residence of half a century.

July opened warmer, with temperature at 80°, but continued and closed agreeably cool, with rains sufficient for garden crops, which came in early.

In August there were frequent rains, with generally cool weather until the 23d, when frost occurred in the neighborhood. In Western Michigan, from 21st to 23d, frosts were reported so severe as to " wipe out the entire crop of cranberries, corn, potatoes and garden truck." The temperature mean of the season was 65°, or a degree below normal. The rainfall, 13 inches, or 3.5 inches above the mean.

The spring of 1878 was early and warm. The first summer month was comparatively cool, with frequent rains until the 25th; winter clothing and fires were comfortable. The thermometer ranged from 50° to 70°. After the 25th it rose to 80° and soon to 86°, and the remainder of the month was warm.

July was a remarkable month, exceptionally warm and close. Showers were frequent and heavy. The wind was often in a northerly quarter, which served to allay the sensible heat; but the mercury was at 80° and upwards for more than twenty-three days, and on the 17th rose to 100°,—the highest on my records. The rainfall amounted to 8.8 inches, almost the normal mean for the summer season, and nearly one-fourth the entire precipitation of the highest years in my series.

August was warm and moist, but without excessive heat, and with many days of rain. The general mean of the summer was only 74°, notwithstanding the exceptionally hot July. The total rainfall was 15 inches, or one-third more than the normal for the season.

Sudden changes and hot and short summers characterize the whole Atlantic side of this continent; yet there is a compensation even in these drawbacks. They stimulate mind and body, and nature herself, to greater energy, and they add that variety and contrast which, according to the old saw, are the spice of life.

July and August, which constitute our true summer, crowd the watering-places with visitants, denizens of the crowded, stifling city, eager for pure air and a glimpse of that nature which the town denies them. No doubt our bilious climate renders any change, even to the country resident, serviceable to health.

But a country home is the best place for the enjoyment of the pleasures of summer. Here are her choicest haunts, here is her true paradise. The season is too short, life itself is too short to be spent in the dry and artificial city, when "every blooming pleasure waits without," to bless those who accept the invitation.

To watch the development of nature's green and growing things, their progress from the first opening bud to matured perfection, to observe the sights and sounds, and inhale the sweet breath of nature in this season of her prodigality, when the trees have their richest dress, the flowers their brightest hues, the birds their sweetest songs, the skies their deepest blue; when the breeze comes laden with choicest odors, and the dews and rains with blessings from above,—these combine to make the brief period which constitutes the summer of this region one of intense delight, more real, more intense from its very briefness and contrasts.

This lake region has been long noted for its clear and brilliant atmosphere, and for those effects which are attendant upon it. Not in famed Italy are the skies so pure, and so deeply blue; nor do the clouds pile up so magnificently, and display such ever-shifting and gorgeous panorama, in any other land. Shall I confess to be a builder of castles in that unsubstantial region; that my imagination sometimes runs riot in those ethereal fields, or

". . . . bestrides the lazy pacing clouds,
And sails upon the bosom of the air?"

Certainly the heavens, whether by night or day, are one of the features which add peculiar attractiveness to a region where mists and fogs seldom obscure their brightness, and no mountains shut from view the cloud-land which lies along the horizon, or bar out the splendors of closing day. To the contemplative mind the clouds are ever a study, and a continued delight and wonder. They compensate, to a great degree, for the absence of mountain scenery, and in their ever changing forms and varying lights they bear a resemblance to their more substantial prototypes.

For excursions into this attractive land frequent opportunity is afforded by the extent of open horizon. Here the clouds accumulate in mountain masses, pile upon pile, until they rival the Alps in grandeur of outline, and they raise lofty peaks, which seem covered with purest snow, far above the region of perpetual frost. At other times they lie in lengthened strata, like distant savannas, with calm oceans beyond, amid islands, which in the setting sun reflect his rays in scarlet, vermilion and gold. Certainly in this level country cloud-land is a most beautiful and attractive land, worthy to be a home for the immortals.

> "Mid yon rich clouds' voluptuous pile
> Methinks some spirit of the air
> Might rest to gaze below awhile,
> Then turn to bathe and revel there."

The beauty of the sunsets in the lake region has been often noticed, and, whatever science may determine as to the causes of the phenomena, it is certain that they are a remarkable feature, which adds greatly to the charm of our summers and autumns. I find in my journal some attempts at description, which may serve to give an idea, though very imperfect, of the characteristic phenomena:

June 20, 1867, closed with a brilliant sunset. The day had been one of the warmest of the season, but not cloudless. Towards evening heavy banks of cumuli hung upon the horizon to the east and south, while along the west lay narrow strata, showing broad openings of sky between, to a height of about thirty degrees. Above these extended a panorama of cirro-cumuli,—almost a "mackerel sky"—heavier below, but becoming more light and fleecy towards the zenith.

When the sun set, the clouds in the western sky became all of pure gold,—the low-lying strata glowing like a furnace, and the same hue lighted up the broken fleeces far into the zenith,—golden fleeces, indeed, worthy the admiration of an Argonaut. The sky seen through the lower strata was a delicate pea-green, graduating into the blue above. Through the golden fleeces the expanse of ether appeared of a depth and vividness of blue seldom equalled. Higher up, the bright lights upon the scattered wavelets gave to the blue empyrean an almost infinity of distance, resembling the star-lighted heavens.

At the same time the mountainous piles on the south and east, reaching from the horizon half way up the zenith, were painted with a deep crimson, whose warm blush met and mingled with the golden tints overhead. Altogether it was a most entrancing spectacle.

Some account of a more than usually phenomenal sunset I copy from my notes of 1864, Nov. 19.

The day had been one of the pleasantest of the late autumn, cold but clear in the morning, clouding up during the latter part of the day, until sunset, when suddenly the western sky became all aglow with gorgeous color. From the point in the horizon where the sun went down a mass of fleecy clouds extended, in the form of an inverted pyramid, to the zenith, and thence across to the opposite horizon. Below, from the same point to its opposite in the east, narrow belts of cloud swept across the sky, forming low arcs. The centre mass, from the horizon to half way overhead, and the lower portions of the belts, presented the most brilliant combination of crimson and scarlet it is possible to conceive; the structure being like piles of wool, sufficiently dense to conceal the sky beyond, and giving increased effect to the coloring by its varying tints. The patches of sky visible between the central mass and the belts was of clear apple-green, shading into the blue.

This splendid spectacle lasted about a quarter of an hour, fading with the daylight. At a little after five o'clock the brightness had disappeared, and the clouds assumed their previous dun hue.

But the phenomenon did not end here. As twilight deepened a faint blush began to tinge the fleecy surface, like colored lights reflected from waves. With the gradually departing daylight the blush deepened into rouge, and in a few minutes the banks and belts of cloud-land were again lighted up, with a splendor of coloring scarcely less brilliant than before, the hue inclining to orange. This new flood of rosy light soon involved the whole heavens, to its very eastern limit, while below the clouds the western and southern horizon glowed with clear gold. For a quarter of an hour this brilliant vision increased momentarily in breadth and intensity, and a full half hour elapsed before it faded entirely away.

I have often seen colors as gorgeous in the western

sky, but never before, in any land, the singular phenomenon of the reappearing of the colors with such splendor after an interval of total absence, nor so long a continuance of the display. No art of man can paint the equal of this gorgeous scene. Scarcely can any conception of man's rise to its reality. It was a scene to remember all one's days.

How does the sunset hour, with its surcease of daily cares, dispose the contemplative mind to drink to the full all this harmony and beauty, and to raise a song of thanksgiving to its author, who has spread upon his curtain of the sky* colors so delicate with those which are so rich and gorgeous. As

> ". . . . fades the glimmering landscape on the sight,
> And all the air a solemn stillness holds,"

what a serenity and peace are breathed over the face of nature, even setting at rest the stormy passions in the heart of man.

Filled are these twilight hours with sweet and tender musings; with memories of the loved and gone, who with us once watched the sun's parting rays, unconscious how soon he was to set to them forever. But behind these dun clouds of the soul are glowing brighter hopes, and the future is gilded with a golden glory.

In the splendor of its setting, parting day has thrown upon the storm clouds his many-colored robes, to give assurance to the world of a benignant morrow.

So, to the just, these are an emblem of hope; that he too, after the storms of life, may sink as calmly to rest,

---

* "Thou deckest thyself with light, as it were with a garment,
And spreadest out the heavens like a curtain."—*Psalm* civ.

and, clad in robe of brightness, rise to a fairer and better day, while the rapt vision will penetrate beyond the veil, and gain some nearer conception of His glory in the heavens who can light up the gateway with such celestial splendors.

AUTUMN-TIME.

". . . . And in the Autumn time
 Earth has no purer and no lovelier clime."
                                        HALLECK.

" Aye, thou art welcome, Heaven's delicious breath!
 When woods begin to wear the crimson leaf,
 And suns grow meek, and the meek suns grow brief,
 And the year smiles as it draws near its death."
                                        BRYANT.

AUTUMN-TIME.

NO period of the year impresses us more sensibly with the rich fulness of nature's blessings than the verging of summer into autumn.

Before the leaves have quite begun to decay, or the trees to throw off their verdant dress, and the harvests are still in the fields, is peculiarly the husbandman's season of joyful promise. Vegetation has perfected its growth, and the juices are now passing into the fruit. The great alchemist has outdone philosophers, and in her wondrous crucibles has perfected that mingling of ingredients which is about to convert her materials into gold.

If the past season has been favorable the farmer now looks with delight upon waving fields whitening in the sun; the lordly maize hanging its wilted tassels, signifying that the ear is receiving the golden glaze of maturity he has so long awaited, "first the blade, then the ear, and now the full corn in the ear." The earth-loving potato is assimilating the starchy mealiness which is its last claim from its mother's bosom. The fat pumpkin begins to glow with the absorbed beams of summer, and the dainty buckwheat is waiting for cooler suns to drop its flowers of pink and white, and display its well-remembered and old-fashioned, three-cornered grains of rusty brown.

The garden, too, has reached its full luxuriance. The purple beet, well filled with sweet juices, the green-leaved

course, and cheat us with an expectation that is doomed to disappointment.

Early New England writers speak of this serene portion of autumn as peculiar to America, hence the name they gave it. But we look in vain for any recognition of it in pages not more than half a century old. It seems to have departed from the land of the Puritans with the vanished forests, and doubtless these had much to do with its former prevalence. The French of Canada called the season " St. Martin's summer," as it came about the time of the calendar day of that saint.

Here too, and in the region of the lakes, its visits have become somewhat like those of the angels, though it has not deserted this, its favorite abode, altogether, as is the case in the Puritan's land. But so many years pass with so little semblance of it, that many even here are apt to look upon its existence as fabulous.

Yet the Indian summer is no myth. It often breaks upon us from the very midst of storm, frost and snow, true to the tradition, that there must first be a "squaw winter" before we can have an "Indian summer." At once the icy blasts are locked securely in their northern caves, the snow melts and the earth dries under a genial sunshine. The calm, still atmosphere is filled with a smoky haze, which hangs like a veil over the landscape. Day after day succeeds of most delicious, dreamy softness; not enervating like the heats of summer, but exhilarating to soul and body. For the rains and the frost have purified the atmosphere, rendering it elastic and bracing. The sun's rays have lost their power to oppress, and bring only enjoyment. How softly his beams fall on all surrounding objects,—the gold without the glitter. What a delicious atmosphere; we can almost. fly in it!

"——how soft the blue,
That throws its mantle o'er the lengthening scene."

Neither Eastern climes nor rural England can produce anything to compare with this balmy sunshine and this glorified landscape, shrouded in the hazy canopy of Indian summer!

Pleasant as our autumns usually are,—the most lovely and enjoyable of all the seasons,—not more than one in three or four presents any period of successive days which take on the character of well-defined Indian summer. Intervals between such years may vary from one to ten. A single fine day, or even many fine, sunny days in October or November, broken by alternating rainy, snowy or frosty ones, do not constitute a period worthy the name. Of the fifty years, from 1835 to 1885, ten are marked on my calendar as having each a full week of well defined Indian summer, viz., 1837, '39, '44, '48, '53, '59, '68, '73, '75 and, '84; two as having eleven to fifteen days, viz., 1840 and '50; two as having thirty days, 1865 and '74, and one 42 days, 1849.

Of the fifteen autumns above named, eight may be classed among those having a generally normal character, both as to temperature and rainfall,—1837, '40, '44, '48, '59, '68, '73 and, '75; six belong to warm and rather dry seasons,—1839, '50, '53, '65, '74 and '84,—in which the rainfall was one-half to two-thirds the normal amount. One—1849—is quite exceptional, having forty-two days of well defined Indian summer. One other season only approaches it, that of 1865, a cold, changeable and dry year, but closing with an autumn exceedingly pleasant and warm; the whole month of November being balmy and delightful, though with comparatively little of the haze which characterizes the true Indian summer.

I have alluded to the autumn of 1849 as remarkable for its long continuance of Indian summer.

The last summer month was warm and accompanied with frequent showers in this locality, while dry weather prevailed at the East and South. September had so little rain that the roads were dusty through the latter part of the month; when strong winds announced the approach of the equinoctial storm, which set in on the 29th with soaking rains.

At the beginning of the third week in October the Indian summer commenced, and continued, with scarcely an interruption to the balmy, hazy atmosphere, until 24th November—a period of seven weeks, when it closed with a dense fog, followed by rain and cold.

The mean temperature of the autumn was 54°, or 4° above the normal; the rainfall, 11 inches, or 3 inches above the average.

The winter which succeeded was rather open, without extreme cold.

The fall season of 1865 followed upon a summer that was very changeable, but cold and dry. September brought unusual warmth,—the real summer. The thermometer for days together was above 80° and showers were frequent, but the dry beds of streams were not filled. Fruit and crops of every kind were abundant, but the former fell early and decayed rapidly. Vines continued to make rampant growth throughout the month. Scarcely any change took place in the foliage, which continued green until near the middle of October. On the 2d of this month a frost came, of sufficient strength to make a little ice. But the month continued mild, with no hard frosts and very little rainfall.

With November we entered upon a mild and delightful "spell," quite Indian summer-like, clear and without frost, except very slight, occasionally, at night. There was no rain, except for a single day. A few days at the close assumed the soft, hazy appearance peculiar to the lovely season, and these continued until 3d December, —the haze deepening into mist, which ended in rain. No storm occurred during the whole autumn.

The summer preceding the autumn of 1874 was of normal character. September was very warm, having a maximum of 97° and a mean temperature of 12° above the normal of the month. The rainfall was only 0.67, being far below the normal of 2.8 inches. South-west winds prevailed. During both this month and October the skies were about equally divided between clear, cloudy and rainy.

October was normal in temperature, the mean being 51°, the maximum 75°, the rainfall only 0.78 inches. September frosts occurred on the 10th and 11th, followed by harder frosts on 13th and 14th. These sadly interfered with the change of the leaf, which had been progressing finely, so that leaves fell rapidly, and trees were soon bare. Clear, sunshiny days succeeded, but cool, with winds varying from north-west to west; the temperature at freezing in early morning, and rising to 65° and 70° at midday. This clear, calm weather prevailed until November 12, without rain, except slight showers. It was accompanied with a smoky haze, the sun rising red, as in a mist, and for many mornings there was a mingled fog and smoke. Fires spread on the marshes in Greenfield and Royal Oak, which were with difficulty suppressed.

On 11th and 13th November occurred night frosts; on the 17th rain, followed by clear and cold weather. The first snow fell on 20th. On the 23d a furious storm, lasting all day. This was general over the United States, east of the Mississippi, and as far south as the Gulf States. The drought continued throughout the following winter, with unusual cold. November was normal, both in temperature and rainfall. The mean temperature of the *season* was $52°$, or $2°$ above normal. The rain fall, 3.8, or 6 inches less than the normal.

Very dry periods occur here, as elsewhere, but severe *drought* is the exception. The average rainfall for the year being 31 or 32 inches, we have years as low as 22 inches. The summer precipitation, whose mean is 9.5 inches, has been—but very rarely—as low as five inches, and the autumn season, whose average is eight inches, has two or three times been as low as four inches, and five or six times as low as six inches, during the past half century.

That droughts have been so extreme that fires, caught in the woods and marshes, have overrun large tracts of country, to the great destruction of timber, there is ample evidence in the past. The Indians were accustomed to take advantage of dry autumns to set fire to the grass and shrubbery on the oaklands, for the purpose of clearing the land of incumbrances to the pursuit of deer and other game. To this cause the sparse timber of the "openings" is in a great degree attributable. Our pine forests, too, have often suffered extensively from fires, both intentional and accidental. The grass of the river marshes, which conceals game, was regularly burned over by the French habitants, taking advantage of those dry spells, which are very common. Our autumnal-night skies are still often lighted by a brilliant glow from the marshes of the river Rouge and the Grand Marais.

The fall of 1828 is said to have been marked by one of those disastrous droughts. In October fires overspread the country, commencing about the middle of the month, while the leaves were on. In many places the soil was so burned out, particularly in the ash swales, that trees fell together in large bodies, through the southern part of Wayne County and northern part of Monroe. Smoke was so dense that houses could not be seen from the roads, and everything exposed gathered stickiness. Rains did not fall until December, when the swamps filled. Vast quantities of hay were consumed, and cattle were left destitute of fodder.

A year of similar destruction, within my personal observation, is that of 1853. The summer had been very warm and dry, with the usual accompaniment of frost, which occurred in the latter part of August. From 11th to 14th of that month the temperature ranged at 90° to 100°. There was no rain during the whole of June and July, except on the single night of 25th July.

In September, fires ran over the marshes in the northern part of this country, burning up about six inches of the peaty soil, and destroying some of the tamarac timber. On the 14th rain fell sufficient to saturate a few inches in depth of soil. This is all that was known here of the equinoctial storm, which visited the south and west portions of the State in very severe and copious deluges.

The drought continued until late in October. For five months, excepting the showers mentioned, no rain fell in quantity sufficient to lay the dust, which was raised in clouds by every passing vehicle, and added to the misty shroud that covered all the face of the earth. With the exception of this dense mist the weather was calm, temperate and enjoyable.

But a more formidable shroud was destined to overwhelm the country. My journal of October 20 records that for several days our city has been involved in clouds of smoke, driven upon us from the surrounding woods and marshes, which are reported on fire in every direction. This smoke, during the prevailing calm weather, settles during the night, and, in combination with aqueous vapor, occasions in the morning a dense fog, sometimes so thick as to render locomotion dangerous. It penetrates the houses, filling lungs, eyes and nose, rendering respiration difficult, and pervading everything with the smoky odor. People are lost in the streets; vehicles run upon the sidewalks. It is worse than the fogs of London.

As the sun attains greater elevation, towards noon, the cloud lifts or disperses, and we enjoy a few rays of sunshine. Lake captains report that the mist lies twenty miles out into Lake Erie.

Towards evening dense, dun clouds are seen rising in the north and west with a very formidable appearance. From all entering thoroughfares travellers bring intelligence of woods on fire, in many places down to the roads. Many fine tracts of timber are burned and fallen. Fences, and in some instances houses, barns and stacks, have become victims to the devouring tyrant. I went out on the Pontiac road, ten miles from the city, to view the scene. The forest was on fire within two miles of Detroit, creating great consternation. Yet but little growing timber had been destroyed, the fires skimming the surface, and burning up everything that was dry. The swamps and marshy spots were most involved, in consequence of the peaty soil, and here the destruction of timber was great, over several thousands of acres. On other roads the devastation was said to be still more widespread and destructive.

On the 21st rain fell, at intervals, all day, and further devastation was stopped. It is probable that the rain itself was a consequence of the great conflagration.

The year 1871 afforded a still more formidable illustration of the effects of a year of drought. During the whole of July and August but little over one inch of rain fell, though the temperature was generally high, and the drought continued into the autumn. The rainfall during September and October was only two inches. In November three inches fell.

Before the middle of September leaves had largely fallen, and the woods wore the livery of autumn. On 17th, 18th, and 19th, heavy frosts occurred, doing much injury. Then followed some hazy weather, but no well defined Indian summer.

Early in October fires spread over the marshes north of Detroit. In consequence of the extreme dryness in the whole North-west extensive forest fires occurred in Wisconsin and Minnesota, which burned over 3000 square miles of territory.

On 8th October began the great fire which destroyed more than half of the city of Chicago, all within twenty-four hours. On the same night, amid the expression of universal sympathy for our sister city, news came that the cities of Holland and Manistee, in Michigan, were in ashes. During the week succeeding followed tidings of even more disastrous fires in other parts of the Peninsula, particularly on the eastern and western coasts. The new County of Huron was almost swept over by the fire-fiend; nearly all its villages on the lake coast were destroyed. The conflagration reached into and over a large part of Sanilac County. At least 5000 inhabitants of these counties were left homeless; farm houses, crops, fences, timber—all were burned up. Many people even perished, unable to escape the swift march of the flames and smoke borne on the wings of a strong wind. This great disaster aroused the sympathies of the whole country, and the substantial aid afforded subsequently enabled the settlers to establish themselves anew, with some of the comforts of life, upon their desolated fields.

But I return to Detroit. For many days, and until nearly the end of the month, the atmosphere of the city was charged with the smoke and scent of burning woods and fields.

The country, too, was destitute of water, wherever no large and permanent streams existed, and great distress resulted. But notwithstanding the prevailing drought the crops universally were good and fruit abundant.

About Nov. 15 snow fell and the weather began to be cold and stormy; on the 24th five inches of snow fell at Detroit, and the atmosphere was freezing cold. Extreme drought continued all through the winter, which was stormy and cold. The entire rainfall of 1871 was only about twenty inches.

The weather notes of a few seasons will serve to show, better than any general description, the ordinary character of our autumns.

The autumn of 1850 succeeded a moist and uncommonly warm summer. On Sept. 24 the equinoctial storm set in, and continued with scarcely an interruption until the 28th. The remainder of the month brought fine weather, which continued uninterruptedly through October, with cold nights. The harvests were unusually abundant and good. Malarial sickness prevailed extensively over the State.

November proved equally pleasant. The latter half accompanied with the hazy atmosphere peculiar to Indian summer, but not of so pronounced a type as that of the year previous. The last week of November brought rain and increased cold. The mean temperature of the season was 52 deg.; rainfall, 5.6 inches.

The autumn of 1872 may be classed as pleasant, with a fine autumnal change. It followed upon a very warm summer, having a rainfall of nearly the average amount, but insufficient for the prevailing dryness. Some heavy rains fell in September, but streams were still low. Several frosts occurred about the middle of the month.

The autumnal change of the leaf was brilliant and protracted. Frosts were few and light until the 25th, following which a strong breeze brought down the leaves in great quantities.

November favored us with a few days of calm, sunny weather, but scarcely any well defined Indian summer. It was preceded by a severe storm on the 17th, which was felt over the Atlantic, as far as England, with loss of many vessels. In our Northern States the storm was accompanied with a heavy fall of snow, blocking the railways. At Detroit only a few inches fell, which did not remain long. The season closed with strong north-west winds, a temperature of eight deg. and two inches of snow.

The mean of the season was 48 deg.; rainfall, six inches.

The fall of 1876 was warm, dry and pleasant; a temperature somewhat below the normal; the rainfall also normal, as was that of the summer. September and October continued rather cool and wet, and without frost until Oct. 15. Until this date foliage was quite green; the autumnal change progressed very slowly, and with little brilliancy. Only a few trees were bare. After a few hard frosts the leaves faded and fell, without the bright and varied colors which so often give a lustre to the closing year.

The fall of 1884 was also warm and dry. No frost occurred in September, yet the trees put on their full-colored dresses, the hickories and tulip trees displaying their glowing yellows, while the maples shed their coats early. This autumn succeeded a dry spring and summer, and was itself two inches below the normal in rainfall. October had all of the usual pleasant character, and was marked by a week of Indian summer at the close. November was also pleasant, and without storm. The mean temperature of the season was five deg. above the average.

I will close these short season-records by those of a single autumn, given more in detail.

The summer of 1839 was very dry, with a severe drought in many parts of the Northern States. August brought rains, blended with slight frosts. My journal of the autumn continues thus:—

Sept. 4. Since 1st inst. warm and dry. Fruit of the old French pear trees ripe and dropping.

Sept. 9. Crops are coming in early, much in advance of the same latitude in New York. Maize is generally ready to be cut.

Sept. 10. Quite cool for the last few days. Yesterday and to-day a high wind, almost a gale.

Sept. 11. Rain last night. Several remarkably brilliant auroras have been observed recently, and the night atmosphere seems to have unusual transparency.

Sept. 12. Frosts last night. Thermometer this morning, 24 deg.

Sept. 13. Ice formed 1-16th inch thick. Morning foggy. Day mild. (This was the first severe frost of the season, and with others which followed sufficed to put an end to vegetation.)

Sept. 15. Rain all day. Have seen no mosquitoes since August.

Sept. 17. Thunder-storm last night, and drizzly rain all day.

Sept. 24. Saw two wild geese flying southward, said to betoken cold weather.

The frosts of a fortnight ago have hastened the autumnal changes in the forest. Maple, linden and ash are quite yellow; leaves of the latter tree strewing the ground.

Sept. 25. More wild geese flying southward.

Sept. 27. Rains for several nights past, ending with heavy frost, and quite a respectable snow-storm.

October enters with a hard frost, whitening the ground and forming ice. The katy-did has been piping merrily for a fortnight past.

Oct. 4. Three days of sunny weather. Yesterday almost as warm as July. Slight rain at night.

Oct. 8. Rain on nights of 6th and 7th. Very warm.

Oct. 10. Since last entry we have had a succession of uncommonly fine, warm days, with a south-west wind and heat often quite oppressive. The autumnal change in the forests has been rapid. Even oaks are in the dry leaf.

Oct. 11. Rain from north-east. Growing colder.

Oct. 13. After a drizzle, yesterday, warm and pleasant again. Crops are generally abundant. Wheat and oats a particularly good yield. Maize was very generally cut by the frost a week too soon for full ripening.

Oct. 14. Forest trees are mostly denuded, or in faded leaf. Poplars and willows only are green.

The squirrel tribe, quails and pheasants are unusually numerous. The former are seen in large bodies on the march. Quails have been so abundant as to be killed with sticks in the streets of Detroit. The warm, sunny days which have succeeded the frosty ones have brought back to life the house flies, which are now almost as numerous as in midsummer.

Birds are still flying around, many in full song. Since 1st inst. I have observed the robin, towee-bunting, wren, woodpeckers (*varius* and *icterocephalus*), bluebird, yellowbird, raven, crow, blackbird, chicadee, peetweet and snowbird.

The river being calm, found to-day by measurement that its level is below the high-water mark of last year 15 inches. This is in harmony with the diminished rainfall of the last two years.

Oct. 20. Cold, with continued easterly wind. Ice formed this morning ⅛ inch thick. The white-fishing season has commenced, but the run is yet small.

Since 13th inst. we have been favored with balmy Indian summer. All nature is hushed and wrapped in a thin, misty robe. Through this the sun's rays fall, robbed of their earlier brilliance and fervor and of a deeper and milder red.

Oct. 27. This delicious weather has continued until to-day, when a shower set in.

Nov. 3. A week of chilly weather since last date.

Nov. 5. A day of rain, after two mild and pleasant days.

Nov. 19. The weather has been clear and delightful, with a few slight frosts. Some rain last week, but the heavens are bright as in summer. In fact, vegetation is making a second growth and strawberries are in bloom.

Nov. 20 and 21. Nights are clear and cold, thermometer down to 9°. The air brisk and clear, with northwest wind.

Nov. 22. This morning the smoke has settled low and filled the atmosphere in spite of low temperature and clear sky. At evening the moon rose red and hazy, and a bright halo was visible around it.

Nov. 23. Ther. at 6 A.M. at 30°. Before sunrise the sky in the east, filled with small mottled clouds, assumed a deep, beautiful crimson blush, reaching nearly to the zenith. The lovely meteor vanished as the sun rose above the horizon. At dusk both rain and hail fell, and a fine rain continued until 9 A.M. of the following day.

Nov. 24. Westerly wind. During the night snow fell, about 2 inches, and drifted, with high wind.

Nov. 25. At 6 A.M. ther. 4°. At 7 A.M. sunk to 0, rising again to 7° during the day.

Nov. 26. Ther. at 7 A.M. 2°. The river is filled with floating ice.

Nov. 29. Cold much moderated; ther. at 6 A.M. 30°. Navigation of the Erie Canal closed to-day.

Nov. 30. Foggy all day.

Soft weather continued several days, with rain and drizzle. The December following was mild and snowless, the roads hard and dusty, the whole winter was one of unusual mildness.

The mean temperature of the autumn of 1839 was 51°, or one deg. above the normal. The rainfall, only 4 inches, or half the normal amount.

THE RIPENING OF THE YEAR.

Ah! 'twere a lot too blest
   Forever in thy colored shades to stray,
Amid the kisses of the soft south-west
   To rove and dream for aye."

BRYANT.

THE RIPENING OF THE YEAR.

THE splendor of the autumnal change varies greatly with the character of the season. Sometimes we escape frosts, except very light ones, until the time prescribed for the fall of the leaf has arrived. Still the trees obey the law of change, and in their falling honors give token of the waning of the year.

Maples are among the first to obey, nor do frosts seem necessary, either to the assumption of their brilliant vestments, or the final putting off of their summer clothing. Individual maples, ashes, and some other trees are often quite bald before their companions have begun to show the " sere and yellow leaf."

If the summer and fall have been dry, this ripening takes place earlier, in consequence. As a rule, but little change occurs in the forest garniture until after a frost of sufficient severity to cut down tender vegetables. Then it comes on rapidly, and soon involves the whole forest, so that there is a sudden and wonderful burst of beauty.

Early in the season the wild grape vines turn yellow, and as they hang among the green foliage, or crown the tree tops in graceful festoons, give a fine, picturesque effect to the forest borders.

The maples are not only among the first to feel the departure of summer, but are the most capricious in their colors. At times they assume a clear yellow, at others a scarlet or crimson dress. This depends somewhat upon the character of the season, but individuals have each their own habit in this respect; the hard or sugar maple inclining oftener to the purple-reds; the soft maple to the yellows and orange.

Other forest trees are more uniform in their autumnal vestments. The hickories and tulips affect the yellow inclining to orange. The former change early, and in the fields rear their piles of golden foliage, like pyramids of sunshine, contrasting beautifully with the still green woods beyond.

The elm is distinguishable by its lemon-yellow. The beech has a somewhat russety, but still golden hue,—mingled amber and buff,—and retains its foliage almost throughout the winter.

Later in the season the oaks mature, and the tints are as varied almost as the species. In maple woods yellows prevail; in oak, reds. The white oak assumes a russety red; swamp oak, all the shades from red to yellow. Some become a clear salmon. The brilliance of the red and scarlet oaks cannot be surpassed, and they are worthy of cultivation, for this quality alone, as an ornament to our fields and grounds. They obey late the law of change, and are in their glory when the beauty of other trees of the forest has passed away.

In some trees the leaves do not take on one prevailing hue, as in many maples, and a few oaks. Not unfrequently one whole side will be red, while the rest of the tree is yellow. Sometimes the top alone is tinged with scarlet or crimson, while the parts below are quite green. Often each leaf presents these several hues in distinct patches or linings;—suits of livery, turned up with crimson and gold.

Of the forest trees of this region particularly noted for

picturesqueness none add more to autumn's triumphs than the pepperidge or tupelo (*Nyssa*). Its horizontal limbs are covered with glossy leaves that change to a lively crimson, making the tree conspicuously beautiful.

So marked are the colors of different species of trees, that one may distinguish them at a great distance,—further than it is possible to do in summer,—and may thus select and count them out from among the other individuals of the forest, the fields and the hill-sides.

In our rambles at this delightful season, we often meet with a surprise. Before the woods have lost their prevailing green, we come suddenly upon some individual which has ripened before his fellows, and presents an extraordinary contrast and splendor of color, striking the vision like a flash of fire. It constitutes the warm point in the picture, which a painter puts in, with pencil dipped in his most glowing reds, to light up a foreground, or relieve a sombre shadow.

In many woods the American ivy, or Ampelopsis, adds finely to the brightness of the early autumn. It loves to clasp around some stately trunk that will lift it into sunshine, and repays the favor by garlanding it with its palmate leaves of deepest purple and crimson.

This vine has become a favorite in European countries, where it serves to enliven the duller glow of their autumns. When one sees anywhere a wall or trellis draped with brilliant red, he may be sure it is the American Ampelopsis.

At this season I know no more delightful ride or ramble than the beech and maple wood. It is lit by a golden gleam which creates a seeming sunshine in the dullest day. Even the fallen leaves spread a lustrous carpet, that gives to the maple forest a more bright and cheerful aspect than it wears in summer. But when a forest of these trees, in the full splendor of their autumnal foliage, is illuminated by the soft rays of the autumn sun, what a marvel of golden pomp! How the soul bathes in it, as in a flood, until, "dazzled and drunk with beauty," it revels in an ecstasy of delight in which it would gladly stay forever.

Some of our commonest shrubs and plants of the woods and fields are among the most brilliant of autumn's children. The dogwood is as beautiful in its full dress as when covered with its profusion of white calixed flowers, in the spring. It early turns a deep Indian red, and retains its color a long time. This shrub and the common sumach are worthy a more conspicuous place in ornamental grounds than many more cherished foreign plants. The latter is beautiful in summer, from its cones of dark red fruit, crowning the rounded summit, and showing among the green leaves like the flowers of the horse-chestnut. But its greatest beauty is in autumn. It commences its display early, and deepens daily, for a fortnight, into a brighter scarlet, until the whole plant glows like fire, conspicuous among the surrounding foliage as is the scarlet tanager among the birds. It fairly illuminates the landscape.

A few of the shrubs assume the royal purple. As the autumn livery of plants is in this country one of their chiefest beauties, I would select, for the lawn and arboretum, as much with reference to this quality as to foliage or bloom at other seasons, and plant with these contrasts in view.

It is noticeable that many trees of foreign origin, such as the peach—which comes to us from a warmer clime—and the cultivated pear and apple, among fruits, retain their greenness much longer than the denizens of our native woods.

The autumn of 1864 was worthy of note for its uncommon succession of beauty. A few glowing tints began to appear, chiefly in the maples, about the 15th of September, through New York and Michigan. The change made very gradual progress. By the middle of October nothing could surpass the splendor of the woodlands; the maples in their very ripeness, and the oaks beginning to color. The landscape resembled a parterre of flowers, exhibiting on the grandest scale all the variety and glow of a flower garden or a conservatory. The ashes and hickories had then mostly dropped their leaves, as had some of the maples. From the 10th to the 18th a few sharp frosts occurred, which hastened the maturity. On the morning of the latter, which brought ice, as the rays of a bright sun struck the exposed side of the trees, though the air was still, the leaves began to fall, in showers, like a snow-storm, covering the ground on that side. An hour or two afterwards the whole surface underneath the hickories, on my lawn, was carpeted with the yellow leaves, and they had ceased to fall. On the 30th of October I note that most of the oaks are still brilliant, but others have become brown, and the glory is fast fading.

Since nature, at this season, wears so smiling a face, and prepares with such gayety for the long sleep of winter,

"What is there saddening in the autumn leaves?"

Why should man repine, as though these were only signs of approaching death?

The season in which we luxuriate in green leaves and flowers is, in this latitude, indeed short. Scarcely more than three months pass from the period of full foliage to the commencement of nature's harvest. We are therefore necessitated to make the most of the latter season, and to enjoy heartily its peculiar charms, which no other land possesses so fully.

And what a season it is for enjoyment! When nature is assuming her many-colored robe the fervid heats of summer are past, and we no longer seek refuge from them in the seclusion of shade and rest. Our more active energies are called forth. We live, with comfort and increased pleasure, in the open air. A softened serenity prevails over the landscape, in harmony with nature's ripened loveliness, interrupted by occasional storms and frosty nights, but culminating to its full proportion in the glorious Indian summer of our climate.

All summer long the leaves have been imbibing the warm sunshine, at the last to render back the gift in one collected and effulgent glow; as if each leaf were a prism, and refracted the rays it has been so long absorbing, into their primitive colors. The dolphin, dying, shines in brightest hues; the dying swan—as poets tell—sings its sweetest song. So the dying day, whose rays have been colorless in the concentrated light, now gilds the whole horizon with its lately imprisoned hues.

At other seasons Nature displays her wealth of beauty in diversified forms; she now luxuriates in color. Her prevailing green is suited to the fiery glow of a summer sun; the more gorgeous tints to the softer light of autumn.

Not only at this season does Nature delight to paint the trees, her crowning glories; she wantons in color, also, in the flowers and fruits. In the latter the green of their unripened summer is exchanged for the brightened hues of maturity, that so attract the eye in the orchards and gardens. In the flowers of the autumn fields she displays, in larger masses than during the earlier months, her taste for colors.

Some of the most conspicuous of these are noticed in the lines of Bryant:

"On the hill the golden-rod, and the aster in the wood,
And the yellow sunflower by the brook, in autumn beauty stood."

Thus is Nature ever in harmony.

If I were a painter, I would take the woods of autumn for my study. With pencil dipped in all the hues of the rainbow, and with simple truth to nature, such landscapes should glow upon my canvas as Rubens or Salvator Rosa never dreamed of.

If I were a poet, my glowing words should describe the woods in autumn. Dewy Iris, as she descends to cut the golden thread of the year, should hover over my page, wafting a thousand colors from her wings.* The lady of my love should not blend with the rose the cold contrast of the lily, but rather be compared with the maple for grace, and like it, should charm with the bloom and perfection of ripened loveliness.

When comes my time to fall, may it be in the mellow autumn of the year, and of life. When the frosts of age have served to deepen whatever is bright and genial in my nature, but before my leaf has become dry, and rustles mournfully in the wild winds of winter.

---

*Vng. Lucid, B. 4.

CPSIA information can be obtained at www.ICGtesting.com
Printed in the USA
LVOW05s2314100114

368935LV00006B/296/P